Date Due

FEB 2 1984		
AUG 0 7 1996		
OCT 1 0 2000		
3 1 MAY 2001		
2 0 DEC 2002		

SERIES
IN
HUMAN
RELATIONS
TRAINING

THE
1976 ANNUAL
HANDBOOK
FOR GROUP
FACILITATORS

(The Fifth Annual)

Edited by

J. WILLIAM PFEIFFER, Ph.D.
Human Relations Consultant
La Jolla, California

JOHN E. JONES, Ph.D.
Human Relations Consultant
La Jolla, California

UNIVERSITY ASSOCIATES, INC.
7596 Eads Avenue
La Jolla, California 92037

PREFACE

In this bicentennial period, we note that twenty-eight years have passed since the serendipitous discovery of the T-group in New Britain, Connecticut. For practitioners in the field of human relations training, those years were marked by excitement and controversy, debate and dissention. "Sensitivity training" had the unique distinction of being attacked simultaneously by the political right and left; "encounter" raised psychiatric eyebrows and provoked harsh critiques; the "third force" of the new humanism worried academic psychologists, legislators, managers, and just about everybody else. Reports of nuns taking off their clothes and key executives crying in "truth sessions" were matched by testimony of significant life changes occurring over a weekend and claims of a coming transformation in human evolution.

Today, the flamboyance has diminished but the excitement remains: the theory of experiential learning grows more elegant; research attesting to the abiding impact of training is available (e.g., Smith, 1975); practitioners continue the creative application of behavioral science principles. We observe a growing maturity in the field of human relations training, a maturity reflected in this 1976 *Annual Handbook for Group Facilitators*. We value the efforts of our contributors and appreciate their patience and collaboration in the editing process. Collectively, our authors have produced work that is sound, tested, and, above all, practical.

Our publishing purpose continues to be making practical material easily available to the group facilitator. For this reason, few restrictions are imposed on the reproduction of the materials in the *Annual*.

The *Annuals* are copyrighted, but users are free to duplicate and modify all materials (forms, charts, structured experiences, descriptions, instruments, work sheets, lecturettes, resources) for educational and training purposes. We do request that a credit line be included.

If, however, materials are to be reproduced in publications or are intended for large-scale distribution, prior written permission of the editors is required.

We are happy to acknowledge the editorial contributions of two members of the University Associates staff. Marion Fusco, managing editor, has had day-to-day editorial and management responsibility for the 1976 *Annual*. She has edited all material, handled much of the contact with contributors, and supervised the course of the *Annual*'s production from the manuscript stage to the finished volume.

Tony Banet, University Associates senior consultant, has made a major contribution to the content of the 1976 *Annual*. He has helped review, prepare, and revise material for publication and is responsible for the section introductions of this volume.

This *Annual* is written and compiled by group facilitators for group facilitators. We encourage readers to submit materials that they believe would be of interest and use to their colleagues. In this way, our Series in Human Relations Training will continue to serve as a clearinghouse for original and adapted ideas.

REFERENCE

Smith, P. B. Controlled studies of the outcome of sensitivity training. *Psychological Bulletin*, 1975, *82*, 597-622.

La Jolla, California
December 1975

J. William Pfeiffer
John E. Jones

UNIVERSITY ASSOCIATES
Publishers and Consultants

 University Associates is an educational organization engaged in human relations training, research, consulting, publishing, and both pre-service and in-service education. The organization consists of educational consultants and experienced facilitators in human relations, leadership training, and organization development.

In addition to offering general laboratory experiences, University Associates designs and carries out programs on a contractual basis for various organizations. These programs fall under the following areas of specialization: human relations training, leadership development, organization development, and community development.

TABLE OF CONTENTS

---

*See the Introduction to the Structured Experiences Section, p. 5, for an explanation of numbering.

THEORY AND PRACTICE

GENERAL INTRODUCTION TO THE 1976 *ANNUAL*

This 1976 *Annual Handbook for Group Facilitators*—the fifth *Annual* to be published—continues the University Associates emphasis on practical, current, high-quality training materials. Group facilitators working in personal growth, humanistic education, leadership and management training, and organization development will find in this collection a balanced variety of resources for program design and implementation.

The 1976 *Annual* continues the basic format and divisions of previous *Annuals*: Structured Experiences, Instrumentation, Lecturettes, Theory and Practice, and Resources. Its selections, however, are entirely new; no *Annual* overlaps in content with any other.

The Structured Experiences section follows the format developed in *A Handbook of Structured Experiences for Human Relations Training*, Volumes I, II, III, IV, and V. The section contains twelve new structured experiences useful in a variety of group training situations.

Instrumentation contains scales and inventories that can be used by facilitators when focused feedback and self-assessment are desired.

Lecturettes are brief, simplified summaries that can be used to supplement structured experiences or to serve as handouts for group participants.

Papers in the Theory and Practice section, longer and more complex than lecturettes, are nevertheless addressed to the practitioner rather than the scholar and provide background reading of current concepts and issues in human relations training. The new University Associates journal, *Group & Organization Studies: The International Journal for Group Facilitators*, scheduled to begin publication in March 1976, will provide additional background material and research studies for the human relations practitioner.

The Resources section offers access to tools—books, research, information, reviews—that the facilitator will find useful.

Many items in this *Annual* have been designed to fulfill the facilitator's need for handout materials. Work sheets are provided for many structured experiences; instruments include inventories, forms, and a workbook; lecturettes are designed to be presented by the facilitator or read by the participant; many Theory and Practice papers are suitable as background information, as are also the surveys and collections in the Resources section.

Brief author biographies are located at the end of each piece in the 1976 *Annual*, and all contributors are listed alphabetically at the end of the book. Titles, mailing addresses, and, where possible, telephone numbers have been included so that *Annual* readers can direct their inquiries and comments to individual authors.

A collection implies both variety and some unevenness. The materials in this *Annual*—which represent both the new and the "classic"—are offered as practical, stimulating sources of relevant information for the group facilitator.

INTRODUCTION TO THE
STRUCTURED EXPERIENCES SECTION

In our series of human relations training publications, we have consistently used the term "structured experience" as a label for those laboratory activities that (a) focus the group process, (b) control extraneous variables, and (c) heighten the probability that certain learnings will occur for participants. Although the learning goals of the structured experience can be specified and the outcomes are somewhat predictable, the structured experience does not dictate *what* a participant *should* learn. Its intent is to facilitate learning that would otherwise be haphazard and diffuse.

Structured experiences abound; with the publication of this *Annual*, we have collected and published 184. Creating new structured experiences that are novel, exciting, and enriching for group participants is one of the joys of human relations training.

The process that a structured experience yields is a function of three elements: the *objectives* of the experience, the *content*, and the *structures* employed to focus learnings. These elements are diagrammed in Figure 1.

Objectives

The objectives or learning goals of a structured experience may include cognitive, affective, and skill-building aspects.

Cognitive: Awareness of content; incorporation and use of the content; generalization; conceptual integration.

Affective: Self-awareness, ownership of feelings, insight, empathy, awareness of inner life, awareness of personal and interpersonal processes.

Skill Building: Development, practice, and implementation of interpersonal skills and techniques such as listening, problem solving, and intervening.

Content

The content areas listed here refer to personal, interpersonal, and group events; however, almost any content area—ranging from learning the concept "3" to the social determinants of Protestant denominationalism—is appropriate for a structured experience.

Ice Breakers: Getting acquainted, presentation of self, first impressions.

Interpersonal Communication: Listening, trust building, open and closed relationships.

Group Problem Solving: Problem solving, decision making, consensus.

Awareness Expansion: Sensory awareness, broadening self-perception, establishing personal goals, enlarging personal boundaries.

Personal Feedback: Giving and receiving feedback, conceptual models, instruments.

Competition and Cooperation: Winning, losing, strategies.

Intergroup Communication: Social perception, contact between diverse groups, sociocultural differences, hierarchies.

Dyads: Two-person transactions, communications, perceptions, partners, marital pairs.

Leadership: Leadership functions, strategies, styles, types of leadership, followership.

Group Process: Task and maintenance functions, observation, intervention practice.

Organization Development: Team building, systems analysis, work groups, production/planning operations.

Figure 1. Dimensions of Structured Experiences[1]

Structures

These activities include:

Constructions: Making or building something, assembling or taking apart puzzles.

Data Collection: Counting, measuring, interviewing, checking resources, instrument scoring, assessing skill levels.

Discussions: Conversations, summarizations, question-and-answer sessions, dialogues.

Experiments: Replication of research paradigms, Gestalt work, playing with hypotheses.

Fantasy: Tapping into internal feedback systems, stories, body trips.

Games: Adaptations of standard games, cards, board games.

Graphics: Collage, body painting, drawings, finger painting, clay sculpture.

Instruments: Inventories, check lists, standardized test batteries.

Media: Monies, charts, audiovisual aids, projective techniques, audiotape, videotape.

Models: Conceptual schemes, diagrams.

Movement and Nonverbal Communication: Milling, dancing, interpersonal sculpture, facial expressions, symbolic communication, body reading.

Role Plays: Play reading, acting, impromptu theater, alter ego, role reversals.

---

[1]Adapted with permission from Doris Helge, *Gamed Social Simulations. A Resource Book for Social Work Educators.* Unpublished thesis, School of Social Work, University of Texas at Austin, 1974.

Simulations: Structured role plays, microcosms, simplification of complex phenomena, community or back-home focus.

Subgroups: Men/women, black/white, old/young, experienced/inexperienced.

Tasks: Ranking, problem solving, writing, decision making.

An appropriate combination of objectives, content, and structure will produce a structured experience that will generate data for learning. The data need to be *published* (participants share their reactions) and *processed* (data are integrated); after that, generalizations and applications are discussed.

CONDUCTING STRUCTURED EXPERIENCES

Some guidelines for the facilitator follow.

1. *Rehearse instructions.* Clear instructions are imperative. Giving step-by-step instructions is preferable to giving a list of directions all at once. It is important not to overload participants with instructions; give them at the point that they are needed.

2. *Give time cues.* Remain in charge of starting, stopping, or interrupting the structured experience. Cues such as "When I give the signal . . . " or "Take five more minutes for . . ." keep the structured experience well paced and focused.

3. *Pre-arrange rooms.* This is often helpful, especially with large groups or in structured experiences dependent on chair arrangement, etc.

4. *Brief observers.* Many structured experiences require observers, who need to know *what* and *how* to observe. The value of observation is considerably enhanced when observers are clear about their task.

5. *"Arrest" the group.* The facilitator needs the group's full attention when he is giving directions and instructions. Focus the group's attention by waiting for quiet, using charts, writing out instructions when necessary.

6. *Put data " in the can."* Lengthy structured experiences generate data that frequently get lost if processing occurs only at the end. Interrupting the process periodically and asking participants to write notes to themselves ("What am I learning about myself right now?") for later use increases data retrieval.

7. *Layer the process.* Process sessions frequently can be focused by discussing the learning from the experience in several "layers." A typical layer might include self—this group—back-home groups.

STRUCTURED EXPERIENCE CATEGORIES

Since a particular structured experience can often be adapted for a variety of training purposes, categorizing structured experiences is somewhat arbitrary. The chart on the following page classifies the 184 structured experiences published by University Associates according to their most common use. Each experience is listed only once, in one of the eleven categories, although any given activity could conceivably be used for several different purposes.

The chart includes the short title for each of our published structured experiences, its number, and the volume and page number where it can be found.

All structured experiences published in our Series in Human Relations Training—the *Annuals* and the *Handbooks*—are numbered consecutively, in order of publication of the volumes: Structured Experiences 1 through 24 appear in Volume I of the *Handbooks*; 25-48 in Volume II; 49-74 in Volume III; 75-86 in the 1972 *Annual*; 87-100 in the 1973 *Annual*; 101-124 in Volume IV; 125-136 in the 1974 *Annual*; 137-148 in the 1975 *Annual*; 149-172 in Volume V; and 173-184 in the 1976 *Annual*.

STRUCTURED EXPERIENCE CATEGORIES

173. LIMERICKS: GETTING ACQUAINTED

Goals

    I. To acquaint and involve participants with one another through nonthreatening physical activity.

    II. To divide a large group into subgroups in a climate of humor and cohesiveness.

Group Size

    An unlimited number of participants, preferably divisible by five.

Time Required

    Approximately thirty minutes.

Materials

    One set of five Limericks Strips, prepared according to the Directions for Making Limericks Strips, for each five participants.

Physical Setting

    A large room in which participants may move about freely.

Process

    I. The facilitator posts a demonstration limerick and informs the participants that each of them is to receive one line of the five-line limerick and that their task is to find the other four members of their limerick group.

    II. Limerick Strips are randomly distributed, and the search begins.

    III. When all quintets have formed, the facilitator asks each subgroup to recite its limerick for the entire group.

    IV. Subgroups are then instructed to proceed with the task that is specified on the back of their set of Limericks Strips.

    V. After ten minutes, the facilitator requests that one member from each group report, in turn, on the group's discussion.

Variations

    I. Couplets or haiku can be used for smaller subgroups.

    II. Prose selections, such as fables, can be used to form larger subgroups.

Similar Structured Experiences: *Vol. I:* Structured Experience 2; *Vol. II:* **27**; *'74 Annual:* **125**; *Vol. V:* **149**; *'76 Annual:* **175**.

Submitted by Elizabeth Racicot. Developed and designed with the assistance of Walter Bates, David P. Dixon, Keith Jeffers, Rick Steel, and Bernie J. Villeneuve.

Elizabeth Racicot is presently on leave of absence from the Canadian International Development Agency in Abidjan, Ivory Coast, West Africa. She will be working on a consulting contract in Ivory Coast, Mali, Niger, and Upper Volta. Mrs. Racicot's background is in anthropology, French language and civilization, and library science.

DIRECTIONS FOR MAKING LIMERICKS STRIPS

Each five-line limerick (see samples following) is typed triple-spaced on a 3″ × 5″ card. On the reverse side of the card, the group's task is typed, as follows:

Your group's task is to discuss individuals' expectations concerning this training event. At the end of ten minutes, the facilitator will ask for a brief report on your discussion.

Each card is then cut into five strips, one limerick line to each strip.

Sample Limericks

He received from some thoughtful relations
A spittoon with superb decorations.
When asked was he pleased,
He grimaced and wheezed,
"It's beyond all my expectorations."

The limerick is furtive and mean;
You must keep it in close quarantine,
Or it sneaks to the slums
And promptly becomes
Disorderly, drunk, and obscene.

The limerick packs laughs anatomical
Into space that is quite economical.
But the good ones I've seen
So seldom are clean,
And the clean ones so seldom are comical!

Elton John stopped off once in Hong Kong
And composed a new national song.
The song that he wrote
Was all in one note,
But it sounded superb on a gong.

There was a young lady named Bright
Whose speed was much faster than light.
She went out one day
In a relative way
And returned on the previous night.

A wonderful bird is the pelican.
His mouth can hold more than his belican.
He can take in his beak
Enough food for a week.
I'm darned if I know how the helican.

A certain young lady named Hannah
Was caught in a flood in Montannah.
As she floated away,
Her beau, so they say,
Accompanied her on the piannah.

There was a young man from the city
Who met what he thought was a kitty.
He gave it a pat
And said, "Nice little cat."
They buried his clothes, out of pity.

God's plan made a hopeful beginning,
But man spoiled his chances by sinning.
We trust that the story
Will end in God's glory
But, at present, the other side's winning.

There was a young girl named Irene
Who was chosen as Stock Exchange Queen,
For when in the mood,
Was successfully wooed
By Merrill Lynch, Fenner, and Beane.

There was an old man from Nantucket
Who kept all his cash in a bucket.
His young daughter Nan
Ran off with a man
And as for the bucket, Nantucket.

A tutor who tooted the flute
Tried to tutor two tooters to toot.
Said the two to the tutor
"Is it harder to toot, or
To tutor two tooters to toot?"

174. LABELING: A GETTING-ACQUAINTED ACTIVITY

Goals

    I. To provide opportunities to become acquainted with other members of a group.

    II. To promote feedback and self-disclosure among participants regarding initial perceptions.

Group Size

    Unlimited.

Time Required

    Approximately one hour.

Materials

    I. Twelve blank name tags, blank labels, or strips of masking tape for each participant.

    II. A copy of the Labeling Category List for each participant.

    III. A copy of the Labeling Interview Sheet for each participant.

    IV. Pencils or felt-tipped markers.

Physical Setting

    A room large enough to allow participants to move around and talk in dyads.

Process

Phase One

    I. The facilitator describes the activity and discusses its goals.

    II. The facilitator presents a lecturette on first impressions.

    III. The facilitator distributes a copy of the Labeling Category List to each participant. He instructs each participant to copy each category on a separate blank name tag, label, or strip of masking tape.

    IV. Participants mill around and choose a person who best fits each category. Participants stick a category label on the clothing of the person they select and engage in a one-minute conversation with that person. (Approximately twenty minutes.)

    V. The facilitator forms groups of five to seven members each and instructs them to discuss their reactions to being categorized and labeled (or not labeled) by others' first impressions. (Approximately fifteen minutes.)

Phase Two

    VI. The facilitator forms dyads, instructing participants to choose someone whom they would like to know better.

VII. When all dyads are formed and seated separately, the facilitator distributes a copy of the Labeling Interview Sheet to each participant and answers procedural questions.

VIII. Dyads are allotted ten minutes (five minutes per person) for interviewing. The facilitator stresses the use of nontraditional questions by the interviewer.

IX. The total group meets together, and each participant introduces his partner.

X. The facilitator leads a discussion on the outcomes of the activity.

Variations

I. Participants can generate their own list of categories.

II. Following the dyadic interviews, groups of six to twelve can be formed for the introductions, when there is a large number of participants. Thus, the experience can be part of a group-building design.

III. Each of the two components of the structured experience can be used separately.

IV. The number of labels given participants may be varied according to the size of the total group.

Similar Structured Experiences: *Vol. I:* Structured Experience 1; *Vol. II:* **42**; *'73 Annual:* **88**; *'74 Annual:* **125**; *'76 Annual:* **174**.

Lecturette Source: *'76 Annual:* "Making Judgments Descriptive."

———————

Submitted by Charles L. Kormanski.

Charles L. Kormanski, Ed.D., *is a counselor for the Counseling and Career Development Center, Altoona Campus, Pennsylvania State University. He is involved in counseling college students, facilitating small-group experiences, and teaching counseling courses for continuing education. Dr. Kormanski's background is in teaching, counseling, and small-group training (theory and practice).*

LABELING CATEGORY LIST

Happy	Fun
Friendly	Sexy
Sincere	Commands Respect
Intelligent	Mysterious
Aloof	Warm
Fatherly	Motherly

LABELING INTERVIEW SHEET

Instructions: Each of you will interview the other. The interviewer will choose five *nontraditional* questions to ask. (Some examples are provided below. You may, however, create your own questions.) Following the first interview, you will reverse roles. After both interviews, you will introduce your partner to the group.

Examples of nontraditional questions:

What is your favorite object?
How do you feel right now?
Whom do you trust the most?
What do you most often dream about?
Where do you go to be alone?
What do you think is very exotic?
How would you define friendship?
When do you feel most affectionate?
What turns you on the most?
What value is most important to you?
When do you feel most comfortable?
What do you expect of me?
If you weren't what you are, what would you be?
When do you feel uncomfortable?
How do you deal with your own anger?
Under what circumstances would you tell a lie?
What is difficult for you to do?
What is a favorite joke of yours?

175. BLINDFOLDS: A DYADIC EXPERIENCE

Goals

I. To demonstrate and experience the need for visual cues in perception and communication.

II. To demonstrate the need for visual cues in the definition of "personal space."

Group Size

Unlimited.

Time Required

Approximately one hour.

Materials

I. A blindfold for each participant.

II. A set of paired Blindfolds Word Cards, one for each participant. (See Directions for Making Blindfolds Word Cards.)

III. A copy of the Blindfolds Discussion Sheet for each participant.

Physical Setting

A room large enough for participants to move about without obstructions.

Process

I. The facilitator briefly discusses the importance of nonverbal cues in typical interactions and the importance of touch when visual contact is not possible.

II. The facilitator forms two equal-sized groups—Group A and Group B. Each participant is then given a Blindfolds Word Card for Group A or Group B respectively. After participants have seen their words, they blindfold themselves.

III. The facilitator explains that the participants' task is to locate the other participant whose word is associated with the one he is holding. By milling around, participants are to come into contact with other individuals by touch and then hold the other person's hand and say their words. If the words do not form a pair, the participants are to keep searching. If the words form a pair, the participants, without removing their blindfolds, are to do the following, in turn:

1. Spend a few moments focusing on their feelings of "personal space" in relation to their partner; exploring an optimal physical distance for communicating with their partner; and making a conscious choice about where they want to be with regard to "personal space."

2. Find out as much as they can about each other through conversation.

IV. The facilitator circulates on the perimeter of the group, keeping disoriented participants from running into obstacles and steering them back toward the nucleus of the activity. He also observes behaviors related to the use and defense of personal space, conversational groupings and orientations, and touching behaviors.

V. After all dyads have been formed, the facilitator allows some time for blindfolded conversation. Then he directs participants to form a mental image of what their dyad partners look like, how they are dressed, and where they are located in the room.

VI. The facilitator instructs participants to remove their blindfolds. He distributes copies of the Blindfolds Discussion Sheet to guide the dyadic processing. (Ten minutes.)

VII. The facilitator leads a general discussion of the experience, relating its outcomes to the goals.

Variations

I. Each word may be given to more than one person so long as the pairing word is given to an equal number of participants. This permits a variety of possible dyadic pairings and, especially for large groups, shortens the time needed to locate partners.

II. If participants know each other, it is helpful to forbid them to identify themselves to each other while blindfolded. This prevents past perceptions from heavily influencing present ones.

Similar Structured Experiences: *Vol. I:* Structured Experience **4, 22;** *Vol. II:* **44;** *Vol. III:* **72;** *Vol. V:* **152.**

Lecturette Sources: *'72 Annual:* "Communication Modes: An Experiential Lecture"; *'74 Annual:* "Five Components Contributing to Interpersonal Communications"; *'76 Annual:* "The Awareness Wheel," "Clarity of Expression in Interpersonal Communication."

Submitted by James I. Costigan and Arthur L. Dirks.

James I. Costigan, Ph.D., *is the chairman of the Department of Speech, Fort Hays Kansas State College, Hays, Kansas. He is a co-author of* Interpersonal Communication: Influences and Alternatives *and is actively engaged in teaching, consulting, and research. Dr. Costigan's background is in interpersonal communication, communication theory, and organizational communication.*

Arthur L. Dirks *is an instructor of communication arts on the faculty of Wayne State College, Wayne, Nebraska. He was previously on the faculty of Fort Hays Kansas State College in Hays, Kansas. Mr. Dirks's background is in interpersonal communication, theater, and broadcasting.*

DIRECTIONS FOR MAKING BLINDFOLDS WORD CARDS

One 3″ x 5″ card is needed for each participant. On the Group A cards are typed general words (nouns), such as "automobile." On the Group B cards are typed specific words that will pair up with the Group A cards, e.g., "Chevrolet." Some examples are:

Group A	*Group B*
dog	collie
color	red
country	France
fruit	peach
flower	petunia
beverage	lemonade
metal	zinc
spice	nutmeg
tool	hammer
tree	oak
cat	Angora
insect	ant
measurement	inch
disease	measles
holiday	Christmas
university	Harvard
gem	diamond
emotion	joy
furniture	chair
automobile	Chevrolet

BLINDFOLDS DISCUSSION SHEET

Personal Space

1. How did you behaviorally manifest the boundaries of your "personal space" to your partner?

2. If your space was transgressed, how did you respond to your partner, verbally or non-verbally?

3. Define the physical manifestations of how you expressed your space to your partner.

Communications

1. What behaviors did you use as substitutes for visual components of communication?

2. What made it easy or difficult to sustain a conversation while blindfolded?

3. What forms of reinforcement did you use to encourage or to discourage your partner to make contact with you?

4. What implications can you draw from this experience concerning those parts of you that "see" nonvisually?

176. SYMBOLIC TOAST: A CLOSURE EXPERIENCE

Goals

    I. To provide closure at the end of a training experience.

    II. To provide an opportunity for participants to give and receive feedback.

    III. To allow each person to receive some personal validation from each member of the group.

    IV. To affirm the personal strengths of the participants.

Group Size

    Eight to twelve participants. Several groups may be directed simultaneously in the same room.

Time Required

    Approximately forty minutes.

Materials

    One paper cup for each participant.

Physical Setting

    Participants are seated in a circle.

Process

    I. The facilitator reminds the participants that they will soon be leaving the group, and he adds that each individual will carry with him some essence of each of the others.

    II. The facilitator gives each participant an empty paper cup. He explains that the participants will fill their cups symbolically with some essence of each of the other group members. He asks them to look around the room and to decide what they would like to capture from each of the other members.

    III. He asks for a volunteer to be the focus of the first "round." Then the facilitator models the process by saying (for example), "John, I wish to capture some of your sensitivity for others."

    IV. The other participants continue the process, focusing on the first volunteer, by telling that individual what *they* wish to take from him. The facilitator encourages each participant to maintain eye contact when communicating.

    V. This process continues until each participant has had the opportunity to volunteer.

    VI. The facilitator instructs the participants to take a moment to review the experience and to focus on what they have taken from or given to each of the others.

VII. The facilitator invites all group members to toast one another with their cups and to "drink" the essence of each member of the group. The facilitator says, "Now each of you has a part of me and I have a part of each of you. The activity is now ended."

Variations

I. For larger groups, instead of focusing on one individual at a time, the participants may be asked to mill about the room, symbolically filling their cups with the essence of each of the other group members.

II. The activity can be focused on both giving and receiving.

Similar Structured Experiences: *Vol. I:* Structured Experience 23; *'72 Annual:* **86;** *Vol. IV:* **104, 107, 114.**

Lecturette Source: *'75 Annual:* "Re-Entry."

Submitted by A. Donald Duncan and Jo F. Dorris.

A. Donald Duncan *is an administrative assistant for human relations for the Yonkers Public School System, Yonkers, New York. His current activities include student and parent training, administrator/teacher staff development, and external consulting. Mr. Duncan's background is in law enforcement (crisis intervention and conflict resolution with multidivergent cultural groups) and in community development and education.*

Jo F. Dorris, Ed.D., *is an associate dean of students and a professor of applied behavioral studies, Oklahoma State University, Stillwater. She is the president of the Oklahoma College Personnel Association and is active as a human relations consultant. Dr. Dorris's background is in adult and college teaching, student affairs, staff development, group facilitation, and organizational consultation.*

177. WILDERNESS SURVIVAL: A CONSENSUS-SEEKING TASK

Goals

    I. To teach effective consensus-seeking behaviors in task groups.

    II. To explore the concept of synergy as it relates to outcomes of group decision making.

Group Size

    Five to twelve participants. Several groups may be directed simultaneously in the same room. (Synergistic outcomes are more likely to be achieved by smaller groups, i.e., five to seven participants.)

Time Required

    Approximately one and one-half hours.

Materials

    I. A copy of the Wilderness Survival Work Sheet for each participant.

    II. A pencil for each participant.

    III. A copy of the Wilderness Survival Group Briefing Sheet for each participant.

    IV. A copy of the Wilderness Survival Answer and Rationale Sheet for each participant.

    V. Newsprint and felt-tipped markers.

Physical Setting

    A room large enough for the entire group to meet and separate rooms or areas in which task groups can work without distracting each other.

Process

    I. The facilitator briefly introduces the activity by explaining its purpose, outline, and origin.

    II. The facilitator distributes copies of the Wilderness Survival Work Sheet. Participants complete the work sheet individually. (Approximately ten minutes.)

    III. Groups are formed, and copies of the Wilderness Survival Group Briefing Sheet are distributed to all participants.

    IV. After participants have read the briefing sheet silently, the facilitator briefly discusses its contents.

    V. Groups work separately on the consensus-seeking task. (Approximately thirty minutes.)

    VI. When all groups have completed their task, the entire group reassembles, with the members of each work group seated together.

VII. The statistics for all groups are posted on a chart such as the following.

Outcome	Group I	Group II	Group III
Range of Individual Scores			
Average of Individual Scores			
Score for Group Consensus			

VIII. Groups discuss their consensus-seeking process and outcomes. The focus should be on behaviors that help or hinder group productivity.

 IX. Each participant receives a copy of the Wilderness Survival Answer and Rationale Sheet. The facilitator announces (and posts) the "correct" answers, and each participant scores his own work sheet. A volunteer in each group scores the group's solution and computes the average for the individual scores within the group.

  X. The facilitator leads a total-group discussion of the process and outcomes; he may include discussions of leadership, compromise, decision-making strategies, psychological climate, roles and applications of the techniques learned.

Variations

See *Volume IV*, Structured Experience 115, for variations.

Similar Structured Experiences: *Vol. I:* Structured Experiences **11, 15;** *Vol. II:* **30;** *Vol. III:* **64;** *72 Annual:* **84;** *Vol. IV:* **115;** *'75 Annual:* **140;** *Vol. V:* **151, 155.**

Suggested Instrument: *'75 Annual:* "Decision-Style Inventory."

Lecturette Sources: *'73 Annual:* "Synergy and Consensus-Seeking"; *'76 Annual:* "A Gestalt Approach to Collaboration in Organizations."

Submitted by Donald T. Simpson.

Donald T. Simpson *is an educational specialist on the staff for management and general education, Marketing Education Center, Eastman Kodak Company, Rochester, New York. He is involved with management development and human relations programs in business and the community. Mr. Simpson's background is in military management, industrial engineering, and continuing education.*

WILDERNESS SURVIVAL WORK SHEET

Here are twelve questions concerning personal survival in a wilderness situation. Your first task is *individually* to select the best of the three alternatives given under each item. Try to imagine yourself in the situation depicted. Assume that you are alone and have a minimum of equipment, except where specified. The season is fall. The days are warm and dry, but the nights are cold.

After you have completed this task individually, you will again consider each question as a member of a small group. Your group will have the task of deciding, *by consensus*, the best alternative for each question. Do not change your individual answers, even if you change your mind in the group discussion. Both the individual and group solutions will later be compared with the "correct" answers provided by a group of naturalists who conduct classes in woodland survival.

	Your Answer	Your Group's Answer
1. You have strayed from your party in trackless timber. You have no special signaling equipment. The best way to attempt to contact your friends is to: a. call "help" loudly but in a low register. b. yell or scream as loud as you can. c. whistle loudly and shrilly.	_____	_____
2. You are in "snake country." Your best action to avoid snakes is to: a. make a lot of noise with your feet. b. walk softly and quietly. c. travel at night.	_____	_____
3. You are hungry and lost in wild country. The best rule for determining which plants are safe to eat (those you do not recognize) is to: a. try anything you see the birds eat. b. eat anything except plants with bright red berries. c. put a bit of the plant on your lower lip for five minutes; if it seems all right, try a little.		
4. The day becomes dry and hot. You have a full canteen of water (about one liter) with you. You should: a. ration it—about a cupful a day. b. not drink until you stop for the night, then drink what you think you need. c. drink as much as you think you need when you need it.	_____	_____
5. Your water is gone; you become very thirsty. You finally come to a dried-up watercourse. Your best chance of finding water is to: a. dig anywhere in the stream bed. b. dig up plant and tree roots near the bank. c. dig in the stream bed at the outside of a bend.	_____	_____

6. You decide to walk out of the wild country by following a series of ravines where a water supply is available. Night is coming on. The best place to make camp is:
   a. next to the water supply in the ravine.
   b. high on a ridge.
   c. midway up the slope.

   _____   _____

7. Your flashlight glows dimly as you are about to make your way back to your campsite after a brief foraging trip. Darkness comes quickly in the woods and the surroundings seem unfamiliar. You should:
   a. head back at once, keeping the light on, hoping the light will glow enough for you to make out landmarks.
   b. put the batteries under your armpits to warm them, and then replace them in the flashlight.
   c. shine your light for a few seconds, try to get the scene in mind, move out in the darkness, and repeat the process.

   _____   _____

8. An early snow confines you to your small tent. You doze with your small stove going. There is danger if the flame is:
   a. yellow.
   b. blue.
   c. red.

   _____   _____

9. You must ford a river that has a strong current, large rocks, and some white water. After carefully selecting your crossing spot, you should:
   a. leave your boots and pack on.
   b. take your boots and pack off.
   c. take off your pack, but leave your boots on.

   _____   _____

10. In waist-deep water with a strong current, when crossing the stream, you should face:
    a. upstream.
    b. across the stream.
    c. downstream.

    _____   _____

11. You find yourself rimrocked; your only route is up. The way is mossy, slippery rock. You should try it:
    a. barefoot.
    b. with boots on.
    c. in stocking feet.

    _____   _____

12. Unarmed and unsuspecting, you surprise a large bear prowling around your campsite. As the bear rears up about ten meters from you, you should:
    a. run.
    b. climb the nearest tree.
    c. freeze, but be ready to back away slowly.

    _____   _____

WILDERNESS SURVIVAL GROUP BRIEFING SHEET

Decision by consensus is a method of problem solving and decision making in groups in which all the parties involved actively discuss the issues surrounding the decision. The group thus pools the knowledge and experience of all its members. Any final decision must be supported by each member of the group. The ideas and feelings of all the members are integrated into a group decision, thus allowing several people to work together on a common problem, rather than producing a "we-they" stand-off.

As you might imagine, decision by consensus is usually difficult to attain and will consume more time than other methods of deciding an issue. As the energies of the group become focused on the problem at hand (rather than on defending individual points of view), the quality of the decision tends to be enhanced. Research indicates, in fact, that this approach to problem solving and decision making results in a significantly higher-quality decision than other methods such as the use of majority power (voting), minority power (persuasion), and compromise.

In the decision-by-consensus process, each group member is asked to:

1. prepare his own position as well as possible prior to meeting with the group (but to realize that the task is incomplete and that the missing pieces are to be supplied by the other members of the group).

2. recognize an obligation to express his own opinion and explain it fully, so that the rest of the group has the benefit of all members' thinking.

3. recognize an obligation to listen to the opinions and feelings of all other group members and to be ready to modify one's own position on the basis of logic and understanding.

4. avoid conflict-reducing techniques such as voting, compromising, or giving in to keep the peace and to realize that differences of opinion are helpful; in exploring differences, the best course of action will make itself apparent.

You have just completed an individual solution to Wilderness Survival: A Consensus-Seeking Task. Now your small task group will decide on a group solution to the same dilemmas. Remember, decision by consensus is difficult to attain, and not every decision may meet with everyone's unqualified approval. There should be, however, a general feeling of support from all members before a group decision is made. Take the time you need to listen for understanding, consider *all* members' views, make your own view known, and be reasonable in arriving at a group decision.

WILDERNESS SURVIVAL ANSWER AND RATIONALE SHEET

Here are the recommended courses of action for each of the situations on the Wilderness Survival Work Sheet. These answers come from the comprehensive course on woodland survival taught by the Interpretive Service, Monroe County (New York) Parks Department. These responses are considered to be the best rules of thumb for most situations; specific situations, however, might require other courses of action.

1. (a.) *Call "help" loudly but in a low register.* Low tones carry farther, especially in dense woodland. There is a much better chance of being heard if you call loudly but in a low key. "Help" is a good word to use, because it alerts your companions to your plight. Yelling or screaming would not only be less effective, but might be passed off as a bird call by your friends far away.

2. (a.) *Make a lot of noise with your feet.* Snakes do not like people and will usually do everything they can to get out of your way. Unless you surprise or corner a snake, there is a good chance that you will not even see one, let alone come into contact with it. Some snakes do feed at night, and walking softly may bring you right on top of a snake.

3. (c.) *Put a bit of the plant on your lower lip for five minutes; if it seems all right, try a little.* The best approach, of course, is to eat only those plants that you recognize as safe. But when you are in doubt and very hungry, you may use the lip test. If the plant is poisonous, you will get a very unpleasant sensation on your lip. Red berries alone do not tell you much about the plant's edibility (unless, of course, you recognize the plant by the berries), and birds just do not have the same digestive systems we do.

4. (c.) *Drink as much as you think you need when you need it.* The danger here is dehydration, and once the process starts, your liter of water will not do much to reverse it. Saving or rationing will not help, especially if you are lying unconscious somewhere from sunstroke or dehydration. So use the water as you need it, and be aware of your need to find a water source as soon as possible.

5. (c.) *Dig in the stream bed at the outside of a bend.* This is the part of the river or stream that flows the fastest, is less silted, deepest, and the last part to go dry.

6. (c.) *Midway up the slope.* A sudden rain storm might turn the ravine into a raging torrent. This has happened to many campers and hikers before they had a chance to escape. The ridge line, on the other hand, increases your exposure to rain, wind, and lightning, should a storm break. The best location is on the slope.

7. (b.) *Put the batteries under your armpits to warm them, and then replace them in the flashlight.* Flashlight batteries lose much of their power, and weak batteries run down faster, in the cold. Warming the batteries, especially if they are already weak, will restore them for a while. You would normally avoid night travel, of course, unless you were in open country where you could use the stars for navigation. There are just too many obstacles (logs, branches, uneven ground, and so on) that might injure you—and a broken leg, injured eye, or twisted ankle would not help your plight right now. Once the sun sets, darkness falls quickly in wooded areas; it would usually be best to stay at your campsite.

8. (a.) *Yellow.* A yellow flame indicates incomplete combustion and a strong possibility of carbon monoxide build-up. Each year many campers are killed by carbon monoxide poisoning as they sleep or doze in tents, cabins, or other enclosed spaces.

9. (a.) *Leave your boots and pack on.* Errors in fording rivers are a major cause of fatal accidents. Sharp rocks or uneven footing demand that you keep your boots on. If your pack is fairly well balanced, wearing it will provide you the most stability in the swift current.

A waterproof, zippered backpack will usually float, even when loaded with normal camping gear; if you step off into a hole or deep spot, the pack could become a lifesaver.

10. (b.) *Across the stream.* Errors in facing the wrong way in fording a stream are the cause of many drownings. Facing upstream is the worst alternative; the current could push you back and your pack would provide the unbalance to pull you over. You have the best stability facing across the stream, keeping your eye on the exit point on the opposite bank.

11. (c.) *In stocking feet.* Here you can pick your route to some degree, and you can feel where you are stepping. Normal hiking boots become slippery, and going barefooted offers your feet no protection at all.

12. (c.) *Freeze, but be ready to back away slowly.* Sudden movement will probably startle the bear a lot more than your presence. If the bear is seeking some of your food, do not argue with him; let him forage and be on his way. Otherwise, back very slowly toward some refuge (trees, rock outcrop, etc.).

178. AL KOHBARI: AN INFORMATION-SHARING MULTIPLE ROLE PLAY

Goals

    I. To study how information relevant to a task is shared within work groups.

    II. To observe problem-solving strategies within work groups.

    III. To explore the effects of collaboration and competition in group problem solving.

    IV. To demonstrate the effects of hidden agendas on group decision making.

Group Size

    An unlimited number of groups of six members each.

Time Required

    Approximately two hours.

Materials

    I. A set of five Al Kohbari Data Sheets for each group, one sheet for each member except Colonel Miller. Each sheet is coded by the number of dots (from one to five) at the end of the first paragraph, and each sheet contains some data that is unique to that sheet.

    II. An Al Kohbari Map and an Al Kohbari Equipment-Specifications Summary Sheet for each participant.

    III. One Al Kohbari Biography Sheet for each group member except those who play Colonel Miller (each receives only the biography for the character he is to role play).

    IV. A set of all six Al Kohbari Biography Sheets (one for each of the six roles) for the member in each group who will play Colonel Miller.

    V. Blank paper and a pencil for each group member.

    VI. One Al Kohbari Problem-Solution Sheet for each participant.

Physical Setting

    A room large enough for all groups to work simultaneously without distracting or overhearing one another. (One large room may be used for instructional and processing phases, with smaller rooms available in which individual groups can work during the problem-solving phase.) It is useful to provide a table and chairs for each group, with extra chairs for observers, if used.

Process

    I. The facilitator informs participants that they will be engaging in a problem-solving activity.

    II. He divides the participants into groups of six. (Additional members may serve as observers.)

    III. The facilitator explains that the groups' task is to recommend a type of armored personnel carrier (APC) to be purchased by the Arab nation of Al Kohbari. He says that one type of

APC is the best choice, considering all available data, but that each group is to make its decision privately and independently.

IV. The facilitator distributes materials, as follows:

1. A set of five different Al Kohbari Data Sheets is given to each group, with each member, except Colonel Miller, receiving a differently coded sheet.

2. Each member of each group (including Colonel Miller) receives an Al Kohbari Map and an Al Kohbari Equipment-Specifications Summary Sheet.

3. Each group member except Colonel Miller receives an Al Kohbari Biography Sheet for the character he is to role play.

4. The Colonel Miller in each group receives six Al Kohbari Biography Sheets—one for each member of the group.

5. All members are given blank paper and a pencil.

V. The facilitator informs members that their group will have one hour in which to make a recommendation. He says that if a group finishes before time is called, its members may silently observe other groups but are not to distract other members or join in another group's process.

VI. When all groups have completed their tasks, or at the end of the hour, the facilitator processes the experience through a discussion of the problem-solving strategies observed, the effects of collaboration and competition in the group, the ways in which information was shared in the group, and the effects that hidden agendas had on the group process.

VII. The facilitator then distributes the Al Kohbari Problem-Solution Sheet and discusses it.

Variations

I. Observers may be assigned to specific groups to provide feedback on individual work styles or may circulate from group to group to provide more generalized data.

II. The facilitator may stress competition between groups by posting the amount of time used by each group in accomplishing its task and by posting the recommendation made by each group.

III. The facilitator may inform participants at the beginning that they each have different information on their data sheets.

IV. The data and problem may be tailored to a particular group of participants, or it may be made more or less complex.

Similar Structured Experiences: *Vol. I:* Structured Experience 12; *Vol. II:* **31**; *'72 Annual:* **80**; *'73 Annual:* **98**; *Vol. IV:* **103, 117**; *'74 Annual:* **133, 135**; *'75 Annual:* **139**; *Vol. V:* **155, 156**.

Lecturette Sources: *'73 Annual:* "Conditions Which Hinder Effective Communication"; *'74 Annual:* "Hidden Agendas."

Submitted by Robert E. Mattingly.

> **Major Robert E. Mattingly** *is a Marine officer instructor and an assistant professor of naval science at the University of Southern California. He teaches undergraduate courses in the evolution of warfare and military history. Major Mattingly is a frequent contributor to professional periodicals. He has served in a variety of command and staff assignments including duty with the Department of State in the Middle East and with the United Nations Command in Korea.*

AL KOHBARI DATA SHEET

Your group has been hurriedly called into session by Ambassador Neumann. Last evening at a diplomatic function, His Highness Prince Abdulla Al Salam (oldest son of the sultan) indicated that the country of Al Kohbari was interested in purchasing armored personnel carriers (APC's) for its ground defense force.

Al Kohbari's principal antagonist and traditional enemy is the currently leftist People's Arabian Democracy of Draban (PADD). PADD's army has recently acquired thirty Soviet BTR-60P personnel carriers. The CIA reports that PADD is negotiating for the purchase of seventy additional BTR's with spare parts and advisers from Iraq. A force of this size would be capable of lifting two full-strength infantry battalions and their organic weapons. Such a capability might alter the precarious balance of power between Al Kohbari and PADD and is certainly of concern for prestige reasons.

The date is 1 July 1976. The ambassador has informed Prince Abdulla that the United States would prefer not to supply additional arms directly to Al Kohbari. The sultan has, however, asked that the U.S. Embassy provide his chief of staff with a recommended APC type. His government apparently intends to use this recommendation as a departure point for negotiations with the manufacturing country. Ambassador Neumann is scheduled to dine with both the sultan and Prince Abdulla this evening and has promised to present a military appraisal at that time.

Background

Both Al Kohbari and PADD are located in the southern portion of the Arabian peninsula. The climate is hot and dry most of the year. Since the two countries achieved their independence from colonial powers in the late 1940's, traditional rivalries have been exacerbated by the discovery of high-grade petroleum in the Al Kohbari coastal plain. The significant topographic features of the two nations are depicted on the map of Al Kohbari. The Irawani River seldom rises higher than five feet but is fast moving. Rainfall is limited to the February-April period and averages six to eight inches per year.

Al Kohbari has agreed to limited airfield use by the U.S. and the U.K., while PADD has provided similar facilities for the U.A.R., Iraq, and the U.S.S.R. The main desert areas are passable by both wheeled and tracked vehicles.

Bridging limitation on the major axis of any military advance is generally twenty tons. Excellent cross-country mobility in any vehicle purchased is highly desirable.

Small arms and ammunition stocks are predominately of U.S. WW II vintage. The Al Kohbari rifle squad is composed of six infantrymen and a squad leader.

It is believed that Al Kohbari's actual requirement for APC's is militarily minimal. An increased anti-armor capability utilizing infantry-type weapons would be cheaper and just as effective. However, since prestige is involved and cost is not a problem, the purchase scheme will doubtless be pursued. A proven design is essential. The vehicle must be able to cross the Irawani and have a close-in, antipersonnel armament capability.

A rough "shopping list" of five possible APC choices and comparison data for the BTR-60P are provided. The Defense Attaché Office working group is headed by Colonel Robert B. Miller, USAF, and includes Lieutenant Colonel Percell A. Collins, USA (Army attaché), Lieutenant Colonel Milton S. Steele, USMC (Naval attaché), Captain James L. Coyle, USA (adviser to the 1st Commando Battalion), Warrant Officer Sam J. Jones, USAF (maintenance adviser to the Royal Al Kohbari Air Corps), and Mr. Harold A. Smoot, assistant counselor for economics, U.S. Embassy. Mr. Smoot has a civilian rank equivalent to lieutenant colonel.

Colonel Miller will present the recommended type of APC to Ambassador Neumann at a private appointment scheduled in one hour.

28

AL KOHBARI DATA SHEET

Your group has been hurriedly called into session by Ambassador Neumann. Last evening at a diplomatic function, His Highness Prince Abdulla Al Salam (oldest son of the sultan) indicated that the country of Al Kohbari was interested in purchasing armored personnel carriers (APC's) for its ground defense force. .

Al Kohbari's principal antagonist and traditional enemy is the currently leftist People's Arabian Democracy of Draban (PADD). PADD's army has recently acquired thirty Soviet BTR-60P personnel carriers. The CIA reports that PADD is negotiating for the purchase of seventy additional BTR's with spare parts and advisers from Iraq. A force of this size would be capable of lifting two full-strength infantry battalions and their organic weapons. Such a capability might alter the precarious balance of power between Al Kohbari and PADD and is certainly of concern for prestige reasons.

The date is 1 July 1976. The ambassador has informed Prince Abdulla that the United States would prefer not to supply additional arms directly to Al Kohbari. The sultan has, however, asked that the U.S. Embassy provide his chief of staff with a recommended APC type. His government apparently intends to use this recommendation as a departure point for negotiations with the manufacturing country. Ambassador Neumann is scheduled to dine with both the sultan and Prince Abdulla this evening and has promised to present a military appraisal at that time.

Background

Both Al Kohbari and PADD are located in the southern portion of the Arabian peninsula. The climate is hot and dry most of the year. Since the two countries achieved their independence from colonial powers in the late 1940's, traditional rivalries have been exacerbated by the discovery of high-grade petroleum in the Al Kohbari coastal plain. The significant topographic features of the two nations are depicted on the map of Al Kohbari. The Irawani River seldom rises higher than five feet but is fast moving. Rainfall is limited to the February-April period and averages six to eight inches per year.

Al Kohbari has agreed to limited airfield use by the U.S. and the U.K., while PADD has provided similar facilities for the U.A.R., Iraq, and the U.S.S.R. The main desert areas are passable by both wheeled and tracked vehicles.

The Al Kohbari ground defense force is composed primarily of tough Bedouins who are intensely loyal to the royal family of Al Kohbari. Until 1969 there were few vehicles of any type. Mechanical skills are generally low, and most maintenance is performed by Pakistanis on a contract basis. Current in-service vehicles are of U.K. and U.S. manufacture. Highly technological APC's could probably not be given adequate maintenance support.

Small arms and ammunition stocks are predominately of U.S. WW II vintage. The Al Kohbari rifle squad is composed of six infantrymen and a squad leader.

It is believed that Al Kohbari's actual requirement for APC's is militarily minimal. An increased anti-armor capability utilizing infantry-type weapons would be cheaper and just as effective. However, since prestige is involved and cost is not a problem, the purchase scheme will doubtless be pursued. A proven design is essential. The vehicle must be able to cross the Irawani and have a close-in, antipersonnel armament capability.

A rough "shopping list" of five possible APC choices and comparison data for the BTR-60P are provided. The Defense Attaché Office working group is headed by Colonel Robert B. Miller, USAF, and includes Lieutenant Colonel Percell A. Collins, USA (Army attaché), Lieutenant Colonel Milton S. Steele, USMC (Naval attaché), Captain James L. Coyle, USA (adviser to the 1st Commando Battalion), Warrant Officer Sam J. Jones, USAF (maintenance adviser to the Royal Al Kohbari Air Corps), and Mr. Harold A. Smoot, assistant counselor for economics, U.S. Embassy. Mr. Smoot has a civilian rank equivalent to lieutenant colonel.

Colonel Miller will present the recommended type of APC to Ambassador Neumann at a private appointment scheduled in one hour.

AL KOHBARI DATA SHEET

Your group has been hurriedly called into session by Ambassador Neumann. Last evening at a diplomatic function, His Highness Prince Abdulla Al Salam (oldest son of the sultan) indicated that the country of Al Kohbari was interested in purchasing armored personnel carriers (APC's) for its ground defense force. . .

Al Kohbari's principal antagonist and traditional enemy is the currently leftist People's Arabian Democracy of Draban (PADD). PADD's army has recently acquired thirty Soviet BTR-60P personnel carriers. The CIA reports that PADD is negotiating for the purchase of seventy additional BTR's with spare parts and advisers from Iraq. A force of this size would be capable of lifting two full-strength infantry battalions and their organic weapons. Such a capability might alter the precarious balance of power between Al Kohbari and PADD and is certainly of concern for prestige reasons.

The date is 1 July 1976. The ambassador has informed Prince Abdulla that the United States would prefer not to supply additional arms directly to Al Kohbari. The sultan has, however, asked that the U.S. Embassy provide his chief of staff with a recommended APC type. His government apparently intends to use this recommendation as a departure point for negotiations with the manufacturing country. Ambassador Neumann is scheduled to dine with both the sultan and Prince Abdulla this evening and has promised to present a military appraisal at that time.

Background

Both Al Kohbari and PADD are located in the southern portion of the Arabian peninsula. The climate is hot and dry most of the year. Since the two countries achieved their independence from colonial powers in the late 1940's, traditional rivalries have been exacerbated by the discovery of high-grade petroleum in the Al Kohbari coastal plain. The significant topographic features of the two nations are depicted on the map of Al Kohbari. The Irawani River seldom rises higher than five feet but is fast moving. Rainfall is limited to the February-April period and averages six to eight inches per year.

Al Kohbari has agreed to limited airfield use by the U.S. and the U.K., while PADD has provided similar facilities for the U.A.R., Iraq, and the U.S.S.R. The main desert areas are passable by both wheeled and tracked vehicles.

The Al Kohbari armed forces are composed of a ground defense force (Army) and a small air defense force (Royal Al Kohbari Air Corps). The Air Corps equipment consists exclusively of aircraft manufactured in the U.S. and the U.K. Two fighter squadrons of F-104 Starfighters are operational. The pilots and ground crews are being trained by a 260-man West German contingent, which provides a pool of maintenance experts.

Small arms and ammunition stocks are predominately of U.S. WW II vintage. The Al Kohbari rifle squad is composed of six infantrymen and a squad leader.

It is believed that Al Kohbari's actual requirement for APC's is militarily minimal. An increased anti-armor capability utilizing infantry-type weapons would be cheaper and just as effective. However, since prestige is involved and cost is not a problem, the purchase scheme will doubtless be pursued. A proven design is essential. The vehicle must be able to cross the Irawani and have a close-in, antipersonnel armament capability.

A rough "shopping list" of five possible APC choices and comparison data for the BTR-60P are provided. The Defense Attaché Office working group is headed by Colonel Robert B. Miller, USAF, and includes Lieutenant Colonel Percell A. Collins, USA (Army attaché), Lieutenant Colonel Milton S. Steele, USMC (Naval attaché), Captain James L. Coyle, USA (adviser to the 1st Commando Battalion), Warrant Officer Sam J. Jones, USAF (maintenance adviser to the Royal Al Kohbari Air Corps), and Mr. Harold A. Smoot, assistant counselor for economics, U.S. Embassy. Mr. Smoot has a civilian rank equivalent to lieutenant colonel.

Colonel Miller will present the recommended type of APC to Ambassador Neumann at a private appointment scheduled in one hour.

AL KOHBARI DATA SHEET

Your group has been hurriedly called into session by Ambassador Neumann. Last evening at a diplomatic function, His Highness Prince Abdulla Al Salam (oldest son of the sultan) indicated that the country of Al Kohbari was interested in purchasing armored personnel carriers (APC's) for its ground defense force. . . .

Al Kohbari's principal antagonist and traditional enemy is the currently leftist People's Arabian Democracy of Draban (PADD). PADD's army has recently acquired thirty Soviet BTR-60P personnel carriers. The CIA reports that PADD is negotiating for the purchase of seventy additional BTR's with spare parts and advisers from Iraq. A force of this size would be capable of lifting two full-strength infantry battalions and their organic weapons. Such a capability might alter the precarious balance of power between Al Kohbari and PADD and is certainly of concern for prestige reasons.

The date is 1 July 1976. The ambassador has informed Prince Abdulla that the United States would prefer not to supply additional arms directly to Al Kohbari. The sultan has, however, asked that the U.S. Embassy provide his chief of staff with a recommended APC type. His government apparently intends to use this recommendation as a departure point for negotiations with the manufacturing country. Ambassador Neumann is scheduled to dine with both the sultan and Prince Abdulla this evening and has promised to present a military appraisal at that time.

Background

Both Al Kohbari and PADD are located in the southern portion of the Arabian peninsula. The climate is hot and dry most of the year. Since the two countries achieved their independence from colonial powers in the late 1940's, traditional rivalries have been exacerbated by the discovery of high-grade petroleum in the Al Kohbari coastal plain. The significant topographic features of the two nations are depicted on the map of Al Kohbari. The Irawani River seldom rises higher than five feet but is fast moving. Rainfall is limited to the February-April period and averages six to eight inches per year.

Al Kohbari has agreed to limited airfield use by the U.S. and the U.K., while PADD has provided similar facilities for the U.A.R., Iraq, and the U.S.S.R. The main desert areas are passable by both wheeled and tracked vehicles.

Al Kohbari has diplomatic missions in France, West Germany, Switzerland, the U.K., and the U.S. These countries, as well as Japan, Taiwan, Pakistan, India, and the Republic of Korea, have representation in the capital of Abu Milhelm.

Small arms and ammunition stocks are predominately of U.S. WW II vintage. The Al Kohbari rifle squad is composed of six infantrymen and a squad leader.

It is believed that Al Kohbari's actual requirement for APC's is militarily minimal. An increased anti-armor capability utilizing infantry-type weapons would be cheaper and just as effective. However, since prestige is involved and cost is not a problem, the purchase scheme will doubtless be pursued. A proven design is essential. The vehicle must be able to cross the Irawani and have a close-in, antipersonnel armament capability.

A rough "shopping list" of five possible APC choices and comparison data for the BTR-60P are provided. The Defense Attaché Office working group is headed by Colonel Robert B. Miller, USAF, and includes Lieutenant Colonel Percell A. Collins, USA (Army attaché), Lieutenant Colonel Milton S. Steele, USMC (Naval attaché), Captain James L. Coyle, USA (adviser to the 1st Commando Battalion), Warrant Officer Sam J. Jones, USAF (maintenance adviser to the Royal Al Kohbari Air Corps), and Mr. Harold A. Smoot, assistant counselor for economics, U.S. Embassy. Mr. Smoot has a civilian rank equivalent to lieutenant colonel.

Colonel Miller will present the recommended type of APC to Ambassador Neumann at a private appointment scheduled in one hour.

AL KOHBARI DATA SHEET

Your group has been hurriedly called into session by Ambassador Neumann. Last evening at a diplomatic function, His Highness Prince Abdulla Al Salam (oldest son of the sultan) indicated that the country of Al Kohbari was interested in purchasing armored personnel carriers (APC's) for its ground defense force. . . . .

Al Kohbari's principal antagonist and traditional enemy is the currently leftist People's Arabian Democracy of Draban (PADD). PADD's army has recently acquired thirty Soviet BTR-60P personnel carriers. The CIA reports that PADD is negotiating for the purchase of seventy additional BTR's with spare parts and advisers from Iraq. A force of this size would be capable of lifting two full-strength infantry battalions and their organic weapons. Such a capability might alter the precarious balance of power between Al Kohbari and PADD and is certainly of concern for prestige reasons.

The date is 1 July 1976. The ambassador has informed Prince Abdulla that the United States would prefer not to supply additional arms directly to Al Kohbari. The sultan has, however, asked that the U.S. Embassy provide his chief of staff with a recommended APC type. His government apparently intends to use this recommendation as a departure point for negotiations with the manufacturing country. Ambassador Neumann is scheduled to dine with both the sultan and Prince Abdulla this evening and has promised to present a military appraisal at that time.

Background

Both Al Kohbari and PADD are located in the southern portion of the Arabian peninsula. The climate is hot and dry most of the year. Since the two countries achieved their independence from colonial powers in the late 1940's, traditional rivalries have been exacerbated by the discovery of high-grade petroleum in the Al Kohbari coastal plain. The significant topographic features of the two nations are depicted on the map of Al Kohbari. The Irawani River seldom rises higher than five feet but is fast moving. Rainfall is limited to the February-April period and averages six to eight inches per year.

Al Kohbari has agreed to limited airfield use by the U.S. and the U.K., while PADD has provided similar facilities for the U.A.R., Iraq, and the U.S.S.R. The main desert areas are passable by both wheeled and tracked vehicles.

The capital city, Abu Milhelm, is a rapidly developing port and commercial center. In order to foster reciprocal development of maritime ties with seafaring nations, the government has a long-standing policy of dealing with such countries to the exclusion of all others. Such relations are especially strong with the U.K. and West Germany.

Small arms and ammunition stocks are predominately of U.S. WW II vintage. The Al Kohbari rifle squad is composed of six infantrymen and a squad leader.

It is believed that Al Kohbari's actual requirement for APC's is militarily minimal. An increased anti-armor capability utilizing infantry-type weapons would be cheaper and just as effective. However, since prestige is involved and cost is not a problem, the purchase scheme will doubtless be pursued. A proven design is essential. The vehicle must be able to cross the Irawani and have a close-in, antipersonnel armament capability.

A rough "shopping list" of five possible APC choices and comparison data for the BTR-60P are provided. The Defense Attaché Office working group is headed by Colonel Robert B. Miller, USAF, and includes Lieutenant Colonel Percell A. Collins, USA (Army attaché), Lieutenant Colonel Milton S. Steele, USMC (Naval attaché), Captain James L. Coyle, USA (adviser to the 1st Commando Battalion), Warrant Officer Sam J. Jones, USAF (maintenance adviser to the Royal Al Kohbari Air Corps), and Mr. Harold A. Smoot, assistant counselor for economics, U.S. Embassy. Mr. Smoot has a civilian rank equivalent to lieutenant colonel.

Colonel Miller will present the recommended type of APC to Ambassador Neumann at a private appointment scheduled in one hour.

AL KOHBARI MAP

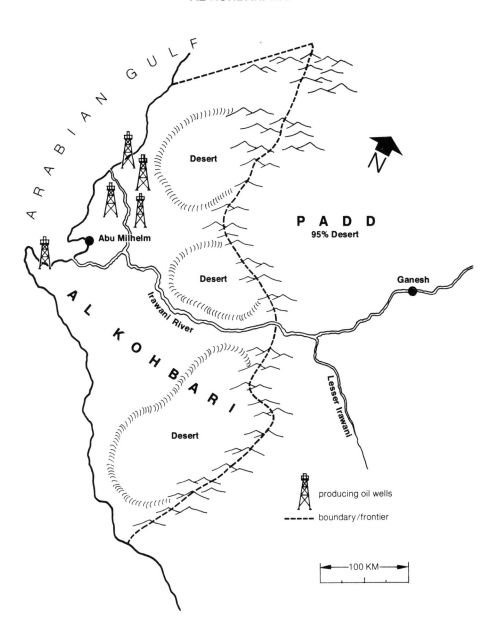

AL KOHBARI EQUIPMENT-SPECIFICATIONS SUMMARY SHEET

BTR-60P (U.S.S.R.) (For Comparison Only)

Crew: 2
Troops: 12
Weight: 10 tons
Height: 2.3 meters
Length: 7.3 meters
Width: 2.8 meters
Road Speed/Range: 80 k.p.h./500 k.p.h.
Propulsion: 8 wheels on land, hydrojet in water, totally amphibious
Armament: 14.5 mm heavy machine gun and 7.62 mm light machine gun in turret (manual traverse)
Power: Two 6-cylinder gasoline engines
Advantages: Fast road speed, amphibious capability, troop capacity.
Disadvantages: Poor cross-country mobility, troops must dismount from top hatches, very light overhead armor, limited night operational capability.

FV 432 APC (United Kingdom)

Crew: 2; 10 infantrymen
Weight: 15.1 tons
Height: 1.88 meters
Length: 5.1 meters
Width: 2.97 meters
Road Speed/Range: 52 k.p.h./580 k.p.h.
Power: Rolls Royce 6-cylinder multifuel, automatic transmission
Armament: One 7.62 mm light machine gun, externally mounted
Propulsion: Fully tracked vehicle
Advantages: Proven design, in service with the Royal Armored Corps since 1965. Can be delivered with 105 mm "Wombat" antitank recoilless rifle, has good night-driving capability, has retriever and command-vehicle variants in production. Spare parts readily available. Good armor protection.
Disadvantages: Rather heavy, relatively slow, cross-country mobility only fair, no amphibious capability. Maintenance intensive.
Cost: £120,000 each, including basic spare parts and track
Delivery: 12 months
Crew training: 12-14 weeks

APC Marder-Schutzenpanzer M-1967 (New) (West Germany)

Crew: 3; 7 infantrymen
Weight: 28.2 tons
Height: 2.86 meters
Length: 7.79 meters
Width: 3.27 meters
Road Speed/Range: 70 k.p.h./600 k.p.h.
Power: Mercedes 6-cylinder, turbocharged diesel
Armament: One 20 mm cannon in rotating turret, two 7.62 mm light machine guns, firing ports for infantrymen
Propulsion: Fully tracked vehicle

Advantages: Wading ability to 2 meters, excellent fire power. Good cross-country mobility, conventional steering, exceptional crew protection and comfort (including ventilation systems and sleeping provision). Full night operational capability. Probably the best all-around NATO APC.
Disadvantages: Very heavy, perhaps overengineered, no amphibious capability, no retriever variant, maintenance intensive.
Cost: DM 950,000 each, exclusive of spare parts
Delivery: 12-14 months
Crew training: 16-20 weeks

APC Type 60 (Improved) (Japan)

Crew: 2; 8 infantrymen
Weight: 12 tons
Height: 1.7 meters
Length: 4.85 meters
Width: 2.4 meters
Road Speed/Range: 45 k.p.h./490 k.p.h.
Power: Mitsubishi V-8 diesel
Armament: .50 caliber heavy machine gun in external mount, .30 caliber light machine gun in hull
Propulsion: Fully tracked vehicle
Advantages: Very low ground pressure, good cross-country mobility, extremely reliable, can be fitted with U.S.-manufactured TOW antitank, wire-guided missile system.
Disadvantages: No amphibious capability, crew comfort is nil, engine compartment and fuel side-by-side near troops, small exit hatches.
Cost: $400,000 each, exclusive of spare parts
Delivery: 6-8 months
Crew training: 10-12 weeks

AMX-10P APC (France)

Crew: 2; 9 infantrymen
Weight: 12.5 tons
Height: 2.37 meters
Length: 5.86 meters
Width: 2.78 meters
Road Speed/Range: 65 k.p.h./620 k.p.h.
Power: Hispano-Suiza, water cooled, multifuel
Armament: 20 mm cannon, 7.62 mm light machine gun (both in enclosed turret)
Propulsion: Fully tracked (a wheeled variant is undergoing tests at present)
Advantages: Excellent cross-country mobility, fully amphibious, excellent fire power, good power-to-weight ratio, currently in full production for French army. An outstanding future appears to await this vehicle.
Disadvantages: A new vehicle not fully debugged, no variants in production, although a number are planned, including a retriever and command vehicle. 20 mm gun had some initial development problems.
Cost: 1,200,000 FF each, exclusive of spare parts
Delivery: 8-10 months (est.)
Crew training: 10-12 weeks

Hagghinds Pbv 302 (Sweden)

Crew: 2; 10 infantrymen
Weight: 13.5 tons
Height: 2.5 meters
Length: 5.4 meters
Width: 2.86 meters
Road Speed/Range: 65 k.p.h./300 k.p.h.
Power: Volvo-Pinta 6-cylinder, supercharged diesel
Armament: 20 mm automatic cannon in handwheel traverse turret
Propulsion: Fully tracked

Advantages: Superior cross-country mobility, excellent armor protection, fully amphibious, high power/weight ratio. Variants include: retriever, command vehicle, bridge layer, artillery-fire control vehicle. Exits through both rear and top. One of the best designed and executed APC's extant.

Disadvantages: No antipersonnel armament (machine guns), relatively short range, hand turret traverse.

Cost: $380,000 (est.), exclusive of spare parts
Delivery: 12-14 months
Crew training: 16-18 weeks

AL KOHBARI BIOGRAPHY SHEET

Warrant Officer Sam J. Jones, USAF

Warrant Officer Jones was born 9 November 1942 in Midville, Georgia. He completed ten years of public school before joining the U.S. Army in 1959. Leaving the Army as a sergeant in 1962, Jones immediately joined the U.S. Air Force. Trained as a maintenance systems noncommissioned officer, Airman Jones rapidly proved to be particularly successful in organizing programs to keep A1E propeller-driven aircraft operational. Promoted to staff sergeant in 1964 and master sergeant in 1966, he spent a total of thirty-six months as a maintenance adviser to the Vietnamese Air Force.

Returning to the United States in 1968, Master Sergeant Jones was appointed a warrant officer and assigned to Offutt Air Force Base, Nebraska. In 1970, Warrant Officer Jones completed his high school equivalency through USAFI. He has attended numerous technical schools and is considered the most knowledgeable member of the U.S. Embassy staff on maintenance matters. Warrant Officer Jones arrived in Al Kohbari eighteen months ago and has established an outstanding working relationship with the German Air Force advisers and technicians who service the Al Kohbari F-104 Starfighters. He has expressed interest in employment with the German contract firm after his retirement in 1979. Colonel Miller is particularly fond of Jones and values his judgment.

Both Lieutenant Colonel Collins and Lieutenant Colonel Steele regard Jones as an excellent mechanic but as totally unmilitary. Jones is married and has two small children who reside in the American compound.

AL KOHBARI BIOGRAPHY SHEET

Lieutenant Colonel Milton S. Steele, USMC

Lieutenant Colonel Steele was born in Santa Carita, California, 26 May 1935. He attended public schools and graduated from Dartmouth College in 1956. Following graduation, Second Lieutenant Steele was commissioned in the Marine Corps Reserve and reported to The Basic School, Quantico, Virginia, for duty.

During the first ten years of his service with the Marines, he was posted to infantry units of the 2nd and 3rd Marine Divisions. Promoted to first lieutenant in 1958 and captain in 1961, he filled virtually all of the command and staff billets in a Marine rifle battalion.

Captain Steele attended the Amphibious Warfare School in 1964, graduating first in a class of 157 officers. Following a tour of duty as commanding officer, Marine Detachment, *USS Little Rock* (a cruiser), Captain Steele reported to the 1st Marine Division in Vietnam. As a company commander and battalion executive officer, Captain Steele participated in a number of major combat operations. He was promoted to major in 1966.

Upon his return to the United States, Major Steele attended the Armed Forces Staff College, Norfolk, Virginia. From 1968 to 1971, Major Steele was assigned to the Marine Corps Development Center, Quantico, where he was project manager for a series of infantry weapons-development projects. Selected for promotion to lieutenant colonel in 1972, he was in the midst of a tour as commanding officer, 2nd Battalion, 5th Marines, when ordered to attaché duty.

Lieutenant Colonel Steele arrived in Al Kohbari 15 September 1974. He is married and has three children. The Steele family resides in the American compound in Abu Milhelm. Lieutenant Colonel Steele is a close friend of Mr. Smoot and Captain Coyle. He considers his tour with the attaché office an interesting but basically unproductive pause in his career.

AL KOHBARI BIOGRAPHY SHEET

Captain James L. Coyle, USA (Armor)

Captain Coyle was born in Bingston, Montana, 26 March 1947. He attended public schools in Montana and Illinois. In 1965, Coyle was appointed to the U.S. Military Academy (West Point) and graduated in 1969, electing to be commissioned in the Armor branch.

After completing the Ranger School, Second Lieutenant Coyle attended the Armor Officer's Basic Course at Fort Knox, Kentucky. While at the school, he wrote a strategic assessment of the Arabian Gulf states that was published in a professional magazine.

Lieutenant Coyle served as a tank platoon commander in an Armor battalion of the 8th United States Army in Korea during 1970-71. He attended the U.S. Army basic intelligence officer course at Fort Huachuca, Arizona, in 1972, graduating second in a class of 134 junior officers. Following an assignment as assistant brigade intelligence officer with the 1st Cavalry Division, Fort Hood, Texas, he was promoted to captain and transferred to his current duties as adviser to the Al Kohbari 1st Commando Battalion.

Captain Coyle has been in Al Kohbari since October 1974. He is well liked and respected by the Bedouin soldiers and has learned a fair amount of Arabic. He is very popular with the U.S. Embassy secretaries.

Captain Coyle is well respected by Lieutenant Colonel Steele. Lieutenant Colonel Collins appears to resent his West Point education and his image as the *bon vivant* of the embassy cocktail circuit.

AL KOHBARI BIOGRAPHY SHEET

Lieutenant Colonel Percell A. Collins, USA (Infantry)

Lieutenant Colonel Collins was born in Warren, Michigan, 25 February 1935. He attended public schools and enlisted in the Army in 1953. Upon completion of recruit training, Private Collins attended the Airborne School and was assigned to a parachute battalion in Germany. Rising to the rank of sergeant, he applied for Officer Candidate School in 1956. Upon graduation, Second Lieutenant Collins was assigned as an infantry officer with the 82nd Airborne Division where he commanded a platoon, served as company executive officer and as a battalion assistant supply officer. He was promoted to first lieutenant in 1957 and captain in 1960.

After attending the Infantry School in 1961, Captain Collins joined the 173rd Airborne Brigade on Okinawa where he served as a company commander and battalion logistics officer. In 1962, he volunteered for duty with the Special Forces. Following the completion of thirteen months of advanced training, Captain Collins served with the 5th Special Forces Group in Indonesia. After a nine-month Vietnamese language course on Okinawa, Captain Collins commanded a Special Forces Detachment in Phouc Long Province, Vietnam.

In 1965, Captain Collins returned to the United States and served as a Special Forces School instructor until 1968. He was promoted to major 1 October 1966.

Major Collins served as battalion operations officer and brigade logistics officer with the 1st Cavalry Division in Vietnam during 1968-69. He is a graduate of the Command and General Staff College, Fort Leavenworth, Kansas.

Promoted to his present rank in 1971, Lieutenant Colonel Collins served on the U.S. Army, Pacific, staff prior to being assigned to Al Kohbari. He is a tough taskmaster and a physical-fitness buff. Lieutenant Colonel Collins has completed ninety-seven credits toward his bachelor's degree. He speaks Vietnamese fluently and has developed a good knowledge of Arabic. Married in 1960, he was divorced in 1968. He has no children. Lieutenant Colonel Collins feels he does most of the work in the Attaché Office and that Colonel Miller is a tired old man.

38   *Copyright © 1976 University Associates, Inc.*

AL KOHBARI BIOGRAPHY SHEET

Mr. Harold A. Smoot, Assistant Counselor for Economics
Embassy of the United States, Al Kohbari

Born in New York City on 9 October 1941, Mr. Smoot attended the Choate School and Yale University.

Upon graduation in 1963 (A.B. in history), Mr. Smoot studied at Trinity College (Dublin) and briefly at the University of Edinburgh (Scotland). In 1965, Mr. Smoot was accepted in the junior officer training program of the U.S. Central Intelligence Agency.

After an initial period of training at CIA headquarters in Langley, Virginia, Mr. Smoot attended the intensive Arabic language course of the Foreign Service Institute in Washington. He served in the political section of the American Embassy in Damascus until that mission was closed in June, 1967. Since that time, Mr. Smoot has been posted to Khartoum, Mogadiscio, and Jidda. His current assignment as assistant economics counselor is a thin cover for his association with the intelligence community. Mr. Smoot speaks excellent Arabic, good French, and passable Italian. He is married and has one small child.

Mr. Smoot's only real military acquaintance is Lieutenant Colonel Steele. He is generally wary of the intelligence role played by the Attaché Office and has little interest in military hardware. Despite his age, Mr. Smoot's rank is relatively high (the equivalent of lieutenant colonel).

AL KOHBARI BIOGRAPHY SHEET

Colonel Robert B. Miller, USAF

Colonel Miller was born in Botwood, New Jersey, on 24 April 1921. He attended public schools and graduated from Springfield College, Springfield, Massachusetts, in 1942. Commissioned in the Army Air Corps in December 1942, he served as a bombardier in B-17's and B-24's flying from England. Postwar assignments took him to various staff billets in the United States.

In 1951, Captain Miller was assigned as a B-29 pilot flying strikes against the North Korean and Chinese Communist forces around the Yalu. Promoted to major in 1952, he was reassigned to the Strategic Air Command where he served in a B-36 heavy bomber squadron and as an air intelligence officer. He was promoted to lieutenant colonel in 1959 shortly after graduation from the Air University.

Lieutenant Colonel Miller spent four years in the Air Force Intelligence Directorate (AFID) as deputy, Soviet Long Range Aviation Estimates Branch. In 1964, he returned to the SAC as a B-52 squadron commander. When his unit deployed to Guam in 1965, Lieutenant Colonel Miller became group executive officer. He flew missions in South Vietnam and Laos during 1965-66.

Promoted to colonel in 1967, he attended the National War College, earning a master's degree in international affairs during off-duty hours. Colonel Miller served in the Air Force Systems Command from 1968 until his assignment as defense attaché in Al Kohbari in April 1973.

Colonel Miller failed selection to brigadier general in 1974. He is married and has three children. His duties as defense attaché are largely ceremonial. He is due for reconsideration for promotion in two months. The decision of the working group is totally his responsibility and will probably affect his fitness/efficiency report, which will be completed by the ambassador within the week.

AL KOHBARI PROBLEM-SOLUTION SHEET

Codes: Y = Yes

N = No

P = Probable

? = Unknown

	Equipment Type				
	FV 432	Type 60	Marder	AMX 10P	Pbv 302
Required Capabilities					
Proven Design	Y	Y	Y	N	Y
Fording Capability of 5'	P	P	Y	Y	Y
Ability to Cross 20-Ton Bridges	Y	Y	N	Y	Y
Antipersonnel Armament	Y	Y	Y	Y	N
Seafaring Exporter	Y	Y	Y	Y	Y
At Least 7 Infantrymen	Y	Y	Y	Y	Y
Positive Reinforcers					
Easy Maintenance	N	P	N	?	?
Uses U.S. WW II Ammo	N	Y	N	N	N
Diplomatic Relations with Al Kohbari	Y	Y	Y	N	N

The Japanese Model APC Type 60 is the best-suited vehicle, based on available data. The British FV 432 is a strong second choice, based on the fact that it fulfills all "required" capabilities.

179. X-Y: A THREE-WAY INTERGROUP COMPETITION

Goals

   I. To explore interpersonal trust.

  II. To demonstrate the effects of cooperation, competition, and betrayal.

 III. To dramatize the advantages of both competitive and collaborative models in intergroup relations.

Group Size

   An unlimited number of three-team clusters, each team comprised of two to five participants.

Time Required

   Approximately two hours.

Materials

   I. A pencil for each team.

  II. A copy of the X-Y Score Sheet for each team.

 III. A copy of each of the X-Y Payoff Schedules I, II, and III for each team.

  IV. Blank paper.

Physical Setting

   Enough space for the three teams in each cluster to meet separately without overhearing or disrupting one another.

Process

   I. The facilitator forms clusters of three teams each and designates the teams in each cluster as A, B, and C. He seats the teams far enough apart so that they cannot overhear the other teams. (The goals of the activity are *not* discussed at this point.)

  II. A copy of the X-Y Score Sheet and a copy of the X-Y Payoff Schedule I are given to each team. The teams study these two sheets. (Five minutes.)

 III. The facilitator reiterates the rules found on the X-Y Score Sheet and answers *procedural* questions. (The team's goal is purposely left ambiguous.)

  IV. The facilitator announces that there will be ten rounds to the activity. He reminds the teams to remember the ground rules and informs them of the amount of time (one minute for each person in the largest team) allotted during each round for the teams to mark their choice for that round. (See the Time Chart for Rounds.)

TIME CHART FOR ROUNDS

Rounds 1-3 (Schedule I)	Decision making: 1 minute per person in the largest team
Between Rounds 3-4	One-way written communication: 5 minutes
Rounds 4-5 (Schedule I)	Decision making: 1 minute per person in the largest team
Between Rounds 5-6	Negotiation: 5 minutes for team strategy and 5 minutes for representatives' meeting
Rounds 6-8 (Schedule II)	Decision making: 1 minute per person in the largest team
Between Rounds 8-9	Two-way written communication: 10 minutes
Rounds 9-10 (Schedule III)	Decision making: 1 minute per person in the largest team

V. The facilitator announces the beginning of round one. At the end of the allotted time, he directs the teams to signal (raise hands) if they have marked their choices. He instructs all unfinished teams to complete the task and then directs each team (1) to share its decision with the other two teams in its cluster, without comments or reactions, and (2) to record the outcomes for round one on its X-Y Score Sheet, according to X-Y Payoff Schedule I.

VI. The facilitator answers any questions about scoring and proceeds with rounds two and three in the same manner (time for marking, reminder to finish, sharing in cluster, scoring).

VII. At the completion of round three, the facilitator announces that before round four is conducted, each team may send a written message to each of the other two teams in its cluster. He stresses that there will be no verbal communication and that no reply will be made to any message. (Five minutes.)

VIII. Rounds four and five are conducted in the same manner as rounds one to three.

IX. At the conclusion of round five, the facilitator distributes X-Y Payoff Schedule II and announces that this form replaces the previous one. A negotiation session is then introduced. Teams are given five minutes to discuss a team strategy. Then five more minutes is allotted, during which time a representative from each team meets with the two representatives from the other teams in the same cluster.

X. Rounds six, seven, and eight are conducted as above, with scoring done according to X-Y Payoff Schedule II.

XI. Before round nine, the facilitator distributes X-Y Payoff Schedule III. He introduces a ten-minute period in which each team may send a written communication to the other two teams in its cluster and may send back a written reply to each of the two messages it receives. (No talking permitted between teams.)

XII. At the end of ten minutes, round nine is conducted, followed by round ten; both are scored according to X-Y Payoff Schedule III.

XIII. The facilitator then conducts a processing session consisting of the following phases:

1. Team members discuss feelings they had about each other and share insights about team functioning. (Ten minutes.)

2. The three teams in each cluster form a group and explore the dynamics that emerged during the activity. (Ten minutes.)

3. The facilitator discusses the goals of the structured experience, relates the outcomes to the goals, and explores the implications of the learning.

Variations

   I. Larger teams can be used to generate more intragroup data.

   II. Team decision-making times can be varied for each round.

   III. Chips, bubble gum, or money can be used as team "winnings."

   IV. Rather than teams comparing their marked choices during each round, a few participants may be designated as "the clearinghouse." Each team sends a "runner" to report the team's choice for the round, and the clearinghouse then awards points according to the X-Y Payoff Schedule for that round.

   V. An additional negotiation session can be permitted between rounds nine and ten.

   VI. During the processing phase, teams may be instructed to form generalizations from key words such as trust, cooperation, collaboration, and betrayal.

   VII. Alternate payoff schedules may be developed.

Similar Structured Experiences: *Vol. II:* Structured Experiences 32, 35, 36; *Vol. III:* 54, 61; *'72 Annual:* 81, 82, 83; *Vol. IV:* 105; *'75 Annual:* 147; *Vol. V:* 150, 160, 161, 163.

Lecturette Sources: *'72 Annual:* "Assumptions About the Nature of Man," "McGregor's Theory X-Theory Y Model"; *'73 Annual:* "Win/Lose Situations"; *'74 Annual:* "Conflict Resolution Strategies"; *'75 Annual:* "Participatory Management: A New Morality."

Submitted by Gustave J. Rath, Jeremy Kisch, and Holmes E. Miller.

Gustave J. Rath, Ph.D., *is a professor of industrial engineering/management sciences and of educational organization development and the director of the Design and Development Center, The Technological Institute, Northwestern University, Evanston, Illinois. He is currently working with churches, police, and educational and health care systems. Dr. Rath's background is in goal setting and the diagnosis, planning, implementation, and evaluation of social systems.*

Jeremy Kisch, Ph.D., *is the chief of psychology at Rockland Psychiatric Center, Orangeburg, New York, and an assistant professor of psychiatry at New York Medical College. Dr. Kisch's background is in clinical psychology and applied behavioral science.*

Holmes E. Miller, Ph.D., *is an assistant professor of operations research and statistics at the Rensselaer Polytechnic Institute, Troy, New York. He is teaching and doing research in the area of operations research applications to health, industrial, and public systems. Dr. Miller's background is in industrial engineering, operations research, and systems analysis.*

X-Y SCORE SHEET

Instructions: For ten successive rounds, the members of your team will choose either an X or a Y. The payoff for each round depends on the pattern of independent choices made by the three teams in your cluster.

Round	Team Choice (Circle)	Pattern of Choices in the Cluster	Team Payoff	Team Balance
1	X Y	_____ X _____Y	$_____	$ _____
2	X Y	_____ X _____Y	_____	_____
3	X Y	_____ X _____Y	_____	_____
4	X Y	_____ X _____Y	_____	_____
5	X Y	_____ X _____Y	_____	_____
6	X Y	_____ X _____Y	_____	_____
7	X Y	_____ X _____Y	_____	_____
8	X Y	_____ X _____Y	_____	_____
9	X Y	_____ X _____Y	_____	_____
10	X Y	_____ X _____Y	_____	_____

Ground Rules: There are three basic rules to be followed during this activity:

1. Members of your team are not to confer with members of the other teams in your cluster, either verbally or nonverbally, unless given specific permission to do so.
2. The members of a team must agree on a single choice for each round of the activity.
3. Members of other teams in your cluster are not to know your team's choice until your team is instructed to reveal it.

X-Y PAYOFF SCHEDULE I

Cluster Choice Pattern	Team Payoffs
3 X's	Lose $1 each
2 X's	Win $2 each
1 Y	Lose $2
1 X	Win $3
2 Y's	Lose $2 each
3 Y's	Win $1 each

X-Y PAYOFF SCHEDULE II

Cluster Choice Pattern	Team Payoffs
3 X's	Lose $2 each
2 X's	Win $5 each
1 Y	Lose $2
1 X	Lose $3
2 Y's	Win $3 each
3 Y's	Win $2 each

X-Y PAYOFF SCHEDULE III

Cluster Choice Pattern	Team Payoffs
3 X's	Lose $2 each
2 X's	Win $4 each
1 Y	Lose $4
1 X	Win $6
2 Y's	Lose $4 each
3 Y's	Win $2 each

180. DISCLOSING AND PREDICTING: A PERCEPTION-CHECKING ACTIVITY

Goals

    I. To aid participants in developing social perception skills.

    II. To familiarize participants with the concept of accurate empathy.

    III. To demonstrate the effects that first impressions can have on perception.

Group Size

    An unlimited number of dyads.

Time Required

    Approximately thirty minutes.

Materials

    I. A copy of the Predicting Work Sheet for each participant.

    II. A pencil for each participant.

Physical Setting

    A room large enough for dyads to meet separately.

Process

    I. The facilitator briefly introduces the activity and instructs participants to form dyads—preferably with persons whom they do not already know well.

    II. The facilitator distributes a copy of the Predicting Work Sheet and a pencil to each participant. He goes over the instructions, topics, and method of scoring. He stresses that the goals of the activity do not include "winning" or "losing."

    III. Participant pairs sit face to face. Round one begins. Without prior discussion, each partner rates his agreement with the statement and his prediction of his partner's rating. The partners then compare the numbers, record the differences, and briefly discuss the topic. (Two to three minutes.)

    IV. The facilitator answers questions of clarification on procedure. Rounds two through twenty are carried out in the same manner, without facilitator interruptions.

    V. Partners total their "difference" scores on their work sheets.

    VI. The facilitator processes the activity with the total group. He points out that the better the partners know each other, the lower their difference scores will be. He leads a discussion of perception and empathy, focusing on the accuracy of participants' predictions, factors (first impressions, stereotyping) that might have influenced predictions, and learnings or insights gained from the activity.

46   *Copyright © 1976 University Associates, Inc.*

Variations

I. Playing cards may be used to indicate rankings. Each member receives a set of ten playing cards (ace and numbered cards) all in one suit (hearts, spades, diamonds, or clubs) and in a suit different from that of his partner. In each round, each member selects a card with a number corresponding to his ranking of the statement and lays it face down. Each member then selects a card with a value corresponding to his prediction of his partner's ranking of the same statement. The cards are then turned face up and the differences are noted on a score sheet.

II. Prior to round one, each participant may tell his partner a pertinent fact about himself (where he is from, what political party he belongs to, etc.) that could form the basis of a stereotype.

III. The activity can be carried out in triads or quartets.

IV. Statements can be written especially for a particular training group.

Similar Structured Experiences: *Vol. I:* Structured Experiences **17, 21**; *Vol. II:* **25, 42, 45**; *Vol. III:* **57, 58, 70**; *Vol. IV:* **116, 118**.

Suggested Instruments: *'72 Annual:* "Interpersonal Relationships Rating Scale"; *'73 Annual:* "Scale of Feelings and Behavior of Love," "Involvement Inventory"; *'74 Annual:* "Interpersonal Communication Inventory," "Self-Disclosure Questionnaire"; *'75 Annual:* "Scale of Marriage Problems."

Lecturette Sources: *'72 Annual:* "Openness, Collusion and Feedback"; *'73 Annual:* "The Johari Window: A Model for Soliciting and Giving Feedback"; *'74 Annual:* "Five Components Contributing to Effective Interpersonal Communications"; *'75 Annual:* "Giving Feedback: An Interpersonal Skill."

Based on material submitted by Jacques Lalanne.

***Jacques Lalanne** is the president of the Institut de Développement Humain, Quebec, Canada. He is training groups of parents, teachers, administrators, and professionals, as well as doing doctoral research on affective and moral development. Mr. Lalanne's background is in teaching, existential counseling, group work, social action, and educational consulting.*

PREDICTING WORK SHEET

Instructions: You are to indicate the degree of your agreement or disagreement with each statement on this work sheet, according to the following scale:

Total   0   1   2   3   4   5   6   7   8   9   Total
Disagreement   Agreement

Your partner will simultaneously indicate his rating of the statement on his work sheet. Then each of you will independently indicate the rating that you predict your partner gave to the statement. You will then compare your ratings and compute the differences between your predictions of each other's ratings and the actual ratings. The numerical differences are your scores for the round. Each "round" should take approximately two to three minutes.

Topic	Your Own Rating	Your Prediction of Your Partner's Rating	Difference Between Your Prediction and Your Partner's Actual Rating
1. History will vindicate Nixon.			
2. Sports teach democratic values.			
3. I like my job.			
4. I try to maintain a balanced diet.			
5. Children should obey their parents.			
6. I vote regularly.			
7. I am careful in handling my money.			
8. I had a happy childhood.			
9. I like to be the "star."			
10. I usually hold my anger inside.			
11. I have a hard time confronting my friends.			
12. I am easily embarrassed in front of groups.			
13. I believe in life after death.			
14. Abortion on demand is the right of every woman.			
15. I consider myself to be very intelligent.			
16. I often share my sexual fantasies.			
17. I am not afraid of dying.			
18. Religion has done more harm than good.			
19. Extramarital sex is natural.			
20. I like my physical appearance.			

Total "Difference" Score _____

181. BOASTING: A SELF-ENHANCEMENT ACTIVITY

Goals

    I. To help participants identify, own, and share their personal strengths.

    II. To explore feelings and reactions to sharing "boasts" with other participants.

    III. To experience the enhanced sense of personal power in announcing one's strengths to others.

Group Size

    No more than thirty participants.

Time Required

    Approximately one hour and fifteen minutes.

Physical Setting

    A room large enough to allow participants to move around and engage in dyadic conversations without distracting one another.

Process

    I. The facilitator presents a lecturette on identifying, "owning," and sharing one's strengths (or talents or achievements) as aspects of personal power. The lecturette focuses on the cultural taboo against boasting and acknowledges fears of violating it or of being ridiculed. The lecturette might conclude with a reading of Herman's poem, "Boast."[1] (Ten minutes.)

    II. The facilitator instructs the group to break into dyads. He announces that the task is to identify and share with each other at least three or four areas of strength that each partner is willing to boast about to other members of the group. The dyads are also asked to focus on and share their feelings of anticipation about the ensuing group activity. (Ten minutes.)

    III. The facilitator directs the participants to mill around in the total group and to share boasts with others. Participants are to be aware of feelings, reactions, and reservations during the experience. (Twenty minutes.)

    IV. The facilitator directs the participants to meet with their partners. (Twenty minutes.) They are instructed to process the experience, using the following guidelines:

        1. How did it feel to share your boasts with other group members?
        2. Which boasts seemed easier and which seemed harder?
        3. Was it easier to share your boasts with some individuals than with others?
        4. How did you share your boasts: proudly? tentatively? with embarrassment? with gusto?

---

[1]S. M. Herman, "Notes on Freedom." In J. W. Pfeiffer & J. E. Jones (Eds.), *The 1972 Annual Handbook for Group Facilitators.* La Jolla, Calif.: University Associates, 1972, p. 219.

5. Did *you* believe what you were saying?

6. How were your boasts received by others, and how did those reactions feel to you?

7. How would you rate each of your boasts on a ten-point "safe to risky" scale? (0 is completely safe, 10 is highly risky.)

8. How did you feel about yourself during the experience, and how are you feeling about yourself now?

V. The facilitator leads a general processing discussion, focusing on what individuals learned or relearned about themselves and how the learning might be applied. (Ten minutes.)

Variations

I. During step III, participants can share their boasts "on stage" to the total group rather than to individuals, with the group encouraged to cheer and applaud.

II. Steps II and IV can be done in triads or quartets rather than in dyads.

Similar Structured Experiences: *'73 Annual:* Structured Experience 90; *'75 Annual:* **143.**

Lecturette Sources: *'72 Annual:* "Risk-Taking and Error Protection Styles"; *'73 Annual:* "The Johari Window: A Model for Soliciting and Giving Feedback"; *'76 Annual:* "Assertion Theory."

Submitted by Jack J. Rosenblum and John E. Jones.

> **Jack J. Rosenblum, J.D.,** *is a human relations consultant in Sunderland, Massachusetts. He is an educational consultant currently pursuing his doctoral degree at the University of Massachusetts School of Education. Mr. Rosenblum's background is in humanistic education, laboratory education, and organization development.*

> **John E. Jones, Ph.D.,** *is the vice president of University Associates, La Jolla, California. He is a co-editor of the University Associates* Handbook *series, the* five Annual Handbooks for Group Facilitators, *and* Group & Organization Studies: The International Journal for Group Facilitators. *Dr. Jones's background is in teaching and counseling, education, and organization and community-development consulting.*

182. THE OTHER YOU: AWARENESS EXPANSION

Goals

   I. To increase personal self-awareness.

  II. To provide participants an opportunity to experiment with new behavior.

 III. To help participants integrate new data into their self-concepts.

Group Size

    Eight to twelve participants for each group facilitator.

Time Required

    Approximately two and one-half hours.

Materials

   I. A pencil and blank sheet of 8½" x 11" paper for each participant.

  II. Colored crayons or felt-tipped markers for each participant.

Process

   I. The facilitator briefly introduces the activity. He distributes paper and a pencil to each person.

  II. The facilitator instructs participants to find a comfortable position and to remain quiet for about a minute.

 III. He then directs participants to write down in a "free-association" way the first responses that come to their minds for the following topics:

1. weapon	11. heroine
2. goddess	12. type of architecture
3. color	13. musical instrument
4. kind of music	14. animal
5. season of the year	15. type of weather
6. article of clothing	16. precious gem
7. fruit	17. piece of furniture
8. geographic location	18. food
9. legendary figure	19. god
10. tool	20. herb or spice
	21. hero

 IV. The facilitator instructs participants to spend a few moments studying their written responses. Based on their insights, they are each then asked to give themselves a new name that reflects their responses.

V. Participants are next directed to place their new name on a sheet of paper and to draw a picture depicting the *essence* of that name—"the other you"—using crayons and/or felt-tipped markers.

VI. Each participant explains his picture to the group, using the first person: "I am (new name) . . ." Other participants may ask for clarification at the end of each presentation.

VII. Following the individual presentations, participants are given a few moments of quiet time to reflect on their "other person."

VIII. Each person is then given five minutes to "be" his other person with the group. This may be done extemporaneously or after a few moments of planning. Other participants may be used as "props." (The idea is for each individual to "try on" this newly surfaced personality, to develop a new level of awareness.)

IX. The facilitator leads the group in a discussion of learnings and their applications.

Variations

I. The structured experience can be either interrupted or stopped at the end of step VI.

II. Step VII can be embellished by staging a theatrical production in which participants create costumes to wear when making their presentations.

III. Participants may create a montage or collage of their new identity instead of drawing a picture.

IV. The facilitator may alter the list of topics to fit the group.

Similar Structured Experiences: *Vol. I:* Structured Experiences **16, 20;** '*72 Annual:* **85.**

Lecturette Sources: '*75 Annual:* "What Is Psychosynthesis?"; '*76 Annual:* "Fantasy: Theory and Technique."

Submitted by Anthony J. Reilly.

Anthony J. Reilly, Ph.D., is a senior consultant with University Associates, La Jolla, California. He coordinates professional development workshops and client consultation. Dr. Reilly's particular interests are in the areas of business, industry, medical systems, and education.

183. CONSULTING TRIADS: SELF-ASSESSMENT

Goals

  I. To assess consultation skills.

  II. To provide practice in one-to-one consultation.

Group Size

  An unlimited number of triads.

Time Required

  Approximately two hours.

Materials

  I. A copy of either the Consultation-Skills Inventory or the Goals for Personal Development Inventory for each participant.

  II. A copy of the Consultation-Skills Observer Sheet for each participant.

  III. Pencils.

Physical Setting

  A room in which triads can work without disturbing one another.

Process

  I. The facilitator briefly discusses the goals of the activity.

  II. Participants complete the inventory. (Approximately fifteen minutes.)

  III. Triads are formed and the participants in each triad identify themselves as A, B, and C.

  IV. The following instructions are given by the facilitator: During the first round, participant A is to be the first "client"; he is to present his results from the inventory. Participant B is to be the first "consultant"; his task is to begin a helping relationship with the "client." Participant C is to be the first "observer"; he receives a copy of the Consultation-Skills Observer Sheet.

  V. Round one is begun. The facilitator stops the process after twenty minutes and instructs participant C to report his observations and lead a discussion for ten minutes.

  VI. Round two begins. Participant B becomes the client, C becomes the consultant, and A becomes the observer. (Thirty minutes.)

  VII. Round three begins; participant C is the client, A is the consultant, and B is the observer. (Thirty minutes.)

  VIII. The triads are instructed to develop one or more generalizations about consulting behaviors that help and that hinder.

IX. The entire group re-forms, and generalizations about consultation skills are elicited from the group. The facilitator then conducts a discussion of the process.

Variations

    I. Instruments other than the inventories suggested may be used.

    II. A discussion of consultation styles can precede triad formation, with participants role playing specific consultation styles.

    III. The check list on the observer sheet can be cast in a numerical-rating response mode for more detailed feedback.

    IV. Participants can be instructed to discuss some real, "back-home" problem rather than their inventory results.

Similar Structured Experiences: *Vol. I:* Structured Experience **8**; *Vol. III:* **50**; *Vol. V:* **152**.

Suggested Instrument: *'73 Annual:* "Helping Relationship Inventory."

Lecturette Sources: *'73 Annual:* "The Johari Window"; *'74 Annual:* "The 'Shouldist' Manager"; *'75 Annual:* "The Supervisor as Counselor."

———————

Submitted by Anthony G. Banet, Jr.

__Anthony G. Banet, Jr., Ph.D.,__ is a senior consultant with University Associates, La Jolla, California. He is a clinical psychologist with experience in community mental health and has consulted with numerous public service agencies. Dr. Banet is also the editor of Creative Psychotherapy: A Source Book.

CONSULTATION-SKILLS INVENTORY

This check list is designed to help you think about various aspects of the behaviors involved in consultation. It gives you an opportunity to assess your skills and to set your own goals for growth and development. To use it best:

1. Read through the list of activities and decide which ones you are doing the right amount of, which ones you need to do more of, and which ones you need to do less of. Make a check for each item in the appropriate place.

2. Some activities that are important to you may not be listed here. Write these activities on the blank lines.

3. Go back over the whole list and circle the numbers of the three or four activities at which you want most to improve at the present time.

	OK	Need to Do More	Need to Do Less
General Skills			
1. Thinking before I talk	_____	_____	_____
2. Being comfortable with my educational background	_____	_____	_____
3. Being brief and concise	_____	_____	_____
4. Understanding my motivation for working in a helping profession	_____	_____	_____
5. Reading group process accurately	_____	_____	_____
6. Separating personal issues and work	_____	_____	_____
7. Listening actively to others	_____	_____	_____
8. Appreciating the impact of my own behavior	_____	_____	_____
9. Being aware of my need to compete with others	_____	_____	_____
10. Dealing with conflict and anger	_____	_____	_____
11. Building an atmosphere of trust and openness	_____	_____	_____
12. Having a clear theory base	_____	_____	_____
_____	_____	_____	_____
Sensing and Diagnosing			
13. Helping clients to discover their own problems	_____	_____	_____
14. Asking direct questions	_____	_____	_____
15. Inspiring the client's confidence in my ability to do the job	_____	_____	_____
16. Willing not to be needed by the client	_____	_____	_____

	OK	Need to Do More	Need to Do Less
17. Offering to find answers to questions	_____	_____	_____
18. Drawing others out	_____	_____	_____
19. Expecting clients to use my solutions	_____	_____	_____
20. Helping clients generate solutions to their own problems	_____	_____	_____
21. Accepting the client's definition of the problem	_____	_____	_____
	_____	_____	_____

Contracting

22. Talking about money and fees without embarrassment	_____	_____	_____
23. Promising only what I can deliver	_____	_____	_____
24. Saying "no" without guilt or fear	_____	_____	_____
25. Working under pressure of deadlines and time limits	_____	_____	_____
26. Setting realistic goals for myself and the client	_____	_____	_____
27. Presenting my biases and theoretical foundations	_____	_____	_____
28. Working comfortably with authority figures	_____	_____	_____
29. Letting someone else take the glory	_____	_____	_____
30. Working with people I do not particularly like	_____	_____	_____
31. Giving in to client restrictions and limitations	_____	_____	_____
32. Assessing personal needs that determine acceptance of the contract	_____	_____	_____
	_____	_____	_____

Problem Solving

33. Stating problems and objectives clearly	_____	_____	_____
34. Summarizing discussions	_____	_____	_____
35. Selling my own ideas effectively	_____	_____	_____
36. Helping clients maintain a logical sequence of problem solving	_____	_____	_____

	OK	Need to Do More	Need to Do Less
37. Challenging ineffective solutions	_____	_____	_____
38. Describing how other clients solved a similar problem	_____	_____	_____
39. Asking for help from others	_____	_____	_____
40. Evaluating possible solutions critically	_____	_____	_____
41. Contributing various techniques for creative problem solving	_____	_____	_____
_____	_____	_____	_____

Implementing

	OK	Need to Do More	Need to Do Less
42. Attending to details	_____	_____	_____
43. Helping clients make use of their strengths and resources	_____	_____	_____
44. Taking responsibility	_____	_____	_____
45. Changing plans when emergencies come up	_____	_____	_____
46. Building and maintaining morale	_____	_____	_____
47. Requesting feedback about the impact of my presentations	_____	_____	_____
48. Controlling my anxiety while I am performing my task	_____	_____	_____
49. Intervening without threatening my clients	_____	_____	_____
50. Intervening at the appropriate time	_____	_____	_____
51. Admitting errors and mistakes	_____	_____	_____
52. Admitting my own defensiveness	_____	_____	_____
_____	_____	_____	_____

Evaluating

	OK	Need to Do More	Need to Do Less
53. Assessing my own contributions realistically	_____	_____	_____
54. Acknowledging failure	_____	_____	_____
55. Feeling comfortable with clients reviewing my work	_____	_____	_____
56. Dealing with unpredicted changes	_____	_____	_____
57. Devising forms, inventories, etc., to aid evaluation	_____	_____	_____

	OK	Need to Do More	Need to Do Less
58. Relying on informal feedback	_____	_____	_____
59. Taking notes, writing up what has been done	_____	_____	_____
60. Letting go when the task is finished	_____	_____	_____
61. Arranging for next steps and follow-up	_____	_____	_____
62. Attributing failure to client's "resistance"	_____	_____	_____
_____	_____	_____	_____

GOALS FOR PERSONAL DEVELOPMENT INVENTORY

This form is designed to stimulate your thinking about your relationships with others and your skills in group situations. It is intended to facilitate your setting your own goals for development. The steps in using it:

1. Read through the list of activities and decide which ones you are doing the right amount of, which ones you should do more of, and which ones you should do less of. Make a check for each item in the appropriate place.

2. Some goals that are not listed may be more important to you than those listed. Write some goals on the blank lines.

3. Go back over the whole list and circle the numbers of the *three* or *four* activities at which you would like to improve most at this time.

	OK	Need to Do More	Need to Do Less
Communication Skills			
1. Talking in the group	————	————	————
2. Being brief and concise	————	————	————
3. Being forceful	————	————	————
4. Drawing others out	————	————	————
5. Listening alertly	————	————	————
6. Thinking before I talk	————	————	————
7. Keeping my remarks on the topic	————	————	————
8. _____	————	————	————
Observation Skills			
9. Noting tension in the group	————	————	————
10. Noting who talks to whom	————	————	————
11. Noting interest level of the group	————	————	————
12. Sensing feelings of individuals	————	————	————
13. Noting who is being "left out"	————	————	————
14. Noting reaction to my comments	————	————	————
15. Noting when the group avoids a topic	————	————	————
16. _____	————	————	————
Problem-Solving Skills			
17. Stating problems or goals	————	————	————
18. Asking for ideas, opinions	————	————	————
19. Giving ideas	————	————	————
20. Evaluating ideas critically	————	————	————

	OK	Need to Do More	Need to Do Less
21. Summarizing the discussion	‗‗‗‗	‗‗‗‗	‗‗‗‗
22. Clarifying issues	‗‗‗‗	‗‗‗‗	‗‗‗‗
23. ‗‗‗‗‗‗‗‗‗‗‗‗‗‗‗‗	‗‗‗‗	‗‗‗‗	‗‗‗‗

Morale-Building Skills

	OK	Need to Do More	Need to Do Less
24. Showing interest	‗‗‗‗	‗‗‗‗	‗‗‗‗
25. Working to keep people from being ignored	‗‗‗‗	‗‗‗‗	‗‗‗‗
26. Harmonizing, helping people reach agreement	‗‗‗‗	‗‗‗‗	‗‗‗‗
27. Reducing tension	‗‗‗‗	‗‗‗‗	‗‗‗‗
28. Upholding rights of individuals in the face of group pressure	‗‗‗‗	‗‗‗‗	‗‗‗‗
29. Expressing praise or appreciation	‗‗‗‗	‗‗‗‗	‗‗‗‗
30. ‗‗‗‗‗‗‗‗‗‗‗‗‗‗‗‗	‗‗‗‗	‗‗‗‗	‗‗‗‗

Emotional Expressiveness

	OK	Need to Do More	Need to Do Less
31. Telling others what I feel	‗‗‗‗	‗‗‗‗	‗‗‗‗
32. Hiding my emotions	‗‗‗‗	‗‗‗‗	‗‗‗‗
33. Disagreeing openly	‗‗‗‗	‗‗‗‗	‗‗‗‗
34. Expressing warm feelings	‗‗‗‗	‗‗‗‗	‗‗‗‗
35. Expressing gratitude	‗‗‗‗	‗‗‗‗	‗‗‗‗
36. Being sarcastic	‗‗‗‗	‗‗‗‗	‗‗‗‗
37. ‗‗‗‗‗‗‗‗‗‗‗‗‗‗‗‗	‗‗‗‗	‗‗‗‗	‗‗‗‗

Facing and Accepting Emotional Situations

	OK	Need to Do More	Need to Do Less
38. Facing conflict and anger	‗‗‗‗	‗‗‗‗	‗‗‗‗
39. Facing closeness and affection	‗‗‗‗	‗‗‗‗	‗‗‗‗
40. Withstanding silence	‗‗‗‗	‗‗‗‗	‗‗‗‗
41. Facing disappointment	‗‗‗‗	‗‗‗‗	‗‗‗‗
42. Withstanding tension	‗‗‗‗	‗‗‗‗	‗‗‗‗
43. ‗‗‗‗‗‗‗‗‗‗‗‗‗‗‗‗	‗‗‗‗	‗‗‗‗	‗‗‗‗

Social Relationships

	OK	Need to Do More	Need to Do Less
44. Competing to outdo others	‗‗‗‗	‗‗‗‗	‗‗‗‗
45. Acting dominant	‗‗‗‗	‗‗‗‗	‗‗‗‗
46. Trusting others	‗‗‗‗	‗‗‗‗	‗‗‗‗

	OK	Need to Do More	Need to Do Less
47. Being helpful	————	————	————
48. Being protective	————	————	————
49. Calling attention to myself	————	————	————
50. Standing up for myself	————	————	————
51. _____	————	————	————

General

	OK	Need to Do More	Need to Do Less
52. Understanding why I do what I do (insight)	————	————	————
53. Encouraging comments on my own behavior (soliciting feedback)	————	————	————
54. Accepting help willingly	————	————	————
55. Making up my mind firmly	————	————	————
56. Criticizing myself	————	————	————
57. Waiting patiently	————	————	————
58. Going off by myself to read or think	————	————	————
59. _____	————	————	————
60. _____	————	————	————

———————

This inventory was developed and written by Edwin C. Nevis and Richard W. Wallen.

CONSULTATION-SKILLS OBSERVER SHEET

Instructions: Check the phrases that describe what you observe.

The consultant:

_____	1. Helps the client to analyze problems.
_____	2. Helps the client to generate solutions.
_____	3. Acts as a clarifier to the client.
_____	4. Acts as a summarizer.
_____	5. Contributes suggestions from experience and knowledge.
_____	6. Gives the client ready-made answers.
_____	7. Assumes that the client has presented the problem accurately.
_____	8. Indicates that he is listening.
_____	9. Picks up on nonverbal cues.
_____	10. Talks more than the client does.
_____	11. Shows interest in the client.
_____	12. Paraphrases.
_____	13. Confronts and/or challenges the client.
_____	14. Collaborates with the client to define problem areas.
_____	15. Helps plan follow-up and next steps.
_____	16. Defines the contract and time limits.

What seemed the *most* helpful thing the consultant said or did?

What behaviors seemed *least* helpful?

Other comments:

184. SEX-ROLE ATTRIBUTES: A COLLECTION OF ACTIVITIES

Activities focused on the sexual-role stereotypes held by group participants can be useful in expanding personal awareness and in exploring the cultural biases and prejudices that the sexes have regarding each other. Listed below are some activities that can be included in personal growth and leadership training designs. They can be adapted to a variety of intergroup situations.

Guidelines. The facilitator should relate the activity to previous activities in the group or to the group's objectives. Voluntariness should be stressed. The facilitator should emphasize that the activities focus on sex-role stereotypes, not on sexual feelings.

Adequate time for processing the experience should be provided.

1. *Adjectives.* Participants are instructed to write down three adjectives that, in their view, most describe a typical member of the opposite sex. Then the participants are asked to write down three adjectives that least describe a typical member of the opposite sex. The facilitator lists the adjectives in rough alphabetical order on four sheets of newsprint (i.e., the most typical female, the least typical female, etc.).

   Small groups segregated by sex are formed and asked to reach consensus on the top five adjectives from each list. The consensus lists are posted and the facilitator leads a discussion of the differences and similarities.

   Variations. (A) Sex-segregated groups can conduct their consensus discussion in a group-on-group arrangement. (B) Participants can provide three adjectives most and least descriptive of their parents.

2. *Acting.* Participants are separated into all-female and all-male groups. The facilitator asks each group to discuss briefly how the members of the opposite sex typically behave—e.g., how they typically walk, sit, gesture, smoke, drink.

   Participants enact nonverbally for a five-minute period their perceptions of the opposite sex. Reactions are discussed in cross-sex subgroups and/or the total group.

3. *Fantasy.* The facilitator guides a fantasy in which group participants imagine they have assumed their opposite-sex role. In the fantasy, the facilitator provides cues for body awareness, activities, social expectations, employment, sex-related behaviors, etc. Participants share their fantasy experience in dyads, small groups, or the large group.

4. *Gender Labels.* From magazines or newspapers, the facilitator collects photographs (twelve to twenty) of animate or inanimate objects and presents them one by one to participants. Participants individually ascribe a gender label ("masculine" or "feminine") to each photograph and record these privately, without discussion. After all photographs have been labeled, the facilitator makes a tally for each photograph. The facilitator leads a discussion.

5. *Drawings.* Men and women are segregated by sex into small groups and asked to provide drawings or collages in response to two questions: how we perceive our own sex and how we believe the opposite sex sees us. Representatives from each group post and explain their drawings or collages. The facilitator leads a discussion after the presentations.

6. *The Only One*. The facilitator forms two circles segregated by sex. A female member joins the all-male circle for a few minutes; simultaneously, a male participant joins the all-female circle. Each participant stays in the opposite-sex circle and nonverbally experiments with postures, closeness, etc. After the activity, participants discuss awareness and feelings produced by being the "only one."

Similar Structured Experiences: *Vol. III:* Structured Experiences **56, 62, 63;** *'73 Annual:* **95.**

Lecturette Source: *'73 Annual:* "Confrontation: Types, Conditions, and Outcomes."

INTRODUCTION TO THE
INSTRUMENTATION SECTION

Despite the inherent difficulty of measuring psychological variables and processes, many devices are available to assess, appraise, evaluate, describe, classify, and summarize the varied aspects of human behavior. In human relations training, these devices are called "instruments"; most of them are pencil-and-paper forms designed to provide feedback and to facilitate self-disclosure.

Methods of psychological assessment can be located on a continuum from "soft" to "hard" data. "Soft" refers to highly subjective data that are difficult to measure; "hard" refers to more objective, quantifiable data. Soft data are not necessarily less valid than hard data, but their validity is more difficult to demonstrate. The instruments most commonly used in human relations training fall in the middle of the spectrum. They include surveys, polls, incomplete-sentence forms, check lists, rating scales, semantic differential scales, inventories, and structured interviews. Tests—instruments that have items with right and wrong answers—and physiological measurements (such as the polygraph or biofeedback) are rarely used in training; unfortunately, however, the methods on the "soft" end of the continuum—such as prejudices and testimonies— frequently are.

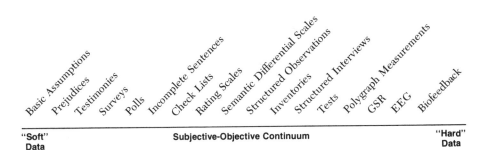

"Soft" Data — Subjective-Objective Continuum — "Hard" Data

Instrumented assessment has many advantages in a training context. An instrument is *objective*. It employs a *common language* so that participants can give standardized responses which are *quantifiable* and *economical* to score and summarize. Instruments are usually based on theory and thereby have *didactic potential*. They *promote involvement*, leading to increased participation and personalized learning.

Instruments have potential disadvantages as well. For many participants, an instrument can be *threatening* because of the information it reveals. It may produce the *false confidence* that a whole personality has been captured by a set of numbers. Instruments lend themselves to *misinterpretation*. They have an *artificial* quality; for many participants, instruments have *unpleasant connotations* with school, grading, and test taking. Some instruments can *overload* participants with irrelevant data.

Careful presentation eliminates or reduces most of the disadvantages of instruments. We regard them as a highly useful component of laboratory design, especially when used in conjunction with structured experiences, which permit participants to share their data, receive feedback and consensual validation, and deepen their understanding of the theory behind the instrument.

INVENTORY OF SELF-ACTUALIZING CHARACTERISTICS (ISAC)

Anthony G. Banet, Jr.

Maslow's construct of the self-actualizing person has been truly seminal in contemporary humanistic psychology. Inspired by his admiration for two of his teachers, Ruth Benedict and Max Wertheimer, Maslow began a study of those characteristics that differentiated the "most remarkable human beings" from ordinary persons. He reviewed the lives of many people, famous and unknown, living and dead, to discover the behaviors that led some human beings to a pattern of excellence in everyday living. His belief in the human capacity to grow in grace and quality shaped the "third force" in psychology, the force that energized the human potential movement.

Maslow never arrived at a precise definition of self-actualization. He viewed it as an ongoing process that involved the "full use and exploitation of talents, capacities, potentialities, etc. Such people seem to be fulfilling themselves and to be doing the best that they are capable of doing . . ." (Maslow, 1970, p. 150). Self-actualizing persons were seen as free of neurotic, psychopathic, or psychotic tendencies; their basic needs for safety, belongingness, love, and self-respect were gratified. Self-actualization is not necessarily to be equated with fame or achievement. The genius of the self-actualizing person is poured into his everyday life. The self-actualizing person is virtuous, in the old sense.

Maslow compiled a list of the virtues of the self-actualizing person that described attitudes, behaviors, and characteristics of the person in the process of developing to his full stature. Self-actualizing persons are not saints. They have many of the "lesser human failings." "They can be boring, stubborn, irritating. They are by no means free from a rather superficial vanity, pride, partiality to their own productions, family, friends and children" (Maslow, 1970, p. 175). In contrast to others, however, the self-actualizing person is aware of his imperfections, owns them, and makes choices about keeping or overcoming the undesirable traits.

In his later writings, Maslow described a life situation beyond self-actualization, in which individuals developed the capacity to transcend their usual experience. These "theory Z" persons are seen as differing in degree from self-actualizing persons, or "theory Y" types (Maslow, 1971b).

INVENTORY OF SELF-ACTUALIZING CHARACTERISTICS

The Inventory of Self-Actualizing Characteristics (ISAC) is based directly on Maslow's descriptions of the self-actualizing person. It is designed for two purposes: to teach in some detail the concept of self-actualization and to provide participants in training situations with a device for measuring their ongoing self-actualizing process. As a self-feedback instrument, the ISAC can be used in any training situation in which a focus on self-appraisal, personal growth, or individual goal setting is desired.

The ISAC consists of seventy-five items, five derived from each of Maslow's fifteen characteristics of self-actualizing persons. Users of the ISAC are asked to decide to what degree each item is accurate or true for them at the current time:

    N (*not at all,* definitely untrue for me);
    O (*occasionally* this is true of me—at least 25% of the time);
    F (*frequently* this is an accurate description of me—about 50% of the time);
    M (*most of the time* this would be descriptive of me);
    H (*highly characteristic,* definitely true for me).

Each response is weighted from a −2 to a +2, giving a possible range of −10 to +10 for each characteristic.

Administration

Instructions are printed on the ISAC. Approximately twenty minutes is required to complete the inventory. Two points should be stressed when the ISAC is introduced.

1. Self-actualization refers to a *process*, not to a fixed state of being. It is a way of experiencing the world; as Maslow says, "self-actualization means experiencing fully, vividly, selflessly with full concentration and total absorption . . . at the moment of experiencing, the person is wholly and fully human" (Maslow, 1971a, p. 45). This present-centeredness (living in the here-and-now) is a continuous event. The ISAC is designed to measure *the extent* to which the participant is involved in the self-actualizing process.

2. The ISAC consists of positive statements. The "social desirability" of each item is in most instances obvious. The instrument can be easily faked; the ISAC yields useful information only when the participant is candid and honest.

Scoring

Participants transfer their letter scores for each item onto the ISAC Score Sheet. For instance, the first characteristic, efficient reality perception, is composed of items 4, 25, 27, 36, and 73. The letter responses to those items are written in the score box.

After all letter responses have been transferred, a numerical value is given to each:

$$N = -2$$
$$O = -1$$
$$F = 0$$
$$M = +1$$
$$H = +2$$

A total score for each characteristic is derived algebraically by adding the numerical values. Score possibilities range from −10 to +10. Total scores are transferred to the ISAC Profile Sheet for easy interpretation.

Interpretation

Scoring is devised so that a score of zero reflects the hypothetical "average" person's ownership of the characteristic. The zero score means that approximately half of the time the person develops the self-actualizing characteristic.

Minus scores indicate that the participant thinks he lacks that particular self-actualizing characteristic. Minus scores indicate an area for growth and practice.

Positive scores indicate that the participant thinks he is engaged in a self-actualizing process in terms of that characteristic.

Group Activities Using the ISAC

Several small-group activities could follow after the administration of the ISAC:

1. Dyads or small groups could share ISAC profiles to attempt to reach consensual validation.
2. Persons with similar low or high scores could be grouped to discuss goal setting, contracting, etc.

OTHER INVENTORIES

Two other inventories based on Maslow's concepts are available. Shostrom's Personal Orientation Inventory (Shostrom, 1974) is a widely used research instrument that can serve as a pre-test or outcome measure. The Self-Actualization Test (Reddin & Sullivan, 1972) is a self-measure of gratified and unmet needs. Valett (1974) has devised a workbook that focuses on concrete, specific self-actualizing behaviors for use in a classroom or group setting.

REFERENCES

Maslow, A. H. *Motivation and personality* (2nd ed.). New York: Harper & Row, 1970.

Maslow, A. H. Self-actualizing and beyond. In A. H. Maslow, *The farther reaches of human nature*. New York: The Viking Press, 1971. (a)

Maslow, A. H. Theory Z. In A. H. Maslow, *The farther reaches of human nature*. New York: The Viking Press, 1971. (b)

Reddin, W. J., and Sullivan, J. B. *The self-actualization test*. Fredericton, New Brunswick, Canada: Organizational Tests, Limited. 1972.

Shostrom, E. L. *Personal orientation inventory manual*. San Diego, Calif.: Educational and Industrial Testing Service, 1974.

Valett, R. *Self-actualization*. Niles, Ill.: Argus Communications, 1974.

Anthony G. Banet, Jr., Ph.D., is a senior consultant with University Associates, La Jolla, California. He is a clinical psychologist with experience in community mental health and has consulted with numerous public service agencies. Dr. Banet is also the editor of Creative Psychotherapy: A Source Book.

INVENTORY OF SELF-ACTUALIZING CHARACTERISTICS (ISAC)
Anthony G. Banet, Jr.

This inventory is designed to give you information about your personal characteristics. Some items reflect concrete behavior, other items are traits or descriptions, and still others are statements of belief or value. Use the inventory to give yourself information about how you view yourself *now*, not how you would like to be.

Directions: As you read each item, decide whether the sentence is true or descriptive of you. Circle the letter to the right of the sentence that most accurately reflects your decision:

N — *Not at all*, definitely untrue for me.
O — *Occasionally* this is true of me—at least 25% of the time.
F — *Frequently* this is an accurate description of me—about 50% of the time.
M — *Most of the time* this would be descriptive of me.
H — *Highly characteristic*, definitely true for me.

1. I meet the needs of other people.	N	O	F	M	H
2. I have fun.	N	O	F	M	H
3. Respecting others is important to me.	N	O	F	M	H
4. My perception of people and situations is accurate.	N	O	F	M	H
5. I know what my biases are.	N	O	F	M	H
6. I like to be a playful child.	N	O	F	M	H
7. Loyalty to my friends is important to me.	N	O	F	M	H
8. My daily life is full of surprises.	N	O	F	M	H
9. I do not need other people.	N	O	F	M	H
10. Class distinctions are unimportant to me.	N	O	F	M	H
11. I am a responsible person.	N	O	F	M	H
12. I like to share myself with others.	N	O	F	M	H
13. I can see the humorous side of serious matters.	N	O	F	M	H
14. I express my anger clearly and directly.	N	O	F	M	H
15. I accept my strengths.	N	O	F	M	H
16. I avoid doing what I believe is wrong.	N	O	F	M	H
17. I strive to keep my life simple and natural.	N	O	F	M	H
18. I am rarely lonely.	N	O	F	M	H
19. I enjoy my own absurdity.	N	O	F	M	H
20. Racial and national differences interest me.	N	O	F	M	H
21. Every day is different for me.	N	O	F	M	H
22. I delight in learning new things.	N	O	F	M	H
23. I can give to others and expect no return.	N	O	F	M	H
24. Nothing is routine for me.	N	O	F	M	H
25. I think clearly.	N	O	F	M	H

26. I believe the end never justifies the means.	N	O	F	M	H
27. I can tolerate chaos and disorder.	N	O	F	M	H
28. Working toward a goal is more enjoyable than attaining it.	N	O	F	M	H
29. I am amused by much of what I experience.	N	O	F	M	H
30. I like to be myself.	N	O	F	M	H
31. I am untroubled by problems with authority.	N	O	F	M	H
32. I experience no pressure to conform to social norms.	N	O	F	M	H
33. I accept my limitations.	N	O	F	M	H
34. The meaning of my life is clear to me.	N	O	F	M	H
35. I enjoy discussing philosophical issues.	N	O	F	M	H
36. I know the difference between what I want and what I need.	N	O	F	M	H
37. I tolerate other people's faults and shortcomings.	N	O	F	M	H
38. My life has a definite purpose.	N	O	F	M	H
39. My major satisfactions come from within.	N	O	F	M	H
40. I can let go of my own interests.	N	O	F	M	H
41. Art, music, and beautiful things strengthen and enrich me.	N	O	F	M	H
42. I believe that supernatural phenomena occur.	N	O	F	M	H
43. I see the positive side of things.	N	O	F	M	H
44. I can make myself at home anywhere.	N	O	F	M	H
45. I have had experiences when I lost my sense of space and time.	N	O	F	M	H
46. I am my own person.	N	O	F	M	H
47. I am aware of the mysterious aspect of life.	N	O	F	M	H
48. Achievement is less important to me than contentment.	N	O	F	M	H
49. I am rarely self-conscious.	N	O	F	M	H
50. Empathy comes easy for me.	N	O	F	M	H
51. I can let things happen without planning.	N	O	F	M	H
52. I do original work.	N	O	F	M	H
53. I know the pain and joy of closeness.	N	O	F	M	H
54. I prize the dignity of all persons.	N	O	F	M	H
55. I am patient with others.	N	O	F	M	H
56. I like to be sexually close to others.	N	O	F	M	H
57. I am an uninhibited person.	N	O	F	M	H
58. Dress and style are unimportant to me.	N	O	F	M	H
59. I have definite moral standards.	N	O	F	M	H
60. I take good care of myself.	N	O	F	M	H
61. I learn something new every day.	N	O	F	M	H
62. I am excited by experimentation and risk taking.	N	O	F	M	H
63. I believe all human beings are members of one big family.	N	O	F	M	H
64. My actions are based on my choices, not needs.	N	O	F	M	H
65. I rarely censor my thoughts.	N	O	F	M	H

66. I can disengage myself from petty concerns.	N	O	F	M	H
67. I am a spiritual person (though not necessarily religious).	N	O	F	M	H
68. I am rarely defensive.	N	O	F	M	H
69. I learn from many different places and persons.	N	O	F	M	H
70. I am never bored.	N	O	F	M	H
71. I am at ease with cultural traditions different from my own.	N	O	F	M	H
72. I have intense inner experiences.	N	O	F	M	H
73. Determining what is real and what is phony is easy for me.	N	O	F	M	H
74. I am objective about most things.	N	O	F	M	H
75. I feel kinship with most people I meet.	N	O	F	M	H

ISAC SCORE SHEET

Instructions: Transfer your letter responses from the ISAC to each of the fifteen scales below and write in the value for each response:

N = −2
O = −1
F = 0
M = +1
H = +2

Sum the values of the items in each scale for a score.

Scale

1. Efficient Reality Perception

Items

4	25	27	36	73

Score

2. Acceptance of Self, Others, Human Nature

Items

15	33	37	60	68

Score

3. Spontaneity, Simplicity, Naturalness

Items

17	24	48	51	65

Score

4. Problem Centeredness

Items

1	35	38	40	49

Score

5. Detachment and Privacy

Items

9	18	30	66	74

Score

6. Autonomy and Independence of Culture and Environments

Items

32	39	44	46	64

Score

7. Freshness of Appreciation

Items

21	41	43	61	70

Score

8. Capacity for Peak Experiences

Items

42	45	47	67	72

Score

9. *Gemeinschaftsgefuhl*

Items

	23	50	54	63	75
letter					
value					

Score

10. Interpersonal Relations

Items

	7	12	53	55	56
letter					
value					

Score

11. Democratic Character Structure

Items

	3	5	10	11	14
letter					
value					

Score

12. Ethical Standards

Items

	16	26	28	34	59
letter					
value					

Score

13. Unhostile Sense of Humor

Items

	2	6	13	19	29
letter					
value					

Score

14. Creativeness

Items

	8	22	52	57	62
letter					
value					

Score

15. Resistance to Enculturation

Items

	20	31	58	69	71
letter					
value					

Score

ISAC PROFILE SHEET

Directions: Enter your total score for each ISAC scale in the box provided, and then chart each score at the appropriate point on the graph.

	Score	−10	−5	0	+5	+10

Scale

1. Efficient Reality Perception

Perceiving the real world accurately; making correct discriminations between the real and the spurious; capacity to deal with facts rather than opinions and wishes; appreciation of the unknown as a source for new learning; willingness to let go of the familiar; lack of obsessiveness.

2. Acceptance of Self, Others, Human Nature

Acceptance of body and body functions; prizing personal strengths; tolerating inadequacies in self and others; lack of defensiveness; a relative lack of overriding guilt, shame, or anxiety; dislike of pretense in self and others; uncritical understanding view of self and others.

3. Spontaneity, Simplicity, Naturalness

Motivated by choice rather than need; in touch with inner feelings and an ability to communicate those feelings effectively to others; an ethical code that is individualized rather than conventional; interest in personal growth and development; appreciation of the simple and unpretentious.

4. Problem Centeredness

Ability to focus on problems outside the self; task oriented; lack of self-consciousness; ability to attend to the needs of others; lack of obsessive introspection; concern with basic questions and philosophical issues.

5. Detachment and Privacy

Liking solitude and time alone more than the average person; reliance on personal judgments; self-determined; objective; power of focusing and concentration; relationships based on choice rather than need, dependency, or manipulation.

Scale	Score	−10	−5	0	+5	+10

6. Autonomy and Independence of Culture and Environments

Independent of material things or others' opinions; self-motivated; disregard of social rewards or prestige; stability in the face of frustrations and adversity; maintaining an inner serenity.

7. Freshness of Appreciation

Capacity for wonder and awe; richness of inner experience; perceiving familiar things as fresh and new; lack of boredom or jadedness; focus on the positive aspects of experience; "original mind"; responsive to beauty.

8. Capacity for Peak Experiences

Capable of intense, transcendent experiences; ability to experience ecstasy, to move beyond space and time; ability to live in a realm of being and beauty; loss of sense of self; experience of opening up to reality and beyond; capacity to be strengthened and enriched by such experiences.

9. *Gemeinschaftsgefuhl*

Feelings of identification, sympathy, and affection for all human beings; desire to be of help to mankind; a posture of forgiveness; a belief that humanity is a large family.

10. Interpersonal Relations

Capacity for intimacy and closeness; capable of great love for others; benevolence, affection toward many people; choice of a small circle of true, loyal friends; concern for the welfare of others; appropriate anger.

11. Democratic Character Structure

Belief in the dignity of all persons; relatively free from biases of class, education, political or religious beliefs, race or color; focus on character rather than physical aspects of other persons; avoidance of scapegoating; clarity about personal anger and its target.

Scale	Score	−10	−5	0	+5	+10

12. Ethical Standards

Strong ethical sense, definite moral standards; clear notion of right and wrong; seeking to do right and avoiding wrongdoing; fixed on ends rather than means.

13. Unhostile Sense of Humor

Sense of humor devoid of hostility, rebellion, or patronizing manner; capacity to laugh at oneself; appreciation of the ridiculous and the absurd; capacity for playfulness.

14. Creativeness

Creativity in everyday life, rather than in artistic endeavors; ability to perceive the true and the real more so than others; creativity that is childlike and playful; having fewer inhibitions or restrictions.

15. Resistance to Enculturation

Detachment from the conventional; lack of distortion around authority and authority figures; transcending racial or national distinctions; unconcerned about what is fashionable or chic; ability to live with and to learn from many cultural influences.

SUGGESTED READINGS

Maslow, A. H. *Motivation and personality* (2nd ed.). New York: Harper & Row, 1970.
Maslow, A. H. *The farther reaches of human nature.* New York: The Viking Press, 1971.

INVENTORY OF ANGER COMMUNICATION (IAC)

Millard J. Bienvenu, Sr.

One of the major components of healthy interpersonal communication is the individual's ability to deal with his own angry feelings and those of others. Some people, through the mechanism of denial, are not aware of their angry feelings and repress them rather deeply. Others, although aware of these feelings, suppress the expression of them, fearing angry responses from others. Many individuals become upset when they simply disagree with others or when others disagree with them. Finally, those individuals who do express angry feelings often do so in destructive ways, e.g., physical violence, insults, and shouting.[1]

The development of the Inventory of Anger Communication (IAC) was an outgrowth of the author's earlier communication scales, the results of which indicated that anger was an inherent yet troublesome aspect of the communication process among individuals. In studying marital communication, the author found that a couple's difficulty in handling their differences and in expressing their anger disrupted their communication process. Some persons avoid venting marital grievances because they have great difficulty handling and tolerating another person's anger. In studying hundreds of premarital couples, the author also found that couples, when angry, either avoided dealing with negative feelings or—the other extreme—withdrew or lost control of their feelings. In other studies of the general population, effective communicators were distinguished from poor communicators by the way they handled their angry feelings.

The IAC has been used as a diagnostic tool in initial interviews, as an aid in ongoing counseling, and as a teaching device in communication classes. It also lends itself to human relations training and to research as a measurement technique.

A 30-item scale, the IAC is intended to identify the subjective and interactional aspects of anger as manifested by the individual. In the *subjective* category, awareness of the expression of anger, intensity of anger, attitudes toward the expression of anger, and the reaction of the individual to his own anger are explored. Items relating to the *interactional* aspects of anger focus on the verbal and physical manner of expressing anger and the manner in which the individual handles it with himself and with others. Subjects respond to the self-inventory by checking one of three possible responses—"Usually," "Sometimes," or "Seldom." The responses to the items are scored from 0 to 3, with a favorable response given the higher score.

Originally, 45 items were formulated from a review of the literature and from the author's communication scales and clinical experiences. To test the validity of the items, they were presented to several psychologists, psychiatrists, and psychiatric social workers. Based on their feedback and on follow-up studies, 15 items were eventually discarded, resulting in the current 30-item version of the inventory.

The IAC is probably best suited for individuals of high school age and older with sufficient mental maturity to attempt to be frank and objective in responding to the items. It can be adapted to either sex and to any marital status.

Engaged in ongoing research, the author would like to collaborate with others using the IAC. A guide to the IAC may be obtained from the author upon request.

---

[1] On the subject of anger, the reader should also refer to "Dealing with Anger" in the Lecturettes section of this *Annual*.

REFERENCES

Bienvenu, M. J., Sr. Measurement of parent-adolescent communication. *The Family Coordinator*, 1969, *18*, 117-121.

Bienvenu, M. J., Sr. Measurement of marital communication. *The Family Coordinator*, 1970, *19*, 26-31.

Bienvenu, M. J., Sr. An interpersonal communication inventory. *The Journal of Communication*, 1971, *21*(4), 381-388.

Bienvenu, M. J., Sr. A measurement of premarital communication. *The Family Coordinator*, 1975, *24*, 65-68.

Millard J. Bienvenu, Sr., Ph.D., is the head of the Department of Sociology and Social Work and the director of the Family Study Center, Northwestern State University, Natchitoches, Louisiana. He has been engaged in ongoing research in the area of family and interpersonal communication. Dr. Bienvenu's background is in marriage and family counseling, teaching, and Gestalt/transactional analysis group therapy.

INVENTORY OF ANGER COMMUNICATION (IAC)
Millard J. Bienvenu, Sr.

Anger is a very basic human emotion that plays an important role in the way we communicate with others. This inventory offers you an opportunity to make an objective self-study of how anger affects you and how you deal with it in your daily contacts with others. This increased awareness on your part may provide insights and clues for feeling more comfortable with yourself and improving your relationships with others. Please do not place your name on this form; if any of the questions are offensive to you, feel free not to answer them.

Directions:

- Please answer each question as quickly as you can according to the way you feel *at the moment* (not the way you usually feel or felt last week).

- Please do not consult with anyone while completing this inventory. You may discuss it with someone after you have completed it. Remember that the value of this form will be lost if you change *any* answer during or after the discussion.

- Honest answers are necessary. Please be as frank as possible, since your answers are confidential.

- Use the following examples for practice. Put a check ($\checkmark$) in *one* of the three blanks on the right to show how the question applies to your situation.

	Yes (usually)	No (seldom)	Some-times
Do you have a tendency to take digs at others?	_____	_____	_____
Do you get very upset when someone disagrees with you?	_____	_____	_____

- The **Yes** column is to be used when the question can be answered as happening *most of the time or usually*. The **No** column is to be used when the question can be answered as *seldom* or *never*.

- The **Sometimes** column should be marked when you cannot definitely answer **Yes** or **No**. *Use this column as little as possible.*

- Read each question carefully. If you cannot give the exact answer to a question, answer the best you can but be sure to answer each one. There are no right or wrong answers. Answer according to the way *you* feel *at the present time*.

	Yes (usually)	No (seldom)	Some-times
1. Do you admit that you are angry when asked by someone else?	_____	_____	_____
2. Do you have a tendency to take your anger out on someone other than the person you are angry with?	_____	_____	_____
3. When you are angry with someone, do you discuss it with that person?	_____	_____	_____

	Yes (usually)	No (seldom)	Some- times
4. Do you keep things in until you finally explode with anger?	_____	_____	_____
5. Do you pout or sulk for a long time (a couple of days or so) when someone hurts your feelings?	_____	_____	_____
6. Do you disagree with others even though you feel they might get angry?	_____	_____	_____
7. Do you hit others when you get angry?	_____	_____	_____
8. Does it upset you *a great deal* when someone disagrees with you?	_____	_____	_____
9. Do you express your ideas when they differ from those of others?	_____	_____	_____
10. Do you have a tendency to be very critical of others?	_____	_____	_____
11. Are you satisfied with the way in which you settle your differences with others?	_____	_____	_____
12. Is it very difficult for you to say nice things to other people?	_____	_____	_____
13. Do you have good control of your temper?	_____	_____	_____
14. Do you become depressed very easily?	_____	_____	_____
15. When a problem arises between you and another person, do you discuss it without losing control of your emotions?	_____	_____	_____

Please go back and circle any questions that were not clear to you.

16. Do you have a tendency to criticize or put down other people?	_____	_____	_____
17. When someone has hurt your feelings do you discuss the matter with that person?	_____	_____	_____
18. Do you have frequent arguments with others?	_____	_____	_____
19. Do you often *feel* like hitting someone else?	_____	_____	_____
20. Do you, at times, feel some anger toward someone you love?	_____	_____	_____
21. Do you have a strong urge to do something harmful?	_____	_____	_____
22. Do you keep your cool (control) when you are angry with someone?	_____	_____	_____
23. Do you tend to feel very bad or very guilty after getting angry at someone?	_____	_____	_____
24. When you become angry, do you pull away or withdraw from people?	_____	_____	_____
25. When someone is angry with you, do you auto- matically or quickly strike back with your own feel- ings of anger?	_____	_____	_____

	Yes (usually)	No (seldom)	Some- times
26. Are you aware of when you are angry?			
27. Provided the timing is appropriate, do you express your angry feelings without exploding?			
28. Do you tend to make cutting remarks to others?			
29. Do you control yourself when things do not go your way?			
30. Do you feel that anger is a normal emotion?			

Please go back and circle any questions that were not clear to you.

CHECK YOURSELF OUT

Directions: Please write down the first thing that comes to your mind when you read the following words or phrases. Be honest with yourself in order to gain the most from this exercise.

1. When people get mad they should _____ .

2. Feeling angry is _____ .

3. People who get angry are _____ .

4. When I get angry I _____ .

5. I get angry when _____ .

6. People make me angry when _____ .

7. When my father got angry he _____ .

8. When my mother got angry she _____ .

9. The best way to describe myself is _____ .

General Information

My age _____   Sex: ☐ Male   ☐ Female   Education _____

Occupation _____   Religion _____

My marital status: ☐ Single ☐ Married ☐ Divorced ☐ Separated ☐ Widowed

In my family, I am(was) the: ☐ Oldest Child ☐ Middle Child ☐ Youngest Child ☐ Only Child

While I was growing up, my parents were: ☐ Married and living together ☐ Separated/divorced
     ☐ One or more deceased

INVENTORY OF ANGER COMMUNICATION
SCORING KEY

Instructions: Look at how you responded to each item in the IAC. In front of the item write the appropriate weight from the table on this page. For example, if you answered "Yes" to item 1, you would find below that you get three points; write the number 3 in front of item 1 in the inventory and proceed to score item 2. When you have finished scoring each of the thirty items, add up your total score.

Scoring Interpretation

Generally, the higher the sum of scores, the more effectively you are handling your angry feelings. Review your answers to each item to see if a pattern of anger expression can be discerned. Attend carefully to the items you marked "sometimes"; they may indicate areas for explanation and work. Discuss your inventory with someone who knows you well for a perception check.

Norms for the Inventory of Anger Communication are not available currently. If you are interested in norm development or more technical information on the inventory, contact the author.

	Yes	No	Sometimes			Yes	No	Sometimes
1.	3	0	2		16.	0	3	1
2.	0	3	1		17.	3	0	2
3.	3	0	2		18.	0	3	1
4.	0	3	1		19.	0	3	1
5.	0	3	1		20.	3	0	2
6.	3	0	2		21.	0	3	1
7.	0	3	1		22.	3	0	2
8.	0	3	1		23.	0	3	1
9.	3	0	2		24.	0	3	1
10.	0	3	1		25.	0	3	1
11.	3	0	2		26.	3	0	2
12.	0	3	1		27.	3	0	2
13.	3	0	2		28.	0	3	1
14.	0	3	1		29.	3	0	2
15.	3	0	2		30.	3	0	2

LEADER EFFECTIVENESS AND ADAPTABILITY DESCRIPTION (LEAD)[1]

Paul Hersey and Kenneth H. Blanchard

Most management writers agree that leadership is a "process of influencing the activities of an individual or group in efforts toward accomplishing goals in a given situation" (Hersey & Blanchard, 1972, p. 68). It is important to note that this definition makes no mention of any particular type of organization; leadership occurs in any situation in which someone is trying to influence the behavior of another individual or group. Thus, everyone attempts leadership at one time or another, whether his activities are centered around a business, an educational institution, a hospital, a political organization, or a family.

The Leader Effectiveness and Adaptability Description (LEAD) can help give individuals some feedback on their own leadership style. Developed at the Center for Leadership Studies, Ohio University, LEAD is designed to measure self-perception of three aspects of leadership behavior: (1) style, (2) style range, and (3) style adaptability or effectiveness.

SUGGESTIONS FOR TRAINERS

In working with the LEAD instrument, trainers will find the following suggestions useful.

1. Administer the LEAD instrument before exposing participants to the theory. Learning the theory first seems to emphasize how one *should* behave rather than how one tends to behave, an emphasis that results in less accurate self-perceptions.

2. Administer the LEAD again at the end of a training session. This gives participants a chance to see how much new knowledge and/or attitudinal change has occurred.[2]

3. Emphasize that LEAD data reflect only self-perceptions and not necessarily the perceptions of individuals' co-workers. Sharing this data with other participants can be a powerful experience when working with ongoing work groups from a particular organization.

4. If individuals are interested in knowing why certain action choices received a plus (+) or minus (−) score on the adaptability or effectiveness aspect of the LEAD, a rationale and analysis booklet can be obtained (Hersey & Blanchard, 1973).

5. After individuals have taken the LEAD, been exposed to the theory, and scored the instrument, it is important for them to practice using the theory. To provide this practice, the *Situational Management Simulator* (Hersey, Blanchard, & Peters, 1972) is a useful training device.[3] It is an exciting, competitive simulation in which participants diagnose when to use a particular leadership style in a series of case incidents. The winning team demonstrates the best diagnostic skills in using the Life-Cycle Theory of Leadership.

---

[1]The development of LEAD, formerly known as the Leader Adaptability and Style Inventory (LASI), is based on the theoretical frameworks presented in Hersey and Blanchard (1972). For more detail on these frameworks, see chapters 4-7. The first publication on the LEAD instrument appeared in the February 1974 issue of *Training and Development Journal* as an article entitled "So You Want to Know Your Leadership Style?"

[2]LEAD profile data, based on the use of the instrument in conjunction with interviews from many different types of organizations over the last several years, were not available at the time of publication of this article. They will be available, however, in a forthcoming 3rd edition of the Hersey and Blanchard text, *Management of Organizational Behavior*.

[3]Information on this simulation can also be obtained from the Center for Leadership Studies, Ohio University, Athens, Ohio 45701.

REFERENCES

Hersey, P., & Blanchard, K. H. *Management of organizational behavior: Utilizing human resources* (2nd ed.). Englewood Cliffs, N.J.: Prentice-Hall, 1972. The 3rd edition of this text should be available in fall, 1976.

Hersey, P., & Blanchard, K.H. *Rationale and analysis of LEAD instruments*. Athens: Center for Leadership Studies, Ohio University, 1973.

Hersey, P., Blanchard, K. H., & Peters, L. G. *Situational management simulator*. Athens, Ohio: Management Education and Development, 1972.

Paul Hersey is the director of the Center for Leadership Studies and a professor of management and organizational behavior at Ohio University. At present he is a Distinguished Visiting Professor at United States International University, San Diego, California. In addition to teaching and research, Mr. Hersey has helped develop managerial training for more than 500 industrial, business, education, and military organizations. Mr. Hersey's background is in teaching, industrial psychology, and leadership training.

Kenneth H. Blanchard, Ph.D., is presently a co-director of the Center for Curriculum and Organizational Development, School of Education, University of Massachusetts, where he is also a professor of leadership and organizational behavior in both the School of Education and the School of Business Administration. He is a consulting editor for the new University Associates journal, Group & Organization Studies: The International Journal for Group Facilitators. Dr. Blanchard is involved in training school administrators and teachers nationally in the areas of motivation, leadership, and change.

LEADER EFFECTIVENESS AND ADAPTABILITY DESCRIPTION (LEAD)
Paul Hersey and Kenneth H. Blanchard

Directions: Assume you are involved in each of the following twelve situations. READ each item carefully and THINK about what you would do in each circumstance. Then CIRCLE the letter of the alternative that you think would most closely describe your behavior in the situation presented. Circle only *one choice.* For each situation, interpret key concepts in terms of the environment or situation in which you most often think of yourself as assuming a leadership role. Say, for example, an item mentions subordinates. If you think that you engage in leadership behavior most often as an industrial manager, then think about your staff as subordinates. If, however, you think of yourself as assuming a leadership role primarily as a parent, think about your children as your subordinates. As a teacher, think about your students as subordinates.

Do not change your situational frame of reference from one item to another. Separate LEAD instruments may be used to examine your leadership behavior in as many different settings as you think helpful.

1. Your subordinates have not been responding to your friendly conversation and obvious concern for their welfare. Their performance is in a tailspin.
   A. Emphasize the use of uniform procedures and the necessity for task accomplishment.
   B. Make yourself available for discussion but do not push.
   C. Talk with subordinates and then set goals.
   D. Be careful not to intervene.

2. The observable performance of your group is increasing. You have been making sure that all members are aware of their roles and standards.
   A. Engage in friendly interaction, but continue to make sure that all members are aware of their roles and standards.
   B. Take no definite action.
   C. Do what you can to make the group feel important and involved.
   D. Emphasize the importance of deadlines and tasks.

3. Members of your group are unable to solve a problem themselves. You have normally left them alone. Group performance and interpersonal relations have been good.
   A. Involve the group and together engage in problem solving.
   B. Let the group work it out.
   C. Act quickly and firmly to correct and redirect.
   D. Encourage the group to work on the problem and be available for discussion.

4. You are considering a major change. Your subordinates have a fine record of accomplishment. They respect the need for change.
   A. Allow group involvement in developing the change, but do not push.
   B. Announce changes and then implement them with close supervision.
   C. Allow the group to formulate its own direction.
   D. Incorporate group recommendations, but direct the change.

5. The performance of your group has been dropping during the last few months. Members have been unconcerned with meeting objectives. They have continually needed reminding to do their tasks on time. Redefining roles has helped in the past.

   A. Allow the group to formulate its own direction.
   B. Incorporate group recommendations, but see that objectives are met.
   C. Redefine goals and supervise carefully.
   D. Allow group involvement in setting goals, but do not push.

6. You stepped into an efficiently run situation. The previous administrator ran a tight ship. You want to maintain a productive situation, but would like to begin humanizing the environment.

   A. Do what you can to make the group feel important and involved.
   B. Emphasize the importance of deadlines and tasks.
   C. Be careful not to intervene.
   D. Get the group involved in decision making, but see that objectives are met.

7. You are considering major changes in your organizational structure. Members of the group have made suggestions about needed change. The group has demonstrated flexibility in its day-to-day operations.

   A. Define the change and supervise carefully.
   B. Acquire the group's approval on the change and allow members to organize the implementation.
   C. Be willing to make changes as recommended, but maintain control of implementation.
   D. Avoid confrontation; leave things alone.

8. Group performance and interpersonal relations are good. You feel somewhat unsure about your lack of direction of the group.

   A. Leave the group alone.
   B. Discuss the situation with the group and then initiate necessary changes.
   C. Take steps to direct your subordinates toward working in a well-defined manner.
   D. Be careful of hurting boss-subordinate relations by being too directive.

9. Your superior has appointed you to head a task force that is far overdue in making requested recommendations for change. The group is not clear about its goals. Attendance at sessions has been poor. The meetings have turned into social gatherings. Potentially, the group has the talent necessary to help.

   A. Let the group work it out.
   B. Incorporate group recommendations, but see that objectives are met.
   C. Redefine goals and supervise carefully.
   D. Allow group involvement in setting goals, but do not push.

10. Your subordinates, usually able to take responsibility, are not responding to your recent redefining of standards.

   A. Allow group involvement in redefining standards, but do not push.
   B. Redefine standards and supervise carefully.
   C. Avoid confrontation by not applying pressure.
   D. Incorporate group recommendations, but see that new standards are met.

11. You have been promoted to a new position. The previous supervisor was uninvolved in the affairs of the group. The group has adequately handled its tasks and direction. Group inter-relations are good.

   A. Take steps to direct subordinates toward working in a well-defined manner.

   B. Involve subordinates in decision making and reinforce good contributions.

   C. Discuss past performance with the group and then examine the need for new practices.

   D. Continue to leave the group alone.

12. Recent information indicates some internal difficulties among subordinates. The group has a remarkable record of accomplishment. Members have effectively maintained long-range goals and have worked in harmony for the past year. All are well qualified for the task.

   A. Try out your solution with subordinates and examine the need for new practices.

   B. Allow group members to work it out themselves.

   C. Act quickly and firmly to correct and redirect.

   D. Make yourself available for discussion, but be careful of hurting boss-subordinate relations.

LEAD SCORING AND INTERPRETATION WORKBOOK

STYLE

Your leadership style (Hersey & Blanchard, 1972, pp. 82-83; 110-112) is the consistent pattern of behavior that you exhibit when you attempt to influence the activities of people. This behavior has been developed over time and is what others learn to recognize as you, the leader, as your style, or as your leadership personality. Others expect and can even predict certain kinds of behavior from you. The pattern generally involves either task behavior or relationship behavior, or some combination of both. These two types of behavior are central to the concept of leadership style.

> *Task Behavior:* The extent to which a leader organizes and defines the roles of individuals and members of his or her group by explaining what activities each is to do as well as when, where and how tasks are to be accomplished. It is further characterized by the extent to which a leader defines patterns of organization, formalizes channels of communication, and specifies ways of getting jobs accomplished.
>
> *Relationship Behavior:* The extent to which a leader engages in personal relationships with individuals or members of his or her group; the amount of socio-emotional support and psychological strokes provided by the leader as well as the extent to which the leader engages in interpersonal communications and facilitating behaviors. (Hersey & Blanchard, 1972, pp. 82-83)[1]

The recognition of task and relationship as two important dimensions of leadership behavior has played an important role in the work of management theorists over the last several decades. These two dimensions have been variously labeled, including such terminology as autocratic/democratic, employee-oriented/production-oriented, and theory X/theory Y.

"Either/Or" Styles of Behavior

For some time, it was believed that task and relationship were "either/or" styles of leadership behavior and, therefore, could be depicted on a continuum ranging from very authoritarian (task-oriented) leadership behavior at one end to very democratic (relationship-oriented) leadership behavior at the other (Tannenbaum & Schmidt, 1957).

In more recent years, the feeling that task and relationship were "either/or" leadership styles has been dispelled. In particular, the leadership studies initiated in 1945 by the Bureau of Business Research at Ohio State University questioned this assumption (Stogdill & Coons, 1957).

Observing the actual behavior of leaders in a wide variety of situations, the Ohio State staff found that leadership styles tended to vary considerably among leaders. Whereas the behavior of some leaders was basically task oriented in character, the behavior of others exhibited socio-emotional support in terms of personal relationships. Other leaders' styles were characterized by both task behavior and relationship behavior. There were even some individuals in leadership positions whose behavior tended to provide little structure or consideration.

No dominant style appeared; instead, various combinations of styles were evident. Thus, it was determined that task and relationship were not "either/or" leadership styles, as the authoritarian-democratic continuum suggested. Instead, these patterns of leadership behavior can be plotted on two separate axes (see Figure 1). Use this figure to score your self-perceptions of your leadership styles and your style range from the LEAD instrument.

DETERMINING LEADERSHIP STYLE

Your perception of your leadership style on the LEAD instrument can be determined in Figure 2. Circle the letter of the alternative action you chose for each situation and then total the number

---

[1]Since our model is an outgrowth of the Ohio State Leadership Studies, these definitions have been adapted from Stogdill and Coons, "Initiating Structure" (task) and "Consideration" (relationship) (1957, pp. 42-43).

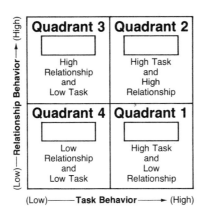

Figure 1. Basic Leadership Behavior Styles

of times an action was used in each of the four subcolumns. The alternative action choices for each situation are not distributed alphabetically but according to the style quadrant a particular action alternative represents.

Quadrant scores from Figure 2 can be transferred to the basic leadership behavior styles in Figure 1. The quadrant numbers in Figure 2 correspond to the quadrant numbers of the model, as follows:

Quadrant (1)—alternative action choices describe Quadrant 1, High Task and Low Relationship Behavior.

Quadrant (2)—alternative action choices describe Quadrant 2, High Task and High Relationship Behavior.

Quadrant (3)—alternative action choices describe Quadrant 3, High Relationship and Low Task Behavior.

Quadrant (4)—alternative action choices describe Quadrant 4, Low Relationship and Low Task Behavior.

Enter the totals associated with each of the four basic leadership styles in the boxes on Figure 1.

Your *dominant leadership style* is defined as the quadrant in which the most responses fall. Your *supporting style* (or styles) is the leadership style that you tend to use on occasion. The frequency of responses in quadrants other than that of your dominant style suggests the number and degree of supporting styles as you perceive them. At least two responses in a quadrant are necessary for a style to be considered a supporting style.

Style Range

Your dominant style plus your supporting styles determine your style range (Hersey & Blanchard, 1972, pp. 121-122). In essence, this is the extent to which *you* perceive your ability to vary your leadership style.

Your style range can be analyzed by examining the quadrants in which your responses to the LEAD occurred in Figure 1 as well as the frequency of these occurrences. If your responses fall only in one quadrant, then you perceive the range of your behavior as limited; if your responses fall in a number of quadrants, you perceive yourself as having a wide range of leadership behavior.

		Alternative Actions			
	1	A	C	B	D
	2	D	A	C	B
	3	C	A	D	B
	4	B	D	A	C
Situations	5	C	B	D	A
	6	B	D	A	C
	7	A	C	B	D
	8	C	B	D	A
	9	C	B	D	A
	10	B	D	A	C
	11	A	C	B	D
	12	C	A	D	B
Quadrant		(1)	(2)	(3)	(4)
Quadrant Scores					

Figure 2. Determining Leadership Style and Style Range

Tri-Dimensional Model

After identifying task and relationship as the two central aspects of leadership behavior, numerous practitioners and writers tried to determine which of the four basic styles was the "best" style of leadership, that is, the one that would be successful in most situations. At one point, High Task/High Relationship (Quadrant 2) was considered the "best" style, while Low Task/Low Relationship (Quadrant 4) was considered the "worst" style (Halpin, 1959; Blake & Mouton, 1964; Likert, 1961).

Yet, research evidence in the last decade clearly indicates that there is no single, all-purpose leadership style (Korman, 1966; Fiedler, 1967). Successful leaders are those who can adapt their behavior to meet the demands of their own unique environment.

If the effectiveness of a leader's behavior style depends on the situation in which it is used, it follows that any of the four basic styles in Figure 1 may be effective or ineffective depending on the situation. *The difference between the effective and the ineffective styles is often not the actual behavior of a leader, but the appropriateness of the behavior to the situation in which it is used.*

In an attempt to illustrate this concept and to build on previous work in leadership, an effectiveness dimension was added to the task and relationship dimensions of earlier leadership models to create the Tri-Dimensional Leader Effectiveness Model (Hersey & Blanchard, 1972, pp. 81-87)[2] presented in Figure 3. (Use this figure to integrate your self-perception scores of your leadership style and style range with your perceived style adaptability from the LEAD instrument.) This model was developed to help practitioners more accurately diagnose the appropriateness of their leadership style (or styles) to specific situations.

---

[2]For a discussion of an early attempt to add an effectiveness dimension to the task and relationship dimensions, see W. J. Reddin, The 3-D Management Style Theory, *Training and Development Journal*, April 1967, pp. 8-17; see also W. J. Reddin, *Management Effectiveness*, New York: McGraw-Hill, 1970.

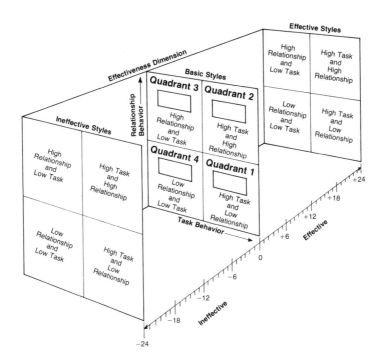

Figure 3. Tri-Dimensional Leader Effectiveness Model

Style Adaptability

The degree to which leadership behavior is appropriate to the demands of a given situation is called style adaptability (Hersey & Blanchard, 1972, pp. 121-123). Someone with a narrow style range can be effective over a long period of time if the leader remains in situations in which his style has a high probability of success. Conversely, a person with a wide range of styles may be ineffective if these behaviors are not consistent with the demands of the situation. *Thus style range is not as relevant to effectiveness as is style adaptability; a wide style range will not guarantee effectiveness.*

Determining Style Adaptability

The degree of style adaptability or effectiveness that you indicate for yourself as a leader can be determined theoretically in Figure 4. Circle the score given each alternative action choice and then calculate the total score as indicated.

A weighting of a +2 to −2 is based on behavioral science concepts, theories, and empirical research. The leadership behavior with the highest probability of success is always weighted a +2. The behavior with the lowest probability of success is always weighted a −2. The second-best alternative is weighted a +1 and the third a −1.

After determining your total score on style adaptability or effectiveness you can integrate this score into the Tri-Dimensional Leader Effectiveness Model (Figure 3) by placing an arrow (→) along the ineffective (−1 to −24) or effective (+1 to +24) dimension of the leadership model that

Alternative Actions

Situations	A	B	C	D
1	+2	−1	+1	−2
2	+2	−2	+1	−1
3	+1	−1	−2	+2
4	+1	−2	+2	−1
5	−2	+1	+2	−1
6	−1	+1	−2	+2
7	−2	+2	−1	+1
8	+2	−1	−2	+1
9	−2	+1	+2	−1
10	+1	−2	−1	+2
11	−2	+2	−1	+1
12	−1	+2	−2	+1
Sub-Total		+	+	+

= Total

Figure 4. Determining Style Adaptability

corresponds to your total score from Figure 4. At this time you may also want to transfer your leadership style and style range scores from Figure 1 to Figure 3 so that all your LEAD data are located together.

SITUATIONAL LEADERSHIP THEORY

The weighting of a +2 to −2 is based on situational analysis using the Life-Cycle Theory of Leadership[3] (Figure 5). This theory is based on a relationship between the amount of direction (task behavior) and the amount of socio-emotional support (relationship behavior) a leader provides, and the followers' level of "maturity."

Followers in any situation are vital, not only because individually they accept or reject the leader, but because as a group they actually determine the personal power of the leader.

Maturity of the Followers or Group

Maturity is defined in Life-Cycle Theory as the capacity to set high but attainable goals (achievement-motivation [McClelland et al., 1953, 1961]), willingness and ability to take responsibility, and education and/or experience of an individual or a group. *These variables of maturity should be considered only in relation to a specific task to be performed.* That is, an individual or a group is not

---

[3]The Life-Cycle Theory of Leadership was developed at the Center for Leadership Studies, Ohio University, Athens, Ohio. It was first published in Hersey and Blanchard (1969).

96

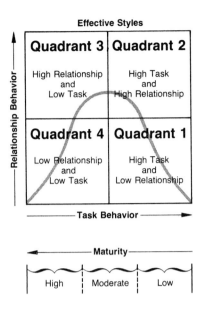

Effective Styles

Quadrant 3	Quadrant 2
High Relationship and Low Task	High Task and High Relationship
Quadrant 4	Quadrant 1
Low Relationship and Low Task	High Task and Low Relationship

← Relationship Behavior →

——— Task Behavior ———→

←——————— Maturity ———————

| High | Moderate | Low |

Figure 5. Life-Cycle Leadership Theory

mature or immature in any *global* sense, only in terms of a specific task. Thus a salesperson may be very responsible in securing new sales, but very casual about completing the paper work necessary to close a sale.

According to Life-Cycle Theory, as the level of maturity of followers continues to increase in terms of accomplishing a specific task, leaders should begin to *reduce* their task behavior and *increase* their relationship behavior until the group is sufficiently mature for the leaders to decrease their relationship behavior (socio-emotional support) as well. Thus, this theory focuses on the appropriateness or effectiveness of leadership styles according to the task-relevant maturity of the followers. This cycle can be illustrated by the bell-shaped curve juxtaposed over the four leadership quadrants in Figure 5.

In Figure 5, the curvilinear function of the cycle would be portrayed on the effective side of the Tri-Dimensional Leader Effectiveness Model. To determine what style is appropriate with a specific individual or group, some benchmarks of maturity have been provided for determining appropriate leadership style by dividing the maturity continuum into three categories—low, moderate, and high.

This theory of leadership states that with people who are low in maturity in terms of accomplishing a specific task, a high task style (Quadrant 1) has the highest probability of success; with people who are of average maturity on a task, moderate structure and moderate-to-high socio-emotional style (Quadrants 2 and 3) appear to be most appropriate; a low-relationship and low-task style (Quadrant 4) has the highest probability of success with people of high task maturity.

ANALYZING TOTAL SCORE

In the LEAD instrument, each of the twelve situations theoretically called for one of the four basic leadership styles depicted in Figure 1. In each case, the situation described something about the maturity level of a work group you might be working with in your role as a leader. Using the Life-Cycle Theory of Leadership as the analytical tool, three of the situations demanded a High Task/Low Relationship action (Quadrant 1), three required a High Task/High Relationship choice (Quadrant 2), three required a High Relationship/Low Task style (Quadrant 3), and finally three asked for a Low Relationship/Low Task style (Quadrant 4).

Thus a person who picked the alternative with the highest probability in all twelve situations would have indicated three style choices in each quadrant and would have received a +24 adaptability or effectiveness score.

The situations in which you chose the theoretically "best" response will have +2 circled on Figure 4. Likewise, the situations in which you chose the theoretically "worst" response will have −2 circled. The situations in which a +1 is circled do not necessarily indicate a theoretically "bad" choice but suggest there was a "better" choice (+2). On the other hand a −1 indicates an inappropriate choice but suggests there was a "worse" choice (−2).

MODIFYING LEVELS OF MATURITY

In attempting to help individuals or groups mature (i.e., encouraging them to take more and more responsibility for performing a specific task), a leader must be careful not to delegate responsibility and/or increase socio-emotional support too rapidly. If this occurs, the individual or group may take advantage and view the leader as a "soft touch." Thus the leader must slowly encourage the maturity of followers on each task that they must perform, using less task behavior and more relationship behavior as they mature and become more willing and able to take responsibility.

When an individual's performance is low on a specific task, one must not expect drastic changes overnight. For a desirable behavior to be obtained, a leader must immediately reward the slightest behavior exhibited by the individual in the desired direction and continue this process as the individual's behavior comes closer and closer to the leader's expectations of good performance. This is a behavior modification concept called *positively reinforcing successive approximations*[4] of a desired behavior.

For example, a sales manager might want to move a salesperson through the cycle so that he or she would assume significantly more responsibility. If the salesperson is normally very dependent on the manager to close a sale, the leader's best bet initially is to reduce some of the structure or close supervision by giving the salesperson an opportunity to assume increased responsibility, e.g., setting up the closing meeting. If this responsibility is well handled, the sales manager should reinforce this behavior with increases in socio-emotional support (relationship behavior). This is a two-step process: first, a reduction in structure and, second, if adequate performance follows, an increase in socio-emotional support as reinforcement. This process should continue until the salesperson is assuming significant responsibility and performing as a mature individual in terms of closing sales. This does not mean that the salesperson's work will have less structure, but rather that the structure can now be internally imposed by the individual instead of being externally imposed by the sales manager. At this point, the cycle as depicted by the Life-Cycle Theory of Leadership in Figure 5 begins to become a backward-bending curve and move toward Quadrant 4 (low-relationship behavior and low-task behavior). Individuals are able not only to structure many of the activities in which they engage while working on a specific task, but also are able to provide their own satisfaction for interpersonal and emotional needs. At this stage of maturity, individuals

---

[4]The most classic discussions of behavior modification, or operant conditioning, have been done by B. F. Skinner. See B. F. Skinner, *Science and Human Behavior*, New York: Macmillan, 1953.

tend to be reinforced positively for their accomplishments when the leader does not look over their shoulder on a specific task and leaves them more and more on their own. It is not that there is less mutual trust and friendship, but rather that less interaction time is needed to prove it with mature individuals.

Although this theory suggests a basic style for different levels of task maturity, it is not a one-way street. When people begin to behave less maturely for whatever reason (e.g., crisis at home, change in work technology), it becomes appropriate for the leader to adjust behavior backward through the Life-Cycle curve to meet the present maturity level of his group. For example, a salesperson is presently working well on his own. Suddenly, the salesperson faces a family crisis that begins to affect his performance on the job. In this situation, it may be appropriate for the manager moderately to increase structure and socio-emotional support (move back toward Quadrant 2) until the individual regains composure.

REFERENCES

Blake, R. R., & Mouton, J. S. *The managerial grid.* Houston, Texas: Gulf, 1964.

Fiedler, F. E. *A theory of leadership effectiveness.* New York: McGraw-Hill, 1967.

Halpin, A. W. *The leadership behavior of school superintendents.* Chicago: Midwest Administration Center, University of Chicago, 1959.

Hersey, P., & Blanchard, K. H. Life-cycle theory of leadership. *Training and Development Journal,* May 1969.

Hersey, P., & Blanchard, K. H. *Management of organizational behavior: Utilizing human resources* (2nd ed.). Englewood Cliffs, N.J.: Prentice-Hall, 1972.

Korman, A. K. "Consideration," "initiating structure," and organizational criteria—a review. *Personnel Psychology: A Journal of Applied Research,* 1966, *19*(4), 349-361.

Likert, R. *New patterns of management.* New York: McGraw-Hill, 1961.

McClelland, D. C., Atkinson, J. W., Clark, R. A., & Lowell, E. L. *The achievement motive.* New York: Appleton-Century-Crofts, 1953.

McClelland, D. C., Atkinson, J. W., Clark, R. A., & Lowell, E. L. *The achieving society.* Princeton, N.J.: D. Van Nostrand, 1961.

Stogdill, R. M., & Coons, A. E. (Eds.). *Leader behavior: Its description and measurement* (Research Monograph No. 88). Columbus: Ohio State University, 1957.

Tannenbaum, R., & Schmidt, W. H. How to choose a leadership pattern. *Harvard Business Review,* March-April 1957, pp. 95-101.

ORGANIZATION BEHAVIOR DESCRIBER SURVEY (OBDS)

Roger Harrison and Barry Oshry

The Organization Behavior Describer Survey (OBDS) was developed to assess the behavior of both line and staff managers and administrators in group and interpersonal situations arising during the course of work. It can be used as a self-evaluation form or to obtain descriptions of behavior from others.

The OBDS was originally developed deductively from Argyris's (1962) theory of interpersonal behavior in organizations. Argyris postulates two kinds of administrative competence: rational-technical competence and interpersonal competence. Rational-technical competence is the ability to meet intellectual knowledge and technical skill requirements of the job; interpersonal competence is the individual's willingness and ability to deal directly and openly with the emotional aspects of interpersonal relationships in the organization.

Argyris's theory is similar to other two-factor theories of organizational behavior, notably Fleishman's Initiating Structure and Consideration, Blake's Managerial Grid, and McGregor's Theory X and Theory Y. Another Fleishman instrument, the Supervisory Behavior Questionnaire, was already available for assessing supervisory behavior on the dimensions of Initiating Structure and Consideration. It focused on supervisor-subordinate relationships and was primarily designed for the first-line level of supervision. In contrast, the OBDS was designed to produce a more general measure of interpersonal behavior, not only downwards in the organization but laterally and upwards as well.

In the first attempt to construct the instrument, twenty items were deductively composed —ten representing rational-technical aspects of interpersonal behavior and ten describing interpersonal competence as defined by Argyris. These items were factor analyzed, using 321 descriptions of managers in a technical manufacturing firm at middle levels of responsibility. Instead of the two expected factors, three important dimensions emerged from the analysis: rational-technical competence (24 percent of the variance), interpersonal competence (22 percent of the variance), and emotional expressiveness (11 percent of the variance).

These results indicated that the expressive and receptive aspects of interpersonal competence were not seen by respondents as closely related to one another. Being open to the ideas and feelings of others was seen as quite different from being open in expression of one's feelings. This seemed an important finding, because it identified another factor beyond the two usually considered important in organizational behavior and because it implied that aspects of interpersonal behavior that trainers and organizational consultants have carelessly tended to think of together may be quite separate processes.

Correlations were calculated between the three scales of the OBDS and the rating on Fleishman's Supervisory Behavior Questionnaire. As expected, the interpersonal competence scale showed moderately high correlations (median = .62) with Fleishman's Consideration Scale. Both the rational-technical and emotional expressiveness scales of the OBDS were moderately correlated with Fleishman's Initiating Structure Scale (median = .47). The emotional expressiveness scale showed negligible correlations with Fleishman's Consideration Scale and lower correlations with the OBDS interpersonal competence scale than with the rational-technical scale. This provided further evidence that the receptive and expressive aspects of interpersonal behavior may be seen quite differently.

Based on these preliminary results, development of the OBDS was carried out. A 36-item questionnaire was constructed, and the descriptions by 189 subordinates of middle managers attending human relations training workshops were factor analyzed. An essentially similar factorial structure was obtained. This was tested by further factor analysis of descriptions of middle managers by fellow participants in a human relations training laboratory (T-group). In this artificial and specialized interaction situation, similar factors were found to those obtained from on-the-job descriptions. The resulting scales are presented here for use in studies of organizational behavior, evaluation of training, and the analysis of interpersonal behavior in groups.

In the current version of the OBDS, four scales are used. These are not altogether independent factorially. The basic factor structure is still three dimensional. However, the items in each of the four scales cluster rather neatly together and have a unity of connotation that argues for separate scoring. The median interscale correlations and reliability estimates of these scales are given in Table 1.

Interscale correlations are based on twelve samples (median N = 51), including:

1. descriptions by fellow members of managers participating in a T-group laboratory,
2. descriptions of industrial managers by self, supervisor, subordinate, and peer,
3. descriptions of managers in an applied research organization by the categories of describers in (2), and
4. descriptions of YMCA executives by the categories of describers in (2).

Table 1. Median Interscale Correlations and Reliability Estimates of OBDS Scales

Scale	Rational-Technical Competence	Verbal Dominance	Consideration	Emotional Expressiveness
Rational-Technical Competence	.73 (pre-post)[1] .83 (split half)[2]	.69	.36	−.03
Verbal Dominance		.71 (pre-post) .84 (split half)	.23	.13
Consideration			.70 (pre-post) .92 (split half)	−.29
Emotional Expressiveness				.70 (pre-post) .89 (split half)

[1]Pre-post correlations are with intervening training experience and are based on eleven samples (median N = 49).
[2]Speaman-Brown split-half reliabilities are based on four samples (median N = 80).

Inspection of Table 1 shows reasonable independence of the scales, with the exception of verbal dominance and rational-technical competence, which are closely related. It is interesting to note the low negative correlation between consideration and emotional expressiveness in view of the attempts by practitioners of laboratory training to encourage increases in behavior on both dimensions. There is, in fact, a consistent tendency in our research for managers who rank high on emotional expressiveness to be seen in generally negative ways by their associates.

The reliabilities reported in Table 1 are adequate, especially considering the shortness of the scales. The pre-post correlations are also evidence of considerable stability, considering that they are based on pre-post time differences averaging two months and that they encompass an intervening human relations training experience designed to produce change along the dimensions measured by the OBDS.

With an instrument measuring behavior through descriptions, it is important to consider not only intradescriber reliability but also to assess interdescriber reliability: the degree of agreement among observers of the same individual's behavior. Accordingly, correlations were calculated between descriptions of the same person by self, supervisor, and subordinate. The findings, presented in Table 2, are based on the same populations as the figures in Table 1.

Table 2. Median Interdescriber Correlations, OBDS Scales

Scale	Correlations Based on Different Roles (13 Samples)		Correlations Based on Same Role (Subordinate) (2 Samples)	
	Median r	Range	r	N
Rational-Technical Competence	.14	−.03 to .27	.39	70
			.24	28
Verbal Dominance	.20	−.05 to .47	.28	61
			.40	22
Consideration	.14	−.07 to .40	.15	69
			.45	26
Emotional Expressiveness	.30	.09 to .56	.50	66
			.56	29

Note: Median N = 53; range of N's: 15 to 66.

These findings are not very encouraging if one hopes to obtain a composite measure from several describers of an individual's interpersonal style in his organizational setting. When compared with the respectable intradescriber reliabilities, these figures are small indeed.

The inclusion of self-subordinate and self-supervisor correlations in this determination may be questioned on the grounds that self-descriptions are more subject to distortion than are descriptions by associates. There is, however, no indication from the distribution of correlations that this is the case. Roughly the same range of relationships was found in those correlations involving self-descriptions as in those based on observations by subordinate and supervisor. The data suggest, rather, that there is in fact considerable inconsistency in personal style, depending on some combination of the perceptual idiosyncracies of the observer and the behavior-determining role relationships between the observer and the individual described. From the data in Table 2, it can be seen that correlations between descriptions by two subordinates of the same supervisor are, on all scales, higher than the median of correlations based on different roles. This suggests that some of the unreliability between raters is indeed due to role relationships that influence interpersonal style. However, even within the same role, the interrater correlations leave a great deal to be desired.

It is also of interest that the correlations tend to be higher for verbal dominance and emotional expressiveness than they do for rational-technical competence and consideration. The items in the latter two scales require a higher degree of inference and refer less directly to observable behavior than do the items in the verbal dominance and emotional expressiveness scales. The more inference we require from the describer, of course, the more we can expect his judgment to be affected by his own psychological processes. For this reason the "best" scale should be one that is based most heavily on concrete descriptions of observable behavior.

In this connection it is interesting to compare Fleishman's Supervisory Behavior Questionnaire with the OBDS. In the study in which the OBDS was first developed we also obtained descriptions on Fleishman's instrument from self, supervisor, peer, and subordinate (N = 50). The median interrater correlations were .39 for initiating structure and .16 for consideration. Thus, the OBDS and the Supervisory Behavior Questionnaire compare favorably in interrater reliability on the consideration dimension, but Fleishman's instrument has a better showing on initiating structure than the OBDS has on verbal dominance, the closest OBDS scale in content.

The rather high mean scores on the OBDS suggest that the responses could be designed to produce a greater spread of scores. For example:

Always = 4
Most of the time = 3
Often = 2
Occasionally = 1
Seldom = 0.

REFERENCE

Argyris, C. *Interpersonal competence and organizational effectiveness.* New York: John Wiley, 1962.

Roger Harrison, Ph.D., *is the vice president for overseas operations, Development Research Associates, Newton Center, Massachusetts. His recent work includes the development of the Autonomy Laboratory and the Positive Power and Influence Workshop. Dr. Harrison lives in England, where he specializes in organization development and in the creation of self-directed methods for educating managers and consultants.*

Barry Oshry, Ph.D., *is the director of Power & Systems Education, NTL Institute for Applied Behavioral Science. He is the developer of the Power & Systems Laboratory, an approach to the study of personal, group, and system power. Dr. Oshry's background is in T-group training, group dynamics, and political psychology.*

ORGANIZATION BEHAVIOR DESCRIBER SURVEY (OBDS)
Roger Harrison and Barry Oshry

Instructions: Listed below are twenty-five descriptions of ways that people behave in staff and problem-solving meetings. Choose an actual person in your organization and select the alternative in each item that comes closest to describing that person's behavior at work. Write an "X" in the appropriate box. Mark only one alternative for each item. Keep in mind that you are limiting yourself to a description of how this person behaves only in *meetings* and *work-oriented situations or conversations.*

The person I am describing is: (check one)

_____ Myself

_____ My superior

_____ My subordinate

_____ Someone who works at the same level as I.

_____ Other (specify) _____

I have known this person for approximately _____ years.

I spend about_____hours per month with this person in *meetings* and/or *work-oriented situations or conversations.*

____ ____ 1. He tries to understand the feelings (anger, impatience, rejection) expressed by others in the group.
　　　　　□ Always　　□ Often　　□ Occasionally　　□ Seldom　　□ Never

____ ____ 2. He shows intelligence.
　　　　　□ Always　　□ Often　　□ Occasionally　　□ Seldom　　□ Never

____ ____ 3. He sympathizes with others when they have difficulties.
　　　　　□ Always　　□ Often　　□ Occasionally　　□ Seldom　　□ Never

____ ____ 4. He expresses ideas clearly and concisely.
　　　　　□ Always　　□ Often　　□ Occasionally　　□ Seldom　　□ Never

____ ____ 5. He expresses his own feelings, e.g., when he is angry, impatient, ignored.
　　　　　□ Always　　□ Often　　□ Occasionally　　□ Seldom　　□ Never

____ ____ 6. He is tolerant and accepting of other people's feelings.
　　　　　□ Always　　□ Often　　□ Occasionally　　□ Seldom　　□ Never

____ ____ 7. He thinks quickly.
　　　　　□ Always　　□ Often　　□ Occasionally　　□ Seldom　　□ Never

____ ____ 8. He is angry or upset when things do not go his way.
　　　　　□ Always　　□ Often　　□ Occasionally　　□ Seldom　　□ Never

____ ____ 9. He is persuasive, a "seller of ideas."
　　　　　□ Always　　□ Often　　□ Occasionally　　□ Seldom　　□ Never

____ ____ 10. You can tell quickly when he likes or dislikes what others do or say.
　　　　　□ Always　　□ Often　　□ Occasionally　　□ Seldom　　□ Never

____ ____ 11. He listens and tries to use the ideas raised by others in the group.
　　　　　□ Always　　□ Often　　□ Occasionally　　□ Seldom　　□ Never

____ ____ 12. He demonstrates high technical or professional competence. He "knows his stuff."
　　　　　□ Always　　□ Often　　□ Occasionally　　□ Seldom　　□ Never

_____ _____ 13. He is warm and friendly with those who work with him.
☐ Always ☐ Often ☐ Occasionally ☐ Seldom ☐ Never

_____ _____ 14. He is able to attract the attention of others.
☐ Always ☐ Often ☐ Occasionally ☐ Seldom ☐ Never

_____ _____ 15. His feelings are transparent; he does not have a "poker face."
☐ Always ☐ Often ☐ Occasionally ☐ Seldom ☐ Never

_____ _____ 16. He comes up with good ideas.
☐ Always ☐ Often ☐ Occasionally ☐ Seldom ☐ Never

_____ _____ 17. He encourages others to express their ideas before he acts.
☐ Always ☐ Often ☐ Occasionally ☐ Seldom ☐ Never

_____ _____ 18. He tries to help when others become angry or upset.
☐ Always ☐ Often ☐ Occasionally ☐ Seldom ☐ Never

_____ _____ 19. He tries out new ideas.
☐ Always ☐ Often ☐ Occasionally ☐ Seldom ☐ Never

_____ _____ 20. He is competitive; he likes to win and hates to lose.
☐ Always ☐ Often ☐ Occasionally ☐ Seldom ☐ Never

_____ _____ 21. He presents his ideas convincingly.
☐ Always ☐ Often ☐ Occasionally ☐ Seldom ☐ Never

_____ _____ 22. If others in the group become angry or upset, he listens with understanding.
☐ Always ☐ Often ☐ Occasionally ☐ Seldom ☐ Never

_____ _____ 23. He offers effective solutions to problems.
☐ Always ☐ Often ☐ Occasionally ☐ Seldom ☐ Never

_____ _____ 24. He tends to be emotional.
☐ Always ☐ Often ☐ Occasionally ☐ Seldom ☐ Never

_____ _____ 25. When he talks, others listen.
☐ Always ☐ Often ☐ Occasionally ☐ Seldom ☐ Never

TOTALS   ☐ R-TC   ☐ VD   ☐ EE   ☐ C

OBDS SCORING AND INTERPRETATION SHEET

Scoring instructions:

1. Go back over your responses to the twenty-five items on the Organization Behavior Describer Survey and assign a number value to each of your responses, using the scale below:

   Always = 4
   Often = 3
   Occasionally = 2
   Seldom = 1
   Never = 0.

   Write the number corresponding to your response on the first blank in front of each item.

2. In the second blank in front of each item, write one of the following codes:

Items	Code
2, 7, 12, 16, 19, 23	R-TC
4, 9, 14, 20, 21, 25	VD
5, 8, 10, 15, 24	EE
1, 3, 6, 11, 13, 17, 18, 22	C

3. Sum the scores of the items for each code and enter them in the four boxes at the end of the instrument.

Interpretation: Your profile of scores describes a person's behavior according to the following four major dimensions.

   R-TC: Rational-Technical Competence. This is the degree to which the person behaves intelligently and quickly, demonstrates competence, has good ideas, tries out new ideas, and offers effective solutions to problems.

   VD: Verbal Dominance. This score reflects your assessment of the degree to which the person tends to behave competitively, persuasively, in an attention-getting manner; presents ideas convincingly; commands attention; and expresses ideas clearly and concisely.

   EE: Emotional Expressiveness. This is the degree to which the person becomes emotional (e.g., acts angry or upset when things do not go his way), expresses his own feelings and emotions, and expresses how he feels about what other people say.

   C: Consideration. This score reflects the degree to which the person listens and responds to the ideas raised by others, encourages others to express their ideas, tries to understand the feelings expressed by others, tries to help when others become angry or upset, listens empathically, is warm and friendly with those who work with him.

Because the four scales do not have an equal number of items, you can make them comparable by utilizing the following procedure:

   1. Copy your four total scores below.

   ☐ R-TC   ☐ VD   ☐ EE   ☐ C

   2. Divide each score by the appropriate number below and enter the result in the boxes.

   ÷6   ÷6   ÷5   ÷8
   ☐ R-TC   ☐ VD   ☐ EE   ☐ C

These scores can be plotted on the following diagram and compared with the norms.

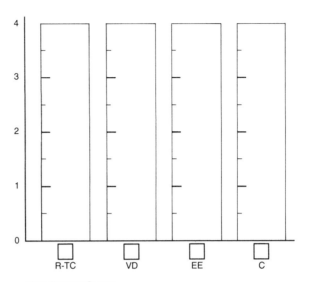

Your Average Scores

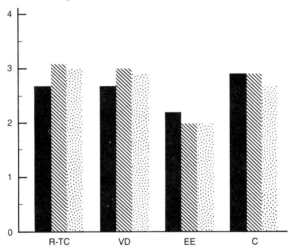

Norms

Combined norms of human relations laboratory
participants, research and development managers,
and YMCA managers (groups virtually identical
on the OBDS)

Self   N = 214

Subordinate   N = 365

Superior   N = 201

INTRODUCTION TO THE
LECTURETTES SECTION

Helping individuals to integrate personal learnings with conceptual material based on theory and research findings is among the most important objectives of human relations training. Reducing the gap between what a participant experiences in the affective sphere and what he understands cognitively is the purpose of lecturettes. They may be used to provide short, succinct statements of principles, models, research findings, or theory. They provide stimuli to which workshop participants can respond with new levels of awareness.

THE EXPERIENTIAL LECTURE

Using input from participants can provide a stimulating and potentially powerful mode for presenting lecture material in a group. We call this approach the "experiential lecture." That is, the lecture "material" is embedded in the learners. It is the facilitator's task to tap that material, to focus it, and to make it come alive conceptually.

There are a number of guidelines to keep in mind if an experiential lecture is to emerge successfully in a training design.

Motivation

The learning climate established must be one that fosters support for participants' contributions. The facilitator should create the lecturette within the context of the group's learning needs. Sequencing is important; the effective lecture provides a bridge between what precedes it and what follows.

Preparation

Participants should be adequately prepared for their role in creating the lecturette. Brainstorming techniques, interviewing fellow participants about a topic, writing down notes to oneself about the topic under consideration can facilitate the unfolding of the lecturette.

Illustration

Specific cases, problems, and anecdotal material provide rich sources of material for the experiential lecture and increase the group's psychological ownership of the final lecturette.

Reaction

The experiential approach gives the facilitator and the participants an opportunity to respond to ideas as they emerge. In addition, by assuming that most questions contain points of view, opinions, or feelings about a particular item, the experiential lecture invites participants to answer questions that are asked during the presentation. Reacting to concepts as they evolve helps to integrate them.

Focus

The facilitator's ability to focus ideas and points of view into a useful frame of reference is a prerequisite for presenting effective experiential lecturettes. Providing a theoretical foundation to understand the behavior elicited over the course of a training event enables participants to validate newly acquired concepts.

Closure

A sense of psychological closure around events or concepts explored during the lecturette is necessary. This enables those involved to move to the next learning opportunity. However, it is unrealistic and, after a point, undesirable, to have complete "closure" on a topic. Concepts should remain open to further examination, fluid rather than static.

USES OF THE EXPERIENTIAL LECTURE

Potential uses for the experiential lecture include the following.

1. To give participants a specific referent as they think about applying new insights to their everyday behavior;
2. To establish a mental set about a particular idea or point of view;
3. To prepare participants to interpret instrumental feedback;
4. To summarize learning experiences.

EFFECTIVENESS OF LECTURETTES

To assess the learning needs of the group and to match those needs with an appropriate lecturette requires the full use of the facilitator's creative powers.

The facilitator must have the capacity to make real *contact* with his audience. Keeping pace with the "vibes" of the audience is necessary—being aware of participants' puzzlements, attending to nonverbal cues concerning boredom or excitement, and responding to such cues make contact easier. Modulating one's voice also helps to keep the group alert and interested. The facilitator's own personal excitement, his sense of having fun and *being with* the group, contributes to the quality of the lecturette presented.

Experiential lecturettes provide an avenue for solid learning and a practical way to blend theory with here-and-now learnings. It is the facilitator's job to diagnose precisely the needs of a learning group, to intervene at the appropriate level, and to follow through with the data generated. By presenting, exploring, and living experiential lecturettes, the trainer gains the flexibility to help his groups reach their learning goals.

DEALING WITH ANGER

Anger is the first emotion human beings experience and the last one we learn to manage effectively. As early as four months of age, the human infant's vague feelings of distress differentiate into recognizable anger; for many of us, a lifetime is spent in denying, suppressing, displacing, or avoiding this troublesome emotional experience. Because anger usually occurs within an interpersonal context, it is a frequent group phenomenon and presents a management challenge to all concerned.[1]

Anger happens when we perceive an external event (object or person) as threatening or when we experience the frustration of unmet expectations. Although anger seems to be a response to something outside of us, it most often is an *intra*personal event: we make ourselves angry. But because anger is so unpleasant and human beings are so adept at projection, we usually attempt to locate the source of our anger outside ourselves with statements such as "You make me angry," "You have irritating habits," "You bother me."

ANGER AND THREAT

When we perceive an external event as threatening to our physical or psychological well-being, a cycle of internal movements is initiated. As the perception is formed, assumptions are made internally about the possible danger of the threat. The assumption is then checked against our perceived power of dealing with the threat. If we conclude that the threat is not very great or that we are powerful enough to confront it successfully, a calm, unflustered response can occur. But if we conclude that the threat is dangerous or that we are powerless to handle it, anger emerges in an effort to destroy or reduce the personal threat and to protect our assumed impotency. The anger cycle can be graphically represented. (See Figure 1.)

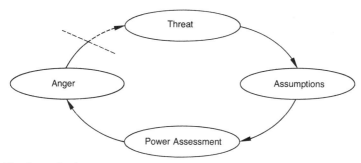

Figure 1. The Anger Cycle

Resentment and Expectations

In the Gestalt view, anger is resentment, an experience accompanying a demand or expectation that has not been made explicit. Unanswered demands or unmet expectations are frustrating; they become another kind of threat, which trips off the anger cycle within us.

---

[1] For a useful instrument dealing with anger, see the "Inventory of Anger Communication" by Millard J. Bienvenu, Sr., in the Instrumentation section of this *Annual*.

Maladaptive Expressions of Anger

Unlike most other feelings, anger has no specific body organs for expression.[2] Physiologically, anger is accompanied by an increase in blood pressure and muscle tightness; psychologically, there are impulses to say aggressive words, strike out, commit violence. But the expression of anger can be so terrifying and threatening that, rather than express it outwardly, we sometimes turn it inward, against ourselves. This short-circuiting of the anger cycle produces distortions of another magnitude: anger turned inward is experienced as guilt; guilt produces feelings of depression, incompetence, helplessness, and, ultimately, self-destruction.

Another common way to short-circuit the anger cycle is to vent the feeling, not at the perceived threatening event, but at someone or something else that is convenient. We are angry at the traffic jam, but we snap at an innocent spouse. The children consistently refuse to meet our expectations, but we kick the dog. We are angry at the group leader, but we complain about the food. Such displacement of angry feeling serves to ventilate but not to resolve: the anger cycle still lacks closure. When displacement becomes generalized to the system, the government, or the state of Western culture, we begin to see the whole world as hostile and we develop a wrathful, attacking behavior style.

Expression of anger can lead to violence; turning it inward produces depression. Displacement is ultimately ineffective and can damage innocent third parties. Repeated failure to close the anger cycle can produce a hostile, cynical, negative view of reality. And even though anger usually occurs in an interpersonal context, it is not an interpersonal event, but self-generated. We make ourselves angry, and there is no one else who can honestly be blamed. Suffering the anger often seems to be the only alternative.

DEALING WITH PERSONAL ANGER

The obvious way to eliminate anger from our lives is to become so personally secure that nothing threatens us. Short of that level of self-actualization, the procedures described here may help.

Owning anger. Acknowledging anger and claiming it as our own behavior is a helpful first step. It increases self-awareness and prevents unwarranted blaming of others. Turning blame and attribution into "I" statements locates the anger where it actually is—inside us. This procedure can help develop a sense of personal power.

Calibrating the response. Anger is not an all-or-nothing experience. It ranges from relatively mild reactions such as "I disagree," "I don't like that," and "I'm bothered," through medium responses such as "I'm annoyed," "I'm pissed off," and "I'm irritated," to intense reactions such as "I'm furious," "I'm enraged," and "I feel like hitting you." Learning to differentiate between levels of anger helps us to assess accurately our capacity for dealing with it.

Diagnosing the threat. What is frightening about the perceived threat? What do I stand to lose? Anger happens because we quickly assume that the situation is dangerous—so quickly that we frequently do not know why the stimulus is threatening. Diagnosing the threat frequently reveals that it is simply a difference in values, opinion, upbringing, or styles of behaving.

Sharing the perceived threat is a way to make the internal anger cycle a public or interpersonal event. It diffuses the intensity of feeling and clarifies our perceptions. It permits us to receive feedback and consensual validation.

Forgiveness involves letting go of the anger and cancelling the charges against the other—and ourselves. Forgiving and forgetting cleans the slate and is a way of opening yourself to future transactions. Forgiveness is a magnanimous gesture that increases personal power.

---

[2]Bodily responses during anger and in sexual arousal are nearly indistinguishable; the only difference is that in sexual arousal, rhythmic muscular movement, tumescence, and genital secretion or ejaculation may occur.

112

DEALING WITH ANOTHER'S ANGER

In interpersonal situations, we often respond to another person's anger, whether or not we have occasioned it, by threatening or frustrating behavior. It frequently happens that we receive another's anger just because we happen to be there. Laura Huxley, in her aptly titled book *You Are Not the Target* (1963), views the anger of another as negative energy that is dumped on us, just as ocean waves dump their energy on the beach.

Anger from another has high potential for hooking us into what is essentially someone else's problem. If we view another's anger as threatening, we start the anger cycle in ourselves, and then we have our anger to deal with, as well as the other person's. To be angry simply because someone else is angry makes no sense, but it frequently happens anyway. Contagion is a usual by-product of intensity.

Anger from another, if responded to appropriately, can increase interpersonal learning and strengthen a relationship. The following steps may be helpful.

Affirm the other's feelings. An old Jules Feiffer cartoon devotes nine panels to one character building up his anger toward another. Finally, he verbally confronts the other with "I hate you, you son of a bitch!" The other character replies, "Let us begin by defining your terms." To *affirm* another's anger is to acknowledge that you are receiving it and to express a willingness to respond. To *disallow* another's anger usually heightens its intensity.

Acknowledge your own defensiveness. Let the other person know what you are feeling. Acknowledge that your own tenseness may lead to miscommunication and distortion. Develop an awareness of the impact of received anger on your body.

Clarify and diagnose. Give and request specific feedback. Distinguish between wants and needs. Check expectations. Discover together who owns what in the situation. When interpersonal needs and wants are out on the table, the resolution of anger becomes more probable.

Renegotiate the relationship. Plan together how similar situations will be dealt with in the future. Contracting to practice new behavior may help eliminate the sources of friction. Acknowledge regret and exchange apologies if that is warranted. Agree on a third-party mediator to help if the two of you are getting nowhere.

Anger does not disappear if we refuse to deal with it; it continues to grow within us. If we deal with anger directly, the discomfort and unpleasantness are compensated by the new learning and self-strengthening that occur. If we deal with it indirectly, we easily trap ourselves into polarization, passivity, "gunnysacking," name-calling, blaming, gaming, and viewing ourselves and our adversary as weak and fragile. Anger is not the worst thing in the world. It is a powerful source of energy, which, if creatively and appropriately expressed, leads to personal growth and improved interpersonal functioning.

SUGGESTED ACTIVITIES

The following activities may be useful in learning to deal with anger.

1. Data can be collected on the methods group members use to deal with anger Statements beginning with "When I'm angry, I . . ." and "I resent . . ." can be classified and used to begin a discussion on anger management and conflict resolutions.

2. A structured fantasy is helpful for members to identify their ogres about anger and anger expression.

3. Anger-producing situations can be role played.

4. The group members can express anger nonverbally (sounds, grunts, gestures, etc.) to determine the intent, impact, and after-effects of expressing anger.

John E. Jones
Anthony G. Banet, Jr.

REFERENCE

Huxley, L. *You are not the target.* New York: Farrar, Straus & Giroux, 1963.

John E. Jones, Ph.D., is the vice president of University Associates, La Jolla, California. He is a co-editor of the University Associates Handbook *series, the five* Annual Handbooks for Group Facilitators, *and* Group & Organization Studies: The International Journal for Group Facilitators. *Dr. Jones's background is in teaching and counseling, education, and organization and community-development consulting.*

Anthony G. Banet, Jr., Ph.D., is a senior consultant with University Associates, La Jolla, California. He is a clinical psychologist with experience in community mental health and has consulted with numerous public service agencies. Dr. Banet is also the editor of Creative Psychotherapy: A Source Book.

ASSERTION THEORY

A friend asks to borrow your new, expensive camera . . . Someone cuts in front of you in a line . . . A salesperson is annoyingly persistent . . . Someone criticizes you angrily in front of your colleagues . . .

For many people these examples represent anxious, stressful situations to which there is no satisfying response. One basic response theory being taught more and more frequently in training programs is a theory called Assertiveness or Assertion.

Some important aspects of Assertion theory include (1) the philosophy underlying assertion, (2) the three possible response styles in an assertive situation, (3) some means of outwardly recognizing these response styles, (4) some functional distinctions between the three styles, and (5) the six components of an assertive situation.

THE PHILOSOPHY OF ASSERTION

Assertion theory is based on the premise that every individual possesses certain basic human rights. These rights include such fundamentals as "the right to refuse requests without having to feel guilty or selfish," "the right to have one's own needs be as important as the needs of other people," "the right to make mistakes," and "the right to express ourselves as long as we don't violate the rights of others" (Jakubowski-Spector, in press).

THREE RESPONSE STYLES

People relate to these basic human rights along a continuum of response styles: nonassertion, assertion, and aggression.

Assertion

The act of standing up for one's own basic human rights without violating the basic human rights of others is termed assertion (Jakubowski-Spector, 1973). It is a response style that recognizes boundaries between one's individual rights and those of others and operates to keep those boundaries stabilized.

When one of her friends asked to borrow Jan's new sports car for a trip, she was able to respond assertively by saying, "I appreciate your need for some transportation, but the car is too valuable to me to loan out." Jan was able to respect both her friend's right to make the request and her own right to refuse it.

Nonassertion

The two alternative response styles represent an inability to maintain adequately the boundaries between one person's rights and those of another. Nonassertion occurs when one allows one's boundaries to be restricted. In Jan's case, a nonassertive response would have been to loan the car, fearing that her friend might perceive her as petty or distrustful, and to spend the rest of the afternoon wishing she had not. Thus, Jan would not have been acting on her right to say no.

Aggression

The third response style, aggression, takes place when one person invades the other's boundaries of individual rights. Aggression, in Jan's case, might sound like this: "Certainly not!" or "You've *got* to be kidding!" Here, Jan would be violating the other person's right to courtesy and respect.

RECOGNIZING RESPONSE STYLES

Some helpful keys to recognizing these nonassertive, assertive, and aggressive response styles in any given situation are (1) the type of emotion experienced, (2) the nonverbal behavior displayed, and (3) the verbal language used.

Emotion

The person responding nonassertively tends to internalize feelings and tensions and to experience such emotions as fear, anxiety, guilt, depression, fatigue, or nervousness. Outwardly, emotional "temperature" is below normal, and feelings are not verbally expressed.

With an aggressive response, the tension is turned outward. Although the aggressor may have experienced fear, guilt, or hurt at one time in the interchange, this feeling has either been masked by a "secondary" emotion such as anger, or it has built up over time to a boiling point. In an aggressive response, the person's emotional temperature is above normal and is typically expressed by inappropriate anger, rage, hate, or misplaced hostility—all loudly and sometimes explosively expressed.

In contrast to the other two response styles, an individual responding assertively is aware of and deals with feelings as they occur, neither denying himself the right to the emotion nor using it to deny another's rights. Tension is kept within a normal, constructive range.

Nonverbal Behavior

Each response style is also characterized by certain nonverbal or body-language cues. A nonassertive response is self-effacing and dependent; it "moves away" from a situation. This response may be accompanied by such mannerisms as downcast eyes, the shifting of weight, a slumped body, the wringing of hands, or a whining, hesitant, or giggly tone of voice.

Aggression represents a nonverbal "moving against" a situation; it is other-effacing and counterdependent. This response may be expressed through glaring eyes, by leaning forward or pointing a finger, or by a raised, snickering, or haughty tone of voice.

Assertion, instead, faces up to a situation and demonstrates an approach by which one can stand up for oneself in an independent or interdependent manner. When being assertive, a person generally establishes good eye contact, stands comfortably but firmly on two feet with his hands loosely at his sides, and talks in a strong, steady tone of voice.

Verbal Language

A third way of differentiating between assertion, nonassertion, and aggression is to pay attention to the type of verbal language being used. Certain words tend to be associated with each style.

Nonassertive words can include qualifiers ("maybe," "I guess," "I wonder if you could," "would you mind very much," "only," "just," "I can't," "don't you think"), fillers ("uh," "well," "you know," "and") and negaters ("it's not really important," "don't bother").

Aggressive words include threats ("you'd better," "if you don't watch out"), put downs ("come *on*," "you must be kidding"), evaluative comments ("should," "bad"), and sexist or racist terms.

Assertive words may include "I" statements ("I think," "I feel," "I want"), cooperative words ("let's," "how can we resolve this"), and empathic statements of interest ("what do you think," "what do you see").

Emotional, nonverbal, and verbal cues are helpful keys in recognizing response styles, but they should be seen as general indicators and not as a means of labelling behavior.

FUNCTIONAL DISTINCTIONS

Outwardly, the three response styles seem to form a linear continuum running from the nonassertive style, which permits a violation of one's own rights; through the assertive style; to the aggressive position, which perpetrates a violation of another's rights.

Functionally, however, as indicated in Figure 1, nonassertion and aggression look both very much alike and very different from assertion. Nonassertion and aggression are dysfunctional not only because they use indirect methods of expressing wants and feelings and fail to respect the rights of *all* people, but also because they create an imbalance of power in which the two positions may mix or even change positions with each other. In refusing to stand up for his rights, the nonassertive responder creates a power imbalance by according everyone else more rights than himself, while the aggressive responder creates a power imbalance by according himself more than his share of rights.

This power imbalance is unstable; the restricted nonassertive responder can accumulate guilt, resentment, or fear until he becomes the aggressive responder in a burst of rage, or he may mix a nonassertive "front" with a subversive "behind the scenes" attempt to "get back" at the person.[1]

The assertive responder seeks a solution that equalizes the balance of power and permits all concerned to maintain their basic human rights. Thus an imbalance of power, caused by a failure to respect the rights of *all* people and perpetuated by the use of indirect methods, creates a very vulnerable position for both the nonassertive and the aggressive responders, while the more functional assertive responder respects all human rights, uses direct methods, and seeks a balance of power.

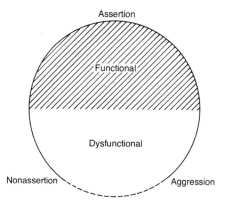

Figure 1. Functional and Dysfunctional Assertive Response Styles[2]

---

[1]The mixed, or indirect, response can range from guilt induction to subversion in style and is represented in Figure 1 by the broken-line area.

[2]Adapted from J. William Pfeiffer and John E. Jones, "Openness, Collusion and Feedback," in J. William Pfeiffer and John E. Jones (Eds.), *The 1972 Annual Handbook for Group Facilitators.* La Jolla, Calif.: University Associates, 1972, p. 199.

COMPONENTS OF AN ASSERTIVE SITUATION

Assertion theory can be helpful in situations in which a person is anxious about standing up for his basic human rights. These situations include saying yes and no with conviction, giving and receiving criticism, initiating conversations, resisting interruptions, receiving compliments, demanding a fair deal as a consumer, dealing with sexist remarks, and handling various other specific situations encountered in one's personal, social, and professional life.

A person may feel capable of being assertive in a situation but make a conscious decision not to be so, because of such things as power issues or the time or effort involved. Before making a decision to be assertive, it is helpful to examine the six components of an assertive situation.

1. The potential asserter's basic human rights and his level of confidence that he has these rights;
2. The specific behavior to which the potential asserter is responding;
3. The potential asserter's feeling reactions to this specific behavior;
4. The specific behavior the potential asserter would prefer;
5. The possible positive and negative consequences for the other person if he behaves as the potential asserter wishes him to behave;
6. The potential consequences of the assertive response for the potential asserter.

Once the situational assertive components have been determined, assertion training techniques provide a means of formulating and enacting an assertive response.

CONCLUSION

Assertion theory offers a model for those who wish to stand up for their own rights without violating the human rights of others. It is a model that can be used in all types of situations—personal, professional, and social—to facilitate honest, direct, functional communication.

Colleen Kelley

REFERENCES

Jakubowski-Spector, P. Facilitating the growth of women through assertive training. *The Counseling Psychologist*, 1973, 4(1), 75-86.

Jakubowski-Spector, P. Self-assertive training procedures for women. In D. Carter & E. Rawlings (Eds.), *Psychotherapy with women*. Springfield, Ill.: Charles C Thomas, in press.

Pfeiffer, J. W., & Jones, J. E. Openness, collusion and feedback. In J. W. Pfeiffer & J. E. Jones (Eds.), *The 1972 annual handbook for group facilitators*. La Jolla, Calif.: University Associates, 1972.

OTHER READINGS

Alberti, R. E., & Emmons, M. L. *Your perfect right: A guide to assertive behavior* (2nd ed.). San Luis Obispo, Calif.: Impact, 1974.

Alberti, R. E., & Emmons, M. L. *Stand up, speak out, talk back!: The key to self-assertive behavior*. New York: Simon & Schuster, 1975.

Bloom, L. L., Coburn, K., & Pearlman, J. *The new assertive woman*. New York: Delacorte, 1975.

Cummings, E., et al. *Assert your self*. Seattle: Seattle-King County N.O.W., 1974.

Fensterheim, H., & Baer, J. *Don't say yes when you want to say no: How assertiveness training can change your life*. New York: McKay, 1975.

Lazarus, A., & Fay, A. *I can if I want to: The direct assertion therapy program to change your life*. New York: William Morrow, 1975.

Osborn, S. M., & Harris, G. G. *Assertive training for women*. Springfield, Ill.: Charles C Thomas, 1975.

Phelps, S., & Austin, N. *The assertive woman*. San Luis Obispo, Calif.: Impact, 1975.

Smith, M. J. *When I say no, I feel guilty*. New York: McKay, 1975.

Colleen Kelley is a human relations consultant in La Jolla, California. Her consulting experience in the human relations field includes workshops, labs, and projects conducted in Mexico, Canada, and France, as well as in the United States. Ms. Kelley's background is in educational psychology, social psychology, and languages.

THE AWARENESS WHEEL

Self-awareness enables a person more effectively to process information he already has, i.e., information about thoughts, feelings, and so forth.

The Awareness Wheel is the major conceptual framework we use for teaching self-awareness. Five types of information are distinguished; these types of information involve somewhat different, though interrelated, cognitive processes (Figure 1).

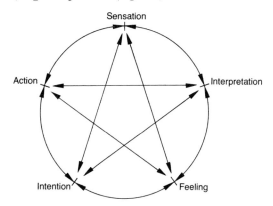

Figure 1. The Awareness Wheel

1. *Sensing* involves receiving data through the senses, e.g., I see, I hear, I touch, I smell, I taste. When a person reports sense data, or sense information, he will make purely *descriptive* statements:

"I see a striped ball."
"I see your muscles tightening."
"I hear your voice becoming louder."

2. *Interpreting* involves assigning meaning to the sense data. Meanings are impressions, conclusions, assumptions, etc. Present sense data are filtered through a framework based on past experiences and interpretations (i.e., stored information). When a person reports interpretive information, he makes inferential statements:

"That striped ball is a soccer ball."
"I think you are scared."
"I don't think you understand what I mean."

3. *Feeling* involves an emotional or affective response to the sense data received and the meaning assigned, e.g., I feel. Usually, feeling involves an actual sensation in some part of the body. A report of feeling information may be either a descriptive or an inferential statement:

"I'm happy."
"I feel scared."
"I think you're upset about something."

4. *Intending* involves what a person wants from a situation. Intention statements indicate the things a person wants to happen or wants to do, or they indicate inferences about another's wants.

"I want to play ball."
"I want to win this argument."
"I think you want me to leave."

5. *Acting* involves actual behavioral response, doing something based on sense data received, meaning assigned, feelings, and intentions. This is the "output" of information processing. One person's output, in turn, becomes "input" for another, i.e., what the other sees, hears, etc. Action includes both verbal behavior and nonverbal behavior.

I act by kicking a soccer ball.
I attack your ideas by saying, "Your thinking is inconsistent."
I ask you, "Are you upset?"

We initially focus on helping participants distinguish among these different types of information and the different cognitive processes involved. But we also clearly point out the interrelationships among the processes. We stress that experience does not necessarily occur in the sequence of sensing, interpreting, feeling, intending, and, finally, acting. Rather, for example, sensing is affected by feeling; i.e., the emotional condition of a person has a major impact on his ability to receive information. As another example, a person's interpretation of the sense data he receives is strongly influenced by his intentions in a situation; thus, he may focus too strongly on some of the sense data and ignore other data.

INCOMPLETE AND INCONGRUENT SELF-AWARENESS

The Awareness Wheel is intended to help participants become conscious of distinctions among different types of information and cognitive process *and* of interrelationships among the different types. When the five different types of information are not interrelated, certain behaviors may occur, resulting in inadequate expressions of self-awareness and ineffective communication. Communication becomes incomplete and/or incongruent.

There are many types of *incomplete* self-awareness, but they all share one characteristic: at least one type of information is missing from a person's awareness. Several common types of incomplete awareness are described here.

1. *Interpret-Act*. This configuration represents a very common behavior pattern, i.e., "assume and do." People who assume and do but have no consciousness of feelings or intentions typically communicate feelings indirectly or without emotion.

2. *Interpret-Feel-Act*. This configuration represents behavior that does not take into account data received from the other person or situation. Since important available information is not recognized, the person's behavior appears to have little relationship to "reality." The person's reactions seem to be based only on internal cues and are not responsive to the other person's communication or the social context. In short, the person seems to be in his "own world."

3. *Confusion of Interpretations with Feelings*. This configuration represents confusion between thoughts and emotions; often, behavior exhibits what might be called "language pollution." For example, a person might say, "I feel that we should decide" or say, while shouting, "I'm not angry, I just think my point is an important one." Sometimes this kind of statement is simply a result of sloppy language, but often it represents a real confusion between thoughts and emotions. This confusion may be manifested in overemotionality or underemotionality or, more generally, in indirect emotional responses.

4. *Sense-Feel-Act*. Behavior based on this configuration indicates little thinking. Actions are basically emotional reactions, that is, an "acting out" of feelings rather than an "acting upon" feelings.

5. *Interpret-Feel.* This configuration involves no action. In essence, the person becomes a patient. Usually the individual's responses are purely reactions to others and, therefore, are controlled by them. The person collects impressions and feelings but seldom translates them into appropriate action. In short, he is not an active agent, making his own choices.

In each of these five configurations, *intention* is not involved. In each case, behavior occurs without the person recognizing his intention in the situation. A sixth configuration does include intention, but other cognitive processes are missing.

6. *Intend-Act.* This configuration represents behavior that is essentially devoid of both interpretation of the other's message and of awareness of one's own emotional reaction to that message. The actions usually express an intention relative to another person, typically an intention to manipulate the other person or control his behavior in some way. Behavior based on this configuration often appears to be cold and calculated.

Besides incomplete awareness, a person can experience *incongruent* awareness. Incongruent awareness happens when two or more parts of the Awareness Wheel are in conflict. For example, a person does not feel good about what he wants (conflict between feelings and intentions). He may ignore the feelings, carry out an action and get what he wants, but the feelings are likely to remain—and along with them, the incongruence. If incongruence is chronic it affects a person's life style.

A person can use incongruence as a "growing point"—finding the incongruent part of his Awareness Wheel and doing something to regain congruent awareness. This may require changing values, expectations, meanings, or intentions or even altering some behavior.

SKILLS IN DISCLOSING SELF-AWARENESS

Making a clear statement about a part of the Awareness Wheel involves a communication skill. Since there are five parts in the Awareness Wheel, five skills are involved in expressing complete awareness:

- making sense statements
- making interpretive statements
- making feeling statements
- making intention statements
- making action statements

A sixth crucial skill is also used when a person discloses complete self-awareness—speaking for self. Speaking for self involves expressing one's *own* sensations, thoughts, feelings, and intentions. The language used in speaking for self is "I," "my," "mine"; e.g., "I see . . . ," "I think . . . ," "My opinion is . . . ," etc. This skill is crucial because it clearly indicates the authority on a person's experience—the person himself. When a person speaks for self, he increases his autonomy, but, at the same time, he takes full responsibility for what he says. Thus, he avoids the two dangers at either extreme of a continuum, *under*responsibility and *over*responsibility.

At one extreme, the underresponsible person does not accept ownership of his thoughts and feelings. He does not even speak for self. He believes his point of view is not important and cannot be useful to self or to others. As a result, he depreciates self and avoids acknowledging his own thoughts, desires, and feelings. He often behaves indirectly to achieve his goals; for example, he may attempt to make others feel guilty because they are overlooking him, hoping to receive the attention he does not ask for directly.

At the other extreme, the overresponsible person tries to speak for another person (e.g., "You are sad") or for everyone (e.g., "Men should be dominant in marriage"). Speaking for others often takes the form of normative appeals; for example, you *should* feel a certain way, or you *ought* to do something. Little or no respect is shown for the other's rights and autonomy. Typically, speaking for the other is an attempt to persuade and manipulate that person into thinking, feeling, or doing something that he would not do if left to his own choosing.

Speaking for self, on the other hand, increases both one's own and the other's personal autonomy and personal responsibility. First, speaking for self clearly indicates that the responsibility for one's own interpretations, feelings, intentions, and actions is self, *not* the other person. And by avoiding speaking for the other, speaking for self leaves room for the other person to report his own perceptions, thoughts, feelings, intentions, and actions—and take responsibility for them.

Sherod Miller
Elam W. Nunnally
Daniel B. Wackman

Sherod Miller, Ph.D., is an assistant professor in the Department of Medicine, University of Minnesota Medical School, Minneapolis. He is a co-author of Alive and Aware: Improving Communication in Relationships *and a co-developer of* Couple Communication. *Dr. Miller's background is in counseling, teaching, family dynamics and development, interpersonal communication, research, and consulting.*

Elam W. Nunnally, Ph.D., is an associate professor at the School of Social Welfare, University of Wisconsin–Milwaukee. He is a co-author of Alive and Aware: Improving Communication in Relationships. *Dr. Nunnally's background is in marital and family counseling, teaching, and research.*

Daniel B. Wackman, Ph.D., is an associate professor and the director of the Communication Research Division in the School of Journalism and Mass Communication, University of Minnesota, Minneapolis. Dr. Wackman's background is in teaching, communication research, and consulting.

INTERPERSONAL FEEDBACK
AS CONSENSUAL VALIDATION OF CONSTRUCTS

A central feature of group process that is frequently discussed is interpersonal feedback. Few attempts, however, have been made to relate the significance of interpersonal feedback in the group situation to the process of individual ideation and its subsequent relationship to behavior (Miller & Porter, 1972; Robinson & Jacobs, 1970).

The fact that giving and receiving feedback is one of the implicit or explicit objectives of a treatment or awareness-oriented group is well documented (Bach, 1966; Ellis, 1973; Miller & Porter, 1972). Because of the emphasis group members give to the exchange of feedback (an interpersonal process that serves to consensually validate reality), the parallel intragroup processes of ideation, construct formation, and inferring are often overlooked.

In our daily interpersonal relationships we form constructs, ideas, or assumptions about others based on the actions of these others. Both the overt and subtle behaviors of others are used as the basis for creating a cognitive framework that is then used to interpret future behavior.

This process of making inferences from behavior is of crucial importance, since the assumptions, once formed, will tend to be resistant to change (Kelly, 1963) and will also shape behavioral responses (Ellis, 1973; Kelly, 1963). It is useful to specify the relationships to behavior of an interpersonal process (consensual validation) and of an intrapersonal process (construct formation) and to suggest relevant activities to foster awareness of these relationships in a group setting. Figure 1 briefly describes this relationship.

As can be seen from Figure 1, once the initial behavior (Behavior I) has set this process in motion, it is difficult to interrupt the flow of interaction that follows.

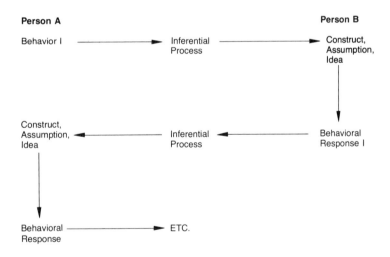

Figure 1. Construct Formation and Behavioral Response

124

CONSENSUAL VALIDATION

In considering feedback, the one asset of a treatment or awareness group that is not available in an everyday situation is validation. Groups such as these allow each group member to validate the inferences he is making concerning an individual's behavior via verbal or nonverbal feedback. An informal "hold" procedure can be established that will enable a group member to check his inferences concerning present ongoing group and individual behavior with the other members of the group. Ideally, this form of validation will also allow group members to become sensitive to and re-evaluate the assumptions they make concerning others. If changes on a conceptual level are made, it could be expected that alternative behavioral responses would also be considered.

APPLICATION

This model could be applied to the behavior of a group and of individuals in a group in a variety of ways.

In any group there are a number of situations in which a group member appears to make inferences about another group member that affect his behavior toward that other member. For example, if Tom interacts with another group member, Sandy, and during this interaction he infers from Sandy's method of presentation (behavior) that she is defensive and at the same time manipulative, the constructs of "defensive" and "manipulative" are then involved in shaping his behavioral response (Behavioral Response I) and his interpretation of further input from Sandy. Thus, he may confront Sandy strongly, saying she is "defensive" and "manipulative." This response then results in inferences being made by Sandy, which result in assumptions on her part concerning her relationship to Tom and perhaps even to the other group members. It is conceivable that the inferences made by Sandy could result in cognitive constructs such as "rejection" or "attack." If this is the case, it might follow that Sandy would contemplate quitting the group (Behavioral Response II). Figure 2 details the example described.

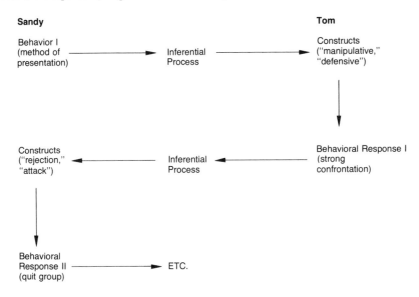

Figure 2. Example of Inferential Process: Construct Formation and Behavioral Response

The "Hold" Procedure

The cyclical nature of the form of interaction described requires that an intervention be made if alternative behavioral responses are to result. A hold-feedback procedure provides a constructive vehicle for group participants to receive and share information concerning their behavior, inferences, and constructs.

If group members observing the interaction between Sandy and Tom provide Sandy with concrete examples of those behaviors that resulted in Tom's forming the constructs "manipulative" and "defensive," alternative methods of presentation might be considered by Sandy. It is also possible that Tom has made faulty inferences. That is, he may have formed constructs concerning Sandy's behavior that are inappropriate or invalid. Feedback to Tom, as the receiver of Sandy's communications, should address the inappropriateness of his inferences, since these will eventually provide the basis for his behavioral response to Sandy. Finally, those involved in the feedback process can provide Sandy with alternative methods of presenting herself and can offer Tom alternative interpretations, if they are warranted.

For example, if the group consensus is that the inferences Tom drew from Sandy's behavior were inappropriate, and if alternative interpretations are offered (i.e., that Sandy's behavior indicates she is scared), Tom's response to her might be support rather than confrontation. Figure 3 shows this process.

This model can be used to provide a conceptual framework for the interpretation of both group and individual behavior. Using this model, awareness groups can serve two important functions. First, through the use of consensual validation, sensitivity to the inferential process and its behavioral ramifications can be created. Second, awareness groups can suggest alternative behavioral responses and provide a nonthreatening environment in which the members can experiment with these responses.

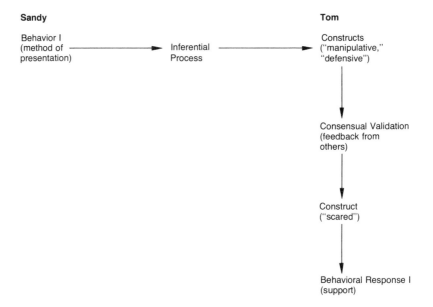

Figure 3. Consensual Validation

SUGGESTED ACTIVITIES

The facilitator may request that group members permit any group member or the group leader to call a "hold" on ongoing group activities. The appropriateness of the inferences being made can then be discussed. Thus, consensual validation may occur through the use of feedback from each group member. In fact, it may be desirable to insist that each member provide feedback in order to facilitate the group validation process.

A number of variations of this activity are possible. For example, it might be agreed to allow a hold for a member desiring validation of his inferences. Another alternative might permit a hold only to allow a group member to identify the constructs he has formed concerning another member. This procedure would require a concrete definition of the behaviors on which the constructs were based.

Donald A. Devine

REFERENCES

Bach, G. R. The marathon group: Intensive practice of internate interaction. *Psychological Reports*, 1966, *18*, 995-1002.

Ellis, A. Rational-emotive therapy. In R. Corsini (Ed.), *Current psychotherapies*. Itasca, Ill.: F.E. Peacock, 1973.

Kelly, G. A. *A theory of personality*. New York: W.W. Norton, 1963.

Miller, C., & Porter, L. *Readings book in laboratories in human relations training*. Washington, D.C.: National Education Association, 1972.

Robinson, M., & Jacobs, H. Focussed video-tape feedback and behavior change in group therapy. *Psychotherapy: Theory, Research, and Practice*, Fall 1970, 7(3), 169-172.

Donald A. Devine, Ph.D., *is the program supervisor for the experimental Community Justice Project, Waterville, Maine. He is currently responsible for the planning and implementation of treatment activities for the project. Dr. Devine's background is in personality theory as it relates to client change, the community, and institutional correctional programming and group dynamics.*

MAKING JUDGMENTS DESCRIPTIVE

Both the literature and the training norms associated with the human potential movement in this country have stressed the value of using descriptive rather than judgmental language. It is useful in providing nonevaluative feedback (Pfeiffer & Jones, 1972; Hanson, 1975). It is helpful in developing a problem-solving rather than a conflictive interaction between parties (Filley, 1975). It tends to evoke factual rather than judgmental responses (Berne, 1961; Harris, 1969). In a counseling or therapeutic context it encourages trust and openness between the parties rather than promoting defensiveness.

There is little doubt about the efficacy of such behavior. The response to the judgmental statement "You are wrong" is likely to be different from and less functional than the response to the descriptive statement "I disagree with you." The former is more likely to evoke anger or defensiveness than the latter. The descriptive statement, instead, is more likely to generate neutral fact gathering and problem solving.

Yet experience indicates that judgments do have to be made and communicated. Words like "good," "bad," "effective," "ineffective," "better," "worse" are a necessary part of human interaction. Supervisors evaluate employee performance. Trainers communicate judgments about group performance. Therapists evaluate client progress. The way in which such judgments are communicated can evoke a wide variety of responses, depending on the form of the statement. What follows are some alternative ways to make what might be called "descriptive judgments." They suggest approaches in communicating evaluations that minimize the threat to the recipient and reduce his defensive reaction.

It is assumed that the performance of the party (an individual or a group) in question has been objectively measured by any reasonably reliable method; the point of concern here is the objective assignment of value statements to measured performance. Thus, the definition of "good" versus "bad" performance is crucial. The elements of the process are twofold: (1) the presence of objective measures that compare actual behavior with some kind of standard and (2) the communication of the standard, the measure, and the judgment to the recipient.

BASES FOR DESCRIPTIVE JUDGMENTS

Comparison with Other Measured Performances

When, for example, a supervisor tells an employee, "You are doing the same kind of work as employees A, B, and C, but last month they each averaged sixty units per hour and you averaged forty units per hour," a comparison with other measured performances is being made. "On that basis I judge your work to be the least effective in the group." In this situation the supervisor has communicated the basis for the judgment, the comparative measurement and relative position among the four workers, and his judgment. The response evoked is likely to be better than if the supervisor merely said, "You are not doing a good job."

A judgment based on a comparison with all other comparable members is an example of what is known as "norm-referenced appraisal" in the testing sense (APA, 1974, p. 19), in which, for example, the position of each individual's score is determined, compared with a mean, and expressed as a standard score. The major criticism of norm-referenced appraisal is that relative position depends on the performance of parties with whom the individual is compared. When used for purposes of judgment, the recipient might well say, "But my work is more like that of employees D, E, and F than employees A, B, and C." This difficulty may be allayed if agreement about the proper comparison parties and about the unit of measurement to be used is obtained prior to the actual measurement and evaluation of performance.

Comparison with an Accepted Standard

A comparison based on this approach involves the use of a generally accepted definition of performance, over which the recipient has no control. For example, a supervisor may say, "We all know that the standard output for a person doing your job is sixty units per hour. You averaged forty units during the last month. On this basis, I judge your work last month to be ineffective." Again, the basis for measurement, the result, and the judgment have been communicated.

This method is one form of "criterion-referenced appraisal." A cutoff score on admission tests used by a university is a similar example. The chief difficulty with criterion-referenced appraisal is the arbitrariness of the criterion level. This problem may be reduced by identifying valid evidence of the value of the standard. Such an approach is *not* likely to be welcome when the person making the judgment relies solely on his status or his experience (e.g., "Speaking as a psychologist . . ." or "In my experience . . .").

Comparison with an A Priori Goal

The use of a standard to which the recipient has agreed prior to actual performance is essential with this method, which is another form of criterion-referenced appraisal. For example, a supervisor may say, "We both agreed last month that an acceptable level of performance for you in your job would be an average of sixty units an hour. You have been averaging forty units over the last month. On that basis I would judge your performance as ineffective." If, on the other hand, the supervisor says, "Your performance has averaged forty units per hour. That is ineffective," the result may be an argument about whether forty units is really good or bad. We should remember that bettors place their bets before a wheel is spun or a race is run. "Good" must be defined prior to behavior if it is to have meaning.

The use of an a priori goal differs from the use of a generally accepted standard, in that the recipient agrees on the definition of "effective" or "good" performance before the activity takes place. Thus it escapes the arbitrariness of an externally imposed standard.

Comparison with Desired Behavior

This approach emphasizes the recipient's actions that have been shown to lead to preferred outcomes. For example, a supervisor may say, "When an employee arrives at work at the 9:00 starting time, presses the activating buttons on the machine for an average of forty minutes an hour, follows the prescribed work cycle, and takes no more than twenty minutes a day for relief breaks, he will average sixty units an hour. You have been late most days and have taken one hour for breaks, so your output has averaged forty units. That is not good behavior."

Such comparisons between planned and actual behavior as an assessment of outcomes are a form of criterion referencing known as "content-referenced appraisal." It differs from the appraisal based on a universal standard or an a priori goal because of its emphasis on the process that leads to desired outcomes. When a known procedure is shown to lead to a desired goal, controlling the performance of the procedure assures the attainment of the goal. Thus, a judgment that the behavior is not being executed automatically suggests that outcomes will not or have not been met.

Content-referenced appraisal depends on a proven connection between behavior and outcomes and on the recipient's acceptance of that connection. Its chief limitation is the lack of consideration of other alternatives. Judgments about failure to follow desired behaviors may be resisted or resented by recipients who have demonstrated alternate behaviors that achieve the same goal. For this reason, content-referenced appraisal should probably be limited to situations where there is only one process to a goal or one clearly superior alternative.

Comparison with Past Performance

A supervisor using this approach might say, "Your performance in the job averaged sixty units a day over the past six months. This month you averaged forty units a day. Your production this month has not been effective." In this case the past performance provides the standard, and deviation from that standard is used as the measure of performance.

This approach is variously identified as "difference-score," "gain-score," or "change-score" analysis. In conventional usage a pre-test is given, a treatment administered, and a post-test given. The two scores are compared, presuming that differences in test scores are a function of the treatment. Various forms of change analysis are widely used in teaching, counseling, and training to make assessments of performance.

Change-score analysis has been variously criticized, and its utility as a valid basis for inference has been rejected by some researchers. The objections are mainly statistical, having to do with the unreliability of such scores. In addition, it is not clear that the change is due to the treatment (or behavior of the party being evaluated).

CONSIDERATIONS

Some of the approaches discussed here suggest useful ways of making judgments descriptive and, therefore, more effective. Change scores do provide descriptive judgments, but they are sufficiently weak as a basis for judgment that their value in appraising performance is minimized. Particular applications may occur, such as the shaping of desired behavior, but equating "good" merely with "better" is not likely to be helpful. Content-referenced appraisal has the limitations already suggested.

However, both norm- and criterion-referenced judgments offer more promising application in the context described here. With the former it is important that the reference parties and the measures used be agreed upon prior to behavior. With the latter it is important that the criterion be acceptable prior to behavior. In both cases, the parties involved are merely defining "good" before the fact—an essential factor in evaluating what "good" is.

Alan C. Filley
Larry A. Pace

REFERENCES

American Psychological Association. *Standards for educational and psychological tests.* Washington, D.C.: Author, 1974.

Berne, E. *Transactional analysis in psychotherapy.* New York: Grove, 1961.

Filley, A. C. *Interpersonal conflict resolution.* Glenview, Ill.: Scott, Foresman, 1975.

Hanson, P. G. Giving feedback: An interpersonal skill. In J. E. Jones & J. W. Pfeiffer (Eds.), *The 1975 annual handbook for group facilitators.* La Jolla, Calif.: University Associates, 1975.

Harris, T. *I'm OK, you're OK.* New York: Harper & Row, 1969.

Pfeiffer, J. W., & Jones, J. E. Openness, collusion, and feedback. In J. W. Pfeiffer & J. E. Jones (Eds.), *The 1972 annual handbook for group facilitators.* La Jolla, Calif.: University Associates, 1972.

Alan C. Filley, Ph.D., is the chairman of the Department of Management, Graduate School of Business, University of Wisconsin–Madison. He is the series editor for the Management Applications Series (Scott, Foresman), the author of Interpersonal Conflict Resolution, and a co-author of Managerial Process and Organizational Behavior. Dr. Filley's background is in research, teaching, and consulting on organizational behavior, conflict resolution, problem solving, and organizational growth.

Larry A. Pace is pursuing his doctoral degree in the Measurement and Human Differences Program, Department of Psychology, University of Georgia, Athens. He is an industrial consultant with various companies. Mr. Pace's background is in psychological measurement, industrial psychology, and univariate and multivariate methods.

LEADERSHIP AS PERSUASION AND ADAPTATION

Group leadership has been of interest to scholars and practitioners in the social sciences since man first began studying his own behaviors. A great deal of attention has been directed toward such questions as "What are the characteristics of task leaders?," "What are the variables that affect the emergence and maintenance of leadership in problem-solving groups?," "What is the best method of training leaders?" As a result of the many different orientations, however, there is a lack of consistency in research findings about leadership. No one really seems to know what "good leadership" is (Lumsden, 1974). Nevertheless, it is essential to understand the nature of leadership and the ways in which we can improve it.

PREVIOUS APPROACHES TO LEADERSHIP

There are several approaches that have been prominent in recent research concerned with the determinants of leadership. The "trait approach," the "situational approach," the "follower approach," and the "contingency model" have been proposed as explanations of the factors that determine leadership in small groups.

The Trait Approach

The first concentrated attempt to define the factors that result in leadership was the "trait approach." Enormous amounts of time and effort were devoted to constructing lists of the physical and psychological attributes believed to differentiate leaders from nonleaders. Unfortunately there was minimal agreement among researchers as to what those distinguishing traits were. The lists of "definitive qualities of leaders" were almost as numerous as the researchers who constructed them. Of several hundred traits studied, only a very few were consistently correlated with leadership (Shaw, 1971). Gouldner (1950) reviewed the empirical investigations related to leadership traits and concluded that "there is no reliable evidence concerning the existence of universal leadership traits" (p. 34). The trait approach is unsatisfactory because it implies that leaders are born, not made.

The Situational Approach

A second perspective on leadership, the "situational approach," holds that it is the social circumstances that command the degree to which any person's leadership potential is exercised. According to this approach the crucial determinant of leadership is the social environment in which leadership is needed. The major claim of the situational approach is that different leadership skills are required in different situations. The deficiency of this approach, however, is that it implies that leaders are born of situations, not of their own abilities.

The Follower Approach

Although the situational approach is currently endorsed by many researchers, a third orientation to leadership has received some acceptance. The "follower approach" maintains that the most effective leaders are those most able to satisfy the needs or desires of a group of followers (Tannenbaum, Weschler, & Massarik, 1974; Sanford, 1950). The follower approach is inadequate because it implies that the emergence and maintenance of leadership is dependent on followers, not on a leader's own skills.

The Contingency Model

By combining ideas from the situational approach and the study of leadership styles, a fourth approach to leadership was developed (Fiedler, 1964). This model maintains that effective leadership depends not only on a leader's personal style, but also on the characteristics of a situation. The contingency model is an exciting step in our understanding of leadership, because it refutes the simplistic and one-dimensional explanations of the earlier approaches. Nevertheless, this model, too, is unsatisfying since it ignores the leader's personal ability to control himself and his situation.

Assumptions of Four Approaches

In order to understand more fully these four approaches to small-group leadership, it is helpful to identify the assumptions on which they are based.

1. The trait approach maintains that a person either does or does not possess the particular traits that are considered to be the determinants of leadership.

2. The situational approach assumes that certain situations call for certain types of leadership and that the leaders will be those who best fit the requirements of a situation. The situational characteristics are viewed as the determinants of leadership.

3. The follower approach holds that the needs of group members determine who will lead. Leadership, then, is a coincidence between the needs of a membership and the abilities that a person happens to possess. The members' needs are assumed to be the key determinants of leadership.

4. The contingency model maintains that personal styles and situational characteristics combine to determine leadership. A "proper match" between styles and situations determines who will lead a group.

These assumptions show that each of the four major approaches to leadership shares a basic orientation: each approach maintains, at least implicitly, that there is a static quality to leadership, a quality that can be isolated and described apart from leaders who operate in particular group situations. A leader's active involvement in the small-group process has been overlooked, ruling out the possibility that a leader can, like any other human being, adapt himself and his behavior in order to enhance his own effectiveness.

A static conception of leadership, therefore, is inaccurate. Small groups are characterized by contingencies—by a lack of certainty regarding events that may occur. Once we acknowledge this dynamic nature of small groups, it becomes clear that a useful theory of leadership must be similarly dynamic. By considering a rhetorical perspective on the process of leading, we can focus on the dynamic nature of leadership and the possibilities for human control over contingent situations.

A RHETORICAL PERSPECTIVE ON LEADERSHIP

As a philosophy of human action, beginning with the writings of ancient thinkers such as Aristotle and Cicero, rhetoric is based on the belief that humans can control their effectiveness through the discovery and management of behaviors that take place in relation to other people. Man is seen as a purposeful agent who can consciously control his own actions and, therefore, the ways in which others respond to him.

A rhetorical perspective on small-group leadership rejects claims that there are static determinants of leadership. Leading is a process, a persuasive process in which a leader achieves effectiveness by the careful selection and management of his actions within a particular group situation. He has the potential to control himself, his situation, and his membership through the use of symbolic behavior. A rhetorical perspective on leadership, then, is characterized by two features: (1) the persuasive nature of the leading process and (2) the recognition that humans can control their environments by adapting to social circumstances.

The Persuasive Process

Leading is an active process that involves making choices regarding behaviors. Presumably a leader has goals for himself, for the individuals in his group, and for the group as a whole. By selecting and implementing behavioral strategies that are designed to lead to these goals, a leader exerts influence and, therefore, engages in persuasion. The leader of a small group *inevitably* effects persuasions by the way he chooses to present himself, by the methods he employs in directing his group's tasks, and by the manner in which he relates to the group members. A leader's choices influence the members' evaluation of him and they, in turn, influence the group's success in reaching collective goals.

The persuasive nature of the leading process has not always been recognized. Some people, for example, persist in claiming that democratic behaviors are not really influences since they imply a "sharing of control." Yet, in choosing to act democratically and not to dominate actively, a leader is exercising influence: he engenders in the group members a certain perception of himself as a leader and of themselves as members of his group. Even the most democratic behaviors are persuasions that reflect a leader's choice of effective behaviors to guide his group. A leader cannot avoid influencing his group. Therefore, identifying and studying the choices of persuasion that must be made by a leader become important: What types of influence does he wish to exert? Whom does he need to persuade? How do his particular choices affect members' perceptions of him and of themselves? How are various persuasive effects achieved by a leader? Leaders should be trained to be *aware of* these choices and to estimate the probable effects of various choices on collective goals.

Control Through Adaptation

A rhetorical perspective on leading also emphasizes the possibility that humans can control their environments through sensitive *adaptation*. People are capable of adjusting themselves in order to be more effective in relation to others. In this orientation it is assumed that a leader can persuade his group members to need what he has to offer, to value the skills that he possesses, to perceive their situation as one in which his guidance is desirable or necessary, to commit themselves to collective goals, and to work together in a satisfactory manner.

Perhaps an example or two will help clarify the view that leaders can adjust themselves, their memberships, and their situations in order to lead more effectively. When Gerald Ford first became President he chose to present himself as a simple, honest man. After the criminal and demoralizing events of Watergate, Ford's apparent honesty and openness were welcomed by a nation weary of deceit and secrecy. However, when Ford's "down-home" presentation became the target of criticism and even ridicule, he began to shift his image. He made more definitive statements and took stronger positions on issues of national policy, altering his self-presentation in ways that he presumably believes to be acceptable or desirable to the voting public.

A newly promoted company president, in taking over a firm that had degenerated into chaos, was at first appreciated and praised for his firmness and positive decision making. When the company was on the road to recovery, however, his tightly controlled, authoritative approach was no longer popular with his employees. He had to adjust his leadership so that it was more relaxed and person centered.

134

These are only two examples of figures whose leadership behaviors are best understood from a rhetorical perspective. We must recognize that leaders, members, and group situations are all flexible and that a rhetorical sensitivity to the methods of persuasion can enhance most people's abilities to lead well. A leader's capacity for adapting himself and his situation through the deliberate management of his behaviors toward others should be emphasized. Such adaptation is desirable as long as it neither jeopardizes one's personal integrity nor results in unethical behavior toward others.

VALUE OF A RHETORICAL PERSPECTIVE

A rhetorical perspective on leadership offers a realistic and useful means for understanding how leaders emerge, how they maintain their power, and how they build effective, cohesive groups.

A second value of a rhetorical perspective is its potential as a strategy for training leaders. Unlike previous methods of training, a rhetorical approach does not provide any "recipes" for success. Instead, it offers potential leaders a useful way of thinking about themselves in relation to a group and its task. By viewing themselves from a rhetorical perspective, leaders could analyze their own behaviors and the situations in which they are to lead. Potential leaders would be able to assess the interplay among the forces of themselves, their goals, their group members, and their group situations. Given a rhetorical orientation to their work, leaders would be able to plan actions that would probably be effective in their particular circumstances.

Every group situation is different—the rules must vary according to the situations and the people involved. A rhetorical perspective on leadership, viewed as a process of persuasion and adaptation, offers a useful method of analysis for leaders of problem-solving groups.

Julia T. Wood

REFERENCES

Fiedler, F. E. A contingency model of leadership effectiveness. In L. Berkowitz (Ed.), *Advances in experimental social psychology.* New York: Academic Press, 1964.

Gouldner, A. (Ed.). *Studies in leadership.* New York: Harper & Row, 1950.

Lumsden, G. An experimental study of the effect of verbal agreement on leadership maintenance in problem-solving discussion. *Central States Speech Journal,* Winter 1974, 25, 270.

Sanford, F. H. *Authoritarianism and leadership.* Philadelphia: Institute for Research in Human Relations, 1950.

Shaw, M. E. *Group dynamics: The psychology of small group behavior.* New York: McGraw-Hill, 1971.

Tannenbaum, R., Weschler, I. R., & Massarik, F. Leadership: A frame of reference. In R. S. Cathcart & L. A. Samovar (Eds.), *Small group communication: A reader* (2nd ed.). Dubuque, Iowa: William C. Brown, 1974.

Julia T. Wood, Ph.D., is an assistant professor in the Division of Speech, University of North Carolina at Chapel Hill. She is particularly interested in the nature of leading behavior as it occurs in task groups. She is currently co-authoring a textbook on small-group discussion. Dr. Wood's background is in college teaching, adult education, and organizational consultation.

ROLE FUNCTIONS IN A GROUP

The members of an efficient and productive group must provide for meeting two kinds of needs—what it takes to do the job, and what it takes to strengthen and maintain the group. Specific statements and behaviors may be viewed at a more abstract level than the content or behavior alone, i.e., in terms of how they serve the group needs.

What members do to serve group needs may be called functional roles. Statements and behaviors which tend to make the group inefficient or weak may be called nonfunctional behaviors.

A partial list of the kinds of contributions or the group services which are performed by one or many individuals is as follows:

A. TASK ROLES (functions required in selecting and carrying out a group task)

1. *Initiating Activity:* proposing solutions, suggesting new ideas, new definitions of the problem, new attack on the problem, or new organization of material.

2. *Seeking Information:* asking for clarification of suggestions, requesting additional information or facts.

3. *Seeking Opinion:* looking for an expression of feeling about something from the members, seeking clarification of values, suggestions, or ideas.

4. *Giving Information:* offering facts or generalizations, relating one's own experience to the group problem to illustrate points.

5. *Giving Opinion:* stating an opinion or belief concerning a suggestion or one of several suggestions, particularly concerning its value rather than its factual basis.

6. *Elaborating:* clarifying, giving examples or developing meanings, trying to envision how a proposal might work if adopted.

7. *Coordinating:* showing relationships among various ideas or suggestions, trying to pull ideas and suggestions together, trying to draw together activities of various subgroups or members.

8. *Summarizing:* pulling together related ideas or suggestions, restating suggestions after the group has discussed them.

B. GROUP BUILDING AND MAINTENANCE ROLES (functions required in strengthening and maintaining group life and activities)

1. *Encouraging:* being friendly, warm, responsive to others, praising others and their ideas, agreeing with and accepting contributions of others.

2. *Gatekeeping:* trying to make it possible for another member to make a contribution to the group by saying, "We haven't heard anything from Jim yet," or suggesting limited talking time for everyone so that all will have a chance to be heard.

Reproduced by special permission from NTL/Learning Resources Corp., *Handbook of Staff Development and Human Relations Training: Materials Developed for Use in Africa* (Revised and Expanded Edition), Donald Nylen, J. Robert Mitchell, and Anthony Stout, pp. 67-70, 1967. The classification system was developed by Morton Deutsch, *The Effects of Cooperation and Competition upon Group Process.* In D. Cartwright & A. Zander, *Group Dynamics—Research and Theory.* Evanston, Ill.: Row Peterson & Co 1960 (2nd Ed.). See also Benne, K. D., & Sheats, P., "Functional Roles and Group Members," *Journal of Social Issues,* 1948, *4,* (2).

3. *Standard Setting:* expressing standards for the group to use in choosing its content or procedures or in evaluating its decisions, reminding group to avoid decisions which conflict with group standards.

4. *Following:* going along with decisions of the group, thoughtfully accepting ideas of others, serving as audience during group discussion.

5. *Expressing Group Feeling:* summarizing what group feeling is sensed to be, describing reactions of the group to ideas or solutions.

C. BOTH GROUP TASK AND MAINTENANCE ROLES

1. *Evaluating:* submitting group decisions or accomplishments to comparison with group standards, measuring accomplishments against goals.

2. *Diagnosing:* determining sources of difficulties, appropriate steps to take next, analyzing the main blocks to progress.

3. *Testing for Consensus:* tentatively asking for group opinions in order to find out whether the group is nearing consensus on a decision, sending up trial balloons to test group opinions.

4. *Mediating:* harmonizing, conciliating differences in points of view, making compromise solutions.

5. *Relieving Tension:* draining off negative feeling by jesting or pouring oil on troubled waters, putting a tense situation in wider context.

From time to time, more often perhaps than anyone likes to admit, people behave in nonfunctional ways that do not help and sometimes actually harm the group and the work it is trying to do. Some of the more common types of such nonfunctional behaviors are described below.

D. TYPES OF NONFUNCTIONAL BEHAVIOR

1. *Being Aggressive:* working for status by criticizing or blaming others, showing hostility against the group or some individual, deflating the ego or status of others.

2. *Blocking:* interfering with the progress of the group by going off on a tangent, citing personal experiences unrelated to the problem, arguing too much on a point, rejecting ideas without consideration.

3. *Self-Confessing:* using the group as a sounding board, expressing personal, nongroup-oriented feelings or points of view.

4. *Competing:* vying with others to produce the best idea, talk the most, play the most roles, gain favor with the leader.

5. *Seeking Sympathy:* trying to induce other group members to be sympathetic to one's problems or misfortunes, deploring one's own situation, or disparaging one's own ideas to gain support.

6. *Special Pleading:* introducing or supporting suggestions related to one's own pet concerns or philosophies, lobbying.

7. *Horsing Around:* clowning, joking, mimicking, disrupting the work of the group.

8. *Seeking Recognition:* attempting to call attention to one's self by loud or excessive talking, extreme ideas, unusual behavior.

9. *Withdrawal:* acting indifferent or passive, resorting to excessive formality, daydreaming, doodling, whispering to others, wandering from the subject.

In using a classification such as the one above, people need to guard against the tendency to blame any person (whether themselves or another) who falls into "nonfunctional behavior." It is more useful to regard such behavior as a symptom that all is not well with the group's ability to satisfy individual needs through group-centered activity. People need to be alert to the fact that each person is likely to interpret such behaviors differently. For example, what appears as "blocking" to one person may appear to another as a needed effort to "test feasibility." What appears to be nonfunctional behavior may not necessarily be so, for the content and the group conditions must also be taken into account. There are times when some forms of being aggressive contribute positively by clearing the air and instilling energy into the group.

E. IMPROVING MEMBER ROLES

Any group is strengthened and enabled to work more efficiently if its members:

1. become more conscious of the role function needed at any given time;

2. become more sensitive to and aware of the degree to which they can help to meet the needs through what they do;

3. undertake self-training to improve their range of role functions and skills in performing them.

POWER

Power is a key ingredient of almost all human relationships, whether person-to-person or system-to-system. In recent years, students of individual and organizational psychology have placed increased emphasis on understanding it and its role. As a result, a variety of definitions have evolved. Suggested here is one comprehensive way of defining power and several perspectives for viewing its magnitude, sources, and character. A clearer understanding of power can be attained by applying this framework to a given relationship; more effective operating strategies can result.

Negative Connotations

To many, the word "power" has a negative connotation, undoubtedly because it is so frequently allied with negative acts. For example, "power" readily comes to mind when one discusses the hold an evil dictator has over his people, but it is only rarely considered when one speaks of the relationship of a mother and her child. Yet, in both cases, very real and considerable power exists; its value is determined in light of the situation in which it is present. Sayings such as "power corrupts" are generalizations, subject to the inaccuracies of such broad statements.

DEFINITION OF POWER

There have been several approaches to describing power and many resulting definitions. Its origin and ingredients will be considered here.

Origin

It is hypothesized that "power" arises from two primary elements—*need* (for a service, for knowledge, for direction, for material) and *means* (a raw material, money, authority, knowledge). The match of a need and a means transforms these two into equal and opposite forces known as *dependence* and *influence*. This is the most easily recognized form of power, which will be labeled "active power."

Since these forces are equal and opposite, it is possible to determine the degree of the resulting power by measuring either influence or dependence. Emerson (1962) equates power with dependence and states that "power resides in dependency" (p. 32). Measuring dependence alone, however, only establishes the strength of activated power. It does not comprehensively assess the effect of peripheral forces of stability and strength.

Ingredients

Other important ingredients of power can be grouped together and termed a power-stability factor. These ingredients, as the name suggests, bear on the stability of the power relationship and its strength and are many and varied. Included in this factor are unfulfilled needs, unutilized means, alternate resources, "do-without" time, and reciprocity.

Unfulfilled needs and *unutilized means* represent important, but often overlooked, potential forces that affect the stability of a power relationship. The drives to fill unspoken needs or to utilize excess means are real. These drives may weaken existing bonds or may strengthen them. For example, if an individual's need for a home improvement loan leads to dealings with a new bank, the relationship between the individual and the bank that holds his mortgage and his savings and checking accounts may be affected. Correspondingly, a tight end in professional football who develops the ability and likes to punt may have his role changed or ask to be traded as a result. Drives such as these vary in strength over time and may not always be present to any significant degree.

Alternate resources are under constant, if not conscious, review by the actors in a power relationship. Are there alternate ways of filling a need? If so, what are the comparative costs—in money, in convenience, in psychological effects? (Thibaut & Kelly, 1959, refer to a comparison-level alternative in treating competing resources.) When considering costs, any penalty for disengagement—such as contractual bonds—must be recognized. Alternate resources are available in most voluntary relationships; e.g., a business that has its yearly income tax made out by accounting firm X may switch to firm Y, perform the task itself with existing personnel, or hire additional personnel.

The *"do-without" time* is most dramatically illustrated in the case of a labor strike, which pits the "do-without" capabilities of the workers against those of the company. The result almost always alters the power relationship between the two systems. This factor is a real consideration in determining power even when it is not tested; the perceived "do-without" time has an impact on power dynamics.

The existence of *reciprocity* between two systems also has a stablizing effect on their relationship. In other words, when each party is influential, as well as dependent, toward the other, the bond between them is stronger. For example, a store may be more willing to provide credit to customers who are likely to increase the amount they purchase because of the credit plan. Both are influential and both are dependent. While reciprocity tends to strengthen a bond between two systems, it is also true that the withdrawal of either a need or a resource by one system often represents a move so major that termination of the relationship results.

The total power that exists between two systems is usually complex, with various influences, dependencies, and stabilizing factors in effect on either side. Some combination of active power and a stability factor is the result.

MAGNITUDE OF POWER

While it is extremely difficult to assign a numerical value to the magnitude of a power relationship, it is possible to assess its relative value and its sources of stability and/or instability. Simply defining the influences and dependencies that exist; labeling them as strong, moderate, or weak; and identifying the factors that may or do affect stability can add depth to a power relationship analysis.

SOURCES OF POWER

If power is born as a result of a union of needs and means, then the primary sources of the needs and means in question must be identified. Needs and means appear in a multitude of forms. Several of the more common are listed here.

Source	Examples
Knowledge	Technical or professional expertise
Resources	Raw materials, money, manpower
Social pressure	Cliques, clubs, gangs, committees
Authority	Policies, elected officials, organizational position
Law	Laws of public domain, civil rights, felony offenses
Norms, values, traditions	Religious beliefs, honesty, social pressures, dress codes, habits
Personal style	Charisma, strong dependence
Coercion	Strikes, riots, mobs

140

Organizationally speaking, all or any of these sources may be pertinent, depending on the segment of the environment concerned. In a manufacturing operation, for example, the plant may rely on the home office for product development (knowledge) and on a paper company for shipping containers that, in turn, supply the product to customers (resources); react to the demands of an ecology group (social pressure); set the amount of production and the number of employees (authority); be influenced by the Food & Drug Administration (law); give out Christmas bonuses and have a summer company picnic (norms, values, traditions); be run by an iron-fisted plant manager (personal style); and be subject to union-instigated work stoppages (coercion).

Taking the time to identify the sources of power can be of enormous benefit in understanding, using, altering, or coping with relationships.

CHARACTER OF POWER

The nature of a power relationship is determined by the characteristics of the systems involved. These characteristics often affect both the visibility and stability of power associations. While many factors could be considered, system energy, permeability (the energy flow across the boundary), adaptability (the ability to change with outside pressures), differentiation (the degree of complexity), and integration (the additive or complementary quality) are used here. A tool for analyzing and describing each characteristic (based on an approach of Oshry, 1971) can be constructed by placing descriptive words and phrases in a matrix showing high or low and positive or negative orientations. (See Figure 1.)

System Energy	Positive	Negative
High	alive, vibrant, creative, alert	violent, explosive, irrational, impetuous
Low	peaceful, simple, elementary	listless, apathetic, dull
Permeability		
High	collaborating, consensual, tending toward teamwork	inefficient, dependent, without initiative, indiscriminate
Low	independent, with initiative	competitive, duplicated, guarded, uncommunicative, filtered
Adaptability		
High	efficient, preplanned, proactive	commanding, controlling, obedient, unquestioning
Low	free, natural, spontaneous	inefficient (regarding environment), rigid, unbending
Differentiation		
High	rich, stimulating, adaptive	diffuse, nonsupportive, competitive
Low	cohesive, unified	simplistic, nonadaptive
Integration		
High	collaborative, supportive	conforming, dull
Low	spirited, independent	competitive, unproductive, combating

Figure 1. Characteristics of Power Systems

It is important to note that the same individual or system will not necessarily be classified in the same quadrant for different characteristics. In fact, there will be frequent deviation in one or more categories.

By analyzing each of these characteristics for both parties of a relationship, several clues can be offered about what sort of approach might help in developing an effective relationship between them. A situation, for example, in which one system is violent and explosive and the other is listless and apathetic will undoubtedly call for a different strategy than if both are creative and vibrant.

Power relationships are complex—their magnitude, their source, and their character need to be considered—but they are well worth defining as an aid in effective dealings between systems.

Dennis C. King
John C. Glidewell

REFERENCES

Emerson, R. M. Power dependence relations. *American Sociological Review*, 1962, 27, 31-41.

Glidewell, J. C. System linkage and distress at school. In *Buffalo Studies in Psychotherapy and Behavioral Change*. Buffalo, N.Y.: State University of New York, 1971.

Glidewell, J. C. A socio-developmental model for community mental health. In Z. Bellak (Ed.), *The concise handbook of community psychiatry and community mental health*. New York: Grune & Stratton, 1973.

Oshry, B. *Work on power characteristics.* Unpublished manuscript, 1971.

Schelling, T. C. *The strategy of conflict.* Boston, Mass.: Harvard University, 1970.

Thibaut, J. W., & Kelly, H. H. *The social psychology of groups.* New York: John Wiley, 1959.

Dennis C. King *is an OD consultant in the Chicago area. He is currently consulting with engineering and manufacturing departments in a consumer products company and a Canadian school system. Mr. King's background includes a degree in engineering, which led to eleven years of manufacturing management. He has been consulting for three years and is pursuing an M.A. in OD at the University of Chicago.*

John C. Glidewell *is a professor of education and social psychology in the Department of Education, University of Chicago. He is a diplomate in industrial and organizational psychology of the American Board of Professional Psychology. Mr. Glidewell's background is in social, community, and organizational psychology, laboratory education, and the study of social change.*

ALTERNATIVES TO THEORIZING

Almost all of us who have been raised in the Western cultural tradition have learned to depend on rationality, logic, and systematic thinking in our dealings with people and situations. Thus, in our culture we have developed magnificent processes for handling great complexity in orderly ways. However, in our often exclusive devotion to the logical and rational we have cut off much of our access to intuition, inspiration, and other noncognitive resources in our lives. Even when we deal with emotions, many of us treat them as "data" to be factored into a rational diagnosis or solution of the "problem."

New Ways of Perceiving

There is much to be gained for the manager and the organization consultant in learning an expanded range of ways of perceiving: letting go of cognitive, intellectual processes from time to time to experience what is happening both within and outside oneself. Parts of our bodies other than our thinking minds—and other ways of perceiving—can and do produce marvelous clues to what life is about, as Eastern religion and philosophy (e.g., Zen and Tao) can show.

Although not normally seen as being relevant to the affairs of organizations, these "new" paths of perception have great applicability and potential for increasing the energy and the capacity for thought and action of managers and others who work in organization environments.

Overemphasis on "Systems" Approaches

At present, organization and management theorists emphasize "systems" approaches to organization dynamics. Systems thinking has become *the* fashionable way of analyzing and treating management problems. For some, the systems way of looking at things has become synonymous with making big abstractions—converting people or process troubles into important-sounding but distant generalities.

The United States Army, for example, is an extremely complex system. A consultant may well estimate that changing the philosophy, policies, and procedures of this entire system would require years of intervention. However, if he focuses on *what* really needs to be done and *who* needs to do it (not to change the whole Army but only the unit he is consulting with), the problem becomes decidedly more manageable.

THE TENDENCY TO "THEORIZE"

Most of us tend to be theorizers, either consciously or unconsciously. People typically have theories about almost everything that goes on from one moment to another in their lives. The theories may be structured and formal or merely loose collections of assumptions. They may focus on significant issues such as U.S. foreign policy or on a minor concern such as whether women ought to precede men when leaving an elevator.

There are, of course, some advantages to having a theory. It can help make the world more predictable and help us feel in control of situations. There may be substantial costs to the theorizing process, however. The very act of mobilizing our theories in order to understand and control what is *going to* happen detaches us from the event itself and our involvement in it. In the act of theorizing we place ourselves partly outside the event as an observer. Thus only part of our awareness and energy is available to deal with what *is* happening.

Theories as Distorting Screens

Our theories can "filter" our thinking and distort our perceptions, functioning as screens between events and our experience of them. The distortions can occur at different points with different consequences.

First, one may theorize before an event, that is, in preparation for it. In this case, the person most often attempts to confirm his theory in the ensuing transactions. Frequently, any aspect of that event that does not fit the pre-established theoretical framework is discounted, distorted, or perhaps not even perceived at all. On the other hand, information that does not fit the theoretical model but is compelling enough to demand notice may threaten the theorizer with the destruction of his model and leave him in confusion, grasping desperately for another model to replace the first.

For example, a highly talented pair of consultants specializing in one of the systems approaches to organization development worked with a group of aerospace engineering managers for several days to focus on the needs of the organization. The work was largely frustrating and unproductive to both the consultants and their client, and the reasons were not difficult to see. The consultants had a *theory* about working with management groups ("managers are unsophisticated about systems"), and the managers had a *theory* about working with organization consultants ("consultants should know best"). The consulting effort failed because neither party could re-examine its assumptions.

When "theory lock-in" occurs in the midst of an event, instead, a slightly different, though related, pattern is revealed. Many people seem compelled to try to "pigeonhole" incoming information into one or another of several possible hypotheses until finally one pigeonhole is declared the winner. Then, once more, subsequent information may be selected to conform with that theory.

Useful Approaches to Theorizing

Appropriate uses of theory and the process of theorizing can, of course, be useful. In Buddhist literature there is an expression that says a wise man will use a raft to cross a river, but once on the other shore he will leave the raft behind. Theories can be treated like the raft: they can be learned and then let go. Sufficient trust in one's internal processes is necessary; when a theory is relevant to the situation, it (or appropriate parts of it) will reoccur to one's mind.

Theorizing can also be useful at the conclusion of an event. Looking back over a series of occurrences and generating some tentative hypotheses about the behavior and organizational interactions of individuals involved in the event may be helpful—if the theorizing does not become restrictive and force subsequent life experiences to be seen in its framework.

EMPHASIS ON A "NOW" RESPONSE

We would do well to learn to live with more ambiguity and with the excitement that comes from being involved as real, live people with other real, live people.

Instead of ignoring his own feelings about and responses to his client, a consultant can learn to respond on a more human, immediate basis. For example, in one recent training workshop, it was not until the consultant honestly stated his own sense of frustration that the client could acknowledge his similar feeling, and progress could be made on the problem.

If we allow ourselves, we can discover that the Eastern principle of "now-ness" can apply to our development as effectively functioning people and to our interactions with other people. If a consultant can, for a moment, give up trying to control and predict where a particular engagement between counselor and counselee ought to go, he might find, more often than not, that a new and surprising clarification will emerge.

144

SUMMARY

There are possibilities for all of us to expand our range of ways of perceiving and of dealing with people and problems. To do so, we need to learn to suspend, temporarily, our logical-rational controls. We need to learn to float with what is happening, to involve ourselves fully, to forget who we are "supposed to be," what our appropriate roles are, what our relationships "ought" to be, what kind of behavior is supposed to be "helpful" and "constructive" and what kind is supposed to be "improper" and "selfish." If we do this, we have the opportunity to discover—to be shocked or surprised, disappointed or delighted. Theories can very often be barriers to an understanding of people's real selves and can inhibit their potential for excitement, creativity, and energy.

SUGGESTED ACTIVITIES

In subgroups of two or four, group members sit in a circle and, in sequence, each reports exactly what he is aware of at that given moment. Each individual begins his statement of awareness with "Right now I am aware of . . ." It is important that participants report their awareness without trying to build rational conversations or to send messages to one another. After the activity has proceeded for a while, the participants can be asked to consider whether their reports of awareness have mostly been focused internally, i.e., on what they have been experiencing within themselves (physically and emotionally) or externally, i.e., on what they have been observing or hearing outside themselves.

In a variation of this approach, each individual makes a statement focusing explicitly on his own experience or on someone else's experience. Thus each participant begins a statement with "Right now I think . . ." or "Right now I feel . . ." or "Right now I see . . ." or "Right now I hear . . .," etc. Or he may begin his statement with "Right now I think *you* feel . . ." or "Right now I imagine *you* think . . . ," etc. The group can then help each member recognize where and how he tends to focus most of his attention—on thinking or feeling, on what is happening with him or on what he imagines is happening with others.

Stanley M. Herman

Stanley M. Herman is a management and organization consultant from Redondo Beach, California. Mr. Herman is one of the developers of authentic management, a Gestalt orientation to organization development.

INTRODUCTION TO THE
THEORY AND PRACTICE SECTION

Hall and Lindzey's classic discussion of psychological theory (1957) continues to make sense when applied to the field of human relations training. By their definition, theory is a cluster of relevant assumptions systematically related to each other and to a set of empirical definitions. Theory serves these functions: it is *heuristic*, that is, capable of generating research and new learning; it *incorporates* known findings into a logically consistent framework; and it *clarifies and simplifies* the complexity of natural or concrete events. An additional primary function of theory is its *utility*—it can be practically applied and used in particular situations.

Theory seems to be the bastard child in the human relations household. Proponents of experience have touted the benefits of "getting out of your head" and "getting in touch with feelings"; critics never fail to single out and view with alarm the apparent and militant anti-intellectualism of group believers. Trainers and group leaders themselves confess the paucity of sound theory and invest their energy in designing imaginative environments and strategies for learning. A caricature of the field comes easily: impulsive groupies getting high on "touchy-feely" games, masking rampant eroticism with pseudoscience.

In our view, however, the bastard child has been a full, if hidden, family member since the beginnings of the field. Contemporary training is the serendipitous offspring of Lewin's action research of the 1940's. Human relations professionals, inspired by Lewin's motto ("If you want to find out how something works, try changing it"), have explored how human interaction works, or does not work, in every conceivable setting. Those explorations have resulted in a respectable collection of data—and the formulation of behavior-based theory. If practice has often raced ahead of planning, if training experiments have sometimes lacked precise hypotheses, it is also true that the first thirty years of human relations training have produced a body of knowledge that more than meets the criteria of social and behavioral science research.

Human relations theory has some special characteristics and some special problems. It is, first of all, *eclectic*. The facilitator is likely to be influenced by learning theory, personality theory, clinical psychology and psychiatry, social psychology, education, organizational behavior, communications, political science, and Eastern mysticism. The diversity of sources is enriching and exciting, but it also makes comprehensiveness, integration, and synthesis difficult.

Secondly, current theory is largely *descriptive*. It organizes and categorizes what is known and attempts to reduce complexity. In the effort to simplify and offer practical assistance, human relations practitioners frequently overlook the fact of individual differences and multiple motivations for human behavior.

Thirdly, current theory is *action oriented*. Theory is used to provide a rationale and framework for interventions in a change process. The emphasis on reaching goals and "making it happen" is laudable, but such a concrete focus often ignores theory's heuristic function of sparking new generalizations and suppositions about what is still unknown. Another Lewin motto ("No action without research, and no research without action") is worth noting here.

We see many tasks ahead for the human relations consultant. A primary one is for consultants to drop their collective defensiveness: human relations training has a respectable tradition, and the lineage includes outstanding theoreticians, researchers, and practitioners. As "practical theorists" (the description Lewin liked) we are challenged on many fronts. Facilitating the change process for individuals, families, organizations, human services, and communities is a difficult, demanding, but worthwhile assignment.

Sound theory in human relations training is vital in order to make the impossible possible. Apollo VII would never have reached the moon in a Ptolemaic universe; a radical rethinking of the planetary system was necessary before the distance of space could be bridged. Our views of inner space also require revision; we need theory to help us perceive what is really there so that our work can serve to enhance the human condition.

The selections in the Theory and Practice section draw from many sources—role theory, education, Gestalt, communications, marital counseling, anthropology, personality theory, and the *I Ching*. They are designed to provide the human relations "practical theorist" with fresh perspectives.

REFERENCE

Hall, C. S., & Lindzey, G. *Theories of personality*. New York: John Wiley, 1957.

CLARITY OF EXPRESSION IN INTERPERSONAL COMMUNICATION

Myron R. Chartier

"Why can't people get things straight?" is a question often asked when communication breaks down. Since many factors contribute to a lack of clarity in communication, no easy answers are available.

FAULTY ASSUMPTIONS

Misunderstandings between persons can occur because of faulty assumptions people make about communication. Two such faulty assumptions are (1) *"you"* always know what *"I"* mean and (2) *"I"* should always know what *"you"* mean. The premise seems to be that since people live or work together, they are or should be able to read each other's minds. Some people believe that since they are transparent to themselves, they are transparent to others as well. "Since I exist, you should understand me," they seem to be saying. Persons who make this assumption often presume that they communicate clearly if they simply say what they please. In fact, they often leave the persons listening to them confused and guessing about the message being communicated. Misunderstanding is common because clarity of communication does not happen.

A third assumption often made is that communication happens naturally, like walking across a room. The communication process, however, is complex, and achieving a correspondence between messages sent and messages received is difficult. Some people ascribe to a "conveyor belt" theory of communication—meaning moves from one head to another with 100-percent accuracy. The shortcoming of a "conveyor belt" theory of communication, however, is that it suggests that meanings are inherent in the words used or messages sent. However, the meaning one person has is never identical to that which another person has because meanings are in people's minds, not in the words they use. Total accuracy in communication would require that two persons have an identical history of shared experiences. Only then could they perceive exactly the same meaning for a given message. Given the reality of different life experiences, this is impossible.

A DEFINITION OF CLARITY

"Getting things straight" is a difficult communication task; yet people must communicate clearly with each other in order to receive information to accomplish the mundane tasks of life and to experience the depths of dialogue with another person.

Fortunately, absolute clarity is unnecessary; *effective communication is accomplished when the amount of clarity or accuracy achieved is sufficient for handling each situation adequately.* According to information theorists, the purpose of communication is to reduce uncertainty. Total accuracy in communication would lead to an absence of uncertainty. However, uncertainty can never be totally eliminated. Accurate or clear communication, then, is designed to reduce uncertainty in a given situation to a point where necessary understanding can occur.

Certain practical principles and guidelines for reducing uncertainty and increasing the accuracy and clarity in interpersonal communication can be suggested. To achieve greater clarity in speaking, the individual should have the desire to do so and want to understand the communication process more completely. The communicator can try to analyze and shape his message according to the following factors: sending and receiving, the communication context, encoding a message, and communication channels. Of course, the degree of clarity achieved in a given situation is likely to result from the combined effects of several of these factors. Since communication is a process, the factors being considered are interrelated, making it difficult to differentiate one from another.

SENDING AND RECEIVING

Several principles and guidelines are observable in any attempt to send a clear message from one person to another. These guidelines can be seen in terms of pictures, attitudes, skills, and the frame of reference.

Pictures

A person needs to have a clear picture of what he hopes to communicate to another individual. The preacher needs a proposition to help him know what he is trying to accomplish with a sermon. The teacher needs instructional objectives to help him know what he wants his pupils to learn. The administrator needs both short- and long-range objectives to help him plan organizational goals and interpret them to his colleagues. Well-stated goals or objectives aid the effective communicator in developing a clear picture of what he wants to say.

This first guideline is particularly valid when dealing with complex, ambiguous, or vague topics. If a topic or idea is unclear to the person sending the message, its lack of clarity is likely to be magnified by the person trying to understand it. Although there are times when a person may find interpersonal communication helpful in clarifying the pictures in his own head, it is imperative that the communicator first be clear about his ideas before he attempts to convince or influence others, give data, or share feelings.

Attitudes

Accuracy in communication varies with the attitudes of the communicators toward their topic. If a person's attitudes are very positive or very negative, the resulting communication tends to be less accurate. Indeed, persons often organize data according to their biases.

Communication clarity is also influenced by the attitudes of the communicators toward each other. It seems reasonable that communication between people who respect or love each other would be more accurate. However, research indicates that accuracy is inversely correlated with either positive or negative attitudes that the communicators hold toward each other. Thus, an analysis of the extent of one's positive or negative attitudes toward the topic and toward the listener is important for clarity and accuracy of communication.

Communication Skills

Clarity of communication is also influenced by the extent to which those listening and those sending are aware of their communication skills. It is possible to evaluate the assumptions one holds about his ability to communicate messages. Persons with careless speech communication habits are often convinced that they are successful communicators because they are able to open their mouths and utter a stream of words. Actual skills in interpersonal communication, however, are quite different. An accurate assessment of one's own communication weaknesses and strengths is important. Often, strengths can be maximized and weaknesses improved. One person may have a sparkling personality that aids him in communication. Another may have a way with words. Yet another may be able to communicate in such a way that others feel he understands them.

The communicator should also try to assess the listening skills of the person receiving the message. Good "hearing" is not necessarily good "listening." As listening is an active rather than a passive process, people's poor listening habits often take the form of daydreaming, defensiveness, inattention, etc.

Psychological Frame of Reference

Because communication is a function of shared or common meanings, meaning does not occur simply because words are spoken. Words have no meaning in and of themselves. Meaning is what people attribute to words; meanings lie within the experiences and feelings of persons. Thus meanings are within people.

Each person is unique. What he is has been determined by his individual experiences and choices in or with his family, friends, school, church, and culture. Each person has his own set of perceptions, thoughts, feelings, and behaviors. This uniqueness has a profound impact upon the success or failure of communication.

It is impossible to know what another person is sensing or feeling. Because a listener can only guess about the communicator's meaning, it is essential that the person speaking avoid basing his communication on unexamined assumptions about that person.

To assess what he is communicating, the sending person needs to know the psychological frame of reference of the person receiving the message. How does the listener see, feel, and act with respect to others and the world? The psychological frame of reference of a child is quite different from that of an adult. Persons from Maine see life differently than do people from California. Some people prefer to quench their thirst with Pepsi-Cola rather than 7-Up; others choose Dr. Pepper. Some people like Henry Kissinger; others intensely dislike him.

People respond quite differently to the words they hear. One person may react warmly to the words "Jesus saves," while another person may become angry and hostile, and yet another may be indifferent and display no strong sentiment. Indeed, what is clear and rational to one person may seem vague and ridiculous to someone else.

A person can increase the clarity of his communication by constantly trying to place himself inside the psychological framework of the other person. He must try to see the communicative situation from the listener's point of view. If the person communicating understands the other person, he can make his communication more relevant to this person's self-understanding and needs.

COMMUNICATION CONTEXT

A second set of factors affecting the clarity of communication is the context in which communication occurs. Is the setting an office, someone's home, or the golf course? Communicating with a professor in his office is altogether different from communicating with a friend at the bowling alley. The rules in the two situations are distinctly different.

The context of communication is important in determining the amount of accuracy needed or possible between persons in a given situation. How much clarity can be achieved is somewhat determined by the persons' communication skills, the number of communication channels available to the person sending, how much repetition he can incorporate into his message, and the nature of the relationship between the persons communicating. Attempting to communicate with a person in another room presents more difficulties for the clarification process than does speaking face-to-face. In short, the speaker needs to develop a realistic expectation for the degree of clarity obtainable in a given context.

ENCODING A MESSAGE

In order to make ideas clear, an individual must encode his message in order to reduce the amount of uncertainty the other person experiences in hearing that communication. Encoding is the process of translating ideas into a message appropriate for delivery. Once ideas are encoded into messages, they become the potential information that can reduce ambiguity in the other person's mind and produce a clearer picture. There are seven principles for increasing the accuracy and clarity of the messages persons use to communicate.

1. Principle of Relevance

Make the message relevant in the terms of the listening party. The most difficult task related to encoding a message is to assemble it in such a way that the words used accurately reflect the picture one intends and, at the same time, fall within the other person's psychological frame of reference. If a listener is to comprehend the sender's message, he must be able to relate the information he is receiving to what he already knows. Therefore, it is important that the message be presented in a context that says to the listener, "This is important and significant for you." This can be done by using the words of the listening person rather than one's own to encode a message. Such a strategy in communication requires adaptability and flexibility in communication behavior, so that, whether speaking to a child, a teenager, an adult, or persons from different cultural and subcultural backgrounds, the communicator employs appropriate behaviors for sending a clear message.

Just as the encoding of a message should be relevant to the person to whom one is speaking, so should it be appropriate to the situation or the context. The content of a conversation in the privacy of a home is not necessarily appropriate for a discussion at a church committee meeting. Even if the topic were the same in both situations, the message would very likely be encoded quite differently.

2. Principle of Simplicity

Reduce ideas to the simplest possible terms. The communicator should employ as few words as possible to communicate his ideas to a listener. Simplicity of language and economy of words are helpful in facilitating clarity of communication. Generally, the simpler the words, the more likely they are to be understood. However, simplicity really relates to the experience of the person receiving the message. What is simple to one person is complex to another. Theological material that is easily understood by the student of theology may seem quite complicated when presented to the layman in a Sunday morning sermon. The effective communicator calculates the extent to which material must be simplified if it is to be understood by those listening, and he uses the principle of simplicity to make sending messages more successful.

3. Principle of Definition

Define before developing, explain before amplifying. Even simple terms can be unclear. Where would a person go, for example, if someone said, "I'll meet you at the side of the building"? Terms more complicated than "side" increase the need for definition and explanation. The use of jargon also creates problems of clarity for those not acquainted with the words. Unfamiliarity with jargon may cause a person to become confused and frustrated in his efforts to understand. He may even stop trying. Unfamiliar or exceptional terms or concepts need to be defined and explained before they are used to make the communicator's message as clear as possible.

4. Principle of Structure

Organize a message into a series of successive stages. Texts on public speaking emphasize the importance of making apparent the order or structure of a message. A well-organized speech, it is said, will increase the audience's understanding. However, there is little research evidence to support such a contention, especially in regard to face-to-face dialogue. Indeed, most people will structure the message in accordance with their own patterns of thinking even as they listen, regardless of how well a message is organized.

What is important is the clarity of thought and the expression of individual parts. In interpersonal communication it is probably best to develop one idea at a time. A message can be "packaged" into a series of stages, with one stage completed before the next is introduced.

Furthermore, the communicator can help the person listening by not overloading him with information. When persons are asked to comprehend too much, they tend to forget or become confused. By developing one idea at a time and taking one step at a time, the person speaking can facilitate accuracy in communication.

5. Principle of Repetition

Repeat the key concepts of the message. The principle of repetition is important. Very important. The words "very important" were repetitive. They repeated the idea of the second sentence in a slightly different manner in order to make the concept clearer. Repetition is particularly important in oral communication, where words are spoken only once. Obviously a communicator should not repeat everything he says since it would bore the listener. However, the person speaking needs to use enough repetition to ensure clear reception of his ideas. Some possible strategies: (a) repeating key ideas, (b) restating difficult ideas, (c) recycling ideas wherever feedback indicates they are weak or misunderstood, and (d) using examples, synonyms, analogies, or periodic summaries. In short, a person should use intentional repetition in his attempts to achieve clarity.

6. Principle of Comparison and Contrast

Relate new ideas to old ideas; associate the unknown with the known. The principle of comparison and contrast is essential to the achievement of clear communication, as understanding comes most often through association—the perception of similarities and differences among objects, events, and people. A person can understand a new, unknown idea more clearly if he is able to relate it to an old, known one.

Discriminating between those elements that rightfully belong to an idea and those that do not will help a listener understand a concept. Comparison helps individuals to identify the similarities in two or more ideas. Contrast helps to point out the differences in two or more ideas. When accurate discriminations occur, clarity in communication emerges: the sharper the discrimination, the greater the clarity.

Helpful devices for presenting comparisons and contrasts include the use of models, metaphors, analogies, and explanations.

7. Principle of Emphasis

Focus on the essential and vital aspects of the communication. Since the transitory nature of interpersonal communication makes it highly susceptible to loss of information, attention should be given to the essential and vital aspects of a message. Communication goals and key points should be sharply focused so as not to submerge the message in details and make it vague, ambiguous, and blurred. The impact of the significant points of a communication can be heightened by speaking louder, using a different tone of voice, pausing, or using various other techniques to captivate the listener. *Reinforcing and underscoring ideas help in developing such impact.* For example: *this last principle is an important one—remember it and use it.*

Communication strategies based on these principles for developing or sending a message will result in a more accurate correspondence of ideas between persons.

COMMUNICATION CHANNELS

Once a message is constructed for sending to another person, it must be sent through a communication channel. Several factors related to communication channels affect clarification in the speaking-listening process. Four of these are discussed here.

Channels Available

An important aspect of communication that affects accuracy and clarity is the number of channels available for sending a message. For example, in a letter only one channel—the written word—is in use. Face-to-face interaction, however, utilizes several channels, e.g., body tension, facial expressions, eye contact, hand and body movements, relative positions of each person, vocal sounds accompanying a verbal message, etc.

To communicate clearly, a person should be aware of the various channels available to him and utilize as many of them as possible. When messages are sent through more than one channel, repetition is increased. As repetition increases, uncertainty is reduced, and the chances for clarity are increased. It is important, however, that whenever multichannel communication occurs, the messages be consistent across all channels or the results will be confusing for the listener.

Feedback

An awareness and use of feedback is important to the communicator. Feedback, which is a term from cybernetic theory, is an essential element in any control process. This phenomenon can be observed in the operation of a self-adjusting camera in which a built-in light meter measures the amount of illumination in the environment and automatically adjusts the camera accordingly. In a comparable manner, feedback can be used to correct and adjust meanings and thus increase communication clarity. A person sending a message should elicit feedback following his communication attempts in order to determine whether the picture received was the one transmitted. On the basis of this feedback, the next step in the communication process can be taken. The following conversation between Joe and Sally is an example of feedback as purposive correction:

Joe: "Feedback is a process of correcting inaccuracy in communication."
Sally: "Do you mean that feedback is simply a process of correcting errors?"
Joe: "Not exactly, although that is a part of what I mean. Feedback is a way of being sure that what I say to you is adequately perceived by you."
Sally: "Now you're really getting complicated. What does 'adequately perceived' mean?"
Joe: "Well, I think 'adequately perceived' means that you understand the idea as I would like for you to understand it."
Sally: "Oh, then you mean that feedback is a device for checking whether or not I got the idea you wanted me to get."
Joe: "Exactly."
Sally: "Do you think I used feedback effectively?"
Joe: "Well, how do you feel about it?"

In the same way that communication clarity can be increased by using a variety of available channels, a number of feedback channels can also be an aid to accuracy.

Noise

Communication accuracy is affected by "noise," a term frequently used to refer to any disturbance that interferes with the sending of a message. Although noise may occur in almost any aspect of the communication process, such interference appears often as an obstruction in the channel between two interacting persons. The interfering noise may be other people talking, the whir of a vacuum cleaner, or the sound of a lawn mower coming through an open window. The greater the noise, the more difficult it becomes to communicate clearly. For this reason it is important for the communicator to find ways of eliminating or reducing sources of distracting noise.

Speed and Pacing

Clarity of communication is related to how much information a channel can carry and a listener can receive at one time. Because the oral channel requires those listening to depend heavily on their memories for comprehension, it is less effective than other channels for handling large amounts of verbal information. Effective lecturers know that it is the rare audience that can absorb more than one or two new ideas. In contrast, the written channel can carry much more verbal information, as it allows individuals to reconsider the material. Therefore, the speed of oral communication must be determined by the listening persons' rate of comprehension. The communicator should pace his message according to the information-processing capacities of the channel and the hearers.

A SUMMARY OF GUIDELINES FOR CLEAR INTERPERSONAL COMMUNICATION

A person wishing to achieve greater clarity in his interpersonal communication should find the following guidelines helpful.

The communicator seeking to improve his communication clarity should:

1. Have a clear picture of what he wants the other person to understand.
2. Analyze the nature and magnitude of his attitudes toward both the topic and the person with whom he is communicating.
3. Assess his own communication skills and those of the person listening.
4. Seek to identify himself with the psychological frame of reference of the person receiving his ideas.
5. Develop a realistic expectation for the degree of clarity obtainable in a given context.
6. Make the message relevant to the person listening by using that person's language and terms.
7. State his ideas in the simplest possible terms.
8. Define before developing and explain before amplifying.
9. Develop one idea at a time, take one step at a time.
10. Use appropriate repetition.
11. Compare and contrast ideas by associating the unknown with the known.
12. Determine which ideas need special emphasis.
13. Use as many channels as necessary for clarity.
14. Watch for and elicit corrective feedback in a variety of channels.
15. Eliminate or reduce noise if it is interfering.
16. Pace his communication according to the information-processing capacities of the channel and the person listening.

. . . .

"I know you believe that you understand what you think I said, but I am not sure that you realize that what you heard is not what I meant."

. . . .

What is clear to you is clear to you and not necessarily to anyone else.

REFERENCES

Combs, A. W., Avila, D. L., & Purkey, W. L. *Helping relationships: Basic concepts for the helping professions*. Boston: Allyn & Bacon, 1971.

Keltner, J. W. *Elements of interpersonal communication*. Belmont, Calif.: Wadsworth, 1973.

McCroskey, J. C., Larson, C. E., & Knapp, M. L. *An introduction to interpersonal communication*. Englewood Cliffs, N.J.: Prentice-Hall, 1971.

Pace, R. W., & Boren, R. R. *The human transaction: Facets, functions, and forms of interpersonal communication*. Glenview, Ill.: Scott, Foresman, 1973.

Ruesch, J. *Disturbed communication: The clinical assessment of normal and pathological communication behavior*. New York: W. W. Norton, 1957.

Satir, V. *Conjoint family therapy* (Rev. ed.). Palo Alto, Calif.: Science & Behavior Books, 1967.

Satir, V. *Peoplemaking*. Palo Alto, Calif.: Science & Behavior Books, 1972.

Stewart, J. (Ed.). *Bridges not walls: A book about interpersonal communication*. Reading, Mass.: Addison-Wesley, 1973.

Myron R. Chartier, Ph.D., *is the director of the doctoral program and an associate professor of ministry, The Eastern Baptist Theological Seminary, Philadelphia, Pennsylvania. He is engaged in relating the behavioral sciences to theology and the practice of ministry. Dr. Chartier's background is in interpersonal, group, and organizational communication as it relates to theory, research, and methodological application.*

156

DESIGNING AND FACILITATING EXPERIENTIAL GROUP ACTIVITIES: VARIABLES AND ISSUES

Cary L. Cooper and Kenneth Harrison

In designing and implementing experiential group activities, certain types of variables need to be considered. These variables can be seen in three major groups: initial, emergent, and evaluative (see Figure 1). Discussed here are the various subdivisions within each type, with specific points of consideration suggested for the facilitator designing an experiential group activity.

INITIAL VARIABLES

Factors to be considered prior to the group activity consist of aims (learning objectives) and the learning environment, including participants, group structure, and the training staff.

Learning Objectives

In designing a group experience, it is important to consider first the general aims or outcome desired and then the specific ways in which people should change, develop, or behave. The following points should be determined.

Standards

- who should set learning standards;
- who should judge the results (participants, facilitators, both of these, outside individuals or groups).

Affective/Conceptual Aims

- the extent to which aims are emotional (usually personal) or conceptual (cognitive).

Short-Term/Long-Term Aims

- how long the group learning is intended to have an effect (days, months, years).

Question of Authority

- who should set learning objectives (facilitator, participants, or both).

Remedial/Developmental Aims

Remedial work tends to focus on a participant's weaknesses, problems, or lacks; developmental work aims on building a participant's strengths. The extent to which the activity is focused in either direction should be considered, as well as the implications of this focus.

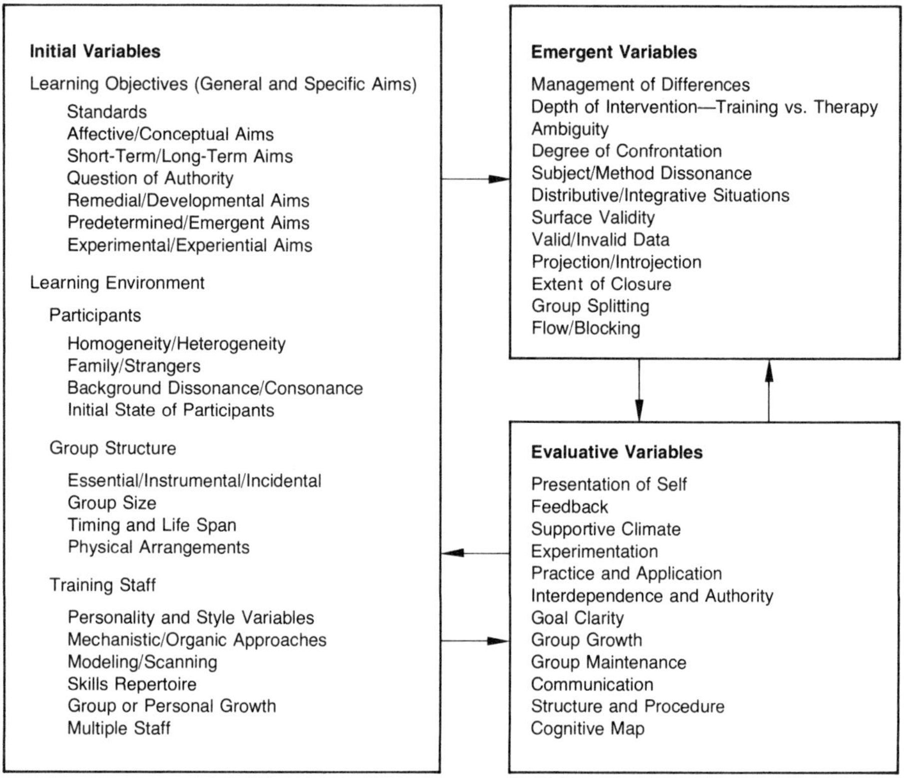
Initial Variables
Learning Objectives (General and Specific Aims)
Standards
Affective/Conceptual Aims
Short-Term/Long-Term Aims
Question of Authority
Remedial/Developmental Aims
Predetermined/Emergent Aims
Experimental/Experiential Aims
Learning Environment
Participants
Homogeneity/Heterogeneity
Family/Strangers
Background Dissonance/Consonance
Initial State of Participants
Group Structure
Essential/Instrumental/Incidental
Group Size
Timing and Life Span
Physical Arrangements
Training Staff
Personality and Style Variables
Mechanistic/Organic Approaches
Modeling/Scanning
Skills Repertoire
Group or Personal Growth
Multiple Staff
Emergent Variables
Management of Differences
Depth of Intervention—Training vs. Therapy
Ambiguity
Degree of Confrontation
Subject/Method Dissonance
Distributive/Integrative Situations
Surface Validity
Valid/Invalid Data
Projection/Introjection
Extent of Closure
Group Splitting
Flow/Blocking
Evaluative Variables
Presentation of Self
Feedback
Supportive Climate
Experimentation
Practice and Application
Interdependence and Authority
Goal Clarity
Group Growth
Group Maintenance
Communication
Structure and Procedure
Cognitive Map

Figure 1. Design and Operational Variables for Group Training

Predetermined/Emergent Aims

- the extent to which learning aims can be determined prior to the experience;
- the possibility of additional aims emerging during the experience;
- the extent to which the facilitator imposes, consciously or otherwise, some aims by his own values and by setting norms.

Experimental/Experiential Aims

The choice between these aims has implications for the training design (e.g., use of observers, data collection, process reviews) and for the facilitator's learning theory or models (e.g., one can experience something and "learn" without discussing that experience afterward). Points to consider:

- the extent to which the activity will be a joint learning experiment, in which the facilitator has a special responsibility (e.g., for helping the group examine data in reviewing its work);
- the extent to which the facilitator allows participants to experience the activity without reviewing their experience.

Learning Environment

The principal components of the learning environment—participants, group structure, and training staff—must often be considered in relation to learning objectives.

Participants

The nature of participants and, especially, the similarities and differences among participants need to be considered. The following items are particularly significant.

Homogeneity/Heterogeneity

Heterogeneity can lead to greater confrontation but can also provide the group with a wider range of resources. Homogeneity, on the other hand, may lead to greater intimacy/affection, but promote less variety. This effect can restrict the number of learning possibilities available to the group.

Family/Strangers

Groups with established relationships (e.g., work groups and family groups) might achieve a greater transfer of learning but might also be reluctant to be entirely open. Instead, participants who are strangers (and unlikely to continue their relationship after the training) may gain greater intimacy and openness at the possible expense of a less effective transfer of learning.

Background Dissonance/Consonance

It is important to consider whether group training is dissonant with the norms and culture of the institutional background within which the activity is to take place. The participants may learn and change their attitudes in ways that are contrary to the ideology of their back-home situations, and the implications of this should be considered. Also, the organizational climate of the aegis under which training is organized may be supportive, hostile, curious, frivolous, skeptical, anxious, or impatient toward group training.

Initial State of Participants

If the initial state of the participants is inaccurately judged, learning may not be optimized. It may be necessary for the facilitator to find ways to check out his initial-state assumptions. Items to be determined:

- the amount of information the facilitators have;
- the assumptions facilitators make about the initial goals, needs, and readiness of the participants.

Group Structure

In assessing design issues, decisions must be made about whether the group is essential, instrumental, or incidental to the learning process; the group size; the timing and life span of the group; and the physical arrangements.

Essential/Instrumental/Incidental

In some training experiences (e.g., interpretive groups) the group itself is a central and essential part of the learning model. In others (e.g., T-groups, encounter groups, etc.) the group is instrumental in the learning process by providing both interaction opportunities and support. In yet other experiences (e.g., Gestalt and counseling), the group is largely incidental, since valuable work can be done as well in pairs, trios, etc. The group may, however, represent an economy or provide further opportunities for participants to learn by observing other individuals and identifying with them.

Group Size

The size of the total group training population is important in designing various learning experiences. One should seriously consider the number of participants desired and the ways in which this population can be divided to achieve various objectives.

Timing and Life Span

Spaced sessions (e.g., two-hour weekly sessions) may produce a less intimate and less person-centered experience, whereas more condensed or intensive sessions (e.g., a one-week residential session) may offer more personal growth. Spaced sessions may allow greater analysis of group dynamics and encourage members to "work through" between sessions (e.g., a couples' group). Defined time limits may encourage participants to express useful information by the end of the allotted time period, but can also establish the facilitator's role as the locus of control or authority of the group. Norms will develop as a result of the following timing parameters:

- the total time allocated to the group experience;
- the time distribution (sessions at regular intervals, one intensive week, etc.);
- session time limits and adherence to limits.

Physical Arrangements

The physical arrangements are a significant consideration in facilitating the learning objectives. For example, a small-group session held in a lecture theater would have an entirely different atmosphere from one held in more intimate surroundings. Physical arrangements include:

- where the groups will work;
- what kind of atmosphere the physical surroundings create (e.g., easy chairs, cushions, etc.);
- how the physical environment can be arranged to support learning objectives.

Training Staff

Issues about staff include personality, style, potential role conflicts, learning models, philosophies, and assumptions. The resolution of these issues is critical to the successful fulfillment of the learning objectives.

Personality and Style Variables

Some facilitators work more readily with their own aggression, some with their affection, and others remain somewhat detached and unemotional. These differences may be justified or rationalized as differences in role perception and style, but they may really be due to personality differences among the staff. Since the models of role conflict and resolution of interpersonal differences in the staff team could influence participants' learning, it is important to review style preferences when selecting a training staff.

Mechanistic/Organic Approaches

If one staff member insists on structuring a group experience, and another wants to respond to group needs spontaneously, the entire experience may suffer. It would be possible, however, to synthesize these two approaches into a more productive compromise.

Modeling/Scanning

Trainers who adopt a learning theory based on modeling might find that they are encouraging noticeable but short-term change. If, instead, they encourage group members to use one another as learning sources, through an approach based on scanning the interaction of group members, participants may *show* less change, although this approach may also prompt major internalized change.

Skills Repertoire

The trainer/facilitator's ability to handle certain types of group experience and his range of competence should be a training consideration.

Group or Personal Growth

Staff disagreement about the level of intervention may create normative problems in that participants receive conflicting messages about the learning objectives of the group. On the other hand, the conflict may provide participants with a wider range and greater breadth of learning. Issues of concern:

- the orientation of the trainer/facilitator toward understanding the dynamics of the group or toward developing the growth potential of the individual;
- whether both orientations can co-exist.

Multiple Staff

The composition of the staff will influence somewhat the norms and learning objectives of the participants. The inclusion of women may provide opportunities for focusing on issues that otherwise might not surface. Items for this variable:

- the number of staff involved;
- the compatibility of the staff;
- inclusion of both men and women;
- inclusion of staff with specific occupational identifications.

EMERGENT VARIABLES

A number of dynamic variables emerge during the learning process in group work. Emergent variables include management of differences, depth and level of interventions, vagueness of direction, confrontation, dissonance in subject and method, distributive/integrative situations, credibility, validity (or nonvalidity) of data, projection and introjection, closure, subdivision of groups, and flow and blocking in learning and communication.

If the facilitator is aware of these variables, he may be more effective in dealing with them as they arise. However, he may also be more likely to provoke or precipitate such issues.

Management of Differences

There are likely to be differences in the starting states, needs, personalities, learning rates, and moods of the participants. Differences and conflict can be a source of creativity. In particular, some participants may want to learn about their own aggression or style of conflict resolution. Occasionally, however, it may be better temporarily to avoid conflict by providing other sources of learning that may ultimately help to resolve the differences, e.g., by splitting the group into compatible subgroups to develop feedback skills before coping with the total group conflict. The facilitator should consider how he and the group cope with differences and conflict—by ignoring them, debating, arguing, fighting, compromising.

Depth of Intervention—Training vs. Therapy

The group may intend to work on issues (e.g., the level of competence in group work) and not become involved in personal or therapeutic issues, but suddenly or gradually the group members may become more introspective, and the hazy boundary between training and therapy is reached.

"Interpretive" interventions would facilitate useful therapy work, whereas "behavioral-data-based" interventions leave options open. Focusing on there-and-then contributions from one member of the group and his personal problems will encourage a therapy-type group; interventions about the here-and-now skills and interpersonal relations between members encourage a training focus.

Therapy is concerned with a person's sense of who he is, how he is, how he got to be that way, and what he could do to change. *Training* is concerned with what a person can do with what he is, how he behaves toward others, and his skill or competence.

Ambiguity

In discovery learning one must cope with ambiguity and uncertainty. Yet some common, recurring themes can be distinguished in T-groups. For example, when the trainer deliberately refuses to be a leader in the group, participants feel the leadership and structure vacuum and usually work to fill it. Participants often expect that the trainer/facilitator should give the group direction and help because he has had previous similar group experience; yet some training models include anxiety as a necessary force in the learning process.

Degree of Confrontation

As an integral part of many learning processes, people are confronted with feedback, evidence, and feelings from other group members and the facilitator. Judging the level of the confrontation is like gauging the difficulty of a jump across a gap—it must not be so small that it is unnoticeable, nor so large that one balks or fails. A confrontation level that is too low may lead to *assimilation* ("That's common sense, I already do/know that"). Too high a level of confrontation may lead to *rejection* ("That's nonsense, I don't agree"). The appropriate level of confrontation leads to *accommodation* ("How can I make sense of that? I am going to work on that"). The facilitator needs to determine:

- elements in the process that provide confrontations;
- how the degree of confrontation can be optimized.

162

Subject/Method Dissonance

It is reasonable and comfortable—consonant—to learn about group dynamics in a group or about interpersonal relations while relating to others. However, it is uncomfortable—dissonant—to tell people to participate or to ask people to discuss their dependence. In the experiential situation, the contract, structure, and method should not be dissonant with the learning aims. Considerations for the facilitator:

- the balance (or lack of it) between what the group is doing and the issues it is working on;
- problems that might arise with a high level of consonance.

Distributive/Integrative Situations

Distributive situations tend to be either analytical (e.g., subdividing issues and distributing the parts among people) or competitive and evaluative (e.g., allocating blame and attributing results to individuals). Integrative situations are usually cooperative or concerned with the Gestalt. Particularly in the use of structured experiences, participants' socialization toward competition can bias group work toward distributive activities. Integration is, however, central to the philosophy of group work. The facilitator needs to consider whether group work and particularly any structured experiences he may use as interventions are likely to work toward distribution or integration.

Surface Validity

Issues of validity and credibility appear very early in group life but become less important later. Unless people feel able to commit themselves initially to the work and life of the group (at least to the extent of making a start), it is difficult to gain their acceptance/commitment. Considerations:

- whether tasks, issues, exercises, and the setting of the group work appear realistic or valid to participants;
- whether members seem credible to each other;
- face credibility of the facilitator—influenced by such factors as age, sex, experience, manner, dress.

Valid/Invalid Data

It is useful for the facilitator to be clear about the ground rules for the validity of data and for him to share and compare his criteria with group members. The most valid data are descriptions of actual behavior ("You sat next to me in every session") or expressions of personal feelings ("I feel warm and strong"). Less valid but complementary data are interpretations ("You sit by me because you feel isolated") and guesses about motives ("You sit by me because you are trying to get to know me"). Interpretations and conjectures about motives cannot be verified—they can only be accepted or denied in comparison with the evidence offered. Their acceptance or denial, however, becomes another valid behavior. Still less valid data are "we" statements where "I" statements would be more accurate ("We all feel anxious, don't we?"); old feedback, which is less valid the farther away from the event it is ("Yesterday I felt angry with you when you talked so much"); and nonspecific generalizations ("Some members of the group just don't listen"). Some tests of data:

- the kind of data valid for the work in progress;
- whether the current data flow in the group is valid or invalid.

Projection/Introjection

In projection, people disclose their own ideas, attitudes, feelings, assumptions, values, skills, and styles to the group and to one another. In introjection, people absorb ideas, feedback, data, etc., from other group members. Projection and introjection can be conscious or unconscious. Often the work in a group proceeds in phases of projection followed by introjection. If this occurs, it may be useful periodically to review the group's progress in these terms.

Extent of Closure

The degree of closure for any issue or incident in the learning process may vary from total open-endedness to a high degree of closure. Both approaches have their difficulties. Low closure can be frustrating and can raise more issues and questions than answers. High closure can lead to encapsulation and elimination—allowing fewer possibilities for individuals to internalize learning. Learning is ultimately personal, and the results of the group's work are vested in individual members as they leave the group. Whatever level of closure the facilitator decides to aim for is likely to be a compromise, based on a judgment of the extent to which closure affects learning and resolution.

Group Splitting

As the group process continues, the initial group-structure variable of size shifts to become an emergent variable. One manifestation is lateness or absenteeism, an issue related to the functioning of the group as well as to the particular individuals. A more obvious form of this issue occurs when members or facilitators suggest that the group split into subgroups or when the group splits spontaneously. In some models (e.g., Bion), it can be considered either as an avoidance mechanism or, if handled as a dichotomy, as a creative polarity. In other models (e.g., encounter), no such negative interpretation is associated with splitting. Dividing into pairs and subgroups is used as a facilitative structural intervention. This issue is related to the initial essential/instrumental/incidental variable, because splitting is less acceptable if the group itself is essential.

Flow/Blocking

At times, the group or some individuals become blocked. They cannot progress and learn only how it feels to be frustrated, impotent, or lacking in skills. These can be useful learning issues, particularly if various styles of responding to a block are explored. At other times the work must flow, feelings must be expressed, and there must be movement.

Flow can be facilitated by such devices as exercises, acting-out, physical and nonverbal expression, and games. Although these may appear "phony" to participants, such contrived measures can often activate genuine results.

The facilitator must be able to cope with learning while he is blocked and must also know how to facilitate flow. He can then determine the implications of his interventions, basing them on the needs of the group and the members, rather than on his own skill bias.

EVALUATIVE VARIABLES

Although the facilitator/trainer has to make certain judgments and decisions before and during group work, the extent to which these judgments should be conscious is debatable. However, the assumption is that more skilled trainers will welcome raising rather than lowering their level of consciousness about their judgment. Such an evaluation is not meant, however, to suggest that intuitive skill and spontaneity are unimportant. This discussion does not recommend any particular model for group work. Rather, it suggests that whatever conscious or unconscious models a facilitator has should be utilized as effectively as possible.

The following are not issues about which the facilitator must make a decision; instead, they offer *criteria* useful in making appropriate judgments about initial and emergent variables. Presenting such a list aims at increasing the clarity with which a facilitator confronts a particular issue and at raising possible alternatives.

Presentation of Self

Until the individual has and uses opportunities to reveal how he perceives, feels, and does things, he has little basis for learning about himself. Often silent members claim they learn by observing and listening to others. In a way this is true, but they are presenting only the "nonincluded" part of themselves. With various results, groups put pressure on silent or nonparticipant members to join in. An effective group climate allows and facilitates self-presentation and does not force conformity to group norms in the method of that presentation.

Feedback

If people learned from experience, older people would clearly be more skilled at relationships and behavior than younger people. How people use their experience is more important than the experience itself. Individuals learn through developing behavior patterns guided by clear and accurate feedback about the effectiveness and appropriateness of their actions. Feedback may come from other participants, the trainer, observers, data-collection instruments, audio- and videotape playback, or task-success elements in a structured experience.

Feedback must be valid data (see emergent variables) and be related to events and actions. Feedback is also more useful if it is relevant to behavior and situations that can be changed or modified. It is easier to change what one *does* than to change what one *is*. For example, "You are a hostile person and should change" is less useful than "If you were less hostile to me, I could work better with you." Negative motives, such as to punish the receiver or to establish the giver's superiority, can often reduce the validity of feedback.

Supportive Climate

An atmosphere of trust and nondefensiveness is necessary for people to risk their ideas and feelings, behave openly, and accept feedback. Each person must be able to risk being himself, right or wrong, effective or ineffective, without feeling he is risking his membership in the group and the acceptance of others. This does not necessarily mean that conflict, anger, or differences should be avoided. Such emotions, indeed, are more acceptable in a supportive climate.

Experimentation

An important possibility in many group training situations is the testing of alternative patterns of behavior and personal relationships. Within a supportive climate and with valid feedback, experimentation can be a key element in changing behavior. Participants may, however, use experimentation defensively: "I did not really feel like that; I only behaved that way to see what you would do." The difference between useful and useless experimentation is that *useful* experimentation concerns one's personal behavior; experimentation with others' behavior is "playing games."

Practice and Application

To gain confidence in his newly acquired behavior, an individual needs to practice it. New behavior needs to be transferred to and retained in situations external to the training situation. This is sometimes referred to as the "re-entry" problem. It is possible and profitable to test actual application if group work is set at intervals (e.g., weekly meetings), since the individual may receive valid feedback on his behavior. Simulated application can be used to deal with an issue concerning the facilitator, including fantasies about applying a new approach to the issue.

Interdependence and Authority

It is important for the group to confront and understand its relationship with the group's authority figure—usually the facilitator/trainer. When this happens, it is a good indicator of progress in the group. If it never occurs, the quality of interdependence is questionable. Overdependency on the facilitator allows members to avoid taking responsibility for their actions and learning. Changes in behavior are then likely to fade when the authority person is not present or if he loses credibility. Interdependence between group members and facilitator is more healthy.

Goal Clarity

It is helpful when participants, groups, and facilitators have some clear goals and purposes. A lack of clear learning goals produces two problems: differences in individual learning needs cannot be handled, and it becomes difficult to determine the extent of progress. Goals are more helpful if related to specific behaviors and actions and checked against feedback. Although clear goals cannot be expected immediately, goal clarification and review should be a continuing process for individuals and for the group.

Group Growth

A group has development needs beyond the collective needs of its members; it needs time and assistance to become mature, effective, and cohesive. A group will often require more man-hours than the same number of individuals working separately or in small subgroups—achieving different, but valued, results. "One-shot" groups are of limited or specialized significance.

Group Maintenance

The need for group maintenance is closely related to group growth. In many group learning models, members can use group maintenance to develop their skills in group diagnosis and group facilitation. Energy invested in group building and maintenance as a preventive rather than repair measure is a positive indicator of group growth.

Communication

Usually only a small proportion of what is said in a group is heard or understood by many of the members. Participants may be thinking about what they want to say next, what they would like to say but will not, what they think the speaker is really saying, or what they are feeling at the moment. Any of these distractions reduce the probability of listening. A positive correction is for group members to slow down the verbal communication rate or make shorter statements that others can check to insure understanding. Checking and nonverbal communication activities are useful in this process.

Structure and Procedure

"Unstructured" groups do not exist. All groups have norms and procedures, and even anarchy is a structure. For example, a T-group is based on certain norms about its form and function.

It is not always sufficiently clear how formal the structure should be and whether it is imposed externally or derived internally. Structures are related to assumptions and values, as well as to participants' abilities to cope with ambiguity. When a group can establish and maintain the degree of structure it needs for effective work and can change the structure as its needs and issues change, group growth is evident.

Cognitive Map

In some group training, theories and conceptual schemes may help participants understand the experience. The behavior of an individual can be seen as based on his interior "map" or schemata, which are not necessarily conscious. However, great benefit and little danger lie in developing a more conscious understanding of one's behavior.

Conceptual material can be introduced by readings, films, lecturettes, and short theory interventions. One of the benefits of using theory material is that it may replace "folklore" notions about a group, e.g., "In any group there will always be one person who will emerge as a leader." One danger in encouraging cognitive development is that some members may use conceptual material inappropriately to defend against or to avoid the experience. Nevertheless, it is usually beneficial for people to comprehend their experience and articulate their insights.

CONCLUSION

The issues and variables we have discussed here are valuable in a number of practical ways. First, they should provide an explicit and systematic guide to help facilitators focus on the issues (initial and evaluative, mainly) that should be considered in *designing* any experiential group activity. Second, they help the training staff of a particular group become more conscious of issues that might *emerge* during the life of the group and identify more clearly the situation in which they currently find themselves. This can also provide a laboratory staff team with a source of comparison to facilitate cohesion in the total learning community. Third, many of these variables and issues can help to highlight issues that should be considered in the designing of a trainer/facilitator *development* program. Also, a careful consideration of these issues can be useful to the individual facilitator in his own development by serving as a possible framework for *self-appraisal*. Finally, many of these variables and issues raise interesting *research* questions about the processes of group functioning. For example, the differentiated effects of spaced vs. massed training sessions or one structure vs. another structure of design might be considered.

The authors' intention here is not to suggest a more mechanistic approach to the design and operation of group training. Experience, intuition, and spontaneity are considered valuable elements in a facilitator's approach. Rather, specific issues have been discussed and clarified to help facilitators consciously analyze some of the significant variables in group training in order to improve their own effectiveness and skill.

Cary L. Cooper, Ph.D., *is F.M.E. Professor of Management Educational Methods in the Department of Management Sciences, Institute of Science and Technology, The University of Manchester, Manchester, England. He is the author of numerous books on group and organization development (e.g.,* T-Groups: A Survey of Research *and* Theories of Group Processes), *the European associate editor of* Interpersonal Development, *and the general editor of a series of John Wiley books entitled* Individuals, Groups, and Organizations. *Dr. Cooper's background is in social psychology, experiential learning groups (T-groups, encounter groups, etc.), organization development, and human relations training for social workers, managers, psychiatrists, and nurses.*

Kenneth Harrison *is a senior lecturer in organizational behavior, Cranfield School of Management, Cranfield, Bedford, England. He teaches MBA students and undertakes management development and OD consultancy in industrial and nonindustrial organizations. Mr. Harrison's background is in group training, organizational psychology, and organization development.*

YIN/YANG: A PERSPECTIVE ON THEORIES OF GROUP DEVELOPMENT

Anthony G. Banet, Jr.

All human groups are living and ever changing. Issues that were critical in the first session evaporate by the fourth session; the excitement of session three is followed by the ennui of session seven. Moods fluctuate, central concerns wax and wane. The group has a life of its own; its primary characteristic is movement. Groups, like individuals, are unique, but all groups share some similar attributes. These observations, made repeatedly by students of groups, are the bases for theories of group development—statements about the flow of group process over time.

The literature in the fields of group psychotherapy, group dynamics, organization development, and human relations training yields an abundance of theories of group development. Tuckman (1965) reviews sixty-two theories; Hill (1973), once a connoisseur of group theories, states that he ended his hobby when his collection numbered over one hundred specimens. Although theories abound and spring from various observational data, underlying similarities can be discerned.

Three different models of group development emerge: the *linear* model, which regards change as a progressive, straight-line function over time; the *helical* (spiral) model, which sees change as a regressive, whirlpool movement from surface to core issues; and the *cyclical* model, which views change as an interplay of yin and yang energy forces. Approaches to a potential integration of these models are here suggested.

FUNCTIONS OF GROUP-DEVELOPMENT THEORIES

Theories of group development serve descriptive and predictive functions. For the group practitioner, the theory also provides a framework for interventions.

On a descriptive level, developmental theory permits the observer to organize his perceptions. During a given slice of group life, verbal behavior, the interaction pattern, emotional climate, or type of content can be characterized and measured. Whatever the observational base, descriptions of group phenomena in a given session can be compared and contrasted with those from a past or future session.

Used predictively, developmental theory enables the observer to forecast the group's future process. The theory describes what *should* be happening, at least under ideal conditions, so that objectives can be set. The predictive aspect offers comfort to the group practitioner: events will not always be as conflicted or sluggish as they appear to be in a given session.

A particular theory also provides the group leader with cues for specific interventions. The leader may want to accelerate the process, slow it down, or freeze or focus it to insure that a group does not avoid or ignore opportunities for learning. Equipped with theory, the leader may plan or design interventions intended to surface and clarify process issues that he regards as important. Developmental theory is a particularly helpful guide to amplifying issues that groups frequently find troublesome: dependency, authority, conflict, power, and intimacy.

Content, Process, and Structure

In a group-development theory, the content, process, and structure of a group are closely interrelated. Content, *what* is being said, verbally and nonverbally, is determined by the group's task, whether it is to make decisions, overcome resistances to growth, or experiment with new behavior. Process refers to *how* a group behaves; process elements include events happening inside individual members, group-level phenomena such as norm development, and contextual (past history, back-home) variables. In the life of a group, content and process are always happening, but the visibility of the process is a function of group structure.

Structure serves as a valve to control the flow of energy between process and content. The structure of the group, which includes such elements as the leader's attitude toward the group and the theory he espouses, determines the extent to which content and process are allowed to interrelate and to influence each other. Structure also includes the group's objectives, the contract between the leader and the group, and the ground rules to which the group subscribes. To a lesser extent, structure also refers to the physical environment in which the group lives.

Group structure can be tight and rigid, permitting no process elements to become part of the group's agenda, or it can be so loose that the process becomes the content, as in a T-group. To some extent, the profusion of group-development theories is a result of the variety of group structures. A loose structure may allow fifteen phases of process to surface; a tight structure, only one or two.

The group's structure enables the practitioner to place a selective value on specific process elements and to make decisions regarding the focus of the group. Each intervention becomes a creative decision to enrich the ongoing content with relevant process phenomena. Too much or too little attention to process endangers the group's task function—its reason for being.

At present, no single theory of group development adequately accounts for all group phenomena reported by observers. Events that are commonplace in a Tavistock conference, for instance, may never surface in a team-building session. Individual "implosions" occur in a Gestalt workshop, but rarely in a communication-skills laboratory. Some groups spend half their life working authority issues; others focus on the issue for only minutes before moving on to long periods of affection and intimacy.

These discrepancies seem attributable to the power of a theory of group development to "make it happen"; that is, the theory, as an observational tool, impacts what is being observed. As Butkovich et al. (1975) state in a recent study, there is a strong "possibility that the group leader's theoretical orientation, as it is reflected in his interpretations and behavior, is causally related to the very group behavior being interpreted" (p. 9).

This contamination by the observer of what is being observed is prevalent in all applied behavioral science. Contamination does not discredit a theory but serves to remind us that "truth" is always filtered through a human observer with built-in biases and distortions. However, contamination does raise the difficult methodological issue that some process elements (transference, for example) may in truth be artifacts of the observational tool employed. What is reported as a group-process event may exist, instead, only in the minds of the intervener. As Lundgren (1971) has demonstrated, the pace and pattern of group process, as well as specific group phenomena, are directly related to the intervention stance prescribed by the leader's theory of group development. Therefore, a primary problem in the study of group development theories is distinguishing between the observer and the data.

Another factor accounting for a less-than-comprehensive theory is that different developmental theories focus on different elements of group process. Theories described here as employing a *linear* model focus on group elements of process: the interaction system, group emotion, then normative system, group culture, and the executive system. The linear model views process as progressive. The *helical* model focuses on contextual elements: transferential, past history aspects of process, including physical and social contacts, emotional and contractual relations, and the

170

individual's attitudes toward authority and control. The helical model views process as regressive. The *cyclical* model focuses and amplifies those process elements contributed by the indivdual member: behavior style; personal feeling state; internalized norms, beliefs, and values; and the ego of the individual. The cyclical model views process as a transcendence of polarities. These elements of process are discussed more fully by Banet (1974).

THE LINEAR MODEL

The group process is viewed by the linear model as an orderly, sequential, progressive movement over time, a straight-line function that passes through predictable phases or stages of growth, paralleling individual growth from conception to maturity. In the linear model, the group is a temporary, intentional community of workers or learners who have banded together to reach some goal. The community life of the group has a definite beginning, middle, and end.

The actual number of phases seen by linear theorists varies considerably, from two (Bennis & Shepherd, 1956) or three phases (Schutz, 1973; Kaplan & Roman, 1963) to ten (Cohen & Smith, 1976) to fifteen (Rogers, 1970). Despite this range of stages, theories embracing the linear model share many similarities. Two representative theories are discussed here: Schutz's theory of interpersonal needs (Schutz, 1967, 1973) and Tuckman's developmental sequence (Tuckman, 1965).

Schutz's Theory

For Schutz, the initial stage of development for the group is the *inclusion* phase. Major inclusion issues revolve around boundaries, building trust and commitment, determining who is a member and who is not, and maintaining individuality while simultaneously being a group member. Group members are motivated by fear, curiosity, excitement, and the need to include or to be included.

As inclusion issues become resolved, the group moves into a *control* phase, in which concerns of power, dominance, authority, and responsibility are prominent. Feelings of anger, helplessness, and incompetency motivate members to deal with personal power, the authority of the leader, and the influence of other group members. This middle phase is critical for all linear models—it is a period in which the group either disintegrates or becomes cohesive. It is a turning point in the life of the group; if the control phase is avoided, denied, or ignored, group development is retarded.

Following the middle phase is a concluding period of *affection*, cohesion, and intimacy. Major issues are (1) how close or how distant group members want to be with each other, (2) giving and receiving warmth, and (3) how much sharing and disclosure is productive and appropriate. When this phase moves toward conclusion, the life of the group begins to terminate. For Schutz, termination involves a reversal of the stages: affectional relations are ended first, then control relations, and finally inclusion.

Tuckman's Sequence

Having reviewed many theories, Tuckman (1965) postulates that the first stage of group life is one of *testing and dependence*. The group orients itself to group living, testing which behaviors are acceptable and which are taboo. Much attention is focused on the group leader, as group members grope to define their task and their boundaries.

Stage two is a period of *intragroup conflict*. Issues of power and competition dominate group life; the mood of the group is highly emotional and rebellious.

When conflict issues are settled, stage three—*group cohesion*—emerges. In the third stage of group life, openness, positive feedback, and expressions of affection are characteristic.

Stage four is described as a period of *functional role-relatedness*. It is a work stage, characterized by a minimum of emotional interaction. The atmosphere of the group encourages and supports task completion; obstacles have been removed in previous stages. When the group completes its task, it terminates.

Tuckman succinctly describes his four phases of group life as "forming, storming, norming, and performing."

Characteristics of the Linear Model

The group elements of process—the interpersonal communications network of the community of learners—are the focus of the linear model. While linear theories recognize that all group members may not be in the same psychological place at the same time, the theories assert that certain critical "barometric events" (Bennis & Shepherd, 1956) bring individual members to a similar awareness; thus, *in general*, the members of a group can be regarded as being in a given phase at a given time. The model implies that all groups, regardless of size or task, deal with the same issues in the same sequence.

The intervention style derived from the linear model emphasizes building awareness of the phases of development, amplifying issues specific to a given phase, and preventing premature movement. In fact, a major concern of interventionists using the linear model is that members will tend to deny the existence of the difficult middle phase (power, control, conflict) in their eagerness to get to a cohesive, affectionate state.

The linear model enjoys broad usage. Many theories describing task groups, social systems, and work teams incorporate the linear view; for Schutz, the phases are most visible in the encounter group (Schutz, 1973). In part, the popularity of the linear model is due to its compatibility with the usual way of regarding personality development: in many such theories, the individual passes through phases until maturity is reached. See, for example, Erikson (1963) and Kohlberg (1964).

Several shortcomings of the linear model should be noted. As Hare (1973) comments, the assumption that a group moves from phase to phase needs further documentation, since linear theorists typically do not discuss the *process* of development in any detail; rather, they simply observe that one phase follows another. The model does not clarify how this sequencing happens, nor does it explain why one group may remain in a given phase for six months, while another passes that stage in three weeks.

The linear model reflects a world view that is peculiar to Western culture. Referring to the linear model as a "staircase" model, Kahn et al. (1974) list some important consequences of viewing development as a progressive, ever-upward moving line: such an attitude suggests that permanence is the only good, and that the top of the line is the only spot worth attaining. As Kahn and his associates see it, the linear model encourages judgment and categorization, rather than acceptance and experiencing, and focuses a group on future events, rather than on the present. In short, the linear model suggests that the destination is more valuable and important than the journey to it.

Theories using the linear model receive a fuller discussion in Bennis and Shepherd (1956), Charrier (1974), Cohen and Smith (1976), Gibbard, Hartman, and Mann (1974), Hare (1973), Jones (1973), Kaplan and Roman (1963), Rogers (1970), Schutz (1973), and Tuckman (1965).

THE HELICAL MODEL

The helical model of group development views the group process as a regressive, spiraling, ever-deepening focus on a few prominent issues peculiar to a given group. The themes and issues worked in the group follow no particular order; once a theme is surfaced, however, it will develop in a fairly predictable pattern, from its surface aspect to its deepest level of significance. Group process moves in a whirlpool fashion; it gains momentum and suctional power as it burrows deeper and deeper.

The group is perceived as a metaphoric tribe which comes together to achieve security, physical safety, and support in times of stress. The group also provides members an opportunity to gain selfhood and significance (Klein, 1968).

At its inception, the group begins a regression away from its obvious, manifest level, down to its latent or hidden meaning. The group acquires allegorical and mythological meaning for its members (Dunphy, 1968); it may begin to recapitulate the dynamics of a primal horde (Ezriel, 1950), a primitive family, or a religious group. In other views, the group is seen as a microcosm (Slater, 1966), a re-enactment of the Oedipal conflict (Gibbard & Hartman, 1973), or the "good breast" of a nuturing mother (Scheidlinger, 1974). This regression to allegorical levels is encouraged by the structure of the group, especially the posture of the leader, in the belief that by reliving past events, a "corrective emotional experience" (Alexander, 1956) will occur, enabling the group and its members to gain a fresh perspective of self and to achieve perceptual and behavioral reorganization.

The group dwells in this regressive space for some period of time. Only after core issues such as dependency, autonomy, aggression, and sexuality are resolved does the group emerge from the depths of the whirlpool to work on present problems and solutions. During the regressive period, the group's process is erratic and disconnected, marked by conflict and motivated by strong, primitive emotionality. The group process re-enacts the turmoil and stress of childhood and adolescence: the flow is choppy and is frequently interrupted by new issues. In its regression, the group develops a cohesion (usually motivated by antagonism toward the leader) and takes on the characteristics of an organism that is in some ways greater than the sum of its parts.

Bion's Theory

Bion (1959) is the principal theorist of the helical model. His central notion is that in every group, two "groups" are actually present: the *work* group and the *basic-assumption* group. The work group is that aspect of group functioning that has to do with the real task of the group. For example, designing a program, passing a resolution, completing a report, or changing behavior are real tasks. But groups do not always function sensibly or productively—they do not always focus on the task. To explain why groups do not always work well, Bion introduced the notion of the basic-assumption group.

Basic assumption is an "as if" term. The group behaves *as if* a certain assumption is basic to its maintenance, growth, and survival. These basic assumptions are covert; they constitute the group's hidden agenda. The basic assumptions derive from the collective repressed feelings of all the group members.

From his experiences in groups, Bion identifies three distinct types of basic assumptions:

1. *Basic-assumption dependency.* The essential aim of this emotional state is to attain security and protection from one individual, usually the leader. The group behaves as if it is stupid, incompetent or psychotic; only a powerful, omniscient, God-like leader can perform the task functions. When the leader fails to meet the (impossible) demands of the group, it expresses its disappointment and hostility in a variety of ways.

2. *Basic-assumption fight-flight.* Here, the group assumes it can survive only if it flees from the task (by withdrawal, regression, or focusing on past history) or if it fights (by aggression, scapegoating, etc.). A leader who is accepted is one who is willing to afford the group an opportunity for flight or aggression.

3. *Basic-assumption pairing.* In this state the basic assumption is that the group has come together for reproductive purposes. Any bond between two or more group members is seen as a sexual bond that will give birth to a Messiah who will save the group by providing it with new life, new thoughts, and a creative way to work on the task. Magic is the solution that is hoped for.

Turquet (1974) has added a fourth type of basic assumption—*basic-assumption oneness*, in which the group seeks to join in a powerful union with an omnipotent force, unobtainably exalted, to surrender itself to passive participation, and thereby to feel " existence," well-being, and wholeness.

The basic-assumption life of the group is oriented inward toward fantasy, not outward toward reality. The basic assumptions are anonymous; they cannot be attributed to any one member. Individuals vary in their readiness (which Bion calls "valency") to combine with a given basic assumption of the group. Some members, as well as the leader, may find it easier to collude with dependency themes, others with flight reactions, etc.

The work group requires concentration, skill, and organization of all resources in the group, as well as cooperation from its members. The basic-assumption group, on the other hand, exists without effort. A group will stay locked into its basic assumptions until some resolution is reached that permits the group to move on to a work level. The basic-assumption life of the group is never exhausted, but it can be deliberately bracketed or suppressed.

An excellent introduction to Bion's theory is provided by Rioch (1970); Colman and Bexton (1975) present extensions and applications of the basic-assumption approach.

Characteristics of the Helical Model

Providing the theoretical basis for many kinds of psychotherapy groups, the helical model has as a major strength its thoroughness in dealing with difficult issues and its unwavering belief that "the child is father to the man." The model attempts to provide group members with an opportunity to reorganize their current personality patterns by correcting the errors of the past. Like the linear model, which avoids the present moment by focusing on the future, the helical model avoids the now, but by focusing on the past. It stresses the belief that the past has much to teach us; we cannot confidently move on until we have digested its lessons. As Santayana said, "Those who do not remember the mistakes of history are condemned to repeat them."

Additionally, the model provides the group with an opportunity to confront the uncomfortable realities of life: pain, suffering, tragedy, and death. Through its focus on history, the model counterbalances the optimism and the idea of progress implicit in the linear model.

The helical model prescribes a central role for the group leader, who functions in the group not as a person but as a role—a role that encourages projection and regression. The coolness and distance of the leader quickly elicit basic-assumption behavior. As the group intensifies, the leader interprets, confronts, and weaves connections between present behavior and past experience, in an effort to make the unconscious conscious.

The intervention stance of helical-model theories focuses on contextual aspects of group process. Past history, emotional relations outside the group, and the individual member's position in relation to authority, responsibility, and control provide the primary process data for the group's considerations.

The leader's central role is a critical shortcoming of helical-model theories. The leader seems constantly to be saying to the group, "I see something you don't see." This posture creates dependency on the perceptual accuracy of the leader and his skill in surfacing and working with unconscious material. This dependency carries the implication that group work is a long-term investment for the group member.

Personality theories that stress the importance of early childhood experience-—psychoanalysis, ego psychology, general psychodynamic theory, and transactional analysis—are compatible with the helical model of change.

Group theories using the helical model can be found in Bion (1959), Burrow (1928), Ezriel (1950), Foulkes and Anthony (1957), Gibbard and Hartman (1973), Saraway (1975), Scheidlinger (1974), Slater (1966), Slavson (1950), Whitaker and Lieberman (1967). For the most part, the psychotherapy group has provided the observational base for these theories.

THE CYCLICAL MODEL

The group process is in constant motion, never at rest, in the cyclical model. The process is continuous and persistent; like the phases of the moon and tides, the seasons, and other natural phenomena, the group life moves through a cycle until it returns, with subtle alterations, to its starting point.

In the cyclical model, the group is a collection of individuals who have gathered together to divine the principle of change that governs their lives and to discover a way to order their behavior in accordance with that principle. The group is less a community than it is a theater—an energy field where individual growth and change unfolds.

No current theory of group development directly defines the cyclical model of change. However, the cyclical model is implied in the practice of those groups that focus on personal, individual change within the group context. The model provides a basis for understanding the Gestalt group and other groups that stress intrapersonal learning.

Philosophical Aspects

Because the cyclical model is not as well known as the linear and helical models, a discussion of its philosophical aspects is provided here. We live in a world of permanent change, where all phenomena are dynamic and in flux. This observation dates back at least to 500 B.C., when Heraclitus in Greece and Confucius in China compared the constant movement of experience to the everchanging flow of a river.

The dynamism of experience has met different responses in Eastern and Western thought. Western thinkers have tended to abstract from experience, "freezing" phenomena so that they can be subjected to scientific investigation. Hence, change tends to be seen in a linear mode, a static progression from phase to phase.

In contrast, the Eastern mode has been to acknowledge the flow of experience and to search for the law of change, itself unchanging, which governs this flow. The name given to this governing principle is *Tao*. *Tao* is one; out of *Tao* comes the energy of yin, the receptive principle, and yang, the active principle. Change is viewed as natural movement and development, in accord with *Tao*. The opposite of change is regression; as H. Wilhelm (1960) puts it, "the opposite of change in Chinese thought is growth of what ought to decrease, the downfall of what ought to rule" (p. 18).

Tao defies definition, as Chung-yuan (1963) states: "The understanding of *Tao* is an inner experience in which distinction between subject and object vanishes. It is an intuitive, immediate awareness rather than a mediated, inferential or intellectual process" (p. 19). The *Tao* is the way, the ultimate principle, the great interfusion of being and nonbeing. Despite this ineffability, the yin/yang energy flowing from *Tao* has acquired highly practical embodiments in Chinese culture: acupuncture, T'ai Chi and other martial arts, centering, calligraphy—all are manifestations of and approaches to *Tao*.

The *I Ching*

Perhaps the most eloquent description of the interplay of yin/yang energy is in the ancient oracle and scripture, the *I Ching*. The *I Ching*, or Book of Changes, applies this concept of change to human phenomena—individual lives, groups, and organizations. It proposes a cyclical theory of change, change as a movement that returns to its starting point. Change is orderly, as is the movement of the tides or the seasons, but its orderliness is not always perceptible. In human situations, the forces of yin and yang produce complex configurations. As a book of wisdom, the *I Ching* invites its user to pursue *Tao*, a state of resonance with the Oneness of actuality (Dhiegh, 1974), by discovering the proper time for correct action.

The *I Ching* has as its basis the two fundamental principles of *yin*, characterized as the receptive and the docile and symbolized by the broken line (— —), and *yang*, characterized as the creative and active and symbolized by an unbroken line (————). In sets of three, the broken and unbroken lines compose the eight *pa kua* (trigrams), signs associated with natural phenomena and basic aspects of human experience.

Combined in all possible ways, the eight *pa kua* produce sixty-four six-line *kua* (hexagrams) which symbolize various elementary aspects of the human condition: primary needs, such as nourishment; personality-development milestones, such as breakthrough, pushing upward, or retreat; social situations, such as marriage, following, conflict; and individual character traits, such as modesty, grace, and enthusiasm. The sixty-four hexagrams comprise a psychological "periodic table of elements" from which immediate, here-and-now situations are composed.

The eight *pa kua* provide descriptions of the basic polarities of life:

1. Ch'ien (≡≡≡), the creative, heaven. The sign is associated with energy, strength, and excitement. It represents the pole of creative power.

2. K'un (≡≡ ≡≡), the receptive, earth, is associated with the womb, nourishment, the great wagon of the earth that carries all life. It represents the pole of yielding, docile receptivity.

3. Chen (≡≡ ≡), the arousing, thunder. It is associated with movement, speed, expansion, and anger. In terms of human polarities, the sign represents confrontation.

4. Sun (≡ ≡≡), the gentle, penetrating wind. It is associated with gentle persuasion, quiet decision making, and problem solving. The sign represents the pole of support.

5. K'an (≡≡≡), the abysmal, water. It is associated with toil, hard work, danger, perseverance, and melancholy. It represents the pole of body and feeling.

6. Li (≡≡≡), the clinging, fire. It is associated with dependency, but also with clarity and perception. It represents the pole of intellect and thought.

7. Ken (≡≡≡), keeping still, the mountain. It is associated with fidelity, meditation, watchfulness. It represents the pole of reflective silence.

8. T'ui (≡≡≡), the joyous, lake. The sign is associated with the pleasures of the mouth —eating, talking, singing. It represents the pole of joyful interaction.

The eight pa kua are arranged in a circle of polar opposites known as the "primal arrangement," or the "mandala of earlier heaven." (See Figure 1.)

Implications for a Theory of Group Process

The philosophy of *Tao* and the forces of yin and yang as presented in the *I Ching* have implications for a theory of group process.

1. The group can be viewed as an energy field demarcated by the basic polarities, as in Figure 1. In each member, and in the group as a whole, there is tension between the apparent choices of creative-receptive, confrontation-support, intellect-feeling, and interaction-silence.

2. Initially, group members attempt to deal with their process by adhering to polar positions. This is an attempt to "freeze" movement, deny change, or place values on the respective polar opposites.

3. Group process proceeds as the group develops awareness of its polarized situation. This awareness leads to a struggle to find creative ways to resolve the interplay of yin and yang forces. Paradoxically, this creative struggle develops two new aspects of group life: the appreciation of the now, and the potential to transcend the polarized field of apparent opposites.

4. The group process is analogous to a roller-coaster ride (Kahn et al., 1974). Energy waxes and wanes; it never stops. The process goes up and down; moments of group life are different from

one another, but not better or worse, immature or more mature. As Kahn et al. (1974) suggest, "at any given moment things are as good and important and worth attending to as they are ever going to be. [The model] urges us to attend to the here-and-now because no future here-and-now is going to be any better, just different" (pp. 43-44). Focus on the now (now-consciousness) is the dynamic unification of past and future in the present moment (Dhiegh, 1974).

5. The group members, by focusing on the now, begin to test synergistic strategies to deal with the apparent polar opposites. Synergy, as defined by Hampden-Turner (1970), refers to "a state of mutual enhancement" between two opposites, an affective and intellectual synthesis that is greater than the sum of its parts.

Synergy allows the group and its members to free themselves from either/or thinking. Synergy is neither compromise nor striving for a "golden mean"; it is a creative combination (conception of a human being from egg and sperm is the highest form of synergy) of opposites to produce something new. Synergy, in the words of Harris (1972), involves grasping a paradox and holding it in creative tension.

6. Groups are unique and idiosyncratic. Each group presents opportunities for growth. Polarities, which are critical issues for some groups or some group members, are nonissues for others. Resolutions or synergistic combinations of polarities will vary from person to person, from group to group.

The cycle of group process follows this course: (1) a struggle to deny change by clinging to polarities, resolved by (2) appreciation of the now and the discovery of the governing principle of change, allowing (3) attempts at synergy to transcend or mutually enhance the polar opposites, followed by (4) the product of the synergy becoming a new pole, awaiting a new struggle to "freeze" change, thereby completing the cycle. The cycle is a dialectic process, subtly changing while remaining much the same.

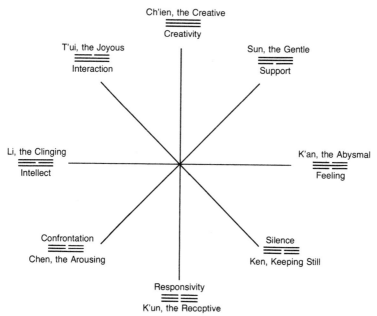

Figure 1. The _Pa Kua_ Arranged as Basic Polarities, the "Primal Arrangement," or the "Mandala of Earlier Heaven"

Characteristics of the Cyclical Model

The intervention stance of the cyclical model focuses on individual-member elements. The major strategy is to amplify minute physical or verbal events so that an appreciation of now and an awareness of polarity can occur. It focuses on the individual's cycle of "becoming, begetting, begoning" (Dhiegh, 1974); as in a theater, only one member or a small cluster of members "perform" at a given time.

The model links human events with other natural phenomena and teaches the ancient philosophy of *Tao*, which aims for personal centeredness and integrity in a world of turmoil and conflict. Central to the cyclical model derived from *I Ching* is the idea that man is in the center of events: it is the individual's responsibility to know the direction of cosmic change and to move in the direction of change, not against it (H. Wilhelm, 1960). The intervention stance reflects this: the group leader provides a constant focus on the individual's responsibility to "own" his change process.

Discussion of the cyclical model of change can be found in Dhiegh (1973, 1974), Fuller (1975), Kahn et al. (1974), and H. Wilhelm (1960). Personality-development theories that imply a cyclical model of change are presented by Allport (1955), Hampden-Turner (1971), and Polster and Polster (1973).

TOWARD INTEGRATION

Cardinal aspects of the three models of change are summarized in Table 1. The models and theories that contain them are attempts to understand what happens in human groups. The observational bases of the models differ. (The table provides an illustration of the old Sufi story of the blind men and the elephant. Each man touched a different part of the beast and concluded that the elephant was like a rug, or a hose, or a pillar.) Questions arise: Can there be one theory of group process? Is integration possible? How can the group practitioner use this abundance of theoretical formulation?

As one option, an integrated theory would offer several benefits. Reducing the profusion of terms would heighten conceptual clarity; a comprehensive view would enable a group to capitalize on all or most of the data it produces. Sharing of techniques derived from different theories would broaden and enrich the practitioner's intervention repertoire.

Some solid attempts at integration have been made. Schutz, although espousing a linear model, has incorporated some cyclical aspects in his interpersonal-needs approach: as a group concludes its movement through stages of inclusion, control, and affection, it recycles and begins working the same issues, but on a different level of intensity and meaning (Schutz, 1973). Kaplan and Roman (1963) postulate that a helical regression occurs before a group enters its linear phases of dependency, power, and intimacy. Bennis and Shepherd (1956) employ a synergistic union of polarities in their initial authority-relations phase, in which dependence and counterdependence themes collide, to be resolved by the emergence of an independence theme. Butkovich and his associates (1975) report a combination of approaches derived from the linear and helical models to understand T-groups and Tavistock groups.

These partial integrations have proved useful in group work, providing insights for the understanding of group phenomena. They do not account sufficiently for the influence of the individual on the group process. Linear and helical models deal primarily with the group; the cyclical model, with the individual. That hybrid creature, the individual-in-the-group, provides the central dilemma for an integrated model.

Eclecticism, a time-honored system in the practical arts, provides another option. Most of us live with a pastiche of conflicting viewpoints and choose, as the situation demands, the one that seems most useful at the moment. We may believe, on an intellectual level, that a chair is a moving collection of molecules, but we expect it to be solid when we sit down. Alas, the theory that simultaneously meets the needs of our head and our behind is a rarity indeed.

178

Table 1. A Summary of the Characteristics of the Linear, Helical, and Cyclical Models of Change

GROUP MODEL

Characteristic	Linear	Helical	Cyclical
Group Movement	Progressive	Regressive	Cyclical
Group Metaphor	Community	Tribe	Theater
Time Focus	Future	Past	Now
Goal	Completion	Corrective Emotional Experience	Synergy
Tension Source	Desire to Improve	Desire to Understand	Desire to Transcend
Intervention Focus	Group Elements	Contextual Elements	Individual Elements
Observation Base	Interpersonal	Historical	Intrapersonal
Representative Theory	Schutz	Bion	*I Ching*
Personality Theory Correlated with Model	Erickson	Freud	Hampden-Turner
Strength	Easy to Understand	Comprehensive	Nature-Based
Drawback	Static	Dependency on Group Leader	Paradoxical
Usual Application	Encounter Groups, Task Groups, Social Systems	Many Psychotherapy Groups	Gestalt Groups, Personal Growth Groups

Eclecticism permits the practitioner to respond to a critical incident in the group by reviewing the objectives of the group and the needs of the members and then selecting the intervention from a theory base that seems most productive for learning. The eclectic stance permits the practitioner to shape his own theory and allows the leader to be present both as a person and a role.

A possible, unfortunate side effect of an eclectic approach is a choppy, uneven flow in the group process. Groups seen through a Tavistock viewpoint in one session, a Gestalt in a second, and an interpersonal-needs theory in the third session can become confused and unproductive.

Scaffold for an Integrated Theory

The following propositions sketch the elements of an integrated model and constitute a first attempt to collate the salient features of several theories. The propositions have as a data base the author's observations of phenomena in psychotherapy, growth, and task groups, as well as the observations and findings of other investigators of group behavior.

The integrated model posits a series of dialectic confrontations, which occur within group members and within the group as a whole. The dialectic consists of interplay between the constructs of yin and yang, viewed as energies in polar opposition to the potential for synergistic fusion.[1] The series of polar confrontations occurs within phases, similar to those described by Tuckman (1965) as "forming, storming, norming, performing." These phases repeat themselves, in a spiraling fashion, until some degree of wholeness or integration is reached, or until the group artificially terminates or abandons its task.

The ancient Chinese scripture *The Secret of the Golden Flower* (R. Wilhelm, 1962) describes a similar intrapersonal dialectic as an individual moves toward enlightenment. This text and Jung's commentary detail a circular movement in which the union of opposites occurs repeatedly until a higher state of consciousness is reached. The cyclical movement continues until all disparate body and human events are integrated (by transcendence or death) into the oneness of *Tao*.[2]

In this integrated model, the confrontation of polarities occurring within individuals is seen as impacting the group constellation as well. The group is not only a theater in which individuals struggle to deal with change; it is also an event in itself that develops and attempts to integrate its energy sources.

The group, as its etymology indicates, is a knot composed of many threads, stronger and more complex than its components.

Appended to the group-process propositions are references to *I Ching kua* that illuminate the dynamics of a particular phase. The *I Ching* serves remarkably well as a guidebook for both the group leader and the group members as they collectively pursue their task. The richness of the *I Ching*'s wisdom applied to group work can only be suggested here, but the text of the eighth *kua*, "Holding Together," may serve to illustrate the advice it offers for beginning groups.

> 8. Pi: Holding Together (Union)
> *The Judgment*
> Holding together brings good fortune
> Inquire of the oracle once again
> Whether you possess sublimity
>   constancy and perseverance;
> Then there is no blame.
> Those who are uncertain gradually join.
> Whoever comes too late
> Meets with misfortune.
>
> What is required is that we unite with others, in order that all may complement and aid one another through holding together. But such holding together calls for a central figure around whom other persons may unite. To become a center of influence holding people together is a grave matter and fraught with grave responsibility. It requires greatness of spirit, consistency and strength. Therefore, let him who wishes to gather others about him ask himself whether he is equal to the undertaking, for anyone attempting the task without a real calling for it only makes confusion worse than if no union at all had taken place.
>
> But when there is a real rallying point, those who at first are hesitant or uncertain gradually come in of their own accord. Late-comers must suffer the consequences, for in holding together the question of the right time is also important. Relationships are formed and firmly established according to definite inner laws. Common experiences strengthen these ties, and he who comes too late to share in these basic experiences must suffer for it. (R. Wilhelm, 1950, p. 36)

Basic Premises of an Integrated Theory

Following are the premises on which this integrated theory is based.

1. Change happens naturally. Change is the interplay of yin and yang energy and not the result of frustration, conflict, disequilibrium, or a search for homeostasis; change simply is.

---

[1]The term "contrapletion," which expresses both the polar opposition and the capacity of the poles to complement or fulfill each other, can be used to describe the yin/yang relationship.

[2]A Western description of polar opposites that define certain personality types can be found in the poet Yeats's *A Vision* (1956). For a brilliant discussion of polar forces operating in society and history, see Thompson's *At the Edge of History* (1972).

2. The group provides a setting for focused and accelerated change. Groups exist to facilitate, intensify, and enrich the change process.

3. The primary task of any group is to respond creatively to change.

4. The energy of individual members and of the group is distributed as yin and yang forces.

   a. *Yin* forces take the form of passivity, docility, receptivity, and simplicity. The yin posture of individuals and of groups is one of waiting to be acted upon, yielding, and accepting.

   b. *Yang* forces take the form of activity, creativity, excitement, and firmness. The yang posture of individuals and groups is one of acting, confronting, and inviting.

5. Every group presents a unique constellation of yin and yang forces, a composite contributed by all group members, including the leader.

Propositions Regarding Group Process

The kaleidoscope provides an image of group process. As yin/yang forces begin to interface, they move subtly and delicately, providing a constant movement through phases. The phases, or movements, are named for appropriate hexagrams from the *I Ching;* each is demarcated by the basic polarities of the mandala of earlier heaven. (See Figure 1.) The sets of polar opposites "govern" a given movement: that is, a given set epitomizes the polar opposition of a given movement.

Initial Movement: *Gathering Together*

The movement is governed by the creative/receptive polarity. The group perceives yang forces residing in the group leader, yin forces residing within itself. The group acclimates itself to its setting; feelings involved are excitement, apprehension, and confusion. The immediate task for the group is developing an awareness and appreciation of the collective situation.

This initial period finds representation in most theories of group development. It involves a basic orientation toward the group situation, a settling in. Major issues revolve around defining self, defining the task, and defining the function of the group and the leader. The movement concludes when there is general agreement that change is in fact possible in the group, whether it is changing behavior, making a decision, or solving a problem.

Kua that illuminate this phase include the following: 1. The Creative; 2. The Receptive; 3. Difficulty at the Beginning; 8. Holding Together; 10. Conduct; 17. Following; 31. Influence; 42. Increase; 45. Gathering Together; and 48. The Well.

Second Movement: *Standstill*

The movement is governed by the thinking/feeling polarity. The awareness of the possibility of change, begun in the initial phase, is now met by a denial of the possibility of and need for change. Group members adhere to one or another polar opposite, dichotomize their options, and develop an either/or mentality. Splits between thinking and feeling, between body and mind are fixated. The feeling level is marked by a clinging dependency on old ways and a resistance to accept the dangers that work and change involve.

This polarizing effect of early group interaction is documented in the work of Myers and Lamm (1975). After some initial effort to alter previously held positions, group members revert to their previous, pre-group stance and fight to maintain it. This phenomenon, variously described as regression or resistance, seems to occur when the group is perceived as an arena wherein bedrock values, beliefs, and worldviews can be challenged.

In the standstill phase occur many of the regressive phenomena described by Bion as the "basic-assumption" group. The movement is marked by tension and working; it begins to change into the following movement when an issue that is of magnitude and moment for most group members emerges.

Kua associated with this phase are the following: 6. Conflict; 12. Standstill; 13. Fellowship with Men; 19. Approach; 29. The Abysmal; 30. The Clinging, Fire; 35. Progress; 44. Coming to Meet; 46. Pushing Upward; and 49. Revolution.

Third Movement: *Biting Through*

The kaleidoscope continues. The third movement is governed by the confrontation/support polarity. Group members develop a greater awareness of possibilities for change. There is a heightened arousal of feeling and a greater need for nourishment. Letting go of polar positions releases power and energy, motivating the group to attempt to grasp the paradox that mutual enhancement of apparent opposites can occur. The group struggles to redistribute yin/yang forces; members impact the leader; the leader impacts the group.

This movement is marked by the emergence of a "both/and" attitude, which replaces "either/or" thinking. Power and authority are seen as residing both in the group and in its members. It is the central period in many theories of group development. When the smoke clears and new learnings (insights, solutions) are apparent, the movement concludes and enters the fourth period.

Kua that illuminate this phase are the following: 6. Conflict; 16. Enthusiasm; 21. Biting Through; 23. Splitting Apart; 33. Retreat; 38. Opposition; 34. Obstruction; 41. Decrease; 51. The Arousing; 57. The Gentle; and 28. Preponderance of the Great.

Fourth Movement: *The Taming Power of the Great*

The movement is governed by the interaction/silence polarity. The group creatively achieves a degree of synergistic fusion. The feelings are focused on enjoyment of the new and the now. Reflective, meditative, incorporating silence coexists with playful and pleasurable interaction with others. The task seems completed; needs are for closure, repose, quiet.

This movement is marked by integration and celebration. Much work is accomplished; previously difficult issues are simply and easily resolved. There are attempts to "freeze" change; a group may end its work here. As it develops awareness that its apparent terminal point also offers the possibility for a new beginning, the group fades into its fifth movement.

Kua associated with this phase are the following: 11. Peace; 20. Contemplation; 26. The Taming of the Great; 27. Nourishment; 32. Duration; 37. The Family; 40. Deliverance; 50. The Caldron; 52. Keeping Still; 58. The Joyous; 61. Inner Truth; and 63. After Completion.

Fifth Movement: *Return*

The circulation is finished, temporarily; the group is at a new starting point. The kaleidoscope is rearranged; new polarities, the recently gained synergistic fusions, provide a field for new beginnings and greater closeness to *Tao*. The cycle spirals onward.

Kua associated with this phase are the following: 24. Return; 34. The Power of the Great; 43. Breakthrough; 49. Dispersion; and 64. Before Completion.

CONCLUSION

This theory is presented to be studied, tested, and then thrown away. As Kahn and his colleagues (1974) observe, theory itself is part of the flow of change: "Even as we grasp it and write it down, it becomes inadequate, melting away" (p. 51).

182

Another Sufi story (Shah, 1972) provides a conclusion. Four persons were given a piece of money. The first was a Persian, who said, "I will use the money to buy *Angur.*" The second was an Arab, who said, "No, because I want *Inab.*" The third was a Turk, who said, "I do not want *Inab,* I want *Uzum.*" The fourth was a Greek. He said, "I want *Stafil.*" Because these four had information but no knowledge, they started to fight.

One person of wisdom present could have reconciled them all by saying, "I can fulfill the needs of all of you, with one and the same piece of money. If you honestly give me your trust, your one coin will become as four, and four at odds will become as one united."

Such a person would know that each in his own language wanted the same thing: grapes.

REFERENCES

Alexander, F. *Psychoanalysis and psychotherapy.* New York: Norton, 1956.

Allport, G. W. *Becoming: Basic consideration for a psychology of personality.* New Haven: Yale University Press, 1955.

Banet, A. G., Jr. Therapeutic intervention and the perception of process. In J. W. Pfeiffer & J. E. Jones (Eds.), *The 1974 annual handbook for group facilitators.* La Jolla, Calif.: University Associates, 1974.

Bennis, W. G., & Shepherd, H. A. A theory of group development. *Human Relations,* 1956, *9,* 415-457.

Bion, W. R. *Experiences in groups.* New York: Basic Books, 1959.

Burrow, T. The basis of group analysis. *British Journal of Medical Psychology,* 1928, *8,* 198-206.

Butkovich, P., Carlisle, J., Duncan, R., & Moss, M. Social system and psychoanalytic approaches to group dynamics: Complementary or contradictory? *International Journal of Group Psychotherapy,* 1975, *25,* 3-31.

Charrier, G. O. Cog's ladder: A model of group development. In J. W. Pfeiffer & J. E. Jones (Eds.), *The 1974 annual handbook for group facilitators.* La Jolla, Calif.: University Associates, 1974.

Chung-yuan, C. *Creativity and Taoism: A study of Chinese philosophy, art and poetry.* New York: Julian Press, 1963.

Cohen, A. M., & Smith, R. D. *The critical incident in growth groups: Theory and technique.* La Jolla, Calif.: University Associates, 1976.

Colman, A. D., & Bexton, W. H. (Eds.). *Group relations reader.* Sausalito, Calif.: GREX, 1975.

Dhiegh, K. A. *The eleventh wing: An exposition of the dynamics of* I Ching *for now.* Los Angeles: Nash, 1973.

Dhiegh, K. A. *I Ching: Taoist book of days,* 1975. Berkeley, Calif.: Shambhala, 1974.

Dunphy, D. C. Phases, roles and myths in self-analytic groups. *The Journal of Applied Behavioral Science,* 1968, *4,* 195-226.

Erikson, E. H. *Childhood and society* (2nd ed.). New York: Norton, 1963.

Ezriel, H. A psycho-analytic approach to group treatment. *British Journal of Medical Psychology,* 1950, *23,* 59-74.

Feldman, R. A., & Wodarski, J. S. *Contemporary approaches to group treatment.* San Francisco: Jossey-Bass, 1975.

Foulkes, S. H., & Anthony, E. J. *Group psychotherapy, the psycho-analytic approach.* Baltimore: Penguin Books, 1957.

Fuller, B. *Synergetics: Explorations in the geometry of thinking.* New York: Macmillan, 1975.

Gibbard, G. S., & Hartman, J. J. The oedipal paradigm in group development: A clinical and empirical study. *Small Group Behavior,* 1973, *4,* 305-354.

Gibbard, G. S., Hartman, J. J., & Mann, R. D. (Eds.). *Analysis of groups.* San Francisco: Jossey-Bass, 1974.

Hampden-Turner, C. *Radical man: The process of psycho-social development.* Cambridge: Schenkman, 1970.

Hare, A. P. Theories of group development and categories for interaction analysis. *Small Group Behavior,* 1973, *4,* 259-304.

Harris, S. J. *The authentic person: Dealing with dilemma.* Niles, Ill.: Argus, 1972.

Hill, W. F., & Grunes, L. A study of development in open and closed groups. *Small Group Behavior,* 1973, *4,* 355-381.

Jones, J. E. A model of group development. In J. E. Jones & J. W. Pfeiffer (Eds.), *The 1973 annual handbook for group facilitators.* La Jolla, Calif.: University Associates, 1973.

Kahn, M., Kroeber, T., & Kingsbury, S. The *I Ching* as a model for a personal growth workshop. *The Journal of Humanistic Psychology,* 1974, *14,* 39-51.

Kaplan, S., & Roman, M. Phases of development in an adult therapy group. *International Journal of Group Psychotherapy,* 1963, *13,* 10-26.

Klein, D. C. *Community dynamics and mental health.* New York: John Wiley, 1968.

Kohlberg, L. Development of moral character and ideology. In M. L. Hoffman (Ed.), *Review of child development research.* New York: Russell Sage, 1964.

Lundgren, D. C. Trainer style and patterns of group development. *Journal of Applied Behavioral Science,* 1971, *7,* 689-709.

Myers, D. G., & Lamm, H. The polarizing effect of group discussion. *American Scientist,* 1975, *63,* 297-303.

Polster, E., & Polster, M. *Gestalt therapy integrated: Contours of theory and practice.* New York: Vintage Books, 1973.

Rioch, M. The work of Wilfred Bion on groups. *Psychiatry,* 1970, *33,* 56-66.

Rogers, C. R. *Carl Rogers on encounter groups.* New York: Harper & Row, 1970.

Saravay, S. M. Group psychology and the structural model: A revised psychoanalytic model of group psychology. *Journal of the American Psychoanalytic Association*, 1975, 23, 69-89.

Scheidlinger, S. On the concept of the "mother-group." *International Journal of Group Psychotherapy*, 1974, 24, 417-428.

Schutz, W. C. *Joy: Expanding human awareness*. New York: Grove Press, 1967.

Schutz, W. C. *Elements of encounter*. Big Sur: Joy Press, 1973.

Shah, I. *Caravan of dreams*. Baltimore: Penguin Books, 1972.

Slater, P. E. *Microcosm: Structural, psychological and religious evolution in groups*. New York: John Wiley, 1966.

Slavson, S. R. *Analytic group psychotherapy*. New York: Columbia University Press, 1950.

Thompson, W. I. *At the edge of history: Speculations on the transformation of culture*. New York: Harper Colophon, 1972.

Tuckman, B. W. Developmental sequence in small groups. *Psychological Bulletin*, 1965, 63, 384-399.

Turquet, P. M. Leadership: The individual and the group. In G. S. Gibbard, J. J. Hartman, & R. D. Mann (Eds.), *Analysis of groups*. San Francisco: Jossey-Bass, 1974.

Whitaker, D. S., & Lieberman, M. A. *Psychotherapy through the group process*. New York: Atherton Press, 1967.

Wilhelm, H. *Change: Eight lectures on the I Ching*. Princeton, N.J.: Princeton University Press, 1960.

Wilhelm, R. (Trans.) *The I Ching* (3rd ed.). Princeton, N.J.: Princeton University Press, 1950.

Wilhelm, R. (Trans.) *The secret of the golden flower*. New York: Harcourt Brace Jovanovich, 1962.

Yeats, W. B. *A vision*. New York: Macmillan, 1956.

Anthony G. Banet, Jr., Ph.D., *is a senior consultant with University Associates, La Jolla, California. He is a clinical psychologist with experience in community mental health and has consulted with numerous public service agencies. Dr. Banet is also the editor of* Creative Psychotherapy: A Source Book.

WORKING WITH COUPLES: SOME BASIC CONSIDERATIONS

Herbert A. Otto

The observations of colleagues and group facilitators make it clear that over the past decade there has been a marked increase in the number of couples who have participated in group experiences. This phenomenon is apparent not only in marriage- and family-enrichment groups, but also in other types of growth groups. The presence of a couple or couples in a group composed of singles, or of people whose spouses are not in attendance, inevitably presents unique problems to the group facilitator. A very different set of conditions and considerations faces the facilitator interested in working with marriage- and family-enrichment groups.

COUPLES IN A GROWTH GROUP

In most growth groups the presence of a couple is noticed by participants almost immediately, and it produces certain expectations. For example: "Are you two going to defend each other if one of you is confronted by the group?"; (if several couples are present) "Are the couples going to form a subgroup within our group?"; "Are couple-related issues going to take up a lot of our time?"; "Are we going to have to play the role of mediator and counselor to you two or between couples?" A very prevalent, usually unexpressed fear is "Are we going to have a fight (between the two members of a couple) on our hands?"

If the facilitator is committed to the presence of a couple (or couples) in a group, *making such expectations of group members explicit is one of the most productive ways of handling this situation.* The following question addressed to the group is useful: "As you know we have a couple (or couples) in our group. What are some of our expectations? What are some of the things we believe may happen and how do we feel about this?"

The "Third Person"

It should be clear to the facilitator that a couple enrolled in a growth group confronts him with the presence of a "third person." This third person is the couple's relationship. In the course of a growth group session, the couple very often will make a bid to have the group work on their relationship or the facilitator will be aware that there is a need to do so. It also often happens that in growth groups the subject of a couple's relationship is inadvertently opened up or becomes the target of a direct inquiry by a participant.

Working with a couple's relationship usually involves a considerable investment of time, energy, and skill. In many, if not most, instances, the couple's unique, individual relationship problem may be only peripherally related—or totally unrelated—to the stated aims and purposes of the group. If this is the case, group members usually resent the considerable investment of time necessary to help a couple.

Dealing with the "Third Person"

Other than asking one member of the couple to leave and enroll in a subsequent growth group, a number of approaches for handling the presence of the "third person" in a group can be suggested.

1. The couple could be separated, each working in a different growth group.

2. The facilitator could meet with the couple in the initial phase of the group's life and make it clear that the aims and purposes of the group do not include working on their relationship.

3. The facilitator could point out to a couple—*at the time the couple makes a bid for help*—that the aims and purposes of the group preclude work on relationship-related problems and issues.

Alternative 2 can be very effective. A preliminary meeting with the couple not only establishes limits and outlines parameters of group function, but it also helps to clarify the couple's expectations. At such time, a couple with severe problems may elect to stay with the growth group and its stated purposes, while making a decision *not* to work in the area of their relationship. Other sources of help can be explored at this time. Thus, the growth group facilitator needs to be clearly aware of the community resources available for counseling help and for marital or family therapy.

The preliminary meeting with a couple also serves as a rough "screen." At times a couple will come to a growth group as a last resort before initiating divorce proceedings. ("We tried everything else—we thought we would try a group before we broke up.") In such instances, the stated purposes of the group may be at considerable variance with the couple's needs, a situation that can then be clarified. However, despite a preliminary meeting and a decision not to work in the area of their relationship, some couples, in the course of group interaction, are drawn into this area. They should then, because of the preliminary meeting, be more able to accept redirection by the facilitator.

Other Areas of Difficulty

Two additional areas of difficulty are frequently associated with a couple's presence in a growth group. The members of a couple appear to inhibit each other and at times even to block each other. They have difficulty communicating openly in each other's presence and in staying in the here-and-now. There is a strong tendency to dwell on past agendas, hurts, traumas, and conflicts. It has also repeatedly been observed that when one member of a couple in a group is at the point of making significant gains in growth or self-realization, the spouse will initiate "diversionary tactics" designed to block potential growth. It would appear that the possibility of personal growth on the part of one spouse is often experienced as threatening by the other, who then makes a move to maintain the status quo. For these and other reasons, it is preferable to separate couples in a growth group.

MARRIAGE-ENRICHMENT AND FAMILY-ENRICHMENT GROUPS

The marriage- and family-enrichment field had its beginnings in the early and mid 1960's, when the first such groups were conducted. One of the major forces in the field is the Roman Catholic Marriage Encounter program, begun in 1967 (Bosco, 1973). It is estimated that by the end of 1975 over half a million couples have attended marriage-enrichment workshops or classes. This is a burgeoning movement. Most of the major religious denominations are active in the field, including program development, leadership training, and the sponsorship of workshops and classes through local churches. Many independent professionals are also entering the field and conducting programs.

In a recent study of marriage- and family-enrichment programs in the United States (Otto, 1975c), the following definition was used:

> *Marriage Enrichment Programs* are for couples who have what they perceive to be a fairly well functioning marriage and who wish to make their marriage even more mutually satisfying. The programs are *not* designed for people whose marriage is at a point of crisis, or who are seeking counseling help for marital problems. Marriage

enrichment programs are generally concerned with enhancing the couple's communication, emotional life, or sexual relationship, fostering marriage strengths, and developing marriage potential while maintaining a consistent and primary focus on the relationship of the couple. (p. 137)

To distinguish the two programs—marriage-enrichment and family-enrichment—the following definition of family-enrichment programs is offered:

Family Enrichment Programs are for parents who have what they perceive to be a fairly well functioning family and who wish to make their family life function even better. The programs are *not* designed for people whose family relationship is at a point of crisis or who are seeking counseling help with family problems. Family-enrichment programs are generally concerned with enhancing the family's communication and emotional life, the parents' sexual relationship and childrearing practices as well as parent/child relationships; and with fostering family strengths and the development of family potential while actively involving the children as an ongoing part of the program. (Otto, 1975c, p. 138)

The majority of family-enrichment programs actively involve the children in much of the experience. A need exists to develop more such programs, since professionals currently seem to prefer conducting marriage-enrichment programs.

Almost all enrichment programs are lead by husband-wife facilitator teams, with a high proportion of professionals. Some programs have extensive training sessions and some forms of certification for lay leaders. For the most part, marriage- and family-enrichment workshops are conducted on weekends, "away from home," in centers or motels. Fees vary, ranging from $10 or $20 per couple to $75 and up.

Both marriage- and family-enrichment programs are currently being offered in many localities. For the most part, marriage-enrichment programs are eclectic and individualistic, drawing on diverse sources and borrowing from each other freely. Contemporary programs can be ranged on a continuum, using the amount of structure built into the program as the main variable. On one end of the continuum would be the Roman Catholic Marriage Encounter program, where there is a maximum of structure, with group interaction restricted to feedback. At the other end of the continuum would be programs utilizing mostly or entirely "sensitivity" or "encounter" sessions. The vast majority of contemporary marriage- and family-enrichment programs are characterized by a considerable amount of structure.

One outgrowth of the movement is the Association of Couples for Marriage Enrichment or ACME (Mace, 1974). This is a national organization founded by the internationally known marriage counselors and pioneers, Dr. David and Vera Mace. ACME has local chapters of couples in many communities. The purpose of the organization is to foster marriage enrichment by couples on an ongoing basis, using local chapters as support groups.

Program Development: Marriage and Family Enrichment

A resource book that surveys the field, describing in detail over twenty program models, is now available (Otto, 1976). There are certain basic considerations in planning programs for couples.

1. It is well to give couples an opportunity to identify individual needs early in the program so that they can move in the direction of meeting these needs.

2. Many, if not most, of the couples attending can profit from work in the areas of communication, including nonverbal communication and listening (Miller et al., 1975). Use of sensory and nonverbal experiences (Otto, 1975b) in this connection is very helpful.

3. It is highly desirable to help couples develop strength-centered attitudes and become aware of each other's personality strengths and resources, as well as marriage and family strengths and potential (Otto, 1969, 1975f).

4. Two other critical areas for couples are creative problem solving (Klemer, 1970) and creative conflict resolution (Bach & Bernhard, 1971).

5. Masters and Johnson and other sexologists have repeatedly said that over half of all marriages suffer from problems of sexual adjustment (Masters & Johnson, 1970). Work in the area of sexual functioning is therefore strongly indicated.

6. Couples need to be given free time and privacy, as well as dyad work and work in the total group in order to maximize growth and learning.

Additional Considerations

If a program of marriage- and family-enrichment classes is to be planned, there are certain additional considerations. First, it is essential that classes be conducted for a minimum of two hours (two-and-a-half hours preferred) with a short break in the middle. If participants set aside an additional half hour for social togetherness or refreshments following the class (without the presence of the facilitator), much gets worked through informally at these post-class sessions. (If the facilitator is present, there is a tendency for participants to single him out to obtain personal counseling or guidance.)

In order to intensify the class experience, "outside assignments" are recommended. These are tasks for couples to complete (usually self-assigned), also called "Action Programs" (Otto, 1975b). Thus the life space outside of the class is effectively utilized for enrichment purposes.

Action programs can also be used in family-enrichment classes that involve children. Since the ages of children attending such programs vary considerably, it is best to have additional room space available. This enables smaller children with a shorter attention span to utilize a playroom from time to time. Also, arrangements can be made for infants or very small children so that parents will have periods of uninterrupted class time.

Homogeneity, Heterogeneity, and Other Issues

Having tried both homogeneous and heterogeneous groups over a number of years, my preference is for heterogeneous groups that include older couples as well as younger, recently married couples. Different age groups have something to contribute to each other. This is less true in the case of couples with teen-age marriages (which are usually beset with problems) and in cases where strong feelings toward authority and the older generation are present.

On occasion, only one member of a couple will come for a marriage-enrichment weekend. This situation makes for a certain awkwardness and difficulty, especially during dyad experiences. If the facilitator discusses this with the participant prior to the group experience and helps group members to clarify their feelings about the presence of a single spouse, this person will usually have a productive weekend experience. The basic premise here is that if one member of a couple changes and grows as a result of the enrichment group, growth can also be triggered in the absent member.

Ancillary Aids

If used appropriately during the life of a group or enrichment group or class, ancillary aids can contribute considerably to the effectiveness of the program. For example, during marriage- and family-enrichment programs to help participants work through their feelings of aggression and hostility, I use Encounter Bats.[1] These are canvas-covered bats that are safe and make a satisfyingly loud "whomp" when they make contact. After being introduced to them, many families purchase and use Encounter Bats at home to work out their feelings.

---

[1]Available from the National Center for the Exploration of Human Potential, 1975.

An effective instrument to foster and enhance open communication is the Now Communication Game[2] for use both at home and in marriage- and family-enrichment groups. The "game"—in reality a chart designed to help convey these communication needs to others—often triggers positive and growth-enhancing interaction between group members. The Sex Communication Game[2] can also be displayed and made available to enrichment-group members near the end of the workshop after the group has worked in the area of sexual enrichment. This instrument helps couples communicate their sexual desires and needs more openly. Finally, the Awareness Communication Chart[2] can be used both in growth groups and enrichment groups. The chart is designed to help group members become aware of and express individual needs and to encourage the fulfillment of these needs during the life of the group. This extensively tested chart is a very effective aid that adds new dimensions to the group experience.

TRAINING FOR AN EMERGENT NEW FIELD

Training programs for facilitators of marriage- and family-enrichment programs are already being conducted by some of the larger organizations in the field, such as the Association of Couples for Marriage Enrichment, and the Minnesota Couples Communication Program, and others. Training involves acquiring skills in group facilitation as well as skills in conducting the particular set of experiences and exercises that compose the program. A background in group counseling, group psychotherapy, or group counseling or therapy with couples and families is helpful. A number of colleges and universities are currently offering such classes and training courses. Fourteen national organizations active in the field of marriage and family enrichment have formed the Council of Affiliated Marriage Enrichment Organizations, which, among other things, is reviewing training standards and qualifications in the field.

IN CONCLUSION

Working with couples in growth groups or in enrichment programs presents many challenges to the facilitator but also offers many rewards and possibilities for personal growth. The marriage- and family-enrichment movement is in a state of rapid growth and expansion, with a wide variety of programs, techniques or experiences, and ancillary aids available to facilitators who wish to develop their own unique program for couples and families.

REFERENCES

Bach, G. R., & Bernhard, Y. M. *Aggression lab: The fair fight training manual.* Dubuque, Iowa: Kendall/Hunt, 1971.

Bosco, A. *Marriage encounter: A rediscovery of love.* St. Meinrad, Ind.: Abbey Press, 1973.

Klemer, R. H. *Marriage and family relationships.* New York: Harper & Row, 1970.

Mace, D., & Mace, V. *We can have better marriages.* Nashville, Tenn.: Abingdon Press, 1974.

Masters, W. H., & Johnson, V. E. *Human sexual inadequacy.* Boston: Little, Brown and Co., 1970.

Miller, S., Nunnally, E., Wackman, D., & Brazman, R. *Minnesota couples communication program: Couples handbook.* Minneapolis, Minn.: Interpersonal Communication Programs, 1975.

Otto, H. A. *More joy in your marriage.* New York: Hawthorn, 1969.

Otto, H. A. *The awareness communication chart.* Beverly Hills, Calif.: Holistic Press, 1975. (a)

Otto, H. A. *Group methods to actualize human potential: A handbook.* Beverly Hills, Calif.: Holistic Press, 1975. (b)

Otto, H. A. *Marriage and family enrichment programs in North America. The Family Coordinator,* 1975, 24, 137-143. (c)

Otto, H. A. *The now communication game.* Beverly Hills, Calif.: Holistic Press, 1975. (d)

Otto, H. A. *The sex communication game.* Beverly Hills, Calif.: Holistic Press, 1975. (e)

Otto, H. A. *The use of family strength concepts and methods in family life education.* Beverly Hills, Calif.: Holistic Press, 1975.(f)

Otto, H. A. *Marriage and family enrichment: New perspectives and programs.* Nashville, Tenn.: Abingdon Press, 1976.

---

[2]Available through Holistic Press, 8909 Olympic Blvd., Beverly Hills, California 90211.

RESOURCES

Association of Couples for Marriage Enrichment, 403 South Hawthorn Road, Winston-Salem, North Carolina, 27103.

The National Center for the Exploration of Human Potential, San Diego, California 92109. Retailer of Encounter Bats.

Herbert A. Otto, Ph.D., *is the chairperson of The National Center for the Exploration of Human Potential, San Diego, California. He is currently lecturing, writing, and conducting training workshops on his group methods, which are designed to actualize human potential. He also conducts a marriage- and family-enrichment program. Dr. Otto's background is in teaching, counseling, and community mental health.*

FANTASY: THEORY AND TECHNIQUE

Anthony G. Banet, Jr., and John E. Jones

As I sit here staring at a blank yellow legal pad, trying to imagine how this opening sentence will sound, my eyes shift to the rugged hillside outside my office window, and I am suddenly reminded of El Greco's View of Toledo. For a few minutes I step into that canvas to explore the terrain and then I shift my gaze to the artist himself as he is painting the picture . . . El Greco is a severe-looking, gray-bearded man with an elongated face . . . his image merges with the tall, shaggy palm tree across the street . . . I start talking to the tree (now El Greco-grandfather-sage) and ask it to tell me about the ocean that it has watched for sixty years. The tree begins to respond . . . The typewriters in the adjoining room recall me to my task; I begin to write.

Reveries — silent movies in our minds, constant streams of images and associations, sounds and words— know no boundaries of space, time, or possibility. Our fantasy lives are always present; like the light in a refrigerator, they are there, waiting, ready for us when we open the door by suspending our attention to outside reality. And like our refrigerators, our fantasy lives can supply us with nourishment and the raw material for creativity and experimentation.

Fantasy (also termed reverie, imagination, or daydreaming), prized by poets and philosophers, has been a phenomenon of human experience since earliest history, but its presence was a source of discomfort and embarrassment for scientific psychologists of the late 1800's, who focused on external behavior and ignored the "black box" inside. In the most benign "scientific" view, fantasy was thought to be useful because it provided diagnostic clues to the secrets of abnormal behavior; more typically, fantasy was seen as a frivolous waste of time, a flirtation with insanity. An idle mind was not only the devil's workshop, it also signaled a possible predisposition to madness. Only in the early 1900's, when some links between fantasy, play, and creativity were discovered in psychoanalytic research, did fantasy activity or "regression in the service of the ego" (as Ernst Kris, 1952, described it) become a respectable subject for psychological inquiry.

Currently, fantasy is alive and well. Some students of human behavior would agree with science fiction writer Ray Bradbury's belief that "the ability to fantasize is the ability to survive" (Hall, 1968, p. 28). As an integral part of Gestalt, encounter, and psychosynthesis theory, fantasy has become a prominent, if not always well-understood, component of change strategies in psychotherapy, personal growth, and group work in general. This paper reviews the development of the diagnostic and therapeutic uses of fantasy in the early work of Freud and Jung and presents a theoretical discussion of fantasy as "personal mythology." Techniques, training considerations, and precautions are described for the group facilitator who wishes to add fantasy to his intervention repertoire.

FANTASY AS A DIAGNOSTIC TOOL

For Freud, the fantasy and dream productions of his patients provided therapeutic insights as well as the basic data for psychoanalytic theory. Freud viewed fantasy and dreams as primary process events generated by the id—primitive wishes and fears that were suppressed by cognition and rationality, the secondary process events generated by the ego. Fantasy and dreams were "the royal road to the unconscious"; the techniques of free association and dream interpretation provided Freud with a window through which he observed the patient's travels on that road.

In Freud's view, fantasies and dreams required interpretation; they were symbolic productions whose obvious, manifest content disguised a hidden, latent level of meaning. The key to interpretation was to regard fantasies as "wish-fulfillments"; according to psychoanalytic theory, human beings are motivated by primitive, socially unacceptable wishes and fears. Beneath the veneer of even the most pleasant fantasies lurk the powerful impulses of sex and aggression.

The Projection Hypothesis

The extraordinary discoveries of Freud prompted other investigators to explore the diagnostic potential of fantasy. The projection hypothesis—that persons unconsciously externalize their wishes, fears, and goals by projecting them onto external stimuli—led to the development of instruments designed to elicit spontaneous fantasy productions from subjects viewing structured, standardized stimuli.

The prototype of projective techniques is Rorschach's inkblot test (Rorschach, 1921). Rorschach presented the ambiguous stimulus of an inkblot to subjects and asked them to report what they saw. Responses were collected, categorized, and interpreted. These fantasy productions provided the interpreter with rich diagnostic information regarding the subject's impulse life, defense system, and strength of emotional controls. The Thematic Apperception Test (TAT), developed by Murray (1938), carried the projective situation further. The TAT required subjects to respond to ambiguous pictures by telling a story based on what is perceived. By categorizing the themes prevalent in the fantasies produced, Murray made inferences regarding the subject's needs, interests, and reality orientation. Today a variety of projective devices is available. These remain the most popular diagnostic tool available to clinicians.

The projection hypothesis has received considerable support from experimental studies. The work of the early Gestalt psychologists (e.g., Kohler, 1925) and later work by the "new school" of perception (e.g., Bruner, 1941) have provided evidence that the internal needs of individuals are directly, if ambiguously, reflected in fantasy life.

FANTASY AS A THERAPEUTIC MODALITY

Jung's Work

Jung regarded fantasy and dreamwork not only as diagnostic tools but also as methods that the patient could use to integrate the layers of self and to advance the work of becoming a person, which he termed the "individuation" process. In Jung's view, growth occurs on two levels: the individual level, in which a person integrates motivations and actions into a harmonious, balanced life; and a transpersonal level, in which an individual makes contact with the collective unconscious—an awareness level that individuals share with the entire human race.

Jung employed several procedures to explore the individual's layers of awareness. All of them involve a focus on fantasy productions.

In *amplification*, the individual subject is asked to record his dream or fantasy and then to make as many associations as possible to a given symbol. The association may include verbal procedures, such as free association, or finger painting, dance, research on a mythological subject, etc. A related technique is *active imagination*, involving a fantasy of entering the given symbol (getting into it, playing with it) and letting the symbol extend itself. In both of these techniques, the subject works with his own, idiosyncratic symbols and meanings.

In a technique Progoff (1973) called *correlation*, symbols from dreamwork and fantasy are matched with real-life situations or outside stimuli. The inner and outer worlds are then allowed to influence each other until some focus or connection is discerned.

192

Jung's belief in the collective unconscious led him to the study of fairy tales, comparative mythology, and religious systems. Information from these sources was brought into the therapeutic session; together, analyst and patient worked with fantasy and myth to pursue the task of personal integration.

Jung's beliefs regarding the healing power of myth and fantasy are discussed by Campbell (1973):

> According to [Jung's] way of thinking, *all* the organs of our bodies—not only those of sex and aggression—have their purposes and motives, some being subject to conscious control, others, however, not. Our outward-oriented consciousness, addressed to the demands of the day, may lose touch with these inward forces; and the myths, states Jung, when correctly read, are the means to bring us back in touch. They are telling us in picture language of powers of the psyche to be recognized and integrated in our lives, powers that have been common to the human spirit forever, and which represent that wisdom of the species by which man has weathered the millenniums. Thus they have not been, and can never be, displaced by the findings of science, which relate rather to the outside world than to the depths that we enter in sleep. Through a dialogue conducted with these inward forces through our dreams and through a study of myths, we can learn to know and come to terms with the greater horizon of our own deeper and wiser, inward self. And analogously, the society that cherishes and keeps its myths alive will be nourished from the soundest, richest strata of the human spirit.
>
> However, there is a danger here as well; namely, of being drawn by one's dreams and inherited myths away from the world of modern consciousness, fixed in patterns of archaic feeling and thought inappropriate to contemporary life. What is required, states Jung therefore, is a dialogue, not a fixture at either pole; a dialogue by way of symbolic forms put forth from the unconscious mind and recognized by the conscious in continuous interaction. (p. 13)

Gestalt

Although Jung pioneered the therapeutic use of purposeful fantasy, currently the use of evoked, goal-oriented fantasy as an integrative, healing modality finds its clearest expression in Gestalt practice and psychosynthesis.

Gestalt therapists employ fantasy as a means to promote contact with disowned parts of self, with fears and expectations. Because of the here-and-now time focus, fantasies in Gestalt work are not merely reported; they are experienced and acted out. The subject is asked to *be* his fantasy so that energy is directed toward making contact with the issue.

Polster and Polster (1974) describe four functions served by fantasy work:

1. *Contact with a resisted event, feeling, or personal characteristic.* In this approach, the person is asked to fantasize in a free-association manner. As certain images become figural, the subject begins to interact with his fantasy production; frequently an assimilation of feelings, a healing of splits, occurs.

2. *Contact with an unavailable person or unfinished situation.* Here, the person visually imagines the presence of, for instance, a dead parent or vanished spouse and begins a conversation with that person. Or a conflictive situation from the past is conjured up, and the subject is asked to take care of his unfinished business. In this technique, closure is sought. In these first two functions, fantasy is "a way of catching up with the past and compensating for errors brought about by blocked expression or overwhelming circumstances" (Polster & Polster, 1974, p. 261).

3. *Exploring the unknown and preparing for the future.* The person rehearses, in fantasy, what he expects to happen in the near future. The rehearsal may be for an upcoming job interview, a confrontation with a feared relative, or other anxiety-laden future events. This type of fantasy seems to develop a repertoire of alertness and preparedness.

4. *Exploring new aspects of the individual.* Here, the person is asked to first imagine and then act out some personal quality that he lacks or has doubts about within himself. For

example, if he is timid, he fantasizes himself as being aggressive and then role plays himself with the new quality.

In Gestalt work, fantasy activity is highly specific and concrete. Other "experiments" used in Gestalt fantasy are discussed by Pfeiffer and Pfeiffer (1975).

Psychosynthesis

The integrated approach of Roberto Assagioli (1971) has as a prime objective the emergence of the self. The overall process is divided into two stages—personal and transpersonal psychosynthesis. On the personal level, the individual "attains a level of functioning in terms of his work and his relationships that would be considered optimally healthy by current standards of mental health" ("What is Psychosynthesis?," 1974, p. WB73). The transpersonal level is concerned with such qualities as a global perspective, altruistic love, and union with others. Psychosynthesis incorporates and modifies approaches from other systems; in many of its techniques, it relies heavily on fantasy production. Fantasy is regarded as a method "to establish two-way communication between the conscious and unconscious aspects of ourselves" ("The Purposeful Imagination," 1975).

In contrast to Gestalt, psychosynthesis employs fantasy in a more playful and expansive manner. Fantasy journeys are designed to awaken hidden potential, promote awareness, resolve conflict situations, and initiate healing processes. Classic and standardized fantasies are also used.

Typifying a standardized fantasy is the technique of symbol projection, in which the person is asked to visualize a standard series of twelve symbolic situations presented verbally by the facilitator. The situations, developed by Leuner (1971), take the subject through a structured fantasy that begins by walking in a meadow. Then the subject, in fantasy, progressively climbs a mountain, follows the course of a stream, visits a house, imagines an ideal person, views animals, walks into a swampy pond, explores a cave, witnesses a volcanic eruption, confronts a lion, and pages through an old picture book. Each fantasy image has specific meanings that are rooted in folklore and mythology; by responding to these images, the person develops awareness of unknown parts of the self.

Psychosynthesis practitioners are devoted to a creative, responsible investigation of fantasy procedures. A regular section of *Synthesis*, the psychosynthesis journal, is focused on fantasy techniques.

Current Research

Many investigators are currently exploring the dimensions of fantasy activity and its relationship to psychological characteristics and body events. Singer (1966) has developed seven categories of daydreaming and has compared the fantasy productions of various age, social-class, and racial groups. Fantasy differences in men and women have been reported by May (1966). Stampfl's implosive therapy employs a highly structured fantasy technique in which persons confront their worst fears (1970). Simonton and Simonton (1975) have reported on the use of fantasy in homeopathic medicine and the management of cancer malignancy.

Recent experimental studies (Lorie & Kryske, 1975) indicate that fantasy production follows a periodic cycle in research subjects. Subjects, wired so that brainwaves and eye movement could be recorded, were asked to report their inner thoughts at five-minute intervals over a ten-hour period. The findings showed a ninety- to one-hundred-minute rhythm for intense fantasy. That is, with no particular provocation or stimulation, normal persons have a continuing inner fantasy production that becomes rather intense every ninety minutes. These intense fantasy periods are associated with a high level of alpha brainwave activity (usually correlated with relaxation) and a low level of eye movement, suggesting attention to internal rather than external stimuli.

It seems likely that future research will continue to explore personality and physiological correlates of fantasy activity. For an overview, see Siegel and West (1975).

FANTASY AS PERSONAL MYTHOLOGY

Fantasy can be seen as the individual's construction of a *personal mythology*, a set of sensory-based symbols that allow us subjectively to interpret our real world and infuse our experience with meaning. Cultural or religious mythologies are the supports of a civilization's cohesion, vitality, and creative powers (Campbell, 1973); analogously, a personal mythology illuminates and strengthens our understanding of our bodies, ourselves, and the world in which we move. More concisely, fantasy tells us the truth about ourselves. Not the literal truth, certainly; not an abstract truth, either, but a metaphoric truth about who we are and where we are psychologically.

Campbell (1968) discusses the emergence of personal mythology as a cultural phenomenon:

> In the past, each civilization was the vehicle of its own long-established mythology, developing in character as its myth was progressively interpreted and elucidated. Today, the individual is the center of his own mythology . . . the individual has an experience of his own—of order, horror, beauty, or even mere exhilaration—which he seeks to communicate through signs; and if his realization has been of a certain depth and import, his communication will have the value and force of living myth. (p. 4)

Personal mythology tells us about our life, "not as it *will be*, or as it *should be*, as it *was*, or as it *never will be*, but as it *is*, in process, *here and now*, inside and out" (pp. 7-8).

Fantasy is a level of awareness and consciousness, a product of personal history and genetic determinants. It can be regarded as a private, intrapersonal language system. On a functional level, fantasy is an ongoing internal feedback process originating in our several selves, transmitting information relating to our motivations, needs, wants, orientations, and aspirations. Skill in generating, using, and understanding fantasy seems to be inborn, but the skill is suppressed by cognitive learning and attention to the outside world. For many adults, the skill needs to be relearned.

Piaget

Piaget's observation of children produced a theory of cognitive development (Piaget, 1950; Leavitt & Doktor, 1970) that postulates that individuals progressively develop through sensory, imagic, and symbolic phases. A *sensory* phase, in which the meaning of the world is mediated primarily by sensory-motor processes, is followed by an *imagic* phase, in which the child can perceive and have visual recollection of stimuli no longer present. The child develops agility in manipulating the fantasy symbols and moves away from manually or tactually dealing with the outside environment.

An elaboration of Piaget's imagic phrase and a description of the fantasy formation process are provided by Langer (1942). In her view, raw sensation (William James's "blooming, buzzing world of confusion") seems to exist only for seconds; even newborns begin to give meaning to sensations, to form pictures or visualizations of what has been experienced. We immediately begin to connect images into a story, just as the first thing we do with words is to tell something, to make a statement. These emerging fantasies mix kinesthetic and auditory sensations with the visual to form a fantasy. As we continue to experience, memory becomes part of the mix, so that fantasy begins to be a cumulative record of our experience of the world, a continuing gloss of metaphor and meaning by which we transform and transcend our raw experience.

Following the sensory and imagic phases is a *symbolic* phase, in which the child begins to use words and numbers to abstract still further from outside reality. In fact, words and numbers begin to acquire a greater reality than internal events or the outside environment as the child grows older. Rationality and the ability to manipulate words and symbols are prized, especially in Western cultures, as the highest achievements to which human beings can aspire; sensory and imagic processes are regarded as aspects of our lower, animal nature. Symbol manipulation moves us further and further from elemental experience; to paraphrase Alan Watts, we develop a preference for eating the menu instead of the dinner.

Symbolic cognition does not, however, terminate the sensory and imagic processes; it only suppresses them. Reclaiming these processes, relearning their value, is the motive behind Perls's dictum to "lose your mind and come to your senses." By suspending symbolic cognition, we can attend to our imagic or fantasy process. Far from being an illusion or imagination's figment, fantasy is closer to the real world of our natural experience than are any culturally determined symbols.

From Fantasy to Myth

Out of fantasy, the individual builds both fairy tales and myths. In her *Philosophy in a New Key*, Langer (1942) distinguishes between the varieties of fantasy: personal fairy tales are attempts to gratify wishes in a utopian setting (Freud's notion of wish-fulfillment); personal myths are attempts to gain a serious envisagement of the fundamental truths about ourselves. Fairy tales are communications about imaginary fulfillment and escape from conflict; myths are communications to help us understand and make moral sense out of our actual experience. Langer (1942) says:

> We do not know just where, in the evolution of human thought, myth-making begins, but it begins somewhere with the recognition of *realistic significance* in a story. In every fantasy, no matter how utopian, there are elements that represent real human relations, real needs and fears which the "happy ending" resolves. Even if the real situation is symbolized rather than stated (a shocking condition may be well disguised, or a mysterious one strangely conceived), a certain importance, an emotional interest, attaches to these elements . . . the great step from fairy tale to myth is taken when not only social forces—persons, customs, laws, traditions—but also cosmic forces surrounding mankind are expressed in the story; when not only relationship of an individual to society, but of mankind to nature, are conceived through the spontaneous metaphor of poetic fantasy. (pp. 144-146)

Historically, fantasy has been viewed as having both a diagnostic and a healing function. Fantasy as personal fairy tale provides diagnostic information about our wishes, fears, aspirations, and motivations. Fantasy as personal mythology can foster the

> centering and unfolding of the individual in integrity, in accord with (a) himself (microcosm), (b) his culture (the mesocosm), (c) the universe (macrocosm), and (d) that awesome ultimate mystery which is both beyond and within himself and all things. (Campbell, 1968, p. 6)

The Vision Quest

Figuring prominently in the puberty rites of the plains Indians (Capps, 1973; Storm, 1972) and other ancient peoples was the *vision quest*. An adolescent boy was sent into the wilderness for a period of meditation and fasting, during which the spirits spoke to him in visions, fantasies, and dreams. He received a name and a vocation from the spirits, as well as predictions of his future. The young boy was prepared for his vision quest by hearing myths told by his elders; he personalized the tribal mythology during his time of solitude. We see in the vision quest a paradigm for the current use of evoked fantasy in a structured growth situation. Even though the fasting and wilderness are missing, the process seems similar.

FANTASY IN GROUP WORK

Fantasy as a structured intervention into individual or group process represents an effort to transpose that process into another key or language. As an intervention, fantasy is the purposeful evocation of inner imagic productions so that personal and group growth goals can be pursued.

Because fantasy interventions produce heightened feelings, the facilitator needs to be knowledgeable regarding the types of fantasy, the techniques of structuring fantasy, training considerations, and precautions for the use of this powerful tool.

Indications for Use

A fantasy intervention is appropriate for these purposes:

To resolve dilemmas or work through an impasse. When verbal transactions are garbled, discussion becomes repetitive, or unvoiced fears stifle process, a fantasy will usually produce fresh data and new solutions.

To tap "deeper" layers or levels. Discussion centering around difficult topics, such as authority, sexuality, or aggression, often stays at a superficial level. Fantasy can move the discussion to a more meaningful level, as well as sanction the expression of difficult feelings.

To focus or personalize learning. Generalized verbal discussion frequently becomes anonymous. Transposing to fantasy promotes ownership and personalized learning.

To play. Group discussions frequently become unnecessarily serious, especially when group members are highly task oriented. Fantasy provides a respite from "work" and produces new data.

To promote creativity. Fantasy frequently helps group members to uncover their originality and gain freshness of perception.

To promote healing. Disruptions, conflict, and interpersonal wounds can often be transposed to an allegoric or metaphoric level and resolved.

To provide cues for intervention. The facilitator will often find it useful to "check in" with his own ongoing fantasy experience to sharpen his reading of the group process and to search for cues for appropriate interventions. A brief fantasy focused on "what I would like to see happen" often brings fresh ideas for creative intervention.

Types of Fantasy

Fantasy interventions can be classified in terms of content, focus, and method of structuring.

Content

Fantasy content refers to *what* the participant is asked to experience. Varieties include:

Narrative fantasies. In this type of fantasy, the content is specified by the facilitator through frequent cues and interruptions into the fantasy-formation process. The structure may be a classic form (e.g., a well-known fairy tale or story) or a simple scenario invented by the facilitator. In the narrative fantasy, the facilitator determines the course of the fantasy by suggestions and specific directions.

Free-form fantasies. Here the content is largely determined by the fantasizer. The facilitator may present minimal initial cues (words, pictures, sounds, etc.) but leaves gaps of silence that participants fill with fantasy productions.

Interactive fantasies enable the fantasizer to speak or move while engaged in fantasy. Much Gestalt technique involves such interaction. Occasionally the fantasy is interrupted, some verbal interaction occurs, and then the participant returns to the fantasy.

Metaphoric fantasies involve fairy-tale characters, supranormal feats and activities, strange and bizarre happenings.

Literal fantasies may visualize actual incidents or persons from the past, present, and future. The emphasis is on "real life" events.

Focus

The facilitator can provide fantasy induction for individuals, pairs, or the entire group. Four major variations of group fantasies are common:

1. Everyone sits in a circle, eyes closed. Someone begins a fantasy involving the entire group. Members contribute to the story as they feel a part of it.
2. One member lies on the floor and begins a fantasy. Other participants join in the fantasy by sitting on the floor and contributing. Individuals may leave the fantasy by getting up from the floor.
3. Group members lie on the floor with their heads together, their bodies forming the spokes of a wheel. Someone begins the fantasy (which may involve only the fantasizer or include other group members), and others contribute as they identify with the story.
4. Members sit in a circle. One member begins a story and then abruptly "passes" the story to the person on his left. The story progresses until all members have had an opportunity to contribute.

Method of Structuring

Several methods for structuring fantasy productions are available.

Spontaneous fantasies are induced by asking the fantasizer to stop his reality process and to check in with his ongoing fantasy process. The intervention ends with the request; no content is specified. Example: "Just close your eyes for a minute and report what is running through your mind."

Triggered fantasies are initiated by the facilitator with brief fantasy "stems." Example: "You are approaching a high brick wall. You look around for a way to get over or around it."

Guided fantasies involve interaction between the facilitator and the fantasizer. Together they develop a scenario; the facilitator assists by asking questions, helping to overcome obstacles, offering support. This fantasy "trip" may cover any variety of subjects, such as getting inside one's body, becoming another person, becoming involved in a cleansing ritual, etc. Examples of guided fantasies are provided by Schutz (1967) and Stevens (1971).

Techniques for Structuring Fantasies

The steps described here have their fullest application in the guided, individual, narrative fantasy, but they are also applicable to all fantasy interventions.

Introduction. The fantasy activity is introduced with descriptions of what will be done, how it will be done, and for what reasons. Sanction is given for a variety of responses—there are no right or wrong ways to have a fantasy.

Climate setting. A quiet, comfortable environment is provided. Participants are encouraged to lie on the floor and close their eyes. Semi-darkness encourages fantasy production. Relaxation, regression, and sensory-awareness techniques help participants to screen out external stimuli. Music often helps to create a peaceful, relaxed mood.

Guiding. The facilitator offers brief, concise cues and directions. He may suggest visualizations, colors, sounds, textures, smells, or activities. The guidance is limited to cues only; responses or feelings are not suggested.

In guiding the fantasy, the facilitator may want to observe participants closely for body reactions, movement, etc. The time focus is kept in the present.

Pacing. Timing and pacing are critical in fantasy production. Allowing too little time truncates the experience for the participant; too much time may distract or blur the focus. Spontaneous fantasies may take only a minute, many triggered fantasies can produce useful material in five minutes or less, a guided fantasy may last twenty or thirty minutes. It is often helpful to give time cues: "In another minute, I will be asking you to leave this place and . . ."

Terminating. The facilitator "returns" the individual or the group to the group room. He calls attention to the real, external situation and gives step-by-step instructions for re-entry. A common termination goes as follows: "In a minute, I want you to return to this room . . . begin stretching your arms and legs and, with your eyes remaining closed and at your own pace, slowly bring yourself to a sitting position . . . when you feel ready, slowly open your eyes."

Sharing. Sharing of the fantasy experience is an important final step. The individual participant can first take some time by himself, reflecting on the experience; dyads or triads can then be formed for interpersonal sharing. As a final step, the sharing can continue in the large group. Fantasy can be an intensely private experience; sanction should be given for sharing only what the participant wants to share. However, some form of sharing is useful because it brings closure.

Training Considerations

The use of fantasy interventions in human relations training should be influenced by several considerations.

Goals. The purpose of the fantasy intervention should be clear to the facilitator and to the participants. In general, the use of fantasy interventions should be consistent with the training objectives and participants' expectations.

Voluntariness and privacy. Participants should participate in fantasy activities voluntarily. Some participants may be fearful of fantasy or believe that they are unable to fantasize. Some participants may want to keep their fantasy productions private. Sanction should be given for nonparticipation and for the privacy of the experience.

Depth and heightened affect. Fantasy frequently serves to develop awareness of difficult issues and suppressed feelings. Care should be taken to offer support and security; the facilitator may need to prepare for expressions of joy, euphoria, sadness, etc. Tears occasionally accompany a moving experience.

Interpretation. Fantasy productions have meaning primarily for the fantasizer. The facilitator may prompt participants to explore or to make associations to ambiguous parts of the fantasy; efforts by the facilitator or other group members to interpret for another should be resisted. Interpretation risks vitiating the fantasy experience. Fantasies do not necessarily *mean* something or *symbolize* something; the fantasy *is* the experience.

Audience effect. Engaging in fantasy activity with a group has different effects: for some participants, fantasy activity is enhanced; for others, it is suppressed. Adequate processing of the experience requires sensitivity on the part of the facilitator, especially for the person having difficulty.

Trust level. Guided fantasies, in particular, require that some degree of trust be present before they are introduced. It is rarely wise to open a group training event with an elaborate fantasy.

Closure. Closure is usually accomplished by providing time for sharing and discussion. Failure to close down the fantasy activity has the same impact as suddenly waking from an absorbing dream and being unable to recall it. At best, it is frustrating; at worst, it can open areas of awareness for which the participant needs follow-through and guidance.

Focus. Fantasy as an intervention promotes intrapersonal awareness, even when done in a group. It may encourage participants to "get into themselves" and stifle interaction. A repeated series of individual guided fantasies can rapidly become boring for the rest of the group, who are reduced to the status of observers.

Precautions

For the participant, fantasy activity is usually a self-regulating experience; that is, he can control his level of participation and involvement. However, for some few group members, fantasy may provide sufficient stimulus for strong emotional reactions. As Polster and Polster (1974) remark, fantasy can initiate a vast renewal of energy, which sometimes cannot be immediately assimilated. These instances and some precautions are discussed here.

Abreaction. In the clinical sense, abreaction refers to the affective reliving of a repressed traumatic experience from the past. The person responds fully to the fantasized event and releases the powerful emotional reaction that the original event prompted. Abreaction is a painful but cathartic experience; it requires close management, privacy, and time to complete the experience. Individuals having an abreaction usually benefit from support and solitude after the experience.

Losing contact boundaries. Occasionally, a group participant will experience a brief, transient psychotic episode during fantasy. The episode may take the form of extended reverie or an unwillingness to leave the fantasy trip. Manifestations of a loss of contact boundaries include disorientation, misperceptions, changes in speech, alterations in visual and auditory perception, and heightened affect. Usually the episode is a pleasant, benign experience. In most instances, it is advisable for a person having this kind of experience to stay in the group. Other participants can provide reality checks, and the presence of others can be supportive and reassuring. In some instances, when the person expresses a desire for solitude, a staff member can stay with him until the episode terminates.

Trances. The group fantasy experience can produce many of the characteristics of a hypnotic trance state. The hypnotic trance, while extensively researched, remains difficult to define; for many investigators, a trance is similar to focused attention. Trance-like phenomena pose no special problem for either the group leader or the participant if the previously discussed training considerations are met.

CONCLUSION

Fantasy is a powerful intervention that enriches individual and group experience by acquainting participants with their "personal mythology." That mythology—and its presentation of metaphoric truth—can support and nourish the individual's search for self-awareness and personal growth. The techniques and methods described here require a respect for fantasy's power and a sense of appropriateness and timing. The responsible facilitator who creatively uses fantasy in group work will tap a source of learning that has impact far beyond the life of the group.

REFERENCES

Assagioli, R. *Psychosynthesis: A manual of principles and techniques.* New York: The Viking Press, 1971.

Bruner, J. S. Personality dynamics and the process of perceiving. In R. R. Blake & G. V. Ramsey (Eds.), *Perception: An approach to personality.* New York: Ronald Press, 1941.

Campbell, J. *The masks of God: Creative mythology.* New York: The Viking Press, 1968.

Campbell, J. The impact of science on myth. In J. Campbell, *Myths to live by.* New York: Bantam, 1973.

Capps, B. *The Indians.* New York: Time-Life Books, 1973.

Hall, M. H. A conversation with Ray Bradbury and Chuck Jones, the fantasy makers. *Psychology Today,* April, 1968, pp. 28-70.

Kohler, W. *Gestalt psychology.* New York: New American Library, 1959.

Kris, E. *Psychoanalytic exploration in art.* New York: International Universities Press, 1952.

Langer, S. *Philosophy in a new key.* New York: Mentor, 1942.

Leavitt, H. J., & Doktor, R. Personal growth, laboratory training, science, and all that: A shot at a cognitive clarification. *Journal of Applied Behavorial Science*, 1970, *6*, 173-179.

Leuner, H. Initiated symbol projection. In R. Assagioli, *Psychosynthesis: A manual of principles and techniques*. New York: The Viking Press, 1971.

Lorie, P., & Kryske, D. F. Ultradian rhythms: The 90-minute clock inside us. *Psychology Today*, April, 1975, *8*, 54-65.

May, R. Sex differences in fantasy patterns. *Journal of Projective Techniques and Personality Assessment*, 1966, *30*, 576-586.

Murray, H. A. *Explorations in personality*. New York: Oxford University Press, 1938.

Pfeiffer, J. W., & Pfeiffer, J. A. A Gestalt primer. In J. E. Jones & J. W. Pfeiffer (Eds.), *The 1975 annual handbook for group facilitators*. La Jolla, Calif.: University Associates, 1975.

Piaget, J. *The psychology of intelligence*. London: Routledge & Kegan Paul, 1950.

Polster, E., & Polster, M. *Gestalt therapy integrated*. New York: Vintage, 1974.

Progoff, I. *Jung, synchronicity and human destiny*. New York: The Julian Press, 1973.

The purposeful imagination. *Synthesis*, 1975, *1*(2), 119-121.

Rorschach, H. *Psychodiagnostics*. Berne, Switzerland: Hans Huber, 1921.

Schutz, W. C. *Joy: Expanding human awareness*. New York: Grove Press, 1967.

Siegel, R. K., & West, L. J. *Hallucinations: Behavior, experience and theory*. New York: John Wiley, 1975.

Simonton, O. C., & Simonton, S. S. Belief systems and management of the emotional aspects of malignancy. *Journal of Transpersonal Psychology*, 1975, *7*, 29-47.

Singer, J. L. *Daydreaming: An introduction to the experimental study of inner experience*. New York: Random House, 1966.

Stampfl, T. G. Implosive therapy: Emphasis on covert stimulation. In D. J. Levis (Ed.), *Learning approaches to therapeutic behavior change*. Chicago: Aldine, 1970.

Stevens, J. O. *Awareness: Exploring, experimenting, experiencing*. Lafayette, Calif.: Real People Press, 1971.

Storm, H. *Seven arrows*. New York: Ballantine, 1972.

What is psychosynthesis? *Synthesis*, 1974, *1*(1), WB70-WB74. Reprinted in J. E. Jones & J. W. Pfeiffer (Eds.), *The 1975 annual handbook for group facilitators*. La Jolla, Calif.: University Associates, 1975.

Anthony G. Banet, Jr., Ph.D., *is a senior consultant with University Associates, La Jolla, California. He is a clinical psychologist with experience in community mental health and has consulted with numerous public service agencies. Dr. Banet is also the editor of* Creative Psychotherapy: A Source Book.

John E. Jones, Ph.D., *is the vice president of University Associates, La Jolla, California. He is a co-editor of the University Associates* Handbook *series, the* five Annual Handbooks for Group Facilitators, *and* Group & Organization Studies: The International Journal for Group Facilitators. *Dr. Jones's background is in teaching and counseling, education, and organization and community-development consulting.*

.

A GESTALT APPROACH TO COLLABORATION IN ORGANIZATIONS

H. B. Karp

Since the early 1950's and the rise of the human relations movement, much emphasis has been placed on the need and importance for collaboration in the organizational setting. While there is much in the current literature to support this view (e.g., Bennis, 1966), an alternate approach, that of Gestalt organization development (OD), has recently been reported on and espoused by Herman (1971),[1] who suggests that the emphasis of organization development should be embodied in the individual rather than in the group. While this different emphasis has great potential for conflict, it also has equally great potential for a positive effect.

Collaboration will produce the greatest payoff in terms of satisfaction and productivity when the individuals participating in the collaborative effort view themselves as individuals at all times. That is, (1) the individual member is clear and concise about what he wants for himself and for the organization, and (2) he can effect and maintain good contact with himself as well as with the others. Contact, simply defined, is the coming together of *me* with something or someone that is *not* me. It is the appreciation of the uniqueness and difference of the other.

Collaboration works among some groups and not among others. When collaboration is "swallowed whole" as a slogan or a panacea for organizational ills, what positive results occur are, at best, temporary—e.g., there may be, temporarily, a slight increase in contributions from the participating members due either to the newness of the approach or to an overzealous conversion to an exciting new "religion" called OD. This is particularly true when the organization adopts a "total-systems approach" and the subtle message becomes: "You damn well better get on board or be viewed as an outcast." The problem with deifying concepts such as collaboration, change, and even personal growth is that the nonbelievers tend to go underground as the converts zealously go forward. This situation often results in the loss of whatever creative efforts the "now-underground" heretics doled out, however sparingly, prior to the great conversion. Nonbelievers, of course, quickly learn the phraseology and how to "play the game" when survival in the organization is at stake.

The issue here is not whether collaboration is a good or bad concept; the issue is *on what successful collaboration is based.* I strongly suggest that collaboration must be based on the recognition of the power that resides in the individual and his right to be himself. If it is not, the result, at best, is a temporary increase in activity, and, at worst, a process that could sap the strength and vitality of the organization.

Consider for a moment the Gestalt notion that the whole is more than the sum of its parts. Implicit in this construct, for me, is the corollary that the maximum potential for the whole (group) can be realized only as the maximum potential for each part (individual) is realized. Thus we have two factors to consider when talking about collaboration: the individual and the group.

---

[1]I wish to express my sincere thanks to Stan Herman for his encouragement and for his criticism of this paper.

THE INDIVIDUAL

Perls (1970), the "father" of Gestalt therapy, defines maturity as "relying on internal rather than external supports" (p. 17); i.e., the more mature an individual is, the more he will rely on his own sense of the situation for guidance when faced with ambiguity or conflict, rather than on the opinions of others. This does not imply that he rejects out of hand what others think or feel; after considering all that is salient, he will decide for himself what he is willing or not willing to do. This developing of maturity, or "centering," as Perls (1972, p. 103) calls it, is the most critical element in the individual's ability to be creative and more productive. It follows then that the more "centered" an individual is, the more he is in touch with his strengths, weaknesses, commitments, priorities, etc., and the more, therefore, he is able to contribute productively to group effort *when that is what is called for.* "Centering" is to Gestalt what "togetherness" is to conventional human relations.

Centering is a *process* that continues for the life of the individual (Perls, 1972) and not something that is easily attained or quickly mastered by the application of a few techniques. It is the process by which the *self* is made known to the individual and accepted by him as unique and valuable. The more an individual is centered, the more he is able to respond effectively to the here-and-now of a situation; the more visible he is as a unique individual; and thus the more he is able to make authentic, and therefore effective, contact with others. While anyone can collaborate, effective collaboration in today's world of organizational complexity and absence of lead time is a direct function of the degree of centeredness that exists for each of the group members.

Most children under the age of six have very little problem in making and maintaining contact, particularly with each other. They seem to display a clear sense of what they want and what they do not want and are open about it; they are constantly excited by encountering new and *different* things; they submit to, but rarely collude with, attempts to block them. I have yet to see a child accept the parental prelude, "I'm doing this to you for your own good!" It would seem that effective contact is a *natural state* and that we have learned to be phony, polite, defensive, agreeable, devious, and the other ways we "should" or "should not" be. Clearly these characteristics are not consistent with what makes for good contact and productive collaborative effort. Workshops designed to deal with the problem of training individuals to become more centered may be a necessary precondition to collaboration in some organizations.

Ten norms for contact can be suggested to focus the attention of individuals on reasons why they are *not* making effective solid contact. There are probably fifty more that could as easily be used.

1. "Talking About" Rather than "Dealing With"

One of the best ways of not dealing with a problem is to talk about it endlessly. A certain amount of "talking about" is necessary to lay out the problem or to explain particular views. However, it becomes destructive when one continues to talk after alternative choices have emerged that can be pursued to deal with the problem.

2. "Should" Rather than "Is"

If we acknowledge the Gestalt assumption that the past is gone and cannot be changed and the future is not yet here, then all we can deal with is the "right here" and "right now." "Shoulds," "oughts," "thou shalt/shalt nots" are interdictions from the past, which may have been effective in the past, but may not be salient to what is going on in the present. (See Herman, 1971.) Clearly, whatever the present situation is, it is somehow different from any situation ever encountered before. By plugging in set rules from the past, the individual is restricting himself, to some degree, since he is not allowing himself to deal with the uniqueness of the present situation.

Instead, when he replaces an "I should" with an "I want," he is making a conscious choice that is geared to the ongoing situation.

3. "I Can't" Instead of "I Won't"

Clearly, there are many things in the organization that the individual cannot do. For example, most managers cannot arbitrarily fire someone, give raises at will, etc. There are, however, many areas where the manager does have much, if not complete, discretionary power. Therefore, if he elects to deny a subordinate's request with an "I can't" when the situation is one in which he really can but chooses not to, then he is telling the subordinate, "I am powerless to do anything to help you." More important, by stating "I can't" when he truly can, he diminishes his own strength; i.e., the more powerless he presents himself, the more powerless he actually becomes. Not only does this tend to erode his influence with his subordinates, it also increases the probability that the subordinate will continue to come back with the same request, or similar ones, in the hope that perhaps now his boss can do something. As long as the boss resorts to the "I can't" position, the subordinate never hears the real underlying issue: "I won't."

4. A Question Instead of a Statement

Questions are obviously quite functional when they represent a request for information. However, when a statement is "politely" masked as a question—e.g., "Don't you agree that . . . ?" or "Wouldn't you think . . . ?"—several outcomes occur that weaken the individual's ability to make solid contact. First, the individual places himself in a "one-down" position by requesting the other's approval to his masked statement. Not only does the statement get lost in the question, the asker has placed himself in the position where he must now listen to the other's answer. In reality, he wanted to have the other person hear something that he had to say. There is also a tendency for the asker to dilute the strength of his original position by phrasing it in terms of a question.

This strategy also creates negative affect in the person to whom the question is addressed. There is the high probability that some confusion will occur if the hearer believes that a question is really being posed; the confusion increases if his answer, should it be other than expected, is met with an argument, generally in the form of another loaded question.

Also, the use of such a question may actually invite the hearer's distrust of the speaker, rather than draw him closer or make him more receptive to the statement.

5. "You," "One," "It," "We," "They," Instead of "I"

There is probably some truth to the old adage "There is safety in numbers"; certainly, there is anonymity. There are times when it is very functional to use pronouns other than "I"; e.g., "you" when I am talking to you, "we" when I am representing the opinion of a group of which I am a member, and so on. However, I can best make myself heard (and hear myself and know where *I* stand) by taking full responsibility for my thoughts, ideas, feelings, etc. This can only be done if I tell you that it is "*I*" saying this to "*you.*"

6. "Yes" Instead of "No"

This norm probably contributes most to an individual losing his centeredness. When an individual says "Yes" or assents by default, when he feels or thinks "No" or agrees when there is little or no cause for agreement, two things happen. First, he commits himself to an action or idea that he truly wants no part of, and makes himself tacitly responsible for the outcomes and a victim to the process. Second, by agreeing when he feels or thinks "No," he withholds his real point of view, which might have been valuable in creating a more desirable outcome.

Hearing "Yes" continually also creates mistrust in the one who is asking for something. Simply put: if I cannot trust you to say "No" when you feel or think "No," then I cannot trust your "Yes" either. If your response to me is always a "Yes," no matter what the request or circumstances, how will I be able to gauge the degree of your support when I *really* need it?

7. On & On & On & On

Repeating the message over and over to create impact is about as effective as repeating a punchline over and over to get a laugh. The general effect of repetition is boredom. Thus, each time the message is repeated by the speaker, its impact becomes increasingly diluted, both for the speaker and for the listeners. This can be demonstrated by choosing a word, preferably an emotionally laden one, and repeating it audibly fifteen times. One can notice the transition from "high impact" to meaningless guttural.

8. "Broadcast" Instead of Contact

Contact is based on directness and impact. Addressing the group (or the ceiling, or the middle of the room) as the means of "getting the message across" to just one or several of the group's members is a sure way to lessen the quality of the impact. If, for example, I, as a manager, want to reprimand you "politely" in the group by saying, "Some of us are not getting the job done," you have every justification for saying to yourself, "He certainly isn't talking to me."

9. Fake Contact

Whether contact is focused on the self or on others, it is difficult to maintain over long periods of time. It is easy for anyone to recall being in a staff meeting, a class, or a conference and suddenly becoming aware that "My God, I've been daydreaming." The body had enough and the mind turned off. When one *starts* to get the signal that he has had enough, he should allow himself to withdraw *totally* for a period of fifteen to thirty seconds—remember the vacation last summer; relive his most recent triumph; once again deliver that devastating rejoinder . . . *anything* that allows him to leave the here-and-now totally for a short period of time. When he comes back into contact, he will be in *total* contact and able to function effectively until the need to withdraw surfaces again. One cannot deal with the need to attend and the need to rest simultaneously. By trying to do both at the same time, one achieves neither. By finishing the one need (withdrawal) completely, the other need (contact) can then be dealt with much more fully. While this may seem awkward at first, a little practice will allow an individual to develop a sense of rhythm between contact and withdrawal that can sustain him for long periods of time when a maximum of concentration is needed.

10. Clarity and Conciseness

This concept embodies the preceding nine. First, until one knows what he wants, he will stand very little chance of getting it. Second, one must be concise; this implies brevity and the lack of qualifying statements preceding the demand. There is no better way of *not* getting what one wants than by preceding a request with something like "You probably won't like this but . . ." or "I know that this might not sound like such a good idea but . . ." and so on.

Internalizing these norms is not a cure-all but a way of starting the centering process that allows people to contact themselves and others more effectively. Unless these norms are internalized by group members, collaborative effort is only a substitute for the real thing.

THE GROUP

In addition to uniting and combining forces that may not have reached a minimum level of maturity, either as individuals or subgroups, another factor contributing to the failure of a collaborative effort is significant: pushing collaboration as a value when it may be violating assumptions of members who do not accept the collaborative model. An effective collaborative group is based on four underlying assumptions.

Enlightened Self-Interest

For a group to function effectively, it must not make unhuman demands on its participants. The individual's question of "What's in it for me?" is a very legitimate one that is also quite valuable for the group. I am *not* speaking disparagingly of altruism or *esprit de corps;* these can be valuable group assets. Individuals, however, will be most committed to solutions that provide each with most of what he wants, in terms of himself or in terms of the organization. Stifling self-interest is one way to prevent group members from contacting what is important for them. Many people will strongly distrust anyone whose only stated motivation is "to want to help" or "to want to do what is best for the group." A person will feel what he feels and will want what he wants regardless of who says that he should or should not. An explicit norm that says "wanting what you want is OK" frees members to be "up front" and more in touch with the factors that are affecting the group's existence.

Contact Based on Differences

This concept has been implicit throughout this discussion, but it should also be explicit, particularly in view of its impact on effective group functioning.

One point needs some cautionary emphasis here. Similarities exist along with differences; liking coexists with disliking; agreeing with disagreeing; fun with friction; and so on. The point is not to make a necessary virtue or "should" out of differences. It is just as necessary to the effective functioning of a group for the members to recognize points of honest agreement and similarity, where they exist, as it is to recognize the differences.

Effective interaction is based on awareness. That is, before contact can be considered, there must first be awareness, i.e., consciousness, that some need or want has arisen or some thing is of interest. Out of the awareness comes energy or excitement, which moves the individual toward the objective. The cycle is complete when the individual has made contact with that objective. For example, as you read this you may suddenly become aware of the fact that you are thirsty. You put down your reading and get up to get a cold beer. When you have quenched your thirst, you are now ready to resume your reading. You have made effective contact with your environment by being aware and attending to your needs as they arose. Had you tried to ignore your thirst and continued to read, you would have become increasingly thirsty and increasingly less able to concentrate on your reading, thereby getting nothing of what you wanted.

Essentially, contact is based on *differences,* not on similarities—me and something that is not me—for example, me and ideas, me and other people, me and food, or even me and me—which is what increased self-understanding is all about.

In terms of group effectiveness, it is essential to focus on differentiation first, by heightening the differences that make each individual unique. Once differentiation has occurred, it is easier to see where everyone stands. This facilitates the integration that results in the final collaborative solution.

The Contract

If emphasis is placed on differences that exist among the members of a group and the necessity for heightening these differences, the question "How do we get our act together?" naturally arises.

Most of us have experienced the difficulties that can arise when trying to reconcile the real differences that occur among the individuals of a group trying to arrive at a collaborative solution. The central concern when dealing with differences or a conflict of any kind is to make certain that all parties are clear and concise about what it is they want. The clearer an individual is about what he initially wants, the easier it will be for him to move from that position to a more suitable one should the situation change or some call for a new approach arise.

The contract is one method of approaching differences. The essence of an effective contract lies in the willingness to deal in the here-and-now with explicit factors. This is true whether the issue be task, maintenance, or something of a highly interpersonal nature.

The contract is highly specific; in reality, it is a demand-response system that is geared to a set time and circumstance with a specific outcome. According to Gestalt theory, each individual always has the option to respond to a demand with (1) "Yes, I will," (2) "No, I won't," or (3) "Yes, I will, under the following circumstances . . ."

The participants must make their respective positions clear. One individual makes a demand of another. The demand must be highly specific in terms of exact behaviors, the time frame the contract covers, the specific outcome expected, and what, if anything, is offered in return. Once this is stated, the other participants now respond individually with one of the three choices already mentioned.

If everyone responds with "I will," then the contract is made and the group can move on with the next order of business. However, if any one individual responds with "I will, under the following circumstances . . .," a countercontract is being offered, which begins the entire process all over again. If any individual's response is "I will not," then the group has several options. The first is to drop the demand, the second is to look for another avenue of approach, and the third is to reconsider the advisability of continuing with a collaborative approach.

A contract broken or not totally fulfilled is more damaging than one never made. A contract is not an end in itself; it is a way to begin and/or proceed *slowly*.

Collaboration as a Situational Alternative

When choosing a collaborative approach, the first thing to consider is who should be included in the effort. Three guidelines can be suggested.

1. *Only individuals who are competent to contribute to the outcome* should be included. All too often individuals have been included in collaborative efforts for many reasons other than that of ability to contribute productively. For example, we may include everyone in the organization because we believe in collaboration as an organizational value; we may include everyone in a specific work unit because the decision will affect the entire unit; we may include the individual because he will feel rejected and left out if we do not. Clearly, without the ability or capability to contribute to a specific outcome, the individual's input can only be neutral at best and damaging at worst.

2. *Only those individuals in the decision-making process who, in some way, will be responsible for the outcome* should be included. An individual can be asked for an opinion or for specific information, both of which can contribute to the final decision, and yet be reasonably excluded from participating in the final decision-making process. Any statement that starts with "I think" can be considered legitimate from any source; but any statement beginning with "we should" or "you should" is not legitimate unless the individual making it will be personally affected by the

208

outcome of that decision. The point here is that, regardless of how competent an individual may be, if he will not be affected by the outcome, his "we should"/"you should" inputs take on the aspect of free advice.

3. *Only individuals who freely wish to collaborate* should be included. Herman (1974a) has pointed out that while collaboration, openness, and trust exist in organizations, so do competitiveness, defensiveness, and distrust. The extent to which one set of conditions pervades the organization is certainly going to be a factor in determining the "organizational climate." It is highly unrealistic, however, to assume that any organization is ever going to function at either extreme. Thus, even in the most zealously converted "Theory Y" organizations there is going to be some internal competition for position, status, or resource; some wariness on the part of individuals when faced with new or unknown conditions; and some honest dislike for other people. Not recognizing these negative conditions is just not being in the here-and-now.

Some people do their best work as individuals, avoiding groups like the plague. Some individuals can turn out their best only under competition. Some people are "toxic" to others, yet are still highly capable of good job performance. To include people who, for whatever reason, do not accept collaboration is a good method for ensuring that the effort will be, to some degree, abortive.

Another factor to be taken into account is that an individual can be competent, responsible for the outcome, and supportive of collaborative effort but just not care, one way or the other, how a particular decision turns out. If his input is needed, it should be derived as quickly and concisely as possible, without forcing him to sit through agonizing hours of debate, argument, conflict, etc., which will only tend to increase his boredom and make him less willing to collaborate on other issues in the future.

If no one wants to collaborate on the project, it is possible that the project should not be handled collaboratively, but individually. A total lack of commitment to a project brings up the question of the advisability of proceeding. If such a project must be undertaken, then any other approach, including an individual one, will probably be more productive than the collaborative one.

CONCLUSION

The critical issue is not which technique, approach, or theory is good or bad, but which of these can get the best results. As long as nothing is totally rejected as a possible alternative, then each individual can generate as many choices for himself as he is capable of doing. As long as the individual is centered and willing to deal with what is happening now, he allows himself the maximum opportunity for effectiveness.

REFERENCES

Bennis, W. *Changing organizations.* New York: McGraw-Hill, 1966.

Herman, S. M. Toward a more authentic manager. *Training and Development Journal,* October, 1971.

Herman, S. M. Notes on freedom. In J. W. Pfeiffer & J. E. Jones (Eds.), *The 1972 annual handbook for group facilitators.* La Jolla, Calif.: University Associates, 1972.

Herman, S. M. The shadow of organization development. In J. W. Pfeiffer & J. E. Jones (Eds.), *The 1974 annual handbook for group facilitators.* La Jolla, Calif.: University Associates, 1974. (a)

Herman, S. M. The "shouldist" manager. In J. W. Pfeiffer & J. E. Jones (Eds.), *The 1974 annual handbook for group facilitators.* La Jolla, Calif.: University Associates, 1974. (b)

Perls, F. S. Four lectures. In J. Fagan & I. L. Shepherd (Eds.), *Gestalt therapy now.* Palo Alto, Calif.: Science and Behavior Books, 1970.

Perls, F. S. *In and out the garbage pail.* New York: Bantam Books, 1972.

H. B. Karp, Ph.D., is an associate professor in the Department of Business Management, Old Dominion University, Norfolk, Virginia. He serves as a consultant to industrial and public service organizations and conducts public and in-house workshops in the United States and Canada. Dr. Karp's background is in organizational psychology, organization development, human motivation, and Gestalt applications to individual and organizational growth.

INTERROLE EXPLORATION

Udai Pareek

Role is a central concept in the understanding of organizational dynamics. It can be conceived as the interface between the person and the organization. In organization development (OD) this important interface region has not been adequately used. Three important OD interventions reported concerning role are those by Dayal and Thomas (1968), Harrison (1971), and Sherwood and Glidewell (1973). The main focus of Role Analysis Technique (Dayal & Thomas, 1968) is to help define a given role in the organization clearly by focusing on the discussion of the purpose of the role, its prescribed and discretionary components, and its linkages with other roles. This technique has been reported to be very useful for role clarification. Role negotiation (Harrison, 1971) and role renegotiation (Sherwood & Glidewell, 1973) are more dynamic interventions, focusing on the help the various roles in an organization can give each other in order to increase their effectiveness. Although these three interventions skirt the problems of role conflict and role stress, they are, nevertheless, very useful for the purpose for which they have been used.

The intervention discussed here is focused on confronting the problems of role conflict and role stress and on evolving strategies of mutual help to cope with these problems among the various roles in an organization. It helps the various role occupants develop joint exploratory strategies. The concepts of role, role stress, and the strategies for coping with role stress are relevant for the intervention.

ORGANIZATIONAL ROLES

The concept of role is the key concept in understanding the integration of the individual with the organization. It is through role that the individual interacts with and becomes (or does not become) integrated with the organization. Katz and Kahn (1966) give role the central place in the organization by defining human organizations as role systems. They use two terms: *office* and *role*.

> Office is essentially a relational concept, defining each position in terms of its relationships to others and to the system as a whole. Associated with each office is a set of activities or expected behaviours. These activities constitute the *role* to be performed, at least approximately, by any person who occupies that office. (p. 173)

Other authors also make a distinction between position, or office, and role. Although Linton (1936), the first among the proposers of the concept of role, viewed the concepts of status and role in an integrated way, the word *role* has been given two meanings. Sometimes the term is used to denote the position a person holds in an organization—along with the expectations derived from that position, e.g., the role of a teacher, a policeman, etc.—and sometimes it is used to describe expected behavior or activities only (for example, the disciplinarian role or evaluator role of a teacher, task and maintenance roles, etc.). Thomas and Biddle (1966) have discussed the various terms used in role theory. In this discussion, the word *role* means any position a person holds in a system (organization), as defined by the expectations that various significant persons, including himself, hold of that position. The term *function* indicates a set of interrelated expectations from a role. In these meanings, "sales manager" is a role, and developing a sales force and customer contact is his function.

As shown in Figure 1, the organization has its own structure and goals, and, similarly, the individual has his personality and needs (motivation). These interact and become integrated to some extent in the role. (Pareek, 1974, discusses role as a central concept in work motivation.)

The overlapping region between the individual and the organization is the role, as illustrated in Figure 2.

Role Space

As suggested by Katz and Kahn (1966), an organization can be defined as a system of roles. However, role itself is a system. From the point of view of an individual, two role systems are important: (1) the system of the various roles the individual occupies and performs and (2) the system of the various roles of which his role is a part and in which his role is defined by other significant roles. The first is called *role space*; the second is known as *role set*.

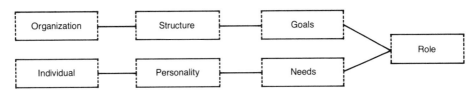

Figure 1. Role as the Integrating Point of the Organization and the Individual

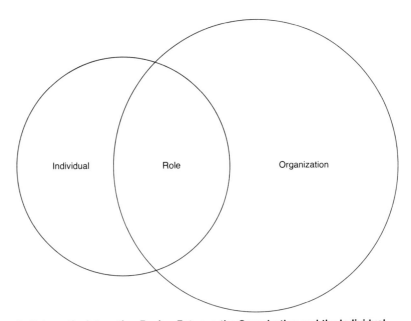

Figure 2. Role as the Interacting Region Between the Organization and the Individual

A person may be a son, a father, a salesman, a member of a club, a member of a voluntary organization, and so on. All these roles make up his role space. In the center of the role space is the self. Just as the concept of role is central to the concept of organizations, the concept of self is central to the concept of role.

> The term "self" refers to the inferences the person makes about the referent for "I." It is a cognitive structure and derives from past experience with other persons and with objects. We define the *self* as the experience of identity arising from a person's inter-behaving with things, body parts, and other persons. (Sarbin & Allen, 1968, p. 523)

The person performs various roles revolving around the self, roles that are at various distances from the self and from each other. These relationships define the role space. Role space, then, is the dynamic interrelationship both between the self and the various roles an individual occupies and among these roles.

The distance between a role and the self indicates the extent to which the role is integrated with the self. When we do not enjoy a particular role or do not get involved in it, there is distance between the self and the role. Goffman (1961) and Ruddock (1969) call it role-distance. "When a person is not fully absorbed in his role behavior and allows it to be seen that this is so, we speak of role-distance" (Ruddock, 1969, p. 14). The phrase *self-role distance*, however, is used here to denote this. Similarly, there may be distance between one role and another role a person occupies. For example, the role of club member may be distant from the role of husband, if the two roles conflict. This I call *interrole distance* or *interrole conflict*.

A role-space map of an individual can, then, be drawn by locating the self in the center and placing the various roles he occupies at various distances from the self and from each other. In Figure 3, the numbers 1 to 9 identify various circles representing distance from the self—1 denoting the least distance and 9 the most distance. Each of an individual's various roles may be located in one of the circles and in one of the four quadrants. For example, if roles A and B are both at a distance of 8 from the self but have maximum distance from each other, both can be located in the circle marked 8, but opposite each other. Self-role and interrole distance are important parts of personality. Some psychologists define personality as a system of action arising out of the interplay of self and role (Ruddock, 1969; Sarbin, 1964).

Banton (1965) has proposed the concepts of basic, general, and independent roles. Basic and general roles are related (e.g., "husband" is a basic role, and "working woman's husband" is a general role). The term *role repertory* is used to indicate a collection of such roles. Ruddock (1969) uses the term *roletree* to indicate a branching network concept. The trunk corresponds to the basic role, the main branches to the general roles, the secondary branches to special roles, and the leaves to the transient roles.

Role Set

As proposed by Merton (1957), *role set* is the "complement of role relationships which persons have by virtue of occupying a particular social status" (p. 369). The term has been widely used in the literature to mean the pattern of relationship between the role being considered and other roles.

The individual's role in an organization is defined by the expectations held by significant roles—including the individual himself—in that organization. The individual's own expectations of his role are termed *reflexive role expectations* by Kahn and Quinn (1970). Katz and Kahn (1966) use the term *focal person* for the individual who occupies the role and *role senders* for persons in the role set of the individual. I use the term *role occupant* for the individual who occupies a particular role and *other roles* for all other roles in the role set of the individual.

A role-set map, like a role-space map, can also be prepared for an individual's role. In this map the role of the role occupant will be in the center, and all other roles can be located at various points on the map. Using a circular model (such as in Figure 3), the roles can be located in the circles marked 1 to 9—1 indicating the roles nearest to the role occupant's role and 9 indicating the roles at the greatest distance from his role. The term *role-role distance* indicates the distance between the role of the role occupant and other roles. The smaller this distance, the higher the *role linkage*, which can be defined as the reverse of role-role distance. Role linkage is an important concept in role satisfaction and role conflict.

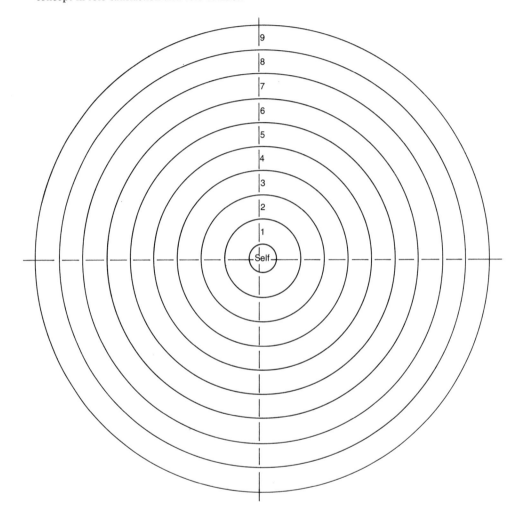

Figure 3. Role-Space Map

214

Role Taking

The process by which the individual establishes identification with the organization is *role taking*. There are two aspects of role taking. One aspect relates to the individual's self-concept and the way he responds to the various expectations held by other roles of his own role. He may react very positively and with great satisfaction to the expectations and fulfill these expectations to the best of his capability. Such a reactive approach will help the individual occupy the role effectively. In contrast, another individual may use the expectations he himself holds of the role he occupies and develop role behavior in which his own expectations play a major role. This is a proactive approach to role performance. Some authors have contrasted these two approaches by calling the first "role taking" and the second "role making."

The other aspect of role taking is concerned with the identification of the self with the role. If the role is so different from the self that the expectations conflict with the self-concept, what I have called self-role distance may result. This aspect of role taking may be called *role acceptance*. Even when there is no evident self-role distance, the degree of role acceptance may be low or high. Sarbin and Allen (1968) have proposed seven levels of intensity of role taking, defining this in terms of how much the individual is able to get into the role. These range from casual roles to the emergence of a moribund person.

Katz and Kahn (1966) have proposed the concept of *role episode* to explain the process of role taking. Role taking involves both role sending (by occupants of other roles) and role receiving (by the role occupant). The role occupant and the other roles (role senders) constantly interact; the process of role sending and role receiving influence the role behavior of the individual. The role senders have expectations on the basis of their perception of the role occupant's behavior. The role occupant acts on the basis of his perception of the role being sent to him. However, his role behavior also influences the expectations of the role senders. Thus, role episode has a feedback loop. Katz and Kahn have elaborated this concept to include interaction between role senders and the role occupant, as well as interpersonal and personality factors. (See Figure 4.)

THE NATURE OF ROLE STRESS

In the role behavior of an individual, several variables are involved—the self, the other roles (role senders), the expectations held by the other roles, the expectations held by the self, roles under-taken and performed by the individual. It is extremely difficult to imagine situations in which there is no conflict among these variables. The very nature of the role has a built-in potential for conflict and stress. Thus, conflict is a natural variable in role performance. Conflict and stress need not, however, be necessarily negative in their effect on the individual and the organization. Some

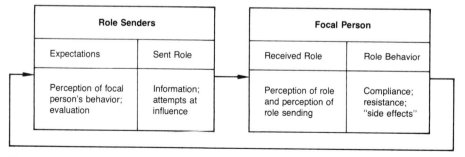

Figure 4. A Model of the Role Episode

amount of stress is necessary for the effective working of both an individual and the organization. It is not the presence or absence of stress that makes the individual or organization effective or ineffective, but the way in which this stress is managed.

The concept of stress has been popular in psychology. Four common terms have been used that are synonymous in meaning: *stress, strain, conflict,* and *pressure.* Lazarus (1966) has defined stress as any force directed at an object. Role conflict has been defined in terms of conflicting expectations. The word *strain* has been used to denote the effect of stress on the individual; the word *pressure* has also been used. It is useful, however, to use these terms interchangeably in order to understand the incompatibility of certain role-related variables, their effects on the individual's behavior, and the efforts he makes in dealing with them.

Several systems of classifications have been used to discuss role conflict and stress. Kahn and Quinn (1970) have classified role stress under three main headings: expectation-generated stress, in which they include role ambiguity and role conflict; expectation-resource discrepancies, in which they include role overload, responsibility-authority dilemma, and inadequate technical information; and role and personality. I find it more functional to use the two main role constellations as areas of conflict and stress.

Role-Space Conflicts

Any conflicts within the field of role space are referred to as role-space conflicts. These conflicts may be the following:

1. *Self-role distance.* If a person occupies a role that he may subsequently find is conflicting with his self-concept, he feels the stress. For example, a usually introverted person, who is fond of studying and writing, may have self-role distance if he accepts the role of salesman in an organization and comes to realize that the expectations held of the role would include his meeting people and being social. Such conflicts are fairly common.

2. *Intrarole conflict.* Since the individual learns to develop expectations as a result of his socialization and identification with significant others, it is quite likely that he sees some incompatibility between two expectations (functions) of his own role. For example, a professor may see incompatibility between the expectations of teaching students and of doing research. Inherently these may not be conflicting, but the individual may perceive them as such.

3. *Role-growth stress.* Just as an individual grows physically, so he also grows in the role he occupies in an organization. With the advancement of the individual, his role changes, and with this change in role, the need for his taking his new role becomes crucial. This is the problem of role growth; it becomes an acute problem especially when an individual has occupied a role for a long time and he enters another role in which he may feel less secure. The new role demands that the individual outgrow his previous role and occupy the new role effectively, and this produces some stress in the individual. In organizations that are expanding rapidly and do not have a systematic strategy of manpower development, managers are likely to experience this stress when promoted to higher positions.

4. *Interrole conflict.* Since the individual occupies more than one role, there may be conflicts between two roles he occupies. For example, an executive often faces a conflict between his organizational role as an executive and his familial role as husband and father. The demands from his wife and children to share his time may be incompatible with organizational demands. Such interrole conflicts are quite frequent in modern society.

Role-Set Conflicts

Conflicts that arise as a result of incompatibility among the expectations held by significant other roles and those held by the individual himself are referred to as role-set conflicts. These conflicts are as follows:

1. *Role ambiguity.* When the individual is not clear about the various expectations people have of his role, he faces the conflict that may be called role ambiguity. Role ambiguity may be due to a lack of information available to the role occupant or a lack of understanding of the cues available to him. Kahn and Quinn (1970) have suggested that role ambiguity may occur in relation to activities, responsibilities, personal style, and norms. They have suggested three loci of role ambiguity: the expectations that role senders hold of the role occupant, the expectations sent by the role sender to the role occupant, and the expectations the role occupant receives and interprets in the light of prior information and experience. They indicate four different kinds of roles that are likely to experience ambiguity: roles new to the organization, roles in expanding or contracting organizations, roles in organizations exposed to frequent changes in demand, and roles in process. Role ambiguity may also result in various other conflicts.

2. *Role overload.* When the role occupant feels that there are too many expectations from the significant roles in his role set, he experiences role overload. This term has been popularized by Kahn et al. (1964). They measured this stress by asking people whether they felt they could possibly finish work given to them during a modified work day and whether they felt that the amount of work they did might interfere with how well it was done. Most executive role occupants experience role overload. Kahn and Quinn (1970) have suggested some conditions under which role overload is likely to occur: in the absence of a mechanism for role integration, in the absence of power of the role occupants, in the large variations in the expected output, and when delegation or assistance cannot procure more time.

3. *Role-role distance.* In a role set, the role occupant may feel that certain roles are psychologically near to him, while some other roles are at a distance. The main criterion of role-role distance is frequency and ease of interaction. When linkages are strong, the role-role distance will be low. In the absence of strong linkages, the role-role distance may be high. The role-role distance can, therefore, be measured in terms of existing and desired linkages. The gap between the desired and the existing linkages will indicate the amount of distance between the two roles.

4. *Role erosion.* A role occupant may feel that some functions he would like to perform are being performed by some other role. The stress felt is called role erosion. Role erosion is the subjective feeling of an individual that some important role expectations he holds of his role are not shared by other roles in his role set. Role erosion is likely to be experienced in an organization that is redefining its role and creating new roles. In one organization, for example, one role was abolished and two roles were created to cater to the executive and planning needs. This led to great stress for the role occupants of both new roles, who felt that their roles had become less important compared to the older role.

Some factors associated with role stress have been identified in research studies. Snock (1966) has reported that the larger the role set of a role occupant, the greater the strain he is likely to experience. Age (younger), experience (less), and size (medium) of the department have been found to be significantly associated with role strain (Richardson, 1973). Lack of empathy and the creation of new roles are two important factors contributing to role stress. However, role variety, i.e., a number of completely dissimilar occupational categories in the organization, has been found to be associated with the ability to cope with uncertainty (Tyler, 1973). Thus, role variety and role specificity (Danet & Gurevitch, 1972) have been found to be two important factors preventing role stress. But the fact remains that the various forms of role stress create problems for the individual and for the organization. However, it is not the presence of stress that may affect the working of the organization, but the way in which stress is managed. The coping behavior of the individual and the organization is important in this respect.

COPING WITH ROLE STRESS

When an individual or an organization experiences role stress, some way of coping with the stress is adopted. Individuals and organizations cannot remain in a continuous state of tension. The strategy adopted may be deliberate and conscious, or, for example, the strategy may be simply to leave the conflict and stress to take care of themselves. This, too, is a strategy, although the individual or the organization may not be aware of it. It is useful for both individuals and organizations to examine what strategy they are using to cope with stress. No strategy at all may lead to a lack of effectiveness. Hall (1972) has reported that simply coping (as opposed to not coping) is important to satisfaction, rather than a particular coping strategy.

Kahn and Quinn (1970) have suggested making a distinction between coping strategies in terms of whether the coping is directed at "the environmental stressors" or "the resultant affect it elicits in the role occupant" (p. 82). For the former, they cited Jahoda (1958) who has distinguished between "passive" adaptation (changes in the self or one's behavior) and "environmental mastery" (active attempts to change the environment). Strategies for coping with the resultant affect of stress—like anger, dissatisfaction, guilt, tension, etc.—could take the form of ego-defensive mechanisms (rationalization, projection, displacement, etc.) or artistic redefinition of the situation (understanding the power of the other role, denying responsibility, minimizing the seriousness of the situation, etc.).

Two Basic Coping Strategies

Broadly classified into two kinds, coping strategies are used either to avoid the stress, in the hope that time will take care of it, or to face the stress and find a solution for it. The first strategy may be called an avoidance strategy. Such a strategy does not contribute to problem solving and, therefore, is dysfunctional. Most avoidance strategies would use defensive behavior and reduce tension but not resolve the problem. Using the term suggested by Golembiewski (1973), these may also be called degenerating strategies, since they lead to a lack of effectiveness on the part of both the individual and the organization.

The other set of strategies uses confrontation as the main approach. Instead of avoiding problems, these strategies help the individual and the organization solve the problem and thus are functional. In Golembiewski's language, they may also be called regenerating strategies since they help the individual and the organization become more functional and increase their self-renewing capacities.

One basic difference between the two sets of strategies is that a confrontation strategy implies that the role occupant believes that he, along with others, can influence the situation, while an avoidance strategy implies that he believes he is not capable of influencing the situation. Gemmill and Heisler (1972) have shown that the greater the belief in one's ability to influence the environment, the lower is the reported job strain.

Applying this broad classification of strategies, there are two ways in which any role conflict or role stress can be managed. Figure 5 summarizes the two main ways of managing the different conflicts discussed earlier.

Role-Space Conflicts

1. *Self-role distance.* The individual may deal with stress in the form of self-role distance in two ways. In the extreme form, the individual may either choose his self-concept and in turn reject the role, or choose his role and in turn reject his self-concept. Many individuals whose self-concept conflicts with the role they occupy in an organization may simply play that role in a routine way to earn their living. They have rejected the role. On the other hand, some other individuals may seriously occupy their roles and, in due time, completely forget their self-concept and play that

218

role effectively, rejecting their self. One important personality characteristic that may influence the decision of the individual to reject the self or the role is inner or other directedness. It has been reported that self-oriented individuals deal with incompatibility by being consistent with their needs while other-directed individuals deal with it by being consistent with prevailing socially induced forces. Both these approaches are dysfunctional. If an individual rejects the role, he is likely to be ineffective in the organization. However, if he rejects the self, he is likely to lose his effectiveness as an individual, perhaps impairing his mental health.

A functional strategy for dealing with this stress is to attempt role integration. The individual may analyze the various aspects of the roles that are causing self-role distance and may begin to acquire skills to bridge this gap or may carry his own self into the role by defining some aspects of the role according to his own skills. In other words, an attempt both to grow in the role and to make the role develop to suit the special capabilities of the person would result in role integration. With this strategy, the individual gets the satisfaction of occupying a role that is nearer to his self-concept. Such an integration is not easy to achieve, but with systematic effort, it can be done.

2. *Intrarole conflict*. Intrarole conflict is both a role-space and a role-set conflict. One way to deal with this stress is to eliminate from the role those expectations that are likely to conflict with other expectations. This is the process of *role shrinkage*, the act of pruning the role in such a way that some expectations can be given up. Although role shrinkage may help avoid the problem, it is a dysfunctional approach, since the advantage of a larger role is lost. Instead, role linkages can be established with other roles and the problem solved by devising some new ways of achieving the conflicting expectations. In this way, the individual can experience both growth and satisfaction. If, for example, a professor is experiencing conflict among three expectations from his role —teaching students, doing research, and consulting with organizations—he may find that the conflict is basically because he does not have enough skills for doing research. He may thus take recourse in role shrinkage. A better way to deal with this problem is to develop role linkages with other colleagues who are good in research and work out an arrangement whereby research is not neglected. Finding more nontraditional and productive ways of doing things may be an even more satisfactory method.

Role Conflict	Avoidance; Dysfunctional, Degenerating Strategies	Confrontation; Functional, Regenerating Strategies
Role-Space Conflicts		
1. Self-role Distance	Self/Role Rejection	Role Integration
2. Intrarole Conflict	Role Shrinkage	Role Linkage, Creativity
3. Role-Growth Stress	Role Fixation	Role Transition
4. Interrole Conflict	Role Elimination and Rationalization	Role Negotiation
Role-Set Conflicts		
1. Role Ambiguity	Role Prescription and Role Taking	Role Clarification and Role Making
2. Role Overload	Prioritization	Role Slimming
3. Role-Role Distance	Role Boundness (Efficient Isolation)	Role Negotiation
4. Role Erosion	Fight for Rights and Rules	Role Enrichment

Figure 5. Two Types of Coping Strategies

3. *Role-growth stress.* When individuals get into new roles as a result of their advancement in the organization or as a result of taking over more challenging roles, there may be a feeling of apprehension because the role is new and may require skills that the role occupant does not have. In such a situation, a usual strategy is to continue to play the previous role about which the individual is sure and which he has been doing successfully. In many cases people at the top management level of an organization continue to play the role of a lower-level manager. A foreman, for example, in due course may become general manager and still play the role of the foreman, with consequent frustrations for the new foreman and for others who expect him to devote his time to more productive aspects. In one organization, for example, after several self-searching sessions, it became clear that the tendency of the senior management level toward close supervision was really a tendency to continue to play old roles. This occurs especially if the individual role requires more new skills that have to be developed, such as planning roles and the role of scanning the environment. In the absence of such skills, the usual tendency is to fall back on old tried-and-tested roles. This is role fixation.

It is nevertheless necessary for people to grow out of their old roles into new ones and face up to new challenges. A more functional way to resolve this conflict is through *role transition*, a phrase borrowed from Burr (1972). Role transition is the process by which a previous role, no matter how successful and satisfying it may have been, is given up to take on a new and more developed role. Burr has suggested that role transition is helped by various processes, including anticipatory socialization, role clarity, substitute gratification, and transition procedure. In order to make role transition more effective, it is necessary to have anticipatory socialization, i.e., preparation for the taking of the new role. This would also include the delegation of responsibility and functions to people below one's own role, so that the person can be free to experiment and to take help in such experimentation from others. Such a process of role transition can be very useful.

4. *Interrole conflict.* The usual approach to dealing with this type of conflict is either to partition the roles clearly, so that a person is a husband or a father when he is at home and an executive when he is in his office, or to eliminate one role, i.e., accepting one role at the cost of the other role. In such a case, the individual takes recourse in rationalization. For example, an executive who neglects his family at home and in this process eliminates his role of father and husband rationalizes the process by thinking that he makes a unique contribution to the company and, therefore, can afford to neglect his family or that he earns enough for his family to pay the price of losing him as a husband and a father. Such rationalizations are part of the process of role elimination. Hall (1972) has used the words *partitioning* and *eliminating* in the sixteen specific behavioral strategies he has identified in dealing with role conflicts. He suggests that these strategies are dysfunctional because they only avoid the problem and do not help individuals confront and resolve the issues.

A more functional approach to the problem is *role negotiation*. Role negotiation has been developed by Harrison (1971) as a technique of dealing with various problems of role conflict. The process of role negotiation is the process of establishing mutuality of roles and getting necessary help to play the roles more effectively and of giving help in turn to the other role. For example, an executive who is not able to find time for his family may sit down and negotiate with his wife and children on how best he can spend time meaningfully within the given constraints. One executive in the largest nationalized bank in India solved the problem by discussing it with his family and working out an arrangement whereby he would give entire Sundays to his family and would not normally accept invitations to dine out unless both the wife and the husband were invited. This negotiation was highly satisfying because neither of the roles had to be sacrificed and eliminated.

Role-Set Conflict

The various coping strategies for each of these four previously identified conflicts are discussed here.

1. *Role ambiguity.* The usual approach to the conflict of role ambiguity is to clarify the roles by writing things on paper. This is *role prescription.* The various expectations are thus defined more clearly, or the individual may remove ambiguity by fitting into the role as described in some expectations. This is the process of role taking. A more functional approach may be to seek clarification from various sources and to define the role in the light of such clarifications. A more creative way is to define the role according to one's own strength and to take steps to make the role more challenging. This is the process of role making.

2. *Role overload.* To deal with the problem of role overload, i.e., a feeling of too many expectations from several sources, the role occupant usually prepares a list of all functions in terms of priorities. This kind of prioritization may help put things in order of importance; however, the problem may be that the functions with which a person is less familiar tend to be pushed lower down the priority list and neglected, while those functions that a person is able to perform without any effort get top priority. This approach, therefore, may be dysfunctional. A more functional approach may be to redefine the role and see which aspects of the role can be delegated to other persons who may be helped to assume these functions, thus helping other individuals to grow also. This may be called role slimming. The role does not lose its vitality in the process of delegating some functions; in fact, the vitality increases with the decrease in obesity.

3. *Role-role distance.* When there is tension between two roles in an organization, the distance between these roles is likely to be large. The linkage in such a case will be weak. The usual tendency in such a stress situation is for each role occupant to play the role most efficiently and avoid interactions. The role occupant conflicts himself to his own role. This may be called *role boundness* (Garg & Parikh, 1975), in which the role occupant voluntarily agrees to be bound by the role. In some organizations individual executives and managers may be highly efficient in their own roles but do not take corporate responsibility; their linkages with other roles are very weak. The individual withdraws in an isolation of efficiency. He gets satisfaction out of playing the individual role effectively and efficiently but does not contribute as much as he could to the overall organization. This approach is thus likely to be dysfunctional. A better method of approach is role negotiation (Harrison, 1971), which can be used for resolving such conflict, as well as the previously discussed interrole conflict.

4. *Role erosion.* The usual reaction to a situation of role erosion is to fight for the rights of the role and to insist on a clarification of roles. However, this is not likely to be functional and helpful, since the basic conflict continues. A better approach may be that of role enrichment. Like job enrichment, the concept of role enrichment involves a vertical loading of the role.

Cummings and ElSalmic (1970) have proposed the idea of role diversity, similar to the concept of role enrichment. According to them, role-set diversity is measured in terms of the number of roles with which the role occupant maintains work relationships. They have reported that a highly diversified role set provides the executive with varied sources of stimulation and, therefore, leads to managerial satisfaction. They found that this variable contributed more to satisfaction than the company size or subunit size.

Role enrichment can be done by analyzing the role systematically and helping the individual see the various strengths in that role and the various challenges that the role contains but that may not be apparent to the individual when he occupies it. Significant role members can help make the role more challenging and satisfying to the role occupant.

INTERROLE EXPLORATION

The various coping strategies outlined make it clear that confrontation strategies are more functional and contribute to the regenerating process. In order to use these strategies it is necessary to work out systematic ways of implementing them. A method evolved and tested in several organizations in India is discussed briefly here.

Interrole exploration (IRE) is used for strengthening various roles in an organization, through a joint effort on the part of these roles. IRE is used for role-set conflicts. Occupants of all the roles in a role set participate in IRE.

The main focus of IRE is on developing confrontation and functional coping strategies for various kinds of role stress. There are various dimensions of interrole interaction that are significant in this connection. IRE is not only a technique of coping with stress, but an approach, a philosophy of working in an organization. The following dimensions are particularly relevant for IRE.

1. *Mutuality versus exclusiveness*. IRE attempts to build mutuality among roles. Giving help and receiving help are possible only in a relationship of mutuality. Davidson and Kelley (1973) have reported the social effect on stress reduction. Mutuality is a function of trust and the perception of the importance and power of the other role as well as of one's own role. (See Figure 6.) If a role occupant perceives his own role or the other role to lack power, other kinds of relationships may develop between the two roles.

2. *Creativity versus conformity*. IRE attempts to stimulate persons in an organization to search for new solutions to the problems they face in working together. The emphasis is on attempting alternative ways of solving a problem. IRE de-emphasizes the use of traditional methods of problem solving, if these methods have not proved to be efficacious. Creativity can be achieved by looking at the problem from different angles, and IRE stresses this. Creativity is related to an internal locus of control. Gemmill and Heisler (1972) have reported that the greater the belief in one's ability to influence the environment, the lower the reported job strain.

3. *Confrontation versus avoidance*. The main philosophy underlying IRE is that problems can be solved if they are brought to the surface and a conscious attempt is made to search for a solution. Instead of avoiding the problems either by not looking at them or by working on nonissues in the organization, IRE attempts to help the various role occupants confront the problems they face in order to find a solution for them. According to this approach, the confrontation of problems is necessary to reach a lasting solution.

4. *Exploration versus expectation of ready-made solutions*. IRE attempts to help people evolve a solution rather than expect any such solution from experts or from persons in the organization. The usual tendency is to look for a ready-made solution to relieve the tension, especially if it is suggested and prescribed by an authority figure like an expert or a member of top management. The underlying philosophy of IRE is that such a solution may not be effective in solving a problem. Effective solutions can come about only through exploration rather than acceptance of an ideal solution. Exploration means a joint effort at understanding the problem and weighing the alternate solutions to that problem.

Perceived Power

		Neither	Only Role Occupant	Only the Other	Both
Trust	Low	Isolation	Coercion	Withdrawal	Exclusiveness and/or Rivalry
	High	Mutual Sympathy	Nurturance	Dependency	Mutuality

Figure 6. Relationship Patterns Under Different Conditions of Trust and Perceived Power

IRE, as an intervention, uses a structured approach with process orientation. Although the various steps involved in IRE are aimed at generating data using structured exercises, the work on these data involves group work, and the solutions can be achieved only through process-oriented work on the problems brought to the surface by the data generated in the structured exercises. By using the structured exercises, the problems and issues of interrole relationships are confronted (Pareek, 1975).

REFERENCES

Banton, M. *Roles.* London: Tavistock, 1965.

Buck, V. E. *Working under pressure.* London: Staples Press, 1972.

Burr, W. R. Role transitions: A reformulation of theory. *Journal of Marriage and the Family,* 1972, *34*(3), 407-416.

Child, J., & Ellis, T. Predictions of variation in managerial roles. *Human Relations,* 1973, *26*(2), 227-250.

Cummings, L. L., & ElSalmic, A. M. The impact of role diversity, job level, and organisational size on managerial satisfaction. *Administrative Science Quarterly,* 1970, *15*(1), 1-11.

Danet, B., & Gurevitch. Presentation of self in appeals to bureaucracy. *American Journal of Sociology,* 1972, *77*(6), 1165-1190.

Davidson, P. O., & Kelly, W. R. Social facilitation and coping with stress. *British Journal of Social and Clinical Psychology,* 1973, *12*(2), 130-136.

Dayal, I., & Thomas, J. M. Operation KPE: Developing a new organisation. *Journal of Applied Behavioral Science,* 1968, *4*(4), 473-506.

Dunkin, M. J. The nature and resolution of role conflicts among male primary school teachers. *Sociology of Education,* 1972, *45*(2), 167-185.

French, J. R. P. Quantification of organizational stress. In *Managing organizational stress.* Princeton, N.J.: Educational Testing Service, 1968.

Garg, P., & Parikh, I. *Profiles in identity.* New Delhi: Rajpal & Sons, 1975.

Gemmill, G. R., & Heisler, W. J. Fatalism as a factor in managerial job satisfaction, job strain, and mobility. *Personnel Psychology,* 1972, *25,* 241-250.

Goffman, E. *Encounters.* New York: Anchor Books, 1961.

Golembiewski, R. T. *Renewing organizations.* Chicago: Peacock, 1973.

Hall, D. T. A model of coping with role conflict: The role of college educated women. *Administrative Science Quarterly,* 1972, *17*(4), 471-486.

Harrison, R. Role negotiation: A tough minded approach to team development. In W. W. Burke & H. A. Hornstein (Eds.), *The social technology of organization development.* Washington, D.C.: NTL Learning Resources Corporation, 1971.

Jahoda, M. *Current concepts in positive mental health.* New York: Basic Books, 1958.

Jones, J. E. Role clarification: A team-building activity. In J. W. Pfeiffer & J. E. Jones (Eds.), *A handbook of structured experiences for human relations training* (Vol. V). La Jolla, Calif.: University Associates, 1975.

Kahn, R. L., et al. *Organizational stress: Studies in role conflict and ambiguity.* New York: John Wiley, 1964.

Kahn, R. L., & Quinn, R. P. Responses to role stress and mediating variables: Role stress: A framework for analysis. In A. McLean (Ed.), *Mental health and work organizations.* Chicago: Rand McNally, 1970.

Katz, D., & Kahn, R. L. *The social psychology of organizations.* New York: John Wiley, 1966.

Lazarus, R. S. *Psychological stress and the coping process.* New York: McGraw-Hill, 1966.

Linton, R. *The study of man.* New York: Appleton-Century-Crofts, 1936.

Merton, R. K. *Social theory and social structure.* Glencoe: Free Press, 1957.

Pareek, U. A conceptual model of work motivation. *Indian Journal of Industrial Relations,* 1974, *10*(1), 15-31.

Pareek, U. *Role effectiveness exercises.* New Delhi: Learning Systems, 1975.

Richardson, A., & Stanton, M. Role strain among sales-girls in a department store. *Human Relations,* 1973, *26*(4), 517-536.

Ruddock, R. *Roles and relationships.* London: Routledge & Kegan Paul, 1969.

Saly, S. M. Organizational role as a risk factor in coronary disease. Administrative Science Quarterly, 1969, *14,* 325-336.

Sarbin, T. R. Role theoretical interpretation of psychological change. In P. Worchel & D. Byrne (Eds.), *Personality change.* New York: John Wiley, 1964.

Sarbin, T. R., & Allen V. L. Role theory. In G. Lindzey & E. Aronson (Eds.), *The handbook of social psychology* (Vol. 2). Reading, Mass.: Addison-Wesley, 1968.

Sherwood, J. J. An introduction to organization development. In J. W. Pfeiffer & J. E. Jones (Eds.), *The 1972 annual handbook for group facilitators.* La Jolla, Calif.: University Associates, 1972.

Sherwood, J. J., & Glidewell, J. C. Planned renegotiation: A norm-setting OD intervention. In W. G. Bennis et al., *Interpersonal dynamics* (3rd ed.). Homewood, Ill.: Dorsey Press, 1973.

Snock, J. D. Role strain in diversified role sets. *American Journal of Sociology,* 1966, *71,* 363-372.

Thomas, E. J., & Biddle, B. J. The nature and history of role theory. In B. J. Biddle & E. J. Thomas (Eds.), *Role theory: Concepts and research.* New York: John Wiley, 1966.

Tyler, W. B. Measuring organisational specialization: The concept of role variety. *Administrative Science Quarterly,* 1973, *18*(3), 383-392.

Udai Pareek, Ph.D., *is a professor of organizational behavior, Indian Institute of Management, Ahmedabad, India. He is the chairman of the Policy Board of the Behavioural Science Center (India) and the chairman of the Board of Directors, Learning Systems. He is also the editor of* Vikalpa: The Journal for Decision Makers *and* Indian Psychological Abstracts, *and a consulting editor for several journals, including* Psychologia *and* Organization and Administrative Science. *Dr. Pareek's background is in education, agricultural and rural change, health and industry, with a focus on process consultancy, change in persons and teams, systems designing, and organization development.*

A CURRENT ASSESSMENT OF OD: WHAT IT IS AND WHY IT OFTEN FAILS

J. William Pfeiffer and John E. Jones

Recently, there has been a great deal of discussion about whether organization development (OD), as a field, is headed toward its own dissolution. A growing number of practitioners are beginning to believe that OD may not crystallize as a profession.

BACKGROUND

Certain conditions have contributed to this development. In economically difficult times, a highly visible target such as an organization development program can easily be cut. There has been a tendency to institutionalize OD rather than to absorb its technology into the culture of organizations, resulting in the establishment of OD programs and departments that are independent of other parts of the organizational structure. By becoming independent, OD programs often make themselves competitive with other programs within the organization.

Also, many consultants have attempted to "sell" OD through routines, packages, solutions, and faddish approaches to the management of change. Although there has been an attempt by both internal and external consultants to legitimize and professionalize the practice of OD, it seems more a strategy for survival than an effort to provide a meaningful, flexible service to a variety of organizations. It is axiomatic that practice in the field of OD has far outstripped the building of theory. Research lags even further behind because of the difficulty in designing controlled studies in complex systems.

Most OD efforts have been aimed at symptoms rather than at large, systemic problems. Human-relations-oriented consultants frequently focus on correlative rather than mediative conditions. That is, a lab may be conducted to work on a trust problem rather than a team session being conducted to solve a production problem.

Definition of OD

Organization development is a term that we find ourselves using less and less because it is becoming relatively meaningless. There is a clear parallel with the now-nearly-forgotten term "sensitivity training," which came to mean too many things and thus ended up meaning nothing.

One of the difficulties with OD is that it has been a popular movement; many people doing traditional training for job enrichment, supervisory-skills training, etc., have found it fashionable to call themselves "organization development" specialists. Yet there is very little agreement as to what the term means.

The chart below indicates what "OD" means to us. What OD *is* may perhaps be most clearly delineated by what OD *is not*. This may be a roundabout way to a definition, but in fact it can also be an effective approach.

Activity	education	training	OD
Focus	the person	the job	the organization

This chart demonstrates the different emphases of education (person focused), training (job focused), and OD (organization focused). That is, the client in OD is *not* the individual, but rather the organization itself. The organization's effectiveness, its capacity to solve problems, its capacity to adapt, its capacity to do an effective job in creating a high quality of life for its employees—these are the central points on which OD focuses.

WHY OD FAILS

The major reason that OD fails may, in fact, be largely one of semantics. In failing adequately to define what OD is, practitioners have failed to define its goals, and in failing to define those goals they have made it virtually impossible to succeed.

Unrealistic Expectations

There are many unrealistic expectations connected with OD. It is frequently seen as a panacea, a cure-all, the new approach to organizational life that will finally rectify all the problems in the organization. This aim is clearly impossible. Such expectations stem from the belief that OD is a *product*, when in fact it is a *process*. OD can never be completed in any particular organization; it is an ongoing process, a way of looking at what is happening, and a way of recycling energy into the creation of a more viable organization.

Inadequate Support

Another reason why OD fails is inadequate or transient top-level support. OD projects are frequently initiated by one senior administrator. If that individual's interest wanes, or he moves on, or the pressures on the organization—financial realities or economic trends—influence him to withdraw his support, or he leaves the organization, the initiative that created the OD program is gone. Thus the people involved with the project may, in fact, find themselves without license to continue.

OD Unreadiness

Organization development often fails because of premature introduction. There is a concept in education called "reading readiness"—that is, children must be cognitively and physically ready to read before they can be taught to read by *any* method. Once the student has reading readiness and is motivated to read, it has been found that most techniques are equally effective. There is an analogous situation regarding organizations. Once an organization has what we call "OD readiness," almost any technique will be successful; inversely, when the organization has not reached that level, no techniques, no approaches, no theoretical models are viable. When members of an organization are lacking in communication skills, collaborative problem solving is highly unlikely. When persons who are deficient interpersonally are convened for problem identification, the processes that ensue often result in a worsening of the situation.

Failure to Follow Through

A remark that consultants often hear from managers is "We've tried OD before, and it won't work here." If a consultant has come into an organization and used such techniques as survey-feedback, sociotechnical systems, management by objectives, transactional analysis, or job enrichment, and has failed to follow through adequately, the organization is unlikely to be favorable toward another OD effort.

Ineffective Use of Consultants

Failure in OD often results from the ineffective use of both internal and external consultants. An effective OD program is a combination of an internal person who understands subtleties, nuances, and organizational pressures, and an external consultant who has the objectivity and the capacity to confront situations as he sees them. It is the linking of these two views, the internal and the external, that leads to effective interventions. OD projects conceived and initiated without adequate external advice and internal support are doomed to failure.

Management Resistance

Another extremely important factor in the failure of OD is frequently overlooked—the resistance of first-line supervisors. One of the major assumptions of OD is that individuals can become more self-directing; this theoretically reduces (or eliminates) the need for first-line supervision. When supervisors recognize that their jobs are in jeopardy, however, they predictably respond in a number of subtle and unsubtle ways to make sure that the OD effort does not succeed. Effective OD ultimately involves major restructuring of supervision.

Size of Organization

One difficulty with OD has to do with the organization's size. Our bias is that organizations of more than one thousand employees (and perhaps those with more than three to four hundred employees) are impervious to OD technology as it is known today. The theoretical models are neither practical nor effective when they are implemented in large systems. Two examples of OD technology scaled for large organizations—survey-feedback and sociotechnical systems—are examples of theory-based interventions that are cumbersome and extremely costly to implement.

The effects of unsuccessful attempts to introduce OD in large organizations are confusion, waste, and uncertainty. In many ways, the theoretical models available are inadequate to deal with larger organizations. This issue needs attention; new models must be postulated and tested.

Unwillingness to Model Behavior

OD is very frequently conceived of as something the other department needs. A president may decide that "something needs to be done" with the marketing group, or a vice president wants some changes within the manufacturing group. A general tendency is for the initiator of the project to exclude himself and his department, making it clear that he does not understand OD. This irony is most clearly present when training departments or OD departments (depending on the size of the system) are very interested in developing other components within their organization but are reluctant to manage their own change. They are usually unwilling to have "outsiders" "tinker" with their system. By not modeling appropriate behavior, OD staffs can make it very difficult for other managers to see that OD programs are meaningful.

Inadequate Skills

OD consultants very frequently are deficient in essential skills. It is our contention that anyone who is going to be a successful OD practitioner *must* be competent to facilitate a personal growth group. The same skills that are required in promoting interpersonal development are absolute prerequisites for an effective OD consultant.

OD consultants typically deny their own power. People helpers in general seem fearful of power, and OD consultants are no exception, viewing power in a distinctly different way than do managers. This difference frequently makes it very difficult to deal with the issue of power within the client system: when power situations arise, consultants often discount their own potency.

Consultants often fail to recognize that they are in a power position because of their role and expertise. They "de-skill" themselves when they deny their power.

OD consultants often fail to learn from other helping professions. For example, it has long been clear that counselor/therapists cannot isolate their own values in dealing with their clients. Nuances, subtleties, inflections, nonverbal cues, are, in fact, reinforcements of a helper's values. Exactly the same thing is true of OD consultants. Most possess humanistic values and are concerned about the quality of life in organizations, but they often pretend that they are free of values with regard to client organizations. Yet the consultant must be in touch with his values and communicate them clearly to systems. Advocacy consultation recognizes this need: know where you stand, be willing to say so, and do not try to hide your values; they are obvious to others.

Much has been made of the concept of process consultation. It has most notably extended OD theory and practice by prescribing an objective role for the consultant. We believe, however, that genuine process consultation is rarely practiced. Advocacy is a part of the individual, and, like any other facet, it can be seen in the process consultant's comments. It is subtly—and sometimes not so subtly—embedded in such things as what he actually observes, what he chooses to comment on, and the interventions he makes. Everything a consultant does implies a valuing process. Skills in successfully advocating humanistic values are generally underdeveloped in OD.

IMMUNITY TO OD

Some organizations seem to be immune to OD. This immunity is most evident in eleemosynary organizations, in which individuals' goals, when fully developed, are often in conflict with the organization's goals. This condition is encountered in churches, schools, service clubs, and other volunteer, nonprofit organizations.

An example can be seen in the university system. The professor's allegiance typically is to his discipline rather than to the institution. Students are frequently only tolerated instead of being seen as the focus of the institution. If an OD consultant were to work with professors to develop their ideal job, it would probably be one in which they would write, consult, travel, study, and not have to deal with either students or the administrative structure that is required to keep the organization going. The conflict between the full development of the individual professor and the prescribed and intended educational purpose of the university makes it difficult, if not impossible, for OD to be implemented successfully.

Another example involves the "Gray Ladies," who volunteer as social companions to hospitalized people. One OD project in a hospital involved an effort to improve the efficiency of the Gray Ladies. The result was that the women "discovered" that their major motivation for being there was not an altruistic desire to help the sick and needy, but their own loneliness and need to be involved. Not too astonishingly, they came to see their activity as an inefficient way to meet their needs, and many of them dropped out of the organization.

These examples illustrate that there are some organizations for which OD technology, as it is currently known, is not inclusive, potent, or definitive enough to augur for success in OD.

EVALUATION

Managers often ask—and we think it is a good question—"Why OD? Does it pay off on the 'bottom line'?" The difficulty is that we do not know. No OD project that we know of can be claimed to be a success on the bottom line. It is impossible to attribute organizational achievement to OD because of the time lag involved between the "treatment" and the "result." In addition, in long-term OD projects there are intervening economic variables that have more impact than OD techniques themselves. Recent examples include the Vietnam War and its impact on the economy, recessionary trends, the growing awareness of ecology, and the dramatic rise in oil prices, all of which, with their gross impact on bottom-line figures, tend to overwhelm any of the subtleties or pay-offs that might be attributable to OD.

As a result, the evaluation of OD is largely intuitional and impressionistic, and there are few managers who are willing to accept this type of evaluation for long. It is, therefore, impossible to "prove" that what OD consultants are doing is effective.

WHAT WE HAVE LEARNED

A number of generalizations can be abstracted from the relatively brief history of OD. Developing a technology of intervening in organizations has led us to the following insights, conclusions, assumptions, cautions, and beliefs.

OD is hard work. Organizations typically take a long time to accumulate the norms, systems, and informal patterns that characterize them. Quick, flashy interventions are not going to induce major, permanent changes.

Organizations inevitably develop; that is, change occurs regardless of the assistance of interventionists. Of course, OD often involves *planned* change, but it is important to recognize that change will occur in any case.

An OD program can become controversial within the organization. It can be seen as part of the problem facing the organization and thought of as a driving force for change. Personnel in the OD department can find themselves in competition for resources with other departments.

OD technology is the proper province of managers. The individuals who are now called OD practitioners might better consider themselves to be essentially educators, preparing managers to utilize OD technology along with other technologies.

What matters is goal attainment. It does not matter who does what, so much as it matters whether the organization's goals are being attained, at what expense, and consistent with what system of values.

An OD profession may be neither needed nor desirable at this time. Certification of internal and external OD specialists is premature. The impetus for controlling the practice of OD is coming from the practitioners rather than the clients.

Values cannot be imposed. When an attempt is made to get people involved in "humanistic" decision making within organizations, what is created is often only a façade of humanism.

OD cannot be sold. Efforts to convince managers and executives to initiate OD programs invariably fail. At best such efforts may make organizations more receptive to future proposals.

Managers will buy almost anything that offers a way out by promising an alleviation of production and human problems. Managers who have not been trained in behavioral science are particularly susceptible to faddish packages that offer high promise of symptom relief.

Applications of behavioral science to organization problems have not been dramatically successful. Behavioral science has been portrayed as a solution to many recurring managerial headaches, but the rapidly changing social and economic environment has made managing more difficult. Theory and research in management science, for example, have not kept up with the rising complexity of the management task. It can be argued that no major behavioral science theory has emerged during the short history of OD.

Premature definition of an emergent activity may affect its development in a deleterious way. If boundaries are put around the field of OD at this time, the development of its technology may be "frozen." Some ambiguous concepts have a heuristic value for a time. Such slogans as "black is beautiful" and "the great society" were useful for fostering inquiry and discussion and lifting our sights, even though they remained ambiguous. As soon as they were defined operationally, they lost their force. There is an analog in medical practice: "Use the new drug quickly before it fails."

Consultants may violate their own values. It is easy for consultants to adopt management practices different from the ones they are advocating and systematically to violate the very values they hope to inculcate within their client systems.

The outsider's perspective may have been overvalued. The external consultant may honestly believe that he has a unique perspective, owing to his grounding in theory and research, but he may neglect to gather the information he needs in order to be sensitive to the culture of the organization. It is easy for him to take "cheap shots" at the organization's norms and processes and equally easy for him to be seen as a management spy, pawn, or dupe.

OD can become elitist. Sometimes OD consultants fail to recognize that their major job is to work themselves out of a job by educating managers in the processes of more effective problem solving.

OD practitioners are prone to jargon. To gloss over a lack of knowledge about the complexity of human systems, many "OD consultants" use "special" language. This severely inhibits communication with clients.

Maintenance is less attractive than new projects. Many OD practitioners are more interested in working with new departments, teams, and problems than they are in the follow-through work needed to maintain the parts of the system with which they have consulted previously.

OD can be boring. Essentially, OD progresses through countless meetings, many of which are focused on problems and processes that have an all-too-familiar ring to them. OD consultants can become insensitive to such issues because of their repetitive quality. Most organizations have chronic, recurrent problems that have no easy solutions. It often takes many meetings and many interactions before effective solutions are generated.

SUGGESTIONS FOR FACILITATORS

The development of the OD "field" to date has a number of implications for group facilitators who are working or want to work with people in organizations. For facilitators to have a long-term, lasting effect on individuals, they must ultimately work within organizations. The implication is to learn how to apply human relations technology to the people problems that recur in organizations. Some suggestions:

1. Negotiate short-term contracts, being careful about promises. In the process of contracting, be explicit about your values.

2. Have a theory that you are able to articulate to clients, and use it as the basis for your work.

3. Develop a varied and eclectic repertoire.

4. Since the most meaningful OD activity is skill building on the part of managers, be prepared to "leave behind" some skills, knowledge, perspectives, and systemic thinking for the people who are charged with identifying and solving problems on a daily basis. Avoid fostering client dependency.

5. Keep a low profile. The objective of any OD consultant is to work himself out of a job. That is, the desirable end is that the organization have within it the resources to carry out its own development without your assistance.

6. Keep your own house in order. It is imperative that OD consultants model a high level of responsibility in both their private and their professional lives. This means that the group facilitator needs, from time to time, to take systematic inventory of his use of his own resources, his own self-actualization, and his own career development.

7. Avoid developing OD *programs;* stress *services* to managers on problem identification, problem solving, and planning.

8. Concentrate on building a base for successful OD through training and consultation. It is usually a mistake to bring people together to work on organizational situations if they do not have minimal skills in self-expression, a feeling of group membership, and enough trust so that problems can be confronted straightforwardly. Training is not only a good way of developing a climate for OD, it also equips organization members with the skills and readiness necessary for the application of OD technology.

9. Be careful what you build. Think systemically, and do not work in an isolated way on what appear to be independent segments of the organization but are, in fact, interdependent parts of a larger system.

10. Work with the priorities that are determined by management. Managers should determine what problems need to be considered within developmental programs, and the entire system rather than some "program" should be accountable for the results.

11. Work to develop a long-term mentality in managers. Consultants should aim at generating within management a larger perspective on change so that particular situations take on their proper significance.

CAVEAT EMPTOR

From this analysis of the current state of the "field" of OD, certain cautions can be pointed out for consumers of consultative services.

1. In OD programs for planned change, things usually get worse before they get better. Often the effort to "pull things apart" in order to study the processes of an organization results in a heightened awareness of its vulnerabilities. People tend to become aware of how decisions are made, how resources are utilized, and so on, and this increased openness can lead to a temporary decline in productivity.

2. Do not hire unknown consultants. It is important to recognize that OD consultation is a highly complex process, and group facilitators who are unprepared to provide services beyond the small-group level may not be qualified to work with managers on systemic analysis and planning.

3. Engage only in short-term contracting. The initial contract with a consultant may be viewed as a "getting acquainted" period, in which both sides test each other before engaging in longer-term arrangements.

4. Do not expect demonstrable results. The unique effects of OD interventions are not visible on the bottom line, and you will have to content yourself with impressionistic evaluations.

5. Run the program yourself. Organizations are managed by executives, not by consultants. It is important that the locus of control in planned-change efforts remain with those persons who are ultimately accountable for outcomes.

6. Do not become dependent on consultants. The consultant should equip you with skills in decision making, but the decisions must be yours.

7. Expect major changes to be slow. Organizations take a long time to get the way they are, and large-scale change efforts that are implemented too rapidly can result in heightened uncertainty and anxiety.

8. Establish some stability while change is being planned. Do not change with each new wind. Organization-assessment efforts should focus not only on identifying problems but

also on the aspects of the organization that are supportive and productive. A common fault in organization diagnosis is to fail to look for organization processes and characteristics that need to be reinforced and sustained.

9. Expect to have a lot of meetings. OD progresses primarily through a series of meetings that involve many people, much time, and a significant expenditure of organization resources.

SUMMARY STATEMENT

OD is nothing but a holistic application of behavioral science. It should be characterized by both creativity and practicality. The stress should be on skills, strategies, and systemic thinking. It follows, then, that if OD fails to survive as an identifiable field and yet the objective of creating greater interpersonal competence within organizations is met, there will be no loss. It seems likely that OD will survive as integrated activities conducted by a variety of professional people rather than by clearly identified "OD practitioners." In the long run, it is immaterial whether there is a distinct professional field called organization development.

J. William Pfeiffer, Ph.D., *is the president of University Associates, La Jolla, California. He is a co-editor of the University Associates* Handbook *series, the* five Annual Handbooks for Group Facilitators, *and* Group & Organization Studies: The International Journal for Group Facilitators. *Dr. Pfeiffer's background is in adult education, internal change-agentry, Gestalt group work, and organization development.*

John E. Jones, Ph.D., *is the vice president of University Associates, La Jolla, California. He is a co-editor of the University Associates* Handbook *series, the* five Annual Handbooks for Group Facilitators, *and* Group & Organization Studies: The International Journal for Group Facilitators. *Dr. Jones's background is in teaching and counseling, education, and organization and community-development consulting.*

INTRODUCTION TO THE
RESOURCES SECTION

"Access to tools," the *Whole Earth Catalog*'s subtitle, also reflects the intent of the *Annual*'s Resources section. Each year adds to the abundance of training materials available to the human relations facilitator; our hope is to provide the reader with a guide to what is current, useful, and worthy of attention.

Included this year: an extensive bibliography of the literature in organization development and planned change; brief accounts of bioenergetics and Hatha Yoga; and reviews of collections of books in the areas of personal growth and development, humanistic education, transactional analysis, and values clarification. Beginning this year, the *Annual* will change its format for book reviews and review primarily *collections* of books on different pertinent topics; reviews of single books will appear in the new University Associates journal, *Group & Organization Studies: The International Journal for Group Facilitators*, beginning with the March 1976 issue.

We are considering a number of projects for this section in future *Annuals*.

- An update of the directory of applied behavioral science consulting organizations, which first appeared in the 1975 *Annual*.
- The development of a directory of academic programs leading to advanced degrees in humanistic psychology and applied behavioral science.
- A review of the small-group literature for 1976-77 (this bibliography will appear every two years).
- A critical review of training "packages."
- An annotated listing of films and audio- and videocassettes applicable to human relations training.

Our aim is to offer up-to-date information, surveys, listings, and reviews useful for the human relations facilitator.

BIOENERGETIC THERAPY

Philip Katz

Fifteen years ago, as a psychotherapy patient, I felt a tightness and a choking sensation in my throat during one session. I was most amazed when my psychoanalytically oriented therapist interpreted my physical reaction as a holding back of crying. I ended the session feeling exhilarated that an analyst could have so much understanding and insight; I sensed that he had come close to a core problem. Unfortunately, the insight was not followed up, and it took me many years and bioenergetic therapy to understand that the choking sensation in my throat was my body's attempt to spare me—and to choke off—the hurt and pain over early experiences. I could not face the hurt and pain directly as long as my throat muscles were spastic and rigid, unable to be shaken back to their elastic state through an organismic, all-consuming crying.

Man's Quest for Health

The never-ending quest for emotional health and freedom has been largely based on an attempt to find relief and release through the mind, intellect, will, guiding principles, formats, technology, or a chemical armamentarium. If we hit on the key, the right button, the precise timing, the accurate dosage, the regulated input, the logical rebuttal, then we can say good-bye to hangups. Wish it were so! The quest is only one example of our culture's blind faith that there is an appropriate technology to deal with all of man's problems and dilemmas and that all we have to do is to find it. However, we must take into account nature's phylogenetic attempt to manage threats to the self, a process that has been going on for millions of years, is rooted in our biology or body structure, and can be dealt with only in a limited way by rational, technological approaches—a relatively recent evolvement in the span of time.

Nature's Response to Threat

Nature has its own responses to different threats to one's being, integrity, selfhood, and sexuality at various developmental levels. When there is a threat to the human infant or child (and even the prenatal organism), the body reacts to maintain its survival. These solutions delimit the human organism in its life functioning. Thus, if the human being is threatened at the early stages of life, the individual instinctively dissociates himself from threatening sensations by shutting off any bodily awareness (and, when consciousness develops, its functionally equivalent psychic counterpart); by binding tension and free-flowing energy into the muscular system; by focusing on ego solutions and ideals to foster the illusion of a lack of threat; and by developing life styles that avoid contact with the threat or that paradoxically and unconsciously re-create paradigms of the original threat situation.

THE BIOENERGETIC APPROACH

Most psychotherapies focus on ego solutions that attempt to increase the ego's control and awareness, to reverse the unwanted behavior or symptoms, and to extend one's range of choice alternatives. The bioenergetic therapist, however, believes that the muscular blockages and their containment of tension and energy, which block off feeling and awareness, must be penetrated and analyzed. Likewise, the disunity of the body has to be reversed so that life energies flow freely and the body becomes integrated and connected. The ego solutions and ideals and the accompanying illusions must be faced and understood.

Another way of viewing bioenergetic therapy is as an attempt to provide a comprehensive clinical-empirical-analytic-intuitive approach that gives full weight to the body structure and uses it as an enormous source of data to reconstruct early life experiences and to formulate hypotheses about the individual's aggressive-assertive function, sexual-genital function, life style and ego functioning, and capacity for tender-longing-love feelings. An individual is rooted in his bodily experiences, sensations, and awareness to the extent that he is rooted in his sexuality and ego and to the extent that he feels a connection to and support from the ground and earth.

What Bioenergetic Therapy Offers

Bioenergetic therapy promises no cures, no easy time in treatment, and no shortcuts. But it does hold out a hope: to the extent that one can surrender to his feelings and deal with his muscular tensions on both physical and psychic levels, life and sexual pleasures improve, delusions are shed for inner truths, good states of feeling become the norm, and feelings of increased vitality and improved physical health occur. To the extent that one can face fully the range of feelings (fear, terror, love, pain, and hurt) that are locked in his hypertonic or hypotonic musculature—which, in turn, reduces his full breathing—he can be free in his life functions.

The Techniques of Bioenergetic Therapy

Attacking the spastic musculature is accomplished through a series of physical exercises such as fixed stress positions, a variety of bodily movements, and vocal release, as well as the palpation of spastic musculature. These physical exercises are integrated with verbal-analytic techniques. The bioenergetic therapist is very much interested in breathing patterns and the points at which blocks to breathing occur (e.g., throat, chest, diaphragm, abdomen); body proportions and balance (e.g., the comparative development of the upper and lower halves of the body); the over- or underdevelopment of body parts (e.g., legs, thighs, pelvis, chest, shoulders); the quality of aggressive-assertive movements (e.g., hitting, kicking); the feeling tone and contact of the eyes (e.g., vacant, sad, longing, bewildered, radiant); the total body message (e.g., "Stay away!" or "Please love me!" or "Screw you!"); the degree of rigidity and flexibility of the total body and body parts. This enormous amount of data is used by the bioenergetic therapist in many ways: for diagnostic purposes, to formulate a treatment plan and select which exercises to use, to follow intuitive cues, and to check therapeutic progress.

The bioenergetic therapist believes that in the body an energy flow exists which swings rhythmically and longitudinally with patterned beats from its source, the solar plexus. The work of Reich (1973a,1973b) with energy forces provides a basic structure as well as departure point for bioenergetic therapists. Supportive evidence for energy forces within the human body comes from the study of electrodynamic force fields within and around the body, studies of the human aura and other auric energies, energy theories from the Far East, Russian scientists' studies of Kirlian photography and bioplasma, and a multitude of clinical and introspective reports.

Bioenergetic Therapy Applied

My opening illustration concerning the neck and its spastic muscles provides an example of bioenergetic therapy. The neck and the waist represent the two constrictions, or "border checkpoints," along the body's longitudinal axis. Thus, energy can be blocked, diverted, or trapped at these points in spastic musculature, shutting off feelings and sensations. A person can be "split off" at the neck level, so that he operates on the "head" level with its emphasis on the mind, the will, or logic. A person such as this may be overcharged in the head (energy can move upward to be used intellectually but may be prevented from moving downward and being released in pleasure) and may appear mechanical and without feeling. Not only can crying be locked in the neck and throat musculature, but so can rage and longing. The breath of life flows through the throat, and interference with this process leads to death, as any predatory animal—and its victim—knows. Thus, repressed death fears are at the level of the throat.

The bioenergetic therapist would employ a series of physical exercises, applying pressure at different levels of the throat to open energy blocks and to achieve improved breathing, which, in turn, will lead to an expression of the repressed feeling and to the release of affect. When, for example, the massive energy used to hold back crying is released and crying becomes a total organismic experience, the individual's breathing, color tone, eye contact, and experience of bodily sensations and aliveness all take on more positive aspects. The infant, unfettered by social constraints and without chronic muscular spasms, "knows" how to release his tensional discomforts by crying literally from head to toe, after which a state of relaxation characterized by slow, deep breathing ensues.

Results

In successful bioenergetic therapy, bodily changes that have functional counterparts in life functioning occur: as hung-up shoulders drop and become naturally rounded, the person no longer carries unwanted responsibilities; as an inflated chest deflates and becomes more relaxed, pretense and self-delusion diminish; as a person's rigid body becomes more flexible, feelings are experienced and choices in life become broader; as a retracted, stiffened pelvis loses its tightness and becomes more motile, both sexual and pleasure functions improve; as a person falls forward (or backward) spontaneously, a debilitating backache disappears; as stiffened legs loosen and take on more color tone, one feels more secure and grounded as a person; as a shoulder girdle immobilized by chronic spasticity loosens and relaxes, the person experiences more sensation and is able to function more aggressively as well as to reach out in a more loving way.

In this bare summary of bioenergetic techniques, as in any summary, nuances are omitted and partial explanations open many questions. This is particularly true for a method that does not follow a "recipe," cookbook technique. The interested reader should be referred to the works of Lowen (1969, 1971) and may obtain a fuller list of readings from the Institute of Bioenergetic Therapy, 144 East 36th Street, New York, N.Y. 10016.

REFERENCES

Lowen, A. *The betrayal of the body*. New York: Macmillan, 1969.

Lowen, A. *Language of the body*. New York: Macmillan, 1971.

Reich, W. *The function of the orgasm* (V. R. Carfagno, Trans.). New York: Farrar, Straus & Giroux, 1973. (a)

Reich, W. *Selected writings of Wilhelm Reich*. New York: Farrar, Straus & Giroux, 1973. (b)

Philip Katz, Ph.D., *is an assistant professor at the University of Bridgeport, Bridgeport, Connecticut, and a member of the Institute of Bioenergetic Analysis. Dr. Katz is in the private practice of clinical psychology. His background is in developmental psychology, body awareness, humanistic education, and school psychology. He also leads workshops in bioenergetic techniques.*

HATHA YOGA

Lorrie Collins Trueblood

Over seven million people of all ages practice some form of Yoga in the United States alone. Some reasons for Yoga's rapidly increasing appeal include (1) today's expanded leisure time, with the opportunity for self-development; (2) disillusionment with traditional forms of philosophy and religion; (3) our culture's overemphasis on material values, which prompts a search for a spiritual balance; (4) the search for an alternative life style that will allow one to live in a fast-paced world; and (5) Yoga's ability to meet the needs of people who desire a healthy way of experiencing well-being, inner peace, and calmness.

Definition

Yoga is an ancient system of self-development that originated in India over two thousand years ago. This philosophic and psychophysiological discipline was codified by the sage Patanjali. He is considered by scholars to be the father of the science of Yoga, having collected and set down in writing the elements of the system in 500 B.C. Yoga translates from the Sanskrit as "yuj," meaning a yoke or a joining of physical, mental, and spiritual forces that lead eventually to self-integration or self-realization.

The goal of Yoga is to know one's self; this is accomplished through eight steps or limbs called "Astanga," which Patanjali suggested that one go through on the path toward self-realization. The eight steps:

1. Yama—nonviolence, nonstealing, right action
2. Niyama—self-purification by discipline
3. Asana—Yogic exercises (asanas)
4. Pranayama—breath control
5. Pratyahara—sensory withdrawal (used as a prelude to meditation)
6. Dharana—concentration
7. Dhyana—meditation
8. Samadhi—an uninterrupted state of meditation, peace, joy

HATHA YOGA

In Sanskrit, Hatha means "Ha," the sun, and "Tha," the moon. The sun represents the positive faces and the moon the negative. These are joined in harmony through deep-breathing techniques and exercises. Hatha Yoga's components are proper breathing, physical exercises, nutrition, concentration, and relaxation. There are literally thousands of postures, of which thirty-two are considered essential. These postures are especially designed to maintain balance in the body; increase blood circulation; promote the flow of energy through the nervous system; remove tension and poisons; stimulate glands and organs; and lead to physical and mental calmness.

Deep Breathing

In Hatha Yoga, breathing is considered the most important function of the body because all other functions depend on it. Control and rhythmic flow of the breath is known as Pranayama. Prana means vital air or absolute energy. This vital force of Prana, according to Yogic philosophy, is found in every living thing, from simple plant life to man.

In classical Yoga texts, the breath is spoken of as the string that controls the kite. The kite in this analogy is the mind and the string is the breath. As the breath moves so moves the mind. If the breath is short and rapid, the mind will work nervously. If the breath is slow and smooth, the mind will become tranquil and peaceful.

Asanas

Exercises (asanas) are coordinated with deep-breathing and relaxation techniques to remove tension. The exercise postures are designed to stretch every part of the body. These are "inner-cises" as well as exercises. The arteries, veins, ligaments, tendons, muscles, tissues, skin, organs, and glands are stimulated, massaged, and toned without strain. Another major benefit is the conservation of vital energy and the reduction of anxiety. The body is slowly deconditioned from old tensions and emotions, causing a release during the process of exercise.

Deep Relaxation

An integral part of Hatha Yoga is deep relaxation. It is believed that ten minutes of deep relaxation builds new body cells and aids in rejuvenation of the entire self. The person consciously tells each part of the body to relax, beginning with the brain center and moving down to the toes and then back up again, all the while breathing slowly and rhythmically. This process can be followed by self-suggestions and mental images of a positive nature, such as picturing oneself on a warm sandy beach listening to the surf roll.

SUMMARY

In brief, Hatha Yoga is a healthy way of exploring one's self in order to experience well-being, calmness, and inner peace.

Swami Sivananda was a famous master as well as a medical doctor in India. He concisely defined the true meaning of Yoga (as quoted by Vishnudevananda, 1971):

> Yoga is a scientific system that makes you master of your senses instead of a slave to them. Yoga is not just standing on your head as many people think, but learning how to stand on your own two feet. Yoga is not a religion, yet it embraces all religions. Yoga can teach the young the wisdom of age and teach the old the secret of youth. Yoga will introduce you to someone you might know . . . yourself.

CLASSES AND TRAINING

The interested person should keep in mind that Yoga is as effective as the teacher is qualified and the student is motivated. A complete listing of centers at which Yoga is taught is available from

Spiritual Community Publications
Box 1080
San Rafael, California 94902.

REFERENCE

Vishnudevananda, S. Lecture given for Yoga Teacher's Training Course, Val Marin, Canada, 1971.

OTHER READINGS

Collins, L. *The beginning Yoga book.* Indianapolis: Santosha Yoga Center, 1975.

Chaudhuri, H. *Integral Yoga.* San Francisco: Institute of Asian Studies, 1965.

Iyengar, B. K. S. *Light on Yoga.* New York: Schocken Books, 1970.

Vishnudevananda, S. *The complete illustrated book of Yoga.* New York: Bell Publishing, 1959.

Lorrie Collins Trueblood *is the director of the Santosha Yoga Center and a co-director of the Human Potential Institute of Indiana, Indianapolis. She is the author of* The Beginning Yoga Chart, The Beginning Yoga Book, *and cassette tapes on* Relaxation, Beginning Yoga, *and* Intermediate Yoga. *Mrs. Trueblood is trained in Hatha and Raja Yoga, elementary and adult education, and educational and organization development consulting. She has an M.A. in educational psychology.*

A REFERENCE LIST FOR CHANGE AGENTS[1]

Larry E. Pate

In 1969, Warren Bennis commented that organization development (OD) was a new and still-emerging field. Bennis's comment is still surprisingly relevant today, especially in terms of our scientific knowledge of the change process. Apart from some very preliminary studies, very little OD research exists. Nonetheless, the situation is beginning to change.

In a 1971 issue of the *Journal of Applied Behavioral Science*, Blake strongly criticized an article on organizational change by Blumberg and Wiener (1971) for the authors' failure to review the literature thoroughly and to include important material relevant to their study. In response, Blumberg (1971) simply stated that he and his co-author were not aware of the material because it had appeared in a relatively obscure journal. Indeed, another writer (Zurcher, 1971) criticized one of Blake's papers on the same grounds and then suggested that such a criticism might easily apply to any researcher in the field. All of these individuals did agree, of course, that a thorough review of the literature on any given topic is necessary for good research and reporting. The purpose here is not to pour salt on wounds, but rather to illustrate the rationale for presenting the material that follows.

Much material has become available during the past few years in the areas of organization development and change. This abundance of material seems to be a direct result of the growing interest and reported successes of several proactive approaches to change. The quantity of material in these areas is so great, in fact, that it is often difficult for writers, change agents, and researchers to keep up with it. Many of us may miss relevant material because we look in the wrong places or because we do not know where to look. The available literature can be useful to more individuals if it is organized into a single document. The purpose of this reference list is to identify some of the recent material in this field, particularly bibliographies and special issues of journals devoted either to the change process or to OD. I have also included a list of professional organizations with interests or activities in OD, a few recommended readings for those just getting started, and a list of nearly six hundred references on change and development, arranged alphabetically by author, that have been published since 1970.

Table 1 lists journals that have published special issues devoted to organizational change, organization development, or other closely related areas. Appropriate information is given for locating each special issue, including the title of the issue (if there is one), and the number of articles is indicated. The 1972 special Summer issue of the *Journal of Contemporary Business*, in particular, is a good reference source. This issue, edited by Wendell French and Cecil Bell, both OD practitioners at the University of Washington, contains articles by Blake, Bowers, Burke, Davis, Gibb, Shepard, and other recognized names in the field. The *Training and Development Journal*, the official journal of the American Society for Training and Development (ASTD), publishes a special issue each year on OD. Virtually every issue of *The Journal of Applied Behavioral Science* and the OD Network's *OD Practitioner* contains articles and information on planned change.

[1]I am indebted to Ken Rowland of the Organizational Behavior Group, University of Illinois at Urbana-Champaign, for his comments and assistance on an earlier draft of this paper.

Table 1. Special Journal Issues on Organization Development and Change

Journal	Year	Vol. (No.)	Relevant Articles	Issue Title
Business Quarterly	1969	*34*(4)	8	Organization development
Educational Technology	1972	*12*(10)	14	Organizational development in the schools
Elementary School Guidance and Counseling	1972	*7*(2)	13	Consultation
Hospital and Community Psychiatry	1972	*23*(6)	5	
International Studies of Management & Organization	1971	*1*(3)	8	Organizational change
Journal of Applied Behavioral Science	1974	*10*(3)	17	Power and social change
	1974	*10*(4)	6	Recent developments in organization development
Journal of Contemporary Business	1972	*1*(3)	7	Organization development: An overview
Journal of Higher Education	1973	*44*(5)	7	Organizational development in higher education
Training & Development Journal	1973	*27*(1)	5	
	1974	*28*(3)	6	Organization development
	1975	*29*(4)	8	Organization development

Finally, University Associates publishes a number of laboratory-related materials that can be useful in the practice of OD.

Table 2 contains a list of eight bibliographies on organization development and change, including the number of references, annotated and otherwise. A complete citation for each bibliography is included in the last section of this paper. Perhaps the most useful of the listed bibliographies is Franklin's (1973) *Organization Development: An Annotated Bibliography* or Pate and Rowland's (1975) *Organizational Change and Development: An Annotated Bibliography;* the least useful, the short one prepared by the Court Studies Division of the National College of the State Judiciary (1972). For those with a special interest in education, Ronald Havelock and others at the University of Michigan have compiled several bibliographies and other materials relevant to the change process. Havelock's (1971) *Bibliography on Knowledge Utilization and Dissemination*, for example, contains about four thousand sources.

Additional and up-to-date information in the OD field can be obtained by applying for membership in or by contacting any of the following professional organizations. Most of these organizations publish journals and offer student memberships at reduced rates.

Organization Development Division, ASTD, P.O. Box 5307, Madison, Wisconsin 53705

Division of Organization Development, Academy of Management, 2002 Crestmont, Norman, Oklahoma 73059

Division 14 (Industrial & Organizational Psychology) of the American Psychological Association, 1200 17th Street, N.W., Washington, D.C. 20036

Table 2. Bibliographies on Organization Development and Change

Bibliography	References	Annotations	Focus
Campbell, et al. (1973)	60	60	Change in education
Franklin (1973)	176	176	Organization development
Murrell and Vaill (1975)	400*	48	Organization development
National College of the State Judiciary (1972)	46	40	Organization development
Pate and Rowland (1975)	60	60	Organization development and change
Reddy (1975)	242		Small-group training
Schmidt (1970)	71		Organization development
Toulouse (1970)	20	20	The future/change

*The category scheme used by these authors causes several references to be listed more than once.

Organization Development Division, International Association of Applied Social Scientists, 1755 Massachusetts Avenue, N.W., Washington, D.C. 20036

OD Network, NTL Institute for Applied Behavioral Science, 1815 N. Fort Meyer Drive, Arlington, Virginia 22209

For newcomers to the field the following titles are essential: (a) the Addison-Wesley series on OD, now consisting of nine volumes,[2] each available in paperback for about $3.50; (b) Argyris (1970), *Intervention Theory and Method: A Behavioral Science View*, available in hardcover for about $10.25; (c) French and Bell (1973), *Organization Development: A Behavioral Science Approach*, available in paperback for about $5.95 and hardcover for about $9.95; (d) Dalton, Lawrence, and Greiner (1970), *Organizational Change and Development*, available in paperback for about $5.95; (e) Huse (1975), *Organization Development and Change*, available in hardcover for about $12.95; (f) Margulies and Raia (1972), *Organizational Development: Values, Process, and Technology*, available in hardcover for about $13.95; and (g) Bennis, Benne, and Chin (1969), *The Planning of Change*, available in hardcover for about $11.95.

REFERENCES[3]

Beckhard, R. *Organization development: Strategies and models.* Reading, Mass.: Addison-Wesley, 1969.

Bennis, W. G. *Organization development: Its nature, origins and prospects.* Reading, Mass.: Addison-Wesley, 1969.

Bennis, W. G., Benne, K. D., & Chin, R. (Eds.). *The planning of change* (2nd ed.). New York: Holt, Rinehart and Winston, 1969.

Blake, R. R. The uses of the past. *Journal of Applied Behavioral Science*, 1971, 7(4), 519-520.

Blake, R. R., & Mouton, J. S. *Building a dynamic corporation through grid organization development.* Reading, Mass.: Addison-Wesley, 1969.

Blumberg, A. Feedback to "Backfeed." *Journal of Applied Behavioral Science*, 1971, 7(6), 775-776.

Lawrence, P. R., & Lorsch, J. W. *Developing organizations: Diagnosis and action.* Reading, Mass.: Addison-Wesley, 1969.

Schein, E. H. *Process consultation: Its role in organization development.* Reading, Mass.: Addison-Wesley, 1969.

Walton, R. E. *Interpersonal peacemaking: Confrontations and third party consultation.* Reading, Mass.: Addison-Wesley, 1969.

Zurcher, L. E. The critic critiqued. *Journal of Applied Behavioral Science*, 1971, 7(6), 778-779.

[2]These nine volumes are Beckhard (1969), Bennis (1969), Blake and Mouton (1969), Galbraith (1973), Lawrence and Lorsch (1969), Roeber (1973), Schein (1969), Steele (1973), and Walton (1969).

[3]Only references not cited in the general bibliography are listed here, to avoid duplication.

ORGANIZATION DEVELOPMENT BIBLIOGRAPHY, 1970–1975

Abad, A. *Management and organization development: A behavioral science approach.* New Delhi: Rachna Prakashan, 1972.

Acker, S. R., & Perlson, M. R. Can we sharpen our management of human resources? *JSAS Catalog of Selected Documents in Psychology,* 1973, *3,* 20. (Ms. No. 313)

Adams, J. D. *Organization development and change.* Washington, D.C.: National Training and Development Service, 1974.

Adams, J. D. (Ed.). *New technologies in organization development: 2* (Originally *Theory and method in organization development: An evolutionary process,* Arlington, Va.: NTL Institute, 1974). La Jolla, Calif.: University Associates, 1975.

Alban, B. Further questions about and by a shadow consultant. *Journal of Applied Behavioral Science,* 1974, *10*(4), 595-597.

Alban, B. T., & Pollitt, L. I. Team building. In T. H. Patten, Jr. (Ed.), *OD–Emerging dimensions and concepts.* East Lansing, Mich: American Society for Training and Development, 1973.

Albanese, R. Overcoming resistance to stability. *Business Horizons,* 1970, *13*(2), 35-42.

Alderfer, C. P. Teaching organizational change to "insiders" and "outsiders." *Professional Psychology,* 1970, *1*(4), 397-401.

Alderfer, C. P. *Existence, relatedness, and growth: Human needs in organizational settings.* New York: Free Press, 1972.

Alderfer, C. P. The relevance of human intellect and organizational power for organization development. In J. D. Adams (Ed.), *New technologies in organization development: 2* (Originally *Theory and method in organization development: An evolutionary process,* Arlington, Va.: NTL Institute, 1974). La Jolla, Calif.: University Associates, 1975.

Alderfer, C. P. Change processes in organizations. In M. D. Dunnette (Ed.), *Handbook of industrial and organizational psychology.* Chicago: Rand McNally, in press.

Allen, R. M., Cortazzo, A. D., & Schwartz, B. J. Hospital improvement project at work. *Mental Retardation,* 1972, *10*(3), 28-29.

Alpander, G. G. Planning management training programs for organizational development. *Personnel Journal,* 1974, *53*(1), 15-25.

Alschuler, A. Toward a self-renewing school. *Journal of Applied Behavioral Science,* 1972, *8*(5), 577-600.

Anderson, J. Giving and receiving feedback. In G. W. Dalton, P. R. Lawrence, & L. E. Greiner (Eds.), *Organizational change and development.* Homewood, Ill.: Irwin-Dorsey, 1970.

Anderson, S. D. OD workshop design: Strategy and techniques. In T. H. Patten, Jr. (Ed.), *OD —Emerging dimensions and concepts.* East Lansing, Mich.: American Society for Training and Development, 1973.

Andrews, J. D. W. Interpersonal challenge: A source of growth in laboratory training. *Journal of Applied Behavioral Science,* 1973, *9*(4), 514-533.

Appelbaum, S. H. Just what should an organizational development specialist do? *Personnel Journal,* 1973, *52*(3), 222-223.

Appelbaum, S. H. A model of organizational diagnosis and development. *Proceedings of the 35th Annual Meeting of the Academy of Management,* August 1975, pp. 107-109.

Appleby, B., & Ford, J. R. The applied social scientist in industry (Working Paper CUSSR-26). Loughborough University of Technology, 1970. Cited by P. A. Clark, *Action research and organizational change.* London: Harper & Row, 1972, p. 155.

Aram, J. D., & Stoner, J. A. F. Development of an organizational change role. *Journal of Applied Behavioral Science,* 1972, *8*(4), 438-449.

Arends, R. I., Phelps, J. H., & Schmuck, R. A. *Organization development: Building human systems in schools.* Eugene, Ore.: Center for Educational Policy and Management, 1974.

Argyris, C. *Intervention theory and method: A behavioral science view.* Reading, Mass.: Addison-Wesley, 1970.

Argyris, C. *Management and organizational development: The path from XA to YB.* New York: McGraw-Hill, 1971.

Argyris, C. The CEO's behavior: Key to organizational development. *Harvard Business Review,* 1973, *51*(2), 55-64. (a)

Argyris, C. *On organizations of the future.* (Professional Paper in Administrative and Policy Studies, Vol. 1, No. 03-001). Beverly Hills, Calif.: Sage, 1973. (b)

Argyris, C. *Behind the front page*. San Francisco: Jossey-Bass, 1974.

Armenakis, A. A., & Feild, H. S. Evolution of organizational change using nonindependent criterion measures. *Personnel Psychology*, 1975, 28(1), 39-44.

Armenakis, A. A., Feild, H. S., & Holley, W. H. An empirical identification of the evaluative problems of organizational development (OD) change agents. *Proceedings of the 34th Annual Meeting of the Academy of Management*, August 1974, p. 50. (Abstract)

Armenakis, A. A., Feild, H. S., & Holley, W. H. Organizational development in a public agency: A case study. *Training and Development Journal*, 1975, 29(4), 52-55.

Armenakis, A. A., Feild, H. S., & Mosley, D. C. Evaluation guidelines for the OD practitioner. *Personnel Journal*, 1975, 54(2), 99-103.

Arnold, J. D. Whither OD in a recessionary economy? *Training and Development Journal*, 1974, 28(3), 3-7.

Aronoff, J., & Litwin, G. H. Achievement motivation training and executive advancement. *Journal of Applied Behavioral Science*, 1971, 7(2), 215-229.

Atkins, S. The ideal expectations survey. *Training and Development Journal*, 1971, 25(3), 38-39.

Audrey, R. F. Power bases: The consultant's vehicle for change. *Elementary School Guidance and Counseling*, 1972, 7(2), 90-97.

Averch, V. R., & Luke, R. A., Jr. The temporary task force: Challenge to organizational structure. *Personnel*, 1970, 47(3), 16-23.

Averch, V. R., & Luke, R. A., Jr. Organization development: The view from within. *Training and Development Journal*, 1971, 25(9), 38-42.

Bakan, D. Should would-be change agents enter politics? *Journal of Applied Behavioral Science*, 1972, 8(3), 363-367.

Barkdull, C. W. Organizing for change. *Michigan Business Review*, 1972, 24(3), 1-4.

Barthol, R. P., & Berry, L. OB strikes out OD: An application of organization development in sports. *Interpersonal Development*, 1973-1974, 4(2), 85-98.

Bartlett, A. C., & Kayser, T. A. (Eds.). *Changing organizational behavior*. Englewood Cliffs, N.J.: Prentice-Hall, 1973. (a)

Bartlett, A. C., & Kayser, T. A. Toward a theory of changing behavior: An elaboration on the role of influence and coercion. In A. C. Bartlett & T. A. Kayser (Eds.), *Changing organizational behavior*. Englewood Cliffs, N.J.: Prentice-Hall, 1973. (b)

Bass, B. M. Organizational life in the 70's and beyond. *Personnel Psychology*, 1972, 25(1), 19-30.

Beck, A. C., Jr., & Hillmar, E. D. OD to MBO or MBO to OD: Does it make a difference? *Personnel Journal*, 1972, 51(10), 827-834. (a)

Beck, A. C., Jr., & Hillmar, E. D. (Eds.). *A practical approach to organization development through MBO*. Reading, Mass.: Addison-Wesley, 1972. (b)

Beckhard, R. Optimizing team-building efforts. *Journal of Contemporary Business*, 1972, 1(3), 23-32.

Beckhard, R. ABS in health care systems: Who needs it? *Journal of Applied Behavioral Science*, 1974, 10(1), 93-106.

Beer, M. The technology of organization development. In M. D. Dunnette (Ed.), *Handbook of industrial and organizational psychology*. Chicago: Rand McNally, in press.

Beer, M., & Huse, E. F. A systems approach to organization development. *Journal of Applied Behavioral Science*, 1972, 8(1), 79-101.

Bellman, G. M. Trains-consults-results: A packaged program to organization change. *Training and Development Journal*, 1971, 25(9), 2-5.

Bennis, W. G. A funny thing happened on the way to the future. *American Psychologist*, 1970, 25(7), 595-608.

Bennis, W. G. An OD expert in the cat bird's seat. *Journal of Higher Education*, 1973, 44(5), 389-398.

Bentley, H. D. Productivity and change. *Personnel Administration*, 1971, 34(5), 4-7; 56-59.

Berlew, D., & LeClere, W. E. Social intervention in Curacao: A case study. *Journal of Applied Behavioral Science*, 1974, 10(1), 29-52.

Blake, R. R., & Mouton, J. S. Change by design: Not by default. *S. A. M. Advanced Management Journal*, 1970, 35(2), 29-34. (a)

Blake, R. R., & Mouton, J. S. OD—fad or fundamental? *Training and Development Journal*, 1970, 24(1), 9-17. (b)

Blake, R. R., & Mouton, J. S. 9,9 sales grid style produces results. *Training and Development Journal*, 1970, 24(10), 4-7. (c)

Blake, R. R., & Mouton, J. S. A behavioral science design for the development of society. *Journal of Applied Behavioral Science*, 1971, *7*(2), 146-163. (a)

Blake, R. R., & Mouton, J. S. The fifth achievement. *Personnel Administration*, 1971, *34*(3), 49-57. (b)

Blake, R. R., & Mouton, J. S. Grid OD: A systems approach to corporate excellence. In H. A. Hornstein, B. B. Bunker, W. W. Burke, M. Gindes, & R. J. Lewicki (Eds.), *Social intervention: A behavioral science approach.* New York: Free Press, 1971. (c)

Blake, R. R., & Mouton, J. S. Interventions, strategies, and styles for the OD-oriented manager. In T. H. Patten, Jr. (Ed.), *OD—Emerging dimensions and concepts.* East Lansing, Mich.: American Society for Training and Development, 1973.

Blake, R. R., & Mouton, J. S. The D/D matrix. In J. D. Adams (Ed.), *New technologies in organization development: 2* (Originally *Theory and method in organization development: An evolutionary process;* Arlington, Va.: NTL Institute, 1974). La Jolla, Calif.: University Associates, 1975.

Blake, R. R., & Mouton, J. S. An overview of the grid. *Training and Development Journal*, 1975, *29*(5), 29-37.

Blohm, H., & Heinrich, L. J. Psychological resistance to the introduction of a corporate planning system: An empirical survey. *International Studies of Management & Organization*, 1971, *1*(3), 311-326.

Blumberg, A. (Ed.). Organizational development in the schools. *Educational Technology*, 1972, *12*(10), 9-62.

Blumberg, A., & Schmuck, R. Barriers to organizational development training for schools. *Educational Technology*, 1972, *12*(10), 30-34.

Blumberg, A., & Wiener, W. One from two: Facilitating an organizational merger. *Journal of Applied Behavioral Science*, 1971, *7*(1), 87-102.

Bolman, L. Laboratory versus lecture in training executives. *Journal of Applied Behavioral Science*, 1970, *6*(3), 323-335.

Bolman, L. The client as theorist: An approach to individual and organization development. In J. D. Adams (Ed.), *New technologies in organization development: 2* (Originally *Theory and method in organization development: An evolutionary process,* Arlington, Va.: NTL Institute,

1974). La Jolla, Calif.: University Associates, 1975.

Bolton, C. K., & Boyer, R. K. Organizational development for academic departments. *Journal of Higher Education*, 1973, *44*(5), 352-369.

Boss, R. W. The not-so-peaceful incident at Peaceful Valley: A confrontation design in a criminal justice agency. *Proceedings of the 35th Annual Meeting of the Academy of Management*, August, 1975, pp. 357-359.

Boston, R. E. Management by objectives: A management system for education. *Educational Technology*, 1972, *12*(5), 49-51.

Bourn, C. J. Planned change in welfare organisation. *Human Relations*, 1973, *26*(1), 113-126.

Boutwell, C. E. Differential staffing as a component in a systematic change process. *Educational Technology*, 1972, *12*(8), 20-24.

Bowers, D. G. OD techniques and their results in 23 organizations: The Michigan ICL study. *Journal of Applied Behavioral Science*, 1973, *9*(1), 21-43.

Bowers, D. G., & Franklin, J. L. Survey-guided development: Using human resources measurement in organizational change. *Journal of Contemporary Business*, 1972, *1*(3), 43-55.

Bowers, D. G., & Seashore, S. E. Changing the structure and functioning of an organization. In W. M. Evan (Ed.), *Organizational experiments: Laboratory and field research.* New York: Harper & Row, 1971.

Bradford, L. P., & Harvey, J. B. Dealing with dysfunctional organization myths. *Training and Development Journal*, 1970, *24*(9), 2-6.

Bradshaw, H. H. The training function: A catalytic model. *Training and Development Journal*, 1972, *26*(7), 14-16.

Braunstein, D. N. Interpersonal behavior in a changing organization. *Journal of Applied Psychology*, 1970, *54*(2), 184-191.

Brimm, M. When is a change not a change? *Journal of Applied Behavioral Science*, 1972, *8*(1), 102-107.

Brown, D. S. The management of advisory committees: An assignment for the 70's. *Public Administration Review*, 1972, *32*(4), 334-342.

Brown, F. G. Organization development in Kansas City. In *First tango in Boston: A seminar on organization change and development.* Washington, D.C.: National Training and Development Service, 1973.

Brown, L. D. "Research Action": Organizational feedback, understanding, and change. *Journal of Applied Behavioral Science*, 1972, 8(6), 697-711.

Brown, L. D. Action research: Hardboiled eggs out of eggheads and hardhats? *Proceedings of the 33rd Annual Meeting of the Academy of Management*, August 1973, pp. 549-555.

Brown, L. D., Aram, J. D., & Bachner, D. J. Interorganizational information sharing: A successful intervention that failed. *Journal of Applied Behavioral Science*, 1974, 10(4), 533-554.

Browne, P. J., & Cotton, C. C. Marginality, a force for the OD practitioner. *Training and Development Journal*, 1975, 29(4), 14-18.

Brynildsen, R. D. Motivation and individual career achievement. In J. D. Adams (Ed.), *New technologies in organization development: 2* (Originally *Theory and method in organization development: An evolutionary process*, Arlington, Va.: NTL Institute, 1974). La Jolla, Calif.: University Associates, 1975.

Buchanan, P. C. Organizational development as a process strategy for change. *Educational Technology*, 1972, 12(10), 10-14.

Bunker, D. R. One more cell in the matrix. *Journal of Applied Behavioral Science*, 1975, 11(3), 281-290.

Burke, W. W. Training organization development specialists. *Professional Psychology*, 1970, 1(4), 354-358.

Burke, W. W. A comparison of management development and organization development. *Journal of Applied Behavioral Science*, 1971, 7(5), 569-579. (a)

Burke, W. W. Organizational development— Here to stay? *Proceedings of the 31st Annual Meeting of the Academy of Management*, August 1971, pp. 170-177. (b)

Burke, W. W. The demise of organization development. *Journal of Contemporary Business*, 1972, 1(3), 57-63. (a)

Burke, W. W. Organization development: Current prospects. *Industrial Training International*, 1972, 7(2), 49-52. (b)

Burke, W. W. The role of training in organization development. *Training and Development Journal*, 1972, 26(9), 30-34. (c)

Burke, W. W. Organization development. *Professional Psychology*, 1973, 4(2), 194-200.

Burke, W. W. Managing conflict between groups. In J. D. Adams (Ed.), *New technologies in organization development: 2* (Originally *Theory and method in organization development: An evolutionary process*, Arlington, Va.: NTL Institute, 1974). La Jolla, Calif.: University Associates, 1975. (a)

Burke, W. W. (Ed.). *New technologies in organization development: 1* (Originally *Contemporary organization development: Conceptual orientations and interventions*, Arlington, Va.: NTL Institute, 1972). La Jolla, Calif.: University Associates, 1975. (b)

Burke, W. W. OD in transition. *Journal of Applied Behavioral Science*, in press.

Burke, W. W., & Hornstein, H. (Eds.). *The social technology of organization development*. Fairfax, Va.: Learning Resources Corporation, 1972.

Burke, W. W., & Schmidt, W. H. Management and organization development: What is the target of change? *Personnel Administration*, 1971, 34(2), 44-56.

Butkovich, P., Sullivan, M., & Astrachan, B. Boundary structures and responses of community mental health centers to pressures for change. *Proceedings of the 33rd Annual Meeting of the Academy of Management*, August 1973, pp. 521-527.

Byrd, R. E. Creative risk taking training: A new tool for human resources development. In T. H. Patten, Jr. (Ed.), *OD—Emerging dimensions and concepts*. East Lansing, Mich.: American Society for Training and Development, 1973.

Calhoon, R. P., & Jerdee, T. H. First-level supervisory training and organizational development. *Public Personnel Management*, 1975, 4(3), 196-200.

Campbell, E. A., Havelock, M. C., Havelock, R. G., Huber, J. C., & Zimmerman, S. Major works on change in education: An annotated bibliography. In R. G. Havelock, *The change agent's guide to innovation in education*. Englewood Cliffs, N.J.: Educational Technology Publications, 1973.

Carlson, J. Consulting: Facilitating school change. *Elementary School Guidance and Counseling*, 1972, 7(2), 83-88.

Carson, W. M. Organization and management development in developing countries. *Industrial Training International*, 1972, 7(10), 305-307.

Carter, R. N. OD strategy for today's training. *Training and Development Journal*, 1975, 29(4), 28-30.

Carvalho, G. F. Installing management by objectives: A new perspective on organizational change. *Human Resources Management*, 1972, 11(1), 23-30.

Chartrand, P. J. *The development of a diagnostic model in two government organizations utilizing modifications of Beckhard's confrontation strategy*. Unpublished master's thesis, Loughborough University of Technology, 1972. (Cited by P. A. Clark, *Action Research and Organizational Change*. London: Harper & Row, 1972, p. 157.)

Cherns, A. B. Can behavioral scientists help managers improve their organizations? *Organizational Dynamics*, 1973, 1(3), 51-67.

Clark, A. W. Sanction: A critical element in action research. *Journal of Applied Behavioral Science*, 1972, 8(6), 713-731.

Clark, J. V., & Krone, C. G. Towards an overall view of organizational development in the early seventies. In J. M. Thomas & W. G. Bennis (Eds.), *Management of change and conflict*. Harmondsworth, England: Penguin, 1972.

Clark, P. A. *Action research and organizational change*. London: Harper & Row, 1972. (a)

Clark, P. A. *Organizational design: Theory and practice*. London: Tavistock, 1972. (b)

Clark, P. A., & Ford, J. R. Methodological and theoretical problems in the investigation of planned organizational change. *Sociological Review*, 1970, 18(1), 29-52.

Clary, T. C. Transactional analysis. *Training and Development Journal*, 1972, 26(10), 14-19.

Clary, T. C. Transactional analysis in organization development. In *First tango in Boston: A seminar on organization change and development*. Washington, D.C.: National Training and Development Service, 1973.

Clary, T. C., & Luke, R. A., Jr. Organizational and individual power. *Training and Development Journal*, 1975, 29(4), 41-51.

Coffee, D. Organizational development or training? *Training and Development Journal*, 1972, 26(5), 12-15.

Conner, D. R. Bridging the gap: OD graduate education. *Training and Development Journal*, 1975, 29(9), 16-19.

Connor, P. E. Values and assumptions in OD: Some critical observations. *Proceedings of the 35th Annual Meeting of the Academy of Management*, August 1975, pp. 348-350.

Conversation: An interview with Chris Argyris. *Organizational Dynamics*, 1974, 3(1), 45-62.

Cooper, C. L. How psychologically dangerous are T-groups and encounter groups? *Human Relations*, 1975, 28(3), 249-260.

Corwin, R. G. Strategies for organizational innovation: An empirical comparison. *American Sociological Review*, 1972, 37(4), 441-454.

Cowen, S., & Rummler, G. A. The management of change: Preparing for automation. *Training and Development Journal*, 1974, 28(5), 42-47.

Crockett, C. The higher education institute: A vehicle for change. *Journal of Higher Education*, 1973, 44(5), 414-425.

Crockett, W. J. Team building—One approach to organizational development. *Journal of Applied Behavioral Science*, 1970, 6(3), 291-306.

Crockett, W. J., Gaertner, R. E., Dufur, M., & White, D. C. OD in a large system. In J. D. Adams (Ed.), *New technologies in organization development: 2* (Originally *Theory and method in organization development: An evolutionary process*, Arlington, Va.: NTL Institute, 1974). La Jolla, Calif.: University Associates, 1975.

Croft, J. C. Organizational development for Thornlea: A communication package and some results. *Journal of Applied Behavioral Science*, 1970, 6(1), 93-106.

Culbert, S. A. Accelerating laboratory learning through a phase progression model for trainer intervention. *Journal of Applied Behavioral Science*, 1970, 6(1), 21-38.

Culbert, S. A. Using research to guide an organization development project. *Journal of Applied Behavioral Science*, 1972, 8(2), 203-236.

Dale, L. A., & Akula, W. G. Managers for a changing society. *Personnel Administration*, 1970, 33(1), 8-16.

Dalton, G. W., Lawrence, P. R., & Greiner, L. E. (Eds.). *Organizational change and development*. Homewood, Ill.: Irwin-Dorsey, 1970.

Davey, N. G. Consultant's role in organizational change. *MSU Business Topics*, 1971, 19(2), 76-79. (a)

Davey, N. G. *The external consultant's role in organizational change.* East Lansing: Graduate School of Business Administration, Michigan State University, 1971. (b)

Davies, R. The grid—A personal experience. *Industrial Training International,* 1970, 5(4), 175.

Davis, K. The management of change: A rogue's gallery. *Supervisory Management,* 1972, 17(8), 25-26.

de Bettignies, H. C., & Boddewyn, J. Introduction: Organizational change. *International Studies of Management & Organization,* 1971, 1(3), 219-221.

Deboer, J. C. *How to succeed in the organization jungle without losing your religion.* Philadelphia: Pilgrim Press, 1972.

Delbecq, A. Sensitivity training. *Training and Development Journal,* 1970, 24(1), 32-35.

DeMichele, J. H. Measuring the effectiveness of laboratory training in organizational development. *Proceedings of the 32nd Annual Meeting of the Academy of Management,* August 1972, pp. 47-48.

Derr, C. B. Organization development in one large urban school system. *Education and Urban Society,* 1970, 2(4), 403-419.

Desatnick, R. L. Developing managers—An integral part of the management process. *Training and Development Journal,* 1970, 24(8), 2-6.

Dienstbach, H. *Dynamik der unternehmungsorganisation: Anpassung auf der grundlage dès planned organizational change.* Wiesbaden, Germany: Betriebswirtschaftlicher Verlag T. Gabler, 1972.

Doryland, C. J. Toward internal consulting policy. *Proceedings of the 34th Annual Meeting of the Academy of Management,* August 1974, p. 17. (Abstract)

Dow, C. J. Organization change and development: The Bellevue experiment with emergency and safety services. In *First tango in Boston: A seminar on organization change and development.* Washington, D.C.: National Training and Development Service, 1973.

Dowling, W. F. To move an organization: The Corning approach to organization development. *Organizational Dynamics,* 1975, 3(4), 16-34.

Driscoll, S. A. Effects of organizational change on the treatment system of a mental hospital (Doctoral dissertation, Syracuse University, 1972). *Dissertation Abstracts International,* 1972. (University Microfilms No. 72-11, 830)

DuBrin, A. J. *The practice of managerial psychology: Concepts and methods for manager and organization development.* New York: Pergamon Press, 1972.

Duffin, R., Falusi, A., Lawrence, P., & Morton, R. B. Increasing organizational effectiveness. *Training and Development Journal,* 1973, 27(4), 37-46.

Duncan, D. M. A systems view of OD. *Organizational Dynamics,* 1974, 2(3), 14-29.

Duncan, R. B. Dimensions to consider in structuring the change agent's role. *Proceedings of the 34th Annual Meeting of the Academy of Management,* August 1974, p. 50. (Abstract)

Dunnette, M. D. Should your people take sensitivity training? *Innovation,* 1970, 14, 42-55.

Dyer, L., & Kochan, T. A. Labor unions and organizational change: A new frontier for OD. *Proceedings of the 34th Annual Meeting of the Academy of Management,* August 1974, pp. 50-51. (Abstract)

Dyer, W. G. *Modern theory and method in group training.* Fairfax, Va.: Learning Resources, 1972. (a)

Dyer, W. G. *The sensitive manipulator: The change agent who builds with others.* Provo, Utah: Brigham Young University Press, 1972. (b)

Dyer, W. G., Maddocks, R. F., Moffitt, J. W., & Underwood, W. J. A laboratory-consultation model for organization change. *Journal of Applied Behavioral Science,* 1970, 6(2), 211-227.

Eddy, W. B. Beyond behaviorism? Organization development in public management. *Public Personnel Review,* 1970, 31(3), 169-175.

Eddy, W. B. From training to organization change. *Personnel Administration,* 1971, 34(1), 37-43.

Eglin, R. Reckitt and Coleman after two years of abrasive reform. *The Director,* 1972, 25(6), 380-383.

Endres, R. E. Successful management of change. *Personnel Administration and Public Personnel Review,* 1972, 1(1), 9-15.

Ends, A. W. A systems approach to organization change in education through school based management. *Proceedings of the 35th Annual Meeting of the Academy of Management,* August 1975, pp. 354-356.

English, J., & Harlow, D. N. How to play two roles and survive. *Proceedings of the 34th Annual Meeting of the Academy of Management,* August 1974, p. 20. (Abstract)

Esbeck, E. S. Organizational change. An inquiry into interdependence (Doctoral dissertation, Case Western Reserve University, 1972). *Dissertation Abstracts International,* 1972. (University Microfilms No. 72-18, 686)

Evans, M. G. Failures in OD programs—What went wrong? *Business Horizons,* 1974, *17*(2), 18-22.

Feitler, F. C., & Lippitt, L. L. A multi-district organizational development effort. *Educational Technology,* 1972, *12*(10), 34-38.

Filley, A. C. Alternative approaches to organizational change. In J. W. McGuire (Ed.), *Contemporary management: Issues and viewpoints.* Englewood Cliffs, N.J.: Prentice-Hall, 1974.

Fink, S. L., Beak, J., & Taddeo, K. Organizational crisis and change. *Journal of Applied Behavioral Science,* 1971, *7*(1), 15-37.

Fitz-enz, J. The case for the organization developer. *Training and Development Journal,* 1971, *25*(1), 30-31.

Fitzgerald, J. In-house staff versus outside consultants. *Proceedings of the 35th Annual Meeting of the Academy of Management,* August 1975, pp. 113-115.

Fitzgerald, T. H. In-house education, reconsidered. *Training and Development Journal,* 1971, *25*(7), 2-8.

Flanders, H. The AT&T Company manpower laboratory, circa 1971. *Proceedings of the 31st Annual Meeting of the Academy of Management,* August 1971, pp. 203-206.

Florez, G. A. Management development—today and tomorrow. *Training and Development Journal,* 1970, *24*(5), 20-24.

Foltz, J. A., Harvey, J. B., & McLaughlin, J. Organization development: A line management function. In J. D. Adams (Ed.), *New technologies in organization development: 2* (Originally *Theory and method in organization development: An evolutionary process,* Arlington, Va.: NTL Institute, 1974). La Jolla, Calif.: University Associates, 1975.

Forbes, R. L., & Nickols, F. W. Educational technology and organizational development: A collaborative approach to organizational change. *JSAS Catalog of Selected Documents in Psychology,* 1975, *5*, 247. (Ms. No. 955)

Ford, C. H. Developing a successful client-consultant relationship. *Human Resource Management,* 1974, *13*(2), 2-11.

Fordyce, J. K., & Weil, R. *Managing with people: A manager's handbook of organization development methods.* Reading, Mass.: Addison-Wesley, 1971.

Forsgren, R., Alpander, G., & Gutman, J. An anatomy of the academy consultant. *Proceedings of the 34th Annual Meeting of the Academy of Management,* August 1974, pp. 18-19. (Abstract)

Foster, M. An introduction to the theory and practice of action research in work organizations. *Human Relations,* 1972, *25*(6), 529-556.

Fox, F. V., Pate, L. E., & Pondy, L. R. Designing organizations to be responsive to their clients. In R. Kilmann, L. Pondy, & D. Slevin (Eds.), *The management of organization design.* New York: American-Elsevier, in press.

Francis, D., & Woodcock, M. *People at work: A practical guide to organizational change.* La Jolla, Calif.: University Associates, 1975.

Franklin, J. L. *Organization development: An annotated bibliography.* Ann Arbor, Mich.: Institute for Social Research, University of Michigan, 1973.

Franklin, J. L. Two approaches to organizational development: A conceptual framework based on judgments of valid information. *JSAS Catalog of Selected Documents in Psychology,* 1974, *4*, 93. (Ms. No. 707)

Franz, E., & Ludekens, B. OD, management development and "future shock." *Industrial Training International,* 1972, *7*(9), 273-275.

French, W. L., & Bell, C. H. A definition and history of organization development: Some comments. *Proceedings of the 31st Annual Meeting of the Academy of Management,* August 1971, pp. 146-153.

French, W. L., & Bell, C. H. A brief history of organization development. *Journal of Contemporary Business,* 1972, *1*(3), 1-8.

French, W. L., & Bell, C. H. *Organization development: Behavioral science interventions for organization improvement.* Englewood Cliffs, N.J.: Prentice-Hall, 1973.

French, W. L., & Hellriegel, D. *Personnel management and organization development.* Boston: Houghton Mifflin, 1971.

Friedlander, F. The primacy of trust as a facilitator of further group accomplishment. *Journal of Applied Behavioral Science,* 1970, *6*(4), 387-400.

Friedlander, F. Congruence in organization development. *Proceedings of the 31st Annual Meeting of the Academy of Management,* August 1971, pp. 153-161.

Friedlander, F., & Brown, L. D. Organization development. *Annual Review of Psychology,* 1974, *25,* 313-341.

Gabriel, P. P. Managing corporate strategy to cope with change. *The Conference Board Record,* 1975, *12*(3), 57-60.

Galbraith, J. R. *Designing complex organizations.* Reading, Mass.: Addison-Wesley, 1973.

Ganesh, S. R. Choosing an OD consultant. *Business Horizons,* 1971, *14*(5), 49-55.

Gannon, M. J., & Paine, F. T. Sources of referral, job orientation, and employee effectiveness. *Proceedings of the 32nd Annual Meeting of the Academy of Management,* August 1972, pp. 36-38.

Gawthrop, L. C. The environment, bureaucracy, and social change: A political prognosis. In A. R. Negandhi (Ed.), *Environmental settings in organizational functioning.* Kent, Ohio: Center for Business and Economic Research, Kent State University, 1970.

Gentry, D. L. Campus recruiters response to the changing educational structure. *Personnel,* 1971, *48*(5), 25-29.

Giacquinta, J. B., London, H. I., & Shigaki, I. S. Implementing organizational changes in urban schools: The case of paraprofessionals. *Journal of Applied Behavioral Science,* 1973, *9*(4), 469-483.

Gibb, J. R. TORI theory: Consultantless team-building. *Journal of Contemporary Business,* 1972, *1*(3), 33-41.

Gilboa, E., Pines, A., & Solomon, L. The wizardry of change agents. *Journal of Applied Behavioral Science,* 1972, *8*(3), 351-360.

Gill, H. S., & Tranfield, D. R. Organization development and the management of training. *Personnel Management,* 1973, *5*(4), 34-35; 37.

Giordano, J., & Giordano, G. Overcoming resistance to change in custodial institutions. *Hospital and Community Psychiatry,* 1972, *23*(6), 183-185.

Glassman, A. M. Team consultation: A revealing analysis. *Proceedings of the 35th Annual Meeting of the Academy of Management,* August 1975, pp. 116-118.

Glenn, R. L., & Morse, L. The Tacoma Police Department teams up for organization development. In *First tango in Boston: A seminar on organization change and development.* Washington, D.C.: National Training and Development Service, 1973.

Golembiewski, R. T. Organizational properties and managerial learning: Testing alternative models of attitudinal change. *Academy of Management Journal,* 1970, *13*(1), 13-31.

Golembiewski, R. T. Toward further development of OD. *Proceedings of the 31st Annual Meeting of the Academy of Management,* August 1971, pp. 183-185.

Golembiewski, R. T. *Renewing organizations: The laboratory approach to planned change.* Itasca, Ill.: F. E. Peacock, 1972.

Golembiewski, R. T. Flexi-time and some of its consequences: A modest structural intervention. *Proceedings of the 34th Annual Meeting of the Academy of Management,* August 1974, p. 51. (Abstract)

Golembiewski, R. T. Some guidelines for tomorrow's OD. In J. D. Adams (Ed.), *New technologies in organization development: 2* (Originally *Theory and method in organization development: An evolutionary process,* Arlington, Va.: NTL Institute, 1974). La Jolla, Calif.: University Associates, 1975.

Golembiewski, R. T., & Blumberg, A. *Sensitivity training and the laboratory approach.* Itasca, Ill.: F. E. Peacock, 1970.

Golembiewski, R. T., & Carrigan, S. B. The persistence of laboratory-induced changes in organization styles. *Administrative Science Quarterly,* 1970, *15*(3), 330-340. (a)

Golembiewski, R. T., & Carrigan, S. B. Planned change in organization style based on the laboratory approach. *Administrative Science Quarterly,* 1970, *15*(1), 79-93. (b)

Golembiewski, R. T., & Carrigan, S. B. Planned change through laboratory methods. *Training and Development Journal,* 1973, *27*(3), 18-27.

Golembiewski, R. T., Hilles, R., & Kagno, M. S. A longitudinal study of flexi-time effects: Some consequences of an OD structural intervention. *Journal of Applied Behavioral Science,* 1974, *10*(4), 503-532.

Golembiewski, R. T., & Munzenrider, R. F. Persistence and change: A note on the long-term effects of an organization development program. *Academy of Management Journal*, 1973, *16*(1), 149-153. (a)

Golembiewski, R. T., & Munzenrider, R. F. Social desirability as an intervening variable in interpreting OD effects. *Proceedings of the 33rd Annual Meeting of the Academy of Management*, August 1973, pp. 534-542. (b)

Golembiewski, R. T., & Munzenrider, R. F. Social desirability as an intervening variable in interpreting OD effects. *Journal of Applied Behavioral Science*, 1975, *11*(3), 317-332.

Golembiewski, R. T., Munzenrider, R. F., Blumberg, A., Carrigan, S. B., & Mead, W. R. Changing climate in a complex organization: Interactions between a learning design and an environment. *Academy of Management Journal*, 1971, *14*(4), 465-481.

Goldman, S., & Moynihan, W. Strategies for consultant-client interface. *Educational Technology*, 1972, *12*(10), 27-30.

Goodstein, L. D. Organizational development as a model for community consultation. *Hospital and Community Psychiatry*, 1972, *23*(6), 165-168.

Goodstein, L. D., & Boyer, R. K. Crisis intervention in a municipal agency: A conceptual case history. *Journal of Applied Behavioral Science*, 1972, *8*(3), 318-340.

Gooler, D. D., & Ely, D. P. The impact of organization on curriculum change. *Educational Technology*, 1972, *12*(10), 39-42.

Greenfield, T. B. Organizations as social inventions: Rethinking assumptions about change. *Journal of Applied Behavioral Science*, 1973, *9*(5), 551-574.

Greenwood, W. The management audit: A systematic diagnostic and appraisal tool for the management consultant. *Proceedings of the 34th Annual Meeting of the Academy of Management*, August 1974, p. 19. (Abstract)

Greiner, L. E. Evolution and revolution as organizations grow. *Harvard Business Review*, 1972, *50*(4), 37-46. (a)

Greiner, L. E. Red flags in organization development. *Business Horizons*, 1972, *15*(3), 17-24. (b)

Greiner, L. E. Evolution and revolution as accounting firms grow. *Journal of Accountancy*, 1973, *136*(4), 88-90.

Greenblatt, M., Sharaf, M. R., & Stone, E. M. *Dynamics of institutional change: The hospital in transition*. Pittsburgh: University of Pittsburgh Press, 1971.

Gross, N., Giacquinta, J. B., & Bernstein, M. *Implementing organizational innovations: A sociological analysis of planned educational change*. New York: Basic Books, 1971.

Grote, R. C. Effect of leadership changes on a work group. *Training and Development Journal*, 1971, *25*(7), 18-21.

Gruber, H., & Niles, J. S. Changing structures for changing times. *Financial Executive*, 1971, *39*(4), 30-34.

Hackman, J. R., & Oldham, G. R. Development of the job diagnostic survey. *Journal of Applied Psychology*, 1975, *60*(2), 159-170.

Hackman, J. R., Oldham, G. R., Janson, R., & Purdy, K. A new strategy for job enrichment. *California Management Review*, 1975, *17*(4), 57-71.

Hage, J., & Aiken, M. *Social change in complex organizations*. New York: Random House, 1970.

Hain, T. Patterns of organizational change (Doctoral dissertation, University of Akron, 1972). *Dissertation Abstracts International*, 1972. (University Microfilms No. 72-25, 697)

Halal, W. E. Organizational development in the future. *California Management Review*, 1974, *16*(3), 35-41.

Hall, D. T., & Mansfield, R. Organizational and individual response to external stress. *Administrative Science Quarterly*, 1971, *16*(4), 533-547.

Hall, R. H. *Organizations structure and process*. Englewood Cliffs, N.J.: Prentice-Hall, 1972.

Hand, H. H., Estafen, B. D., & Sims, H. P., Jr. How effective is data survey and feedback as a technique of organization development? An experiment. *Journal of Applied Behavioral Science*, 1975, *11*(3), 333-347.

Harris, A. The TORI model of change and the changing woman. *Training and Development Journal*, 1975, *29*(8), 22-27.

Harris, J. C. A case study of an action-research consultant style of intervention in organization development (Doctoral dissertation, University of Massachusetts, 1973). *Dissertation Abstracts International*, 1973. (University Microfilms No. 73-6679)

Harrison, R. Choosing the depth of organizational intervention. *Journal of Applied Behavioral Science*, 1970, *6*(2), 181-202.

Harrison, R. Research on human relations training: Design and interpretation. *Journal of Applied Behavioral Science*, 1971, *7*(1), 71-85.

Harrison, R. Training internal OD consultants in industry. *Industrial Training International*, 1972, *7*(5), 152-153.

Harrison, R. Developing autonomy, initiative and risk taking through a laboratory design. In J. D. Adams (Ed.), *New technologies in organization development: 2* (Originally *Theory and method in organization development: An evolutionary process*, Arlington, Va.: NTL Institute, 1974). La Jolla, Calif.: University Associates, 1975.

Hart, H. A. The Grid appraised—Phases 1 and 2. *Personnel*, 1974, *51*(5), 44-59.

Harvey, J. B. Organization development as a religious movement. *Training and Development Journal*, 1974, *28*(3), 24-27.

Havelock, R. G. *Bibliography on knowledge utilization and dissemination.* Ann Arbor, Mich.: Center for Research on Utilization of Scientific Knowledge, University of Michigan, 1971.

Havelock, R. G. A critique: Has OD become a social technology? *Educational Technology*, 1972, *12*(10), 61-62. (a)

Havelock, R. G. *Training for change agents: A guide to the design of training programs in education and other fields.* Ann Arbor, Mich.: Institute for Social Research, University of Michigan, 1972. (b)

Havelock, R. G. *The change agent's guide to innovation in education.* Englewood Cliffs, N.J.: Educational Technology Publications, 1973.

Hayes, W. G., & Williams, E. I., Jr. Supervisory training—An index of change. *Public Personnel Review*, 1971, *32*(3), 158-163.

Heisler, W. J. Patterns of OD in practice. *Business Horizons*, 1975, *18*(1), 77-84.

Heller, F. A. Group feedback analysis as a change agent. *Human Relations*, 1970, *23*(4), 319-339.

Helmich, D. L., & Brown, W. B. Successor type and organizational change in the corporate enterprise. *Administrative Science Quarterly*, 1972, *17*(3), 371-381.

Herman, S. M. Toward a more authentic manager. *Training and Development Journal*, 1971, *25*(10). 8-10. (a)

Herman, S. M. What is this thing called organization development? *Personnel Journal*, 1971, *50*(8), 595-603. (b)

Herman, S. M. The shadow of organization development. In J. W. Pfeiffer & J. E. Jones (Eds.), *The 1974 annual handbook for group facilitators*. La Jolla, Calif.: University Associates, 1974.

Hersey, P., & Blanchard, K. H. Cultural changes: Their influence on organizational structure and management behavior. *Training and Development Journal*, 1970, *24*(10), 2-3.

Hersey, P., & Blanchard, K. H. The management of change: Change and the use of power. *Training and Development Journal*, 1972, *26*(1), 6-10. (a)

Hersey, P., & Blanchard, K. H. The management of change: Change through behavior modification. *Training and Development Journal*, 1972, *26*(2), 20-24. (b)

Hersey, P., & Blanchard, K. H. The management of change: Planning and implementing change. *Training and Development Journal*, 1972, *26*(3), 28-33. (c)

Herzberg, F. The wise old Turk. *Harvard Business Review*, 1974, *52*(5), 70-80.

Heskett, J. L. Sweeping changes in distribution. *Harvard Business Review*, 1973, *51*(2), 123-132.

Hess, F., & Greenstein, G. Organizational development: An idea whose time has come. *Educational Technology*, 1972, *12*(10), 57-60.

Hill, M. The manager as change agent. *Personnel Journal*, 1971, *50*(1), 60-63.

Hill, R. The "unfreezing" of a cigarette giant. *International Management*, 1973, *28*(7), 46-49.

Hillmar, E. D. Where OD and MBO meet. *Training and Development Journal*, 1975, *29*(4), 34-38.

Hirsch, G. P. The challenge of change. *Industrial Training International*, 1972, *7*(3), 82-87.

Hofstede, G. Perceptions of others after a T group. *Journal of Applied Behavioral Science*, 1975, *11*(3), 367-377.

Hollis, J. W., & Krause, F. H. Effective development of change. *Public Personnel Management*, 1973, *2*(1), 60-69.

Hornstein, H., Bunker, B. B., Burke, W. W., Gindes, M., & Lewicki, R. J. (Eds.). *Social intervention: A behavioral science approach*. New York: Free Press, 1971.

Hornstein, H. A., Bunker, B. B., & Hornstein, M. G. Some conceptual issues in individual and group-oriented strategies of intervention into organizations. *Journal of Applied Behavioral Science*, 1971, 7(5), 557-567.

Huse, E. F. *Organization development and change.* St. Paul, Minn.: West, 1975.

Huse, E. F., & Beer, M. Eclectic approach to organizational development. *Harvard Business Review*, 1971, 49(5), 103-112.

Iman, S. C. Fenlon works: The effects of organizational development (Doctoral dissertation, University of Michigan, 1973). *Dissertation Abstracts International*, 1973. (University Microfilms No. 73-11, 156)

Ivancevich, J. M. A longitudinal assessment of management by objectives. *Administrative Science Quarterly*, 1972, 17(1), 126-138.

Ivancevich, J. M. Changes in performance in a management by objectives program. *Administrative Science Quarterly*, 1974, 19(4), 563-574.

Jenks, R. S. An action-research approach to organizational change. *Journal of Applied Behavioral Science*, 1970, 6(2), 131-150.

Jenks, R. S. An internal change agent's role in restructuring university governance. *Journal of Higher Education*, 1973, 44(5), 370-379.

Johns, E. A. *The sociology of organizational change.* New York: Pergamon Press, 1973.

Jones, G. N. *Planning, development, and change: A bibliography on development administration.* Honolulu: East-West Center Press, 1970.

Jones, J. E., & Pfeiffer, J. W. (Eds.). *The 1973 annual handbook for group facilitators.* La Jolla, Calif.: University Associates, 1973.

Jones, J. E., & Pfeiffer, J. W. (Eds.). *The 1975 annual handbook for group facilitators.* La Jolla, Calif.: University Associates, 1975.

Joure, S. A., Frye, R. L., Green, P. C., & Cassens, F. P. Examples of over-use of sensitivity training. *Training and Development Journal*, 1971, 25(12), 24-26.

Just what should an organizational development specialist do? *Personnel Journal*, 1973, 52(3), 222-223.

Kahn, R. L. Organizational development: Some problems and proposals. *Journal of Applied Behavioral Science*, 1974, 10(4), 485-502.

Karras, E. J. Training—A link to organizational change. *Training and Development Journal*, 1973, 27(5), 12-14.

Katcher, D. A. Consulting from within. *California Management Review*, 1972, 14(4), 36-44.

Katz, D., & Georgopoulos, B. S. Organizations in a changing world. *Journal of Applied Behavioral Science*, 1971, 7(3), 342-370.

Kaufman, H. *The limits of organizational change.* University, Ala.: University of Alabama Press, 1971.

Kegan, D. L. Organizational development: Description, issues and some research results. *Academy of Management Journal*, 1971, 14(4), 453-464. (a)

Kegan, D. L. Trust, openness and organizational development: Short-term relationships in research and development laboratories and a design for investigating long-term effects (Doctoral dissertation, Northwestern University, 1971). *Dissertation Abstracts International*, 1971. (University Microfilms No. 71-30, 852) (b)

Kegan, D. L., & Rubenstein, A. H. Trust, effectiveness and organizational development: A field study in R & D. *Journal of Applied Behavioral Science*, 1973, 9(4), 498-513.

Kennedy, J. H. "Just among us consultants . . ." *The Conference Board Record*, 1973, 10(5), 61-64.

Kerr, S. Some modifications in MBO as an OD strategy. *Proceedings of the 32nd Annual Meeting of the Academy of Management*, August 1974, pp. 39-42.

Kilmann, R. H. An organic-adaptive organization: The MAPS method. *Personnel*, 1974, 51(3), 35-47.

Kilmann, R. H., & McKelvey, B. The MAPS route to better organization design. *California Management Review*, 17(3), 23-31.

Kimberly, J. R., & Nielsen, W. R. The impact of organizational development on organizational productivity: An empirical analysis. *Proceedings of the 16th Annual Conference of the Midwest Academy of Management*, April 1973.

Kimberly, J. R., & Nielsen, W. R. Organization development and change in organizational performance. *Administrative Science Quarterly*, 1975, 20(2), 191-206.

King, A. S. Experimenter effects in organizational change. *Proceedings of the 17th Annual Meeting of the Midwest Academy of Management*, April 1974, pp. 124-142.

King, A. S. Expectation effects in organizational change. *Administrative Science Quarterly*, 1974, 19(2), 221-230.

Kingdon, D. R. The management of complexity in a matrix organization: A socio-technical approach to changing organizational behavior (Doctoral dissertation, University of California, Los Angeles, 1970). *Dissertation Abstracts International*, 1970. (University Microfilms No. 70-14, 294)

Kirkpatrick, D. L. Resistance to change. *Training and Development Journal*, 1973, 27(3), 42.

Klein, S. M., Kraut, A. I., & Wolfson, A. Employee reactions to attitude survey feedback: A study of the impact of structure and process. *Administrative Science Quarterly*, 1971, 16(4), 497-514.

Kolb, D. A., & Boyatzis, R. E. On the dynamics of the helping relationship. *Journal of Applied Behavioral Science*, 1970, 6(3), 267-289.

Kolb, D. A., & Frohman, A. L. An organization development approach to consulting. *Sloan Management Review*, 1970, 12(1), 51-65.

Koprowski, E. J. Improving organization effectiveness through action research teams. *Training and Development Journal*, 1972, 26(6), 36-40.

Korten, D. C. *Planned change in a traditional society: Psychological problems of modernization in Ethiopia.* New York: Praeger, 1972.

Kraft, P., & Dettelback, W. W. Organization change through job enrichment. *Training and Development Journal*, 1971, 25(8), 2-6.

Kraft, R. H. P., & Padro, S. Educational planning as a vehicle for systems change. *Educational Technology*, 1972, 12(2), 44-49.

Kreinik, P. S., & Colarelli, N. J. Managerial Grid human relations training for mental hospital personnel. *Human Relations*, 1971, 24(1), 91-104.

Kreps, G. A. Change in crisis-relevant organizations: Police departments and civil disturbances. *American Behavioral Scientist*, 1973, 16(3), 356-367.

Kristensen, R. E. The role of the change agent in community development. *Training and Development Journal*, 1974, 28(10), 13-19.

Krone, C. Open systems redesign. In J. D. Adams (Ed.), *New technologies in organization development: 2* (Originally *Theory and method in organization development: An evolutionary process*, Arlington, Va.: NTL Institute, 1974). La Jolla, Calif.: University Associates, 1975.

Kuriloff, A. H. *Organizational development for survival.* New York: American Management Association, 1972.

Labovitz, G. H. Organizing for adaptation. *Business Horizons*, 1971, 14(3), 19-26.

Lassey, W. R. (Ed.). *Leadership and social change.* La Jolla, Calif.: University Associates, 1971.

Lawler, E. E., III, Hackman, J. R., & Kaufman, S. Effects of job redesign: A field experiment. *Journal of Applied Social Psychology*, 1973, 3(1), 49-62.

Lazarus, H. The American Telephone & Telegraph Company manpower laboratory. *Proceedings of the 31st Annual Meeting of the Academy of Management*, August 1971, pp. 194-202.

Leach, W. B., & Owens, V. W. Training and the change agent role model. *Training and Development Journal*, 1973, 27(10), 40-47.

Leader, G. C. Interpersonally skillful bank officers view their behavior. *Journal of Applied Behavioral Science*, 1973, 9(4), 484-497.

Leary, M. Training strategies for industrial relations change. *Industrial Training International*, 1973, 8(5), 150-153.

Leavitt, H. J., & Doktor, R. Personal growth, laboratory training, science, and all that: A shot at a cognitive clarification. *Journal of Applied Behavioral Science*, 1970, 6(2), 173-179.

Lehman, L. Organizational change and the teacher. *Educational Technology*, 1972, 12(10), 52-54.

Levin, J. M. Manager development: A psychological perspective. *Personnel Journal*, 1973, 52(2), 121-127.

Levine, D. M., Derr, C. B., & Junghans, R. P. Educational planning with organizational development: A people-involving approach to systemic planning. *Educational Technology*, 1972, 12(10), 14-26.

Levinson, H. A psychologist looks at executive development. In G. W. Dalton, P. R. Lawrence, & L. E. Greiner (Eds.), *Organizational change and development.* Homewood, Ill.: Irwin-Dorsey, 1970.

Levinson, H. Easing the pain of personal loss. *Harvard Business Review*, 1972, 50(5), 80-88.

Levinson, H. *The great jackass fallacy.* Boston: Harvard Business School, Division of Research, 1973.

Levinson, H., Sashkin, M., & Burke, W. W. Organization development pro and con: III. Discussion. *Professional Psychology*, 1973, 4(2), 200-208.

Lewicki, R. J., & Alderfer, C. P. The tensions between research and intervention in intergroup conflict. *Journal of Applied Behavioral Science*, 1973, *9*(4), 424-449.

Lieberman, M. A., Yalom, I. D., & Miles, M. B. *Encounter groups: First facts*. New York: Basic Books, 1973.

Lippitt, G. L. Developing life plans. *Training and Development Journal*, 1970, *24*(5), 2-7.

Lippitt, G. L. Criteria for selecting, evaluating and developing consultants. *Training and Development Journal*, 1972, *26*(8), 12-17. (a)

Lippitt, G. L. Once more—OD. *Industrial Training International*, 1972, *7*(8), 252-253. (b)

Lippitt, G. L. *Visualizing change: Model building and the change process*. Fairfax, Va.: NTL Learning Resources, 1973. (a)

Lippitt, G. L. What do you mean by OD?—What does OD mean to you? *Industrial Training International*, 1973, *8*(2); 44. (b)

Lippitt, G. L. Teaching consulting skills in the regular curriculum—A report. *Proceedings of the 34th Annual Meeting of the Academy of Management*, August 1974, p. 19. (Abstract)

Lippitt, G. L. Model building: An organization development technology. In J. D. Adams (Ed.), *New technologies in organization development: 2* (Originally *Theory and method in organization development: An evolutionary process*, Arlington, Va.: NTL Institute, 1974). La Jolla, Calif.: University Associates, 1975. (a)

Lippitt, G. L. Training for a changing world. *Training*, 1975, *12*(5), 46-49. (b)

Lippitt, G. L., & This, L. ITORP: Implementing the organization renewal process. *Training and Development Journal*, 1970, *24*(7), 10-15.

Lippitt, G. L., This, L. E., & Bidwell, R. G. (Eds.). *Optimizing human resources: Readings in individual and organization development*. Reading, Mass.: Addison-Wesley, 1971.

Lippitt, R., & Lippitt, G. L. Consulting process in action. *Training and Development Journal*, 1975, *29*(5), 48-54; *29*(6), 38-41.

London, J. The consistency of management in organizational change. *Personnel Journal*, 1974, *53*(5), 363-366.

Lucas, H. C., Jr., & Plimpton, R. B. Technological consulting in a grass roots, action oriented organization. *Sloan Management Review*, 1972, *14*(1), 17-36.

Luckham, A. R. Institutional transfer and breakdown in a new nation: The Nigerian military. *Administrative Science Quarterly*, 1971, *16*(4), 387-405.

Luke, R. A., Jr., Block, P., Davey, J. M., & Averch, V. R. A structural approach to organizational change. *Journal of Applied Behavioral Science*, 1973, *9*(5), 611-635.

Lundberg, C. C. Planning the executive development program. *California Management Review*, 1972, *15*(1), 10-15. (a)

Lundberg, C. C. Toward a model of social change. *Proceedings of the 32nd Annual Meeting of the Academy of Management*, August 1972, pp. 53-57. (b)

Mack, H. Evaluating the organization development effort. *Training and Development Journal*, 1974, *28*(3), 42-47.

Mackenzie, K. D. Organizational change. In J. W. McGuire (Ed.), *Contemporary management: Issues and viewpoints*. Englewood Cliffs, N.J.: Prentice-Hall, 1974.

Maguire, L. M. *An annotated bibliography of the literature on change*. Philadelphia: Research for Better Schools, 1970. (a)

Maguire, L. M. *Observations and analysis of the literature on change: With reference to education*. Philadelphia: Research for Better Schools, 1970. (b)

Mahler, W. *Diagnostic studies*. Reading, Mass.: Addison-Wesley, 1974.

Maier, N. R. F., Solem, A. R., & Maier, A. A. *The role-play technique: A handbook for management and leadership practice*. La Jolla, Calif.: University Associates, 1975.

Mancke, R. B. Iron ore and steel: A case study of the economic causes and consequences of vertical integration. *Journal of Industrial Economics*, 1972, *20*(3), 220-229.

Mangham, I. L., Shaw, D., & Wilson, B. *Managing change: A practical guide to organization with examples drawn from ICI (Petrochemicals Division)*. London: British Institute of Management, 1971.

Margulies, N. Implementing organizational change through an internal consulting team. *Training and Development Journal*, 1971, *25*(7), 26-33. (a)

Margulies, N. The myth and magic in organization development. *Proceedings of the 31st Annual Meeting of the Academy of Management*, August 1971, pp. 177-182. (b)

Margulies, N. The myth and magic in OD. *Business Horizons*, 1972, *15*(4), 77-82. (a)

Margulies, N. Organizational development in a university setting: Some problems of initiating change. *Educational Technology*, 1972, *12*(10), 48-52. (b)

Margulies, N. Organizational development and changes in organization climate. *Public Personnel Management*, 1973, *2*(2), 84-92.

Margulies, N., & Raia, A. P. *Organizational development: Values, process, and technology.* New York: McGraw-Hill, 1972.

Margulies, N., & Wallace, J. *Organizational change: Techniques and applications.* Glenview, Ill.: Scott, Foresman, 1973.

Marrow, A. J. (Ed.). *The failure of success.* New York: Amacom, 1972.

Marrow, A. J., Bowers, D. G., & Seashore, S. E. *Management by participation: Creating a climate for personal and organizational development.* New York: Harper & Row, 1967.

Mather, A. F. ECHO: A framework for organization development. *Training and Development Journal*, 1973, *27*(1), 40-46.

Mather, A. F., & Schuttenberg, E. M. A team development project. *Training and Development Journal*, 1971, *25*(2), 15-19; 22-24.

Maurice, J. *Le changement au sein des enterprises. Structures et processus.* Genève, Switzerland: Droz, 1971.

Maxwell, S. R., & Evans, M. G. An evaluation of organizational development: Three phases of the Managerial Grid. *Journal of Business Administration*, 1973, *5*(1), 21-35.

Mazze, E. M., & Thompson, J. T., Jr. An organization development design for personnel management. *Training and Development Journal*, 1973, *27*(1), 48-53. (a)

Mazze, E. M., & Thompson, J. T., Jr. Organization renewal: Case study of a marketing department. *MSU Business Topics*, 1973, *21*(3), 39-44. (b)

McFeely, W. M. Multilayered management. *The Conference Board Record*, 1971, *8*(3), 25-29.

McFeely, W. M. *Organization change: Perceptions and realities.* New York: The Conference Board, 1972.

McGill, M. E. Correctness or correctability: Toward contemporary contextual criteria of effective organizational intervention. *Proceedings of the 32nd Annual Meeting of the Academy of Management*, August 1972, pp. 49-52.

McGill, M. E. Action research designs for training and development. *Proceedings of the 33rd Annual Meeting of the Academy of Management*, August 1973, pp. 542-549.

McWhinney, W. H. Some reservations. *Journal of Applied Behavioral Science*, 1972, *8*(1), 107-109.

Meyers, W. R. The politics of evaluation research: The Peace Corps. *Journal of Applied Behavioral Science*, 1975, *11*(3), 261-280.

Miles, R. E. Organization development. In G. Strauss, R. E. Miles, C. C. Snow, & A. S. Tannenbaum (Eds.), *Organizational behavior research and issues.* Madison, Wis.: Industrial Relations Research Association, 1974.

Miles, R. E. *Theories of management: Implications for organizational behavior and development.* New York: McGraw-Hill, 1975.

Mill, C. R. OD in a macrosystem: A three-year progress report. In J. D. Adams (Ed.), *New technologies in organization development: 2* (Originally *Theory and method in organization development: An evolutionary process*, Arlington, Va.: NTL Institute, 1974). La Jolla, Calif.: University Associates, 1975.

Miller, A., Tillinghast, C., III, Garrison, J., & Bell, C. H. Boise Cascade's organization renewal project. *Proceedings of the 31st Annual Meeting of the Academy of Management*, August 1971, pp. 185-194.

Miller, J. G. Living systems: The organization. *Behavioral Science*, 1972, *17*(1), 1-182.

Mills, D. Q. Industrial relations and the theory of human resources management. *Sloan Management Review*, 1970, *12*(1), 1-14.

Miner, J. B. The OD-management development conflict. *Business Horizons*, 1973, *16*(6), 31-36.

Moan, F. E. Does management practice lag behind theory in the computer environment? *Academy of Management Journal*, 1973, *16*(1), 7-23.

Moore, L. F. Myths, fallacies and realities in organizational development. *Canadian Personnel and Industrial Relations Journal*, 1972, *19*(5), 25-30.

Moore, M. L. Task components of the commitment process. In T. H. Patten, Jr. (Ed.), *OD —Emerging dimensions and concepts.* East Lansing, Mich.: American Society for Training and Development, 1973.

Moore, W. C. Before you try to make a change. *Supervisory Management,* 1971, *16*(8), 23-24.

Morgan, C. P., Schneier, C., & Beatty, R. Diagnosing organizations: New fad or new technology in management consulting. *Proceedings of the 34th Annual Meeting of the Academy of Management,* August 1974, p. 17. (Abstract)

Morgan, F., Jr. Organization development in a troubled economy. *Training and Development Journal,* 1975, *29*(4), 3-6.

Morgan, J. S. *Managing change: The strategies of making change work for you.* New York: McGraw-Hill, 1972.

Mosley, D. C., & Green, T. B. Nominal grouping as an organization development technique. *Training and Development Journal,* 1974, *28*(3), 30-37.

Mouton, J. S., & Blake, R. R. Behavioral science theories underlying organization development. *Journal of Contemporary Business,* 1972, *1*(3), 9-22.

Mrazek, C. Political security and tough-mindedness: Essentials for the internal change agent. In T. H. Patten, Jr. (Ed.), *OD—Emerging dimensions and concepts.* East Lansing, Mich.: American Society for Training and Development, 1973.

Muczyk, J. P. A controlled field experiment measuring the impact of MBO on performance data. *Proceedings of the 35th Annual Meeting of the Academy of Management,* August 1975, pp. 363-365.

Mullan, C., & Gorman, L. Facilitating adaptation to change: A case study in retaining middle-aged and older workers at Aer Lingus. *Industrial Gerontology,* 1972, *15*, 20-39.

Murray, D., & Schmuck, R. The counselor-consultant as a specialist in organization development. *Elementary School Guidance and Counseling,* 1972, *7*(2), 99-104.

Murrell, K. L., & Vaill, P. B. *Organization development sources and applications.* Washington, D.C.: American Society for Training and Development, 1975.

Nadler, D. A., Jenkins, G. D., Mirvis, P. H., & Macy, B. A. A research design and measurement package for the assessment of quality of work interventions. *Proceedings of the 35th Annual Meeting of the Academy of Management,* August 1975, pp. 360-362.

Nadler, D. A., & Pecorella, P. A. Differential effects of multiple interventions in an organization. *Journal of Applied Behavioral Science,* 1975, *11*(3), 348-366.

Napier, H. S. Deputy president: Top management in 1982. *Personnel Journal,* 1973, *52*(8), 714-719.

Narver, J. C. Rational management responses to external effects. *Academy of Management Journal,* 1971, *14*(1), 99-115.

Nath, R. Sensitivity training and management education. *Proceedings of the 31st Annual Meeting of the Academy of Management,* August 1971, pp. 206-208.

Nath, R. New directions in organization development. *Proceedings of the 32nd Annual Meeting of the Academy of Management,* August 1972, pp. 34-35.

National College of the State Judiciary, Court Studies Division. *Organization development: A selected and annotated bibliography.* Reno, Nev.: Author, 1972.

National Training and Development Service. *First tango in Boston: A seminar on organization change and development.* Washington, D.C.: Author, 1973.

Nedd, A. N. B. Psychological set and individual response to change (An exploratory study of some psychological and situational determinants of behavioral tendencies toward organizational change) (Doctoral dissertation, Cornell University, 1971). *Dissertation Abstracts International,* 1971. (University Microfilms No. 71-7372) (a)

Nedd, A. N. B. The simultaneous effect of several variables on attitudes toward change. *Administrative Science Quarterly,* 1971, *16*(3), 258-269. (b)

Nielsen, W. R., & Kimberly, J. R. The impact of organizational development on the quality of organizational output. *Proceedings of the 33rd Annual Meeting of the Academy of Management,* August 1973, pp. 527-534.

Nord, W. R. The failure of current applied behavioral science—A Marxian perspective. *Journal of Applied Behavioral Science,* 1974, *10*(4), 579-594.

Oates, D. New shapes for the organization. *Management Review*, 1971, 60(9), 30-32.

Olmosk, K. E. Seven pure strategies of change. In J. W. Pfeiffer & J. E. Jones (Eds.), *The 1972 annual handbook for group facilitators*. La Jolla, Calif.: University Associates, 1972.

O'Neill, M. E., & Martensen, K. R. *Criminal justice group training: A facilitator's handbook*. La Jolla, Calif.: University Associates, 1975.

Ono, T. Modernization of business administration in Japan. *International Studies of Management & Organization*, 1971, 1(3), 274-291.

Organizing for change. *Nations Schools*, 1971, 88(5), 57-61.

O'Rourke, P. So, we ought to get started on OD. *Training and Development Journal*, 1972, 26(1), 21.

O'Rourke, P., & Peterson, L. Why won't OD phase II just happen? *Training and Development Journal*, 1973, 27(1), 22-28.

Owens, J. Organizational conflict and team-building. *Training and Development Journal*, 1973, 27(8), 32-39.

Pagès, M. Bethel culture, 1969: Impressions of an immigrant. *Journal of Applied Behavioral Science*, 1971, 7(3), 267-284.

Partin, J. J. (Ed.). *Current perspectives in organization development*. Reading, Mass.: Addison-Wesley, 1973. (a)

Partin, J. J. Emerging perspectives about organization planning and development. *Training and Development Journal*, 1973, 27(1), 8-17.(b)

Pate, L. E., & Rowland, K. M. Organizational change and development: An annotated bibliography. JSAS *Catalog of Selected Documents in Psychology*, 1975, 5, 259. (Ms. No. 973)

Pate, L. E., & Rowland, K. M. Current OD theory and practice: Some references and comments. *Management Bibliographies & Reviews*, in press.

Patten, T. H., Jr. OD, MBO, and the R/P system: A new dimension in personnel administration. *Personnel Administration*, 1972, 35(2), 14-23.

Patten, T. H., Jr. Relating learning theory to behavior change in organizations—Part I. *Industrial Training International*, 1973, 8(7), 216-218.

Patten, T. H., Jr. Relating learning theory to behavior change in organizations—Part II. *Industrial Training International*, 1973, 8(8), 245-247.

Patten, T. H., Jr. (Ed.). *OD—Emerging dimensions and concepts*. East Lansing, Mich.: American Society for Training and Development, 1973.

Patten, T. H., Jr., Skjervheim, T. F., & Shook, J. L. *Characteristics and professional concerns of organization development practitioners*. Madison, Wis.: American Society for Training and Development, 1973.

Perrow, C. Is business really changing? *Organizational Dynamics*, 1974, 3(1), 31-44.

Peters, E. B. Beating snakes back into their holes: Consultant initiation of supervisory training for organizational problem solving. *Proceedings of the 34th Annual Meeting of the Academy of Management*, August 1974, p. 18. (Abstract)

Petrow, C., Stern, T., & Levinson, H. The quiet revolution at Foggy Bottom. *Management Review*, 1971, 60(12), 4-14.

Pettigrew, A. M. Towards a political theory of organizational intervention. *Human Relations*, 1975, 28(3), 191-208.

Pfeiffer, J. W., & Heslin, R. *Instrumentation in human relations training*. La Jolla, Calif.: University Associates, 1973.

Pfeiffer, J. W., & Jones, J. E. (Eds.). *A handbook of structured experiences for human relations training* (5 vols.). La Jolla, Calif.: University Associates, 1969-1975.

Pfeiffer, J. W., & Jones, J. E. (Eds.). *The 1972 annual handbook for group facilitators*. La Jolla, Calif.: University Associates, 1972.

Pfeiffer, J. W., & Jones, J. E. (Eds.). *The 1974 annual handbook for group facilitators*. La Jolla, Calif.: University Associates, 1974.

Pfeiffer, J. W., & Jones, J. E. *Reference guide to Handbooks and Annuals*. La Jolla, Calif.: University Associates, 1975.

Pheysey, D. C. Off course considerations in training. *Personnel Management*, 1972, 4(12), 26-29.

Pierro, H. P., Jr. Applying the Managerial Grid to a real-life sales situation. *Training and Development Journal*, 1973, 27(11), 20-27.

Placek, P. J. Welfare workers as family planning change agents and the perennial problem of heterophily with welfare clients. *Journal of Applied Behavioral Science*, 1975, 11(3), 298-316.

Plovnick, M., Fry, R., & Rubin, I. New developments in OD technology: Programmed team development. *Training and Development Journal*, 1975, 29(4), 19-25.

Plovnick, M. S., Steele, F., & Schein, E. H. Expanding professional design education through workshops in the applied behavioral sciences. *Journal of Higher Education*, 1973, *44*(5), 380-388.

Podnos, I. The "consultative" method of training. *Personnel*, 1971, *48*(5), 53-59.

Podnos, I. What is consultative training? *Supervisory Management*, 1972, *17*(1), 12-16.

Posthuma, A. B., & Posthuma, B. W. Some observations on encounter group casualties. *Journal of Applied Behavioral Science*, 1973, *9*(5), 595-608.

Pritchett, P. Employee attitude surveys: A natural starting point for organization development. *Personnel Journal*, 1975, *54*(4), 202-205.

Quick, T. L. *Your role in task force management: The dynamics of corporate change.* Garden City, N.Y.: Doubleday, 1972.

Raia, A. P. Organizational development—Some issues and challenges. *California Management Review*, 1972, *14*(4), 13-20.

Randall, L. K. Common questions & tentative answers regarding organization development. *California Management Review*, 1971, *13*(3), 45-52.

Reddin, W. J. Managing organisational change. *Industrial Training International*, 1970, *5*(3), 132-134.

Reddy, W. B. A bibliography of small group training, 1973-1974. In J. E. Jones & J. W. Pfeiffer (Eds.), *The 1975 annual handbook for group facilitators.* La Jolla, Calif.: University Associates, 1975.

Rehfuss, J. A. Training, organizational development, and the future organization. *Public Personnel Review*, 1971, *32*(2), 118-121.

Reid, T. A., & Marinaccio, A. D. A perspective on organizational development: The open line project. *Proceedings of the 81st Annual Convention of the American Psychological Association*, 1973, 8, pp. 965-966.

Reilly, A. J., & Jones, J. E. Team-building. In J. W. Pfeiffer & J. E. Jones (Eds.), *The 1974 annual handbook for group facilitators.* La Jolla, Calif.: University Associates, 1974.

Rhodes, J. An approach to organisation development. *Industrial Training International*, 1970, *5*(10), 407-408.

Richetto, G. M. Organizations circa 1990: Demise of the pyramid. *Personnel Journal*, 1970, *49*(7), 598-603.

Rimler, G. W. Can management survive OD? *Proceedings of the 35th Annual Meeting of the Academy of Management*, August 1975, pp. 119-121.

Roeber, R. J. C. *The organization in a changing environment.* Reading, Mass.: Addison-Wesley, 1973.

Roos, L. L., Jr., & Roos, N. P. Administrative change in a modernizing society. *Administrative Science Quarterly*, 1970, *15*(1), 69-78.

Ross, J. D., & Hare, G. Organization development in local government: Results of an IPA grant. In *First tango in Boston: A seminar on organization change and development.* Washington, D.C.: National Training and Development Service, 1973.

Ross, R. OD for whom? *Journal of Applied Behavioral Science*, 1971, *7*(5), 580-585.

Rowsow, J. M. (Ed.). *The worker and the job: Coping with change.* Englewood Cliffs, N.J.: Prentice-Hall, 1974.

Rubin, I., Plovnick, M., & Fry, R. Initiating planned change in health care systems. *Journal of Applied Behavioral Science*, 1974, *10*(1), 107-124.

Runyon, J. H. Of human stress and organizational change. *Canadian Personnel and Industrial Relations Journal*, 1972, *19*(5), 18-22.

Rush, H. M. *Organization development: A reconnaissance.* New York: The Conference Board, 1973.

Sadler, P. J. Designing an organization structure: A behavioral science approach. *Management International Review*, 1971, *11*(6), 19-33.

Sadler, P. J., & Barry, B. A. *Organizational development: Case studies in the printing industry.* Harlow, England: Longmans, 1970.

Sage, D. What to do before the trainer comes. *Training and Development Journal*, 1973, *27*(6), 30-33.

Sainsaulieu, R. The impact of technical change on the norms of interpersonal relations among workers. *International Studies of Management & Organization*, 1971, *1*(3), 292-310.

Salinas, A. D. R. Executive development programs and behavioral and attitudinal changes of program conductors and professors. *Public Personnel Review*, 1972, *33*(1), 33-36.

Sanford, N. Whatever happened to action research? *Journal of Social Issues*, 1970, *26*(4), 3-23.

Sashkin, M. Organization development practices. *Professional Psychology*, 1973, *4*(2), 187-194.

Sayles, L. Technological innovation and the planning process. *Organizational Dynamics*, 1973, *2*(1), 68-80.

Schacht, H. B. The impact of change in the seventies. *Business Horizons*, 1970, *13*(4), 29-34.

Schaffer, R. H. Management development through management decisions. *Personnel*, 1972, *49*(3), 29-38.

Schmidt, W. H. (Ed.). *Organizational frontiers and human values*. Belmont, Calif.: Wadsworth, 1970.

Schmuck, R. A. Developing collaborative decision-making: The importance of trusting, strong and skillful leaders. *Educational Technology*, 1972, *12*(10), 43-47.

Schmuck, R. A. Some uses of research methods in organization development projects. *Viewpoints*, 1974, *50*(3), 47-59.

Schmuck, R. A., & Miles, M. B. (Eds.). *Organization development in schools*. Palo Alto, Calif.: National Press, 1971.

Schmuck, R. A., Murray, D., Smith, M. A., Schwartz, M., & Runkel, M. *Consultation for innovative schools: OD for multiunit structure*. Eugene, Ore.: Center for Educational Policy and Management, 1975.

Scholtes, P. R. Contracting for change. *Training and Development Journal*, 1975, *29*(4), 8-12.

Schröder, M. The shadow consultant. *Journal of Applied Behavioral Science*, 1974, *10*(4), 579-594.

Schwartz, A. C. Planning for change: What's the best technique? *Personnel*, 1970, *47*(4), 47-54.

Scurrah, M. J., Shani, M., & Zipfel, C. Influence of internal and external change agents in a simulated educational organization. *Administrative Science Quarterly*, 1971, *16*(1), 113-120.

Seashore, S. E., & Bowers, D. G. Durability of organizational change. *American Psychologist*, 1970, *25*(3), 227-233.

Selfridge, R. J., & Sokolik, S. L. A comprehensive view of organization development. *MSU Business Topics*, 1975, *23*(1), 46-61.

Selfridge, R. J., & Sokolik, S. L. When OD comes to your company. *Supervisory Management*, 1975, *20*(2), 24-34.

Sheflen, K. C., Lawler, E. E., & Hackman, J. R. Long-term impact of employee participation in the development of pay incentive plans: A field experiment revisited. *Journal of Applied Psychology*, 1971, *55*(3), 182-186.

Shepard, H. A., & Davis, S. Organization development in good times and bad. *Journal of Contemporary Business*, 1972, *1*(3), 65-73.

Sheposh, J. P., Abrams, A. J., & Licht, M. H. Assessment by technical personnel of the role of the change advocate. *Journal of Applied Psychology*, 1975, *60*(4), 483-490.

Sherwood, J. J. An introduction to organization development. In J. W. Pfeiffer & J. E. Jones (Eds.), *The 1972 annual handbook for group facilitators*. La Jolla, Calif.: University Associates, 1972.

Shetty, Y. K. Is there a best way to organize a business enterprise? *S.A.M. Advanced Management Journal*, 1973, *38*(2), 47-52.

Shirley, R. C. A model for analysis of organizational change. *MSU Business Topics*, 1974, *22*(2), 60-68.

Shirley, R. C. An interactive approach to the problem of organizational change. *Human Resource Management*, 1975, *14*(2), 11-19.

Short, L. E. Planned organizational change. *MSU Business Topics*, 1973, *21*(4), 53-61.

Sikes, W. W., Schlesinger, L. D., & Seashore, C. Developing change agent teams on campus. *Journal of Higher Education*, 1973, *44*(5), 399-413.

Simmons, M. The role of the organization development consultant. *Industrial Training International*, 1972, *7*(2), 53-56.

Sims, H. P., Jr. The business organization, environment, and T-group training: A new viewpoint. *Management of Personnel Quarterly*, 1970, *9*(4), 21-27.

Smith, M. B. Beyond journalistic scouting: Evaluation for better programs. *Journal of Applied Behavioral Science*, 1975, *11*(3), 290-297.

Smith, P. B. Controlled studies of the outcome of sensitivity training. *Psychological Bulletin*, 1975, *82*(4), 597-622.

Smith, P. J. Organisational development. *Industrial Training International*, 1970, *5*(7), 310-311; 331.

Sokolik, S. L. Organization development: Its meaning for the professional trainer. *MSU Business Topics*, 1973, *21*(1), 65-70.

Soltis, R. J. A systematic approach to managing change. *Management Review*, 1970, 59(9), 2-11.

Sperling, K. Getting OD to really work. *Innovation*, 1971, 26, 38-45.

Steele, F. I. Can T-group training change the power structure? *Personnel Administration*, 1970, 33(6), 48-53.

Steele, F. I. Physical settings and organizational development. In H. Hornstein, B. B. Bunker, W. W. Burke, M. Gindes, & R. J. Lewicki (Eds.), *Social intervention: A behavioral science approach*. New York: Free Press, 1971.

Steele, F. I. *Physical settings and organization development*. Reading, Mass.: Addison-Wesley, 1973.

Steele, F. *Consulting for organizational change*. Amherst, Mass.: University of Massachusetts Press, 1975. (a)

Steele, F. *The open organization: The impact of secrecy and disclosure on people and organizations*. Reading, Mass.: Addison-Wesley, 1975. (b)

Steele, F. I., Zand, D. E., & Zalkind, S. S. Managerial behavior and participation in a laboratory training process. *Personnel Psychology*, 1970, 23(1), 77-90.

Stokes, R. A company fit to live in. *Personnel Management*, 1971, 3(8), 33-35.

Strauss, G. Organizational development: Credits and debits. *Organizational Dynamics*, 1973, 1(3), 2-19.

Stuart-Kotzé, R. A situational change typology. *Industrial Training International*, 1972, 7(12), 380-383. (a)

Stuart-Kotzé, R. A situational change typology. *Training and Development Journal*, 1972, 26(1), 56-60. (b)

Sutton, R. L. Cultural context and change agent organizations. *Administrative Science Quarterly*, 1974, 19(4), 547-562.

Swaab, A. M. Organizational change and the principal. *Educational Technology*, 1972, 12(10), 55-57.

Swartz, D. Similarities and differences of internal and external consultants. *Proceedings of the 34th Annual Meeting of the Academy of Management*, August 1974, p. 17. (Abstract)

Tagliere, D. A. Organalysis. *Training and Development Journal*, 1972, 26(4), 30-36.

Tagliere, D. A. What an executive should know about organization development. *Training and Development Journal*, 1975, 29(7), 34-40.

Tannenbaum, R. Organizational change has to come through individual change. *Innovation*, 1971, 23, 36-43.

Taylor, J. C. The conditioning effects of technology on organizational behavior in planned social change (Doctoral dissertation, University of Michigan, 1970). *Dissertation Abstracts International*, 1970. (University Microfilms No. 70-14, 659)

Taylor, J. C. Some effects of technology in organizational change. *Human Relations*, 1971, 24(2), 105-123. (a)

Taylor, J. C. *Technology and planned organizational change*. Ann Arbor, Mich.: Institute for Social Research, University of Michigan, 1971. (b)

Taylor, J. C., & Bowers, D. G. *Survey of organizations: A machine-scored standardized questionnaire instrument*. Ann Arbor, Mich.: Institute for Social Research, University of Michigan, 1972.

Taylor, J. E., & Bertinot, E. An OD intervention to install participative management in a bureaucratic organization. *Training and Development Journal*, 1973, 27(1), 18-21.

Teamwork through conflict. *Business Week*, March 20, 1971, pp. 44-45; 48; 50.

Teuber, E. B. Emergence and change of human relations groups. *American Behavioral Scientist*, 1973, 16(3), 378-390.

Thomas, J. M., & Bennis, W. G. (Eds.). *Management of change and conflict*. Harmondsworth, England: Penguin, 1972.

Thurley, K. E. Planned change in bureaucratic organizations. *International Studies in Management & Organization*, 1971, 1(3), 253-273.

Tichy, N. An interview with Roger Harrison. *Journal of Applied Behavioral Science*, 1973, 9(6), 701-726.

Tichy, N. An interview with Max Pagès. *Journal of Applied Behavioral Science*, 1974, 10(1), 8-26.

Torczyner, J. The political context of social change: A case study of innovation in adversity in Jerusalem. *Journal of Applied Behavioral Science*, 1972, 8(3), 287-317.

Toronto, R. S. General systems theory applied to the study of organizational change (Doctoral dissertation, University of Michigan, 1972). *Dissertation Abstracts International*, 1972. (University Microfilms No. 72-15, 019)

Toronto, R. S. A general systems model for the analysis of organizational change. *Behavioral Science*, 1975, *20*(3), 145-156.

Toulouse, J. Annotated bibliography. In W. H. Schmidt (Ed.), *Organizational frontiers and human values*. Belmont, Calif.: Wadsworth, 1970.

Tranfield, D. Organisation development—An opportunity for the training manager. *Industrial Training International*, 1971, *6*(1), 28-31.

Tranfield, D., & Gill, J. How to OD—Part I. *Industrial Training International*, 1973, *8*(5), 159-161. (a)

Tranfield, D., & Gill, J. How to OD—Part II. *Industrial Training International*, 1973, *8*(6), 181-182; 185. (b)

Tregoe, B. B. What is OD? *Training and Development Journal*, 1974, *28*(3), 16-23.

Tribus, M. Software of change. *Personnel Administration*, 1970, *33*(2), 8-16.

Tripp, R. S. Establishing a viable consulting interface: A practical construct. *Proceedings of the 34th Annual Meeting of the Academy of Management*, August 1974, p. 18. (Abstract)

Underhill, R. S. Multi-level OD in government organizations. In *First tango in Boston: A seminar on organization change and development*. Washington, D.C.: National Training and Development Service, 1973.

Using the Managerial Grid to ensure MBO. *Organizational Dynamics*, 1974, *2*(4), 54-65.

Utterback, J. M. The process of technological innovation within the firm. *Academy of Management Journal*, 1971, *14*(1), 75-88.

Vaill, P. B. O.D.: A grammatical footnote. *Journal of Applied Behavioral Science*, 1971, *7*(2), 264. (a)

Vaill, P. B. *The practice of organization development*. Madison, Wis.: American Society for Training and Development, 1971. (b)

Vaill, P. B. Practice theories in organization development. *Proceedings of the 31st Annual Meeting of the Academy of Management*, August 1971, pp. 161-170. (c)

Vaill, P. B. Practice theories in organization development. In J. D. Adams (Ed.), *New technologies in organization development: 2* (Originally *Theory and method in organization development: An evolutionary process*, Arlington, Va.: NTL Institute, 1974). La Jolla, Calif.: University Associates, 1975.

Vansina, L. S. Improving international relations and effectiveness within multinational organizations. In J. D. Adams (Ed.), *New technologies in organization development: 2* (Originally *Theory and method in organization development: An evolutionary process*, Arlington, Va.: NTL Institute, 1974). La Jolla, Calif.: University Associates, 1975.

Varney, G. H., & Lasher, H. J. Surveys and feedback as a means of organization diagnosis and change. In T. H. Patten, Jr. (Ed.), *OD—Emerging dimensions and concepts*. East Lansing, Mich.: American Society for Training and Development, 1973.

Walton, R. E., & Warwick, D. P. The ethics of organization development. *Journal of Applied Behavioral Science*, 1973, *9*(6), 681-698.

Walter, G. A. Some criteria for ethical organizational development. *Proceedings of the 35th Annual Meeting of the Academy of Management*, August 1975, pp. 351-353.

Warrick, D. D. Future developments in organization development. *Proceedings of the 35th Annual Meeting of the Academy of Management*, August 1975, pp. 366-368.

Weick, K. E. Conceptual trade-offs in studying organizational change. In J. W. McGuire (Ed.), *Contemporary management: Issues and viewpoints*. Englewood Cliffs, N.J.: Prentice-Hall, 1974.

Weisbord, M. R. A businesslike approach to OD. *Journal of Applied Behavioral Science*, 1974, *10*(1), 60-61. (a)

Weisbord, M. R. The gap between OD practice and theory—And publication. *Journal of Applied Behavioral Science*, 1974, *10*(4), 476-484. (b)

Weisbord, M. R. A mixed model for medical centers: Changing structure and behavior. In J. D. Adams (Ed.), *New technologies in organization development: 2* (Originally *Theory and method in organization development: An evolutionary process*, Arlington, Va.: NTL Institute, 1974). La Jolla, Calif.: University Associates, 1975.

Weisbord, M., Lamb, H., & Drexler, A. *Improving police department management through problem-solving task forces: A case study in organization development.* Reading, Mass.: Addison-Wesley, 1974.

Weitzel, W. T., & Whitely, W. T. The relationship between climate and effectiveness in an organization undergoing a joint merger-facilitation process. *Proceedings of the 35th Annual Meeting of the Academy of Management,* August 1975, pp. 369-371.

Weldon, W. Four change strategies. *Training and Development Journal,* 1973, 27(7), 16-18.

Weller, J. M. The involuntary partisans: Fire departments and the threat of conflict. *American Behavioral Scientist,* 1973, 16(3), 368-377.

Werther, W. B., & Weihrich, H. Refining MBO through negotiations. *MSU Business Topics,* 1975, 23(3), 53-59.

Wessman, F. The group construct: A model for OD interventions. *Personnel,* 1973, 50(5), 19-29.

Wessman, F. One more time: Will OD survive? *Training and Development Journal,* 1974, 28(3), 14-15.

Whisler, T. L. *Information technology and organizational change.* Belmont, Calif.: Wadsworth, 1970.

White, O., Jr. *Psychic energy and organizational change.* (Sage Professional Paper in Administrative and Policy Studies, Vol. 1, No. 03-001). Beverly Hills, Calif.: Sage, 1973.

Widing, J. W., Jr. Reorganizing your worldwide business. *Harvard Business Review,* 1973, 51(3), 153-160.

Wieland, G. F. Effects of surveys on organizational members. *Psychological Reports,* 1972, 30(2), 513-514.

Williams, P. M. A look at the goals of organization development programs. *Proceedings of the 32nd Annual Meeting of the Academy of Management,* 1972, pp. 43-46.

Williams, R. Stress in the wake of change. *Personnel Management,* 1970, 2(10), 42-45.

Wilson, J. E., Morton, R. B., & Mullen, D. P. The trend in laboratory education for managers—Organization training or sensitivity? *Training and Development Journal,* 1972, 26(6), 18-25.

Yeager, J. C. Mainsprings of change: On being orientally oriented. *Training and Development Journal,* 1975, 29(8), 41-50.

Yien, S. Employee participation in organizational decision making and acceptance of planned change (Doctoral dissertation, Michigan State University, 1971). *Dissertation Abstracts International,* 1971. (University Microfilms No. 71-12, 011)

Zaltman, G., Duncan, R., & Holbeck, J. *Innovations and organizations.* New York: John Wiley, 1972.

Zand, D. E. Collateral organization: A new change strategy. *Journal of Applied Behavioral Science,* 1974, 10(1), 63-89.

Zeira, Y. Is external management training effective for organizational change? *Public Personnel Management,* 1973, 2(6), 400-407.

Zeira, Y. Training the top-management team for planned change. *Training and Development Journal,* 1974, 28(6), 30-35.

Larry E. Pate *is a visiting assistant professor in the Department of Management, University of Nebraska–Lincoln. He is a Ph.D. candidate in organizational behavior at the University of Illinois, Urbana-Champaign, and received his B.A. and M.S. degrees from the University of California, Irvine. Mr. Pate's research interests are in motivation, leadership, job design, and organization development.*

HUMANISTIC EDUCATION: A REVIEW OF BOOKS SINCE 1970

Patricia A. Schmuck and Richard A. Schmuck

We have participated during the last two decades as teachers, researchers, writers, and consultants attempting to ameliorate and make more productive the human relationships in our schools. Recently, we also participated as parents in the creation of an alternative school within a public system for our own two children. We persist in our efforts to write about such changes, and we are not alone. Indeed, the growth of published analyses and methods for humanizing schooling during the last two decades has been gargantuan. Had we been asked to prepare a review like this some ten or fifteen years ago, for instance, our choice of books would have been severely limited. Naturally, we could have had any number of the large output by John Dewey on progressivism, along with advocates of the child-centered curriculum, and the supporters of the whole-child perspective. Also, we could have drawn from such significant volumes as Miles's *Learning to Work in Groups* (1959), Thelen's *Education and the Human Quest* (1960), Bruner's *The Process of Education* (1961), Neill's *Summerhill* (1960), and Moustakas' *The Alive and Growing Teacher* (1959). But now in 1975, as we commenced this review, we were faced with choices from among more than fifty books in a pluralistic movement that itself is coming of age, a movement now primarily known as "humanistic education."

A Broad Spectrum of Choices

Most participants involved in this movement have tended to agree on what schools *should* be like. Humanized schools should have a social environment that supports interpersonal encounters and whole-person interactions. They should have classrooms in which ideas, facts, and feelings are openly and authentically expressed; in which conflict is brought out into the open, discussed, and collaboratively worked on; in which personal feelings share equal prominence with intellectual activity; and in which learning activities integrate the individual interests and concerns of students with the learning requirements of the district and state. Perhaps most important to the philosophical base of the humanistic educator is the principle that all participants—the teachers, administrators, students, and even the parents—should be legitimate, full-fledged members of the school. All should be respected for having both unique intellectual resources and a myriad of feelings.

But contemporary participants in this movement are not primarily philosophers or moralizers, nor are they simply rehashing the questions and answers of the past. And the writers of books on humanistic education are no longer only theory-oriented academics. Practicing teachers, administrators, and even journalists and popular essayists are preparing their critiques and recommendations. Along with this increased breadth of participation, an expansion in audiences has simultaneously occurred. Books on humanistic education are now being prepared for policy bodies, interested citizens, parents, volunteer aides, and students. More and more, these books are on center stage in a world that has become increasingly concerned about the quality of life—whether it involves air and water or interpersonal and community life.

Along with this increased legitimacy and acceptance, humanistic educators now, more than in the past, base their analyses and action recommendations on the research findings of the behavioral sciences. Thus, the burgeoning of social psychology, for instance, has offered many new intellectual resources for understanding how classrooms and school organizations are operating and how to adapt them effectively to contemporary students, while simultaneously working toward the values of the humanistic philosophers.

The books we considered for review, amounting to no less than fifty, came from this broad spectrum of possibilities.

Before 1970

Books on humanistic education that gained notoriety before 1970 were prepared by muckrakers and ideologists. Muckrakers such as Kozol (1967), Herndon (1965), and Kohl (1967) depicted in vivid detail and with a penetrating style the brutalities and insensitivities that were occurring within the public schools of our major cities. At the same time ideologists such as Freire (published first in English in 1970) and Illich (1970) prepared very powerful revolutionary books, virtually giving up on the public school as an effective and moral institution. Both sets of writers argued for radically new organizational patterns that would bring the public school out of its traditional hierarchical polity into a more pluralistic and democratic relationship with the society and the world. These writings gave energy to the educational pioneers who were attempting to establish private alternative schools and free schools. Many of the muckrakers and ideologists knew very well what they did *not* want our schools to be; some had a rather clear notion of what our schools *should* be; but hardly any had clear cognitive maps and procedures in mind to humanize our existing schools.

Three reformist books did appear toward the end of the 60's that were both muckraking and ideological in character, but at the same time reasonable and practical. They helped to bring humanistic education into focus for a large audience and thus to legitimize criticism of schools and school improvement. The first, *Freedom to Learn* (1969) by Carl Rogers, made a distinctive analytical and action-oriented contribution to humanizing the schools and was studied by many professionals. The second was *Schools Without Failure* by Glasser (1969). His psychiatric status helped to legitimize the fact that schools can damage youngsters psychologically; thousands of practicing teachers were introduced first-hand to his "magic circle." The third contribution brought the muckraking, ideological, and practical emphases to an apex of national notoriety. In 1970, Charles Silberman's three-year Carnegie study entitled *Crisis in the Classroom* reached the top of the best-seller list. Humanistic education was by then a thoroughly acceptable orientation for both professional educators and the public at large.

The Selections for This Review

The books chosen for this review have appeared since 1970. They go beyond muckraking and do not present only ideological arguments. They attempt to make practical recommendations. Moreover, they are based on scientific analysis and strive to connect what is already known about schools and learning with what could be.

We have chosen books to emphasize different aspects of the school enterprise from the humanistic point of view. For example, some books focus on the integration of feelings and thoughts within the psyches of students and teachers, some focus more on a humanistic curriculum, others analyze humane interaction patterns and group processes in the classroom, and some focus on the school's functioning as an organization. Of course, no book that is comprehensively practical can be very easily categorized in any of these ways. All of the books share implicit respect for planned change of a humanistic nature in mainstream, public schools.

INTEGRATING THE AFFECTIVE AND THE COGNITIVE

Perhaps the most outstanding theme of humanistic educators is their criticism that traditional academic life is weighted too much on the cognitive side and that life in public schools should be brought closer to a fifty-fifty, cognitive-affective balance. The following five books taken together constitute a thorough theoretical and practical overview of how affective and cognitive psychological processes can be integrated within the classroom.

Learning to Feel–Feeling to Learn
by Harold C. Lyon, Jr.
Columbus, Ohio: Charles E. Merrill, 1971. 321 pp., $7.95.

Lyon presents an easy-to-follow conceptual guide to many connections between humanistic psychology as a discipline and the psychological processes of the classroom. Writing under the sponsorship of Carl Rogers, Lyon has compiled a reservoir of people, places, concepts, and even lesson plans, using the psychological concepts of May, Maslow, Rogers, and Jourard (along with his own personal growth experiences as an inhibited ex-military man) to exhort teachers to take both the students' feelings and their own into consideration at the same time. His central thesis is that educators should recognize that pleasure, spontaneity, and feelings are as vital to one's life as, if not more vital than, intellectual achievements, for adults as well as for children.

Teachers who are not very knowledgeable about the intricate links between feeling and thinking will find this book stimulating and convincing. Moreover, the book is so nicely organized, dotted with captivating case studies, and so appropriately personal that more experienced readers will also be attracted to it. However, Lyon's book is obviously limited in the practical know-how presented. It offers little advice about how teachers might arrange sequences of classroom experiences that would help them and their students build better connections both interpersonally and between the cognitive and the affective parts of themselves.

Human Teaching for Human Learning:
An Introduction to Confluent Education
by George Brown.
New York: The Viking Press, 1971. 298 pp., $8.50.

One must turn to Brown for practical specificity. Whereas Lyon's strength is in the exposition of the ideas of third-force psychology, Brown eschews theoretical discussion in favor of detailed descriptions of how teachers might proceed to integrate the cognitive and affective realms within the daily classroom curriculum. Especially replete with examples from education, Brown presents actual units prepared by teachers and also gives a bird's-eye view of his methods in action; for example, one chapter is in the form of a diary of one day in the life of a high school teacher.

Furthermore, he goes beyond these very down-to-earth case-studies of success by describing the pitfalls of trying to implement particular practices of affective education without careful diagnosis, planning, and implementation. Brown argues that the teachers who cannot provide an intelligent and understanding conceptual scheme for their affective techniques will likely create problems for their students and themselves.

Left-Handed Teaching: Lessons in Affective Education
by Gloria Castillo.
New York: Praeger, 1974. 223 pp., hardbound, $7.50; paperbound, $2.95.

Brown's work is very nicely picked up and expanded for the elementary level by Castillo, who was a participating early-childhood teacher in Brown's initial Ford Esalen project. Her strength lies in demonstrating with vivid detail how the standard curriculum of the typical elementary school lends itself easily to the introduction of dozens of curriculum techniques. For that reason, a creative elementary teacher, after a cursory view of the book, might think that there really is very little new here. But that would be a hasty conclusion.

Castillo's personal experiences in linking the cognitive and the affective are clearly sequenced and can bring helpful insights to others. Her intense struggles to achieve authenticity with students and always to stay close to the here-and-now with them provide themes of general interest today. Along with her personal revelations and her development of a down-to-earth humanistic psychology, the book offers ten useful lesson plans on such topics as sensory awareness, communication, aggression, nature, and space.

The Lonely Teacher
by Peter Knoblock and Arnold Goldstein.
Boston: Allyn and Bacon, 1971. 154 pp., $3.95.

In a less personal but more general way than Castillo, Knoblock and Goldstein ask us to become more aware of the intrapsychic lives of teachers. They emphasize that while acting in the role of teacher, a person gets scared, sad, and mad; can become angry or glad; and has various likes, dislikes, and unique sensitivities. They go on to show that the way schools are organized helps to increase many negative feelings that teachers are reporting today. The individuated-autonomous social structure of the school organization gives rise to teachers' feelings of separation and loneliness, and, as a consequence, many teachers are preoccupied with a search for community. The authors' implication is that affective richness and support for students would be increased if organizational arrangements for teachers would stress a sense of staff cohesiveness, security, and emotional support.

Human Relations Development: A Manual for Educators
by George M. Gazda.
Boston: Allyn and Bacon, 1973. 194 pp., hardbound,$9.95; paperbound, $4.95.

The focus on the affective life of teachers in the previous books is nicely supplemented by Gazda's emphasis on teacher skill development. Emotional security and staff cohesiveness can go far toward helping teachers to humanize their classrooms; however, particular interpersonal and human relations skills become necessary for full implementation of a confluent curriculum. Developing the ideas and techniques of Rogers, Truax, and Carkhuff, Gazda presents a well-explained model and numerous practical activities for teachers in such humanistic behaviors as accurately estimating how the other is feeling, acting warmly and nonpossessively at the same time, and authentically stating one's own feelings and thoughts. Gazda's basic rationale is that increased self-understanding will facilitate more effective interpersonal actions, provided the teacher has well-developed skills in perceiving and responding. He presents numerous practical exercises that teachers can use in attempting to improve their interpersonal competencies. And in so doing, Gazda implicitly argues that the integration of the affective and the cognitive is ultimately achieved through behavioral practice.

THE CURRICULUM IN HUMANISTIC EDUCATION

What sets humanistic education as a distinctive entity apart from many other subdisciplines within the personal growth movement is the inclusion of curriculum development. The systematic refinement of educational goals, assessment techniques, instructional procedures, and methods of obtaining feedback have become focal in this movement. The following three books capture the diverse flavor of the current offerings.

Toward Humanistic Education: A Curriculum of Affect
by Gerald Weinstein and Mario D. Fantini (Eds.).
New York: Praeger, 1970. 228 pp., $7.00.

Building on the kinds of lesson plans and classroom activities presented by Brown and Castillo, these authors provide a model for curriculum development in humanistic education. In contrast to many other curriculum experts in humanistic education, Weinstein and Fantini show how a humanistic curriculum can be developed.

The model involves four key parts: (1) identifying and diagnosing the attributes of the learners, (2) designing a teaching-learning strategy, (3) implementing the learning activities, and (4) investigating the outcomes. Each of these parts is refined, and methods of developing a humanistic curriculum come alive for the reader. Through the presentation of transcripts of actual teaching situations, the book dramatically presents the joys and struggles of building personally relevant and satisfying vehicles for learning. The book's contribution, however, is largely theoretical; volumes such as the following two should be added for specificity and practicality in relation to the study of a humanistic curriculum.

Clarifying Values Through Subject Matter:
Applications for the Classroom
by Merrill Harmin, Howard Kirschenbaum, and Sidney B. Simon.
Minneapolis, Minn.: Winston Press, 1973. 146 pp., $2.95.

Adding to their previous work on values clarification, Harmin and Simon join with Kirschenbaum in this book to present some very specific activities on how the standard curricula taught currently in most schools can be altered to help students clarify their personal values. Their model includes three essential variables: (1) facts, (2) concepts, and (3) values. It helps students to define these and to differentiate among the three, using a variety of media. The book provides concrete examples to show how the identification of facts, concepts, and values can be interwoven into diverse academic subjects.

An important contribution of their orientation to humanistic education is the distinction drawn between clarification and indoctrination. The authors argue convincingly that clarification of one's values can be facilitated by learning to use particular skills in defining and analyzing values, being presented with value choices, and carefully debriefing the thoughts and feelings experienced in making the choices.

Eggs and Peanut Butter: A Teacher's Scrapbook
by David Weitzman.
Menlo Park, Calif.: Word Wheel Books, 1974. 156 pp., $5.95.

Weitzman's volume is an excitingly prepared scrapbook of a teacher's classroom activities in an inner-city school. Its nontraditional format, eye-catching graphics, and curriculum practices will entice a teacher's curiosity and interest. Although the volume is not theoretical, and at points it is psychologically naive, its strength lies in its potpourri of effective curriculum ideas. The varieties include (1) role play for students on how the earth has changed from the beginning to the present, (2) episodes indicating how particular kinds of inquiry teaching can be negatively used to manipulate and exploit students, (3) the Five Square Cooperation exercise to change a group's functioning, and (4) a meaningless list of dates that can be transformed into a meaningful historical sequence. Weitzman shows what can happen when teachers risk being more open and personal with their students and have effective curriculum activities with which to work.

HUMANIZING CLASSROOM INTERACTION

The 1960's and 70's witnessed a monumental rise in the production of research on group dynamics. The next three books show how the problem of humanizing classroom interaction, both between teacher and students and among students, is beginning to get some analysis and answers.

Tough and Tender Learning
by David Nyberg.
Palo Alto, Calif.: Mayfield, 1971. 186 pp., $2.95.

This delightfully whimsical, yet penetratingly serious, volume presents a philosophical backdrop for the application of group-dynamics theory and practice to the classroom. Nyberg sees the typical classroom as a human stage where important interpersonal events are constantly occurring and where the participants either do not know what feelings are present or do not want to admit that they know. The central issue in humanizing the classroom is the opening of the three figurative boxes that confine and restrict classroom learning. The first constraint is the Quincy Box (the architectural plan that has sponsored self-contained classrooms). The second is the Black Box (the never-never land that mediates stimuli and responses). The third is the Shadow Box (where emotions are hidden and only ideas are considered appropriate for the classroom). Nyberg promises to help teachers open this "Black Quincy Shadow Box," and he largely keeps his promise. With appropriate degrees of wit and a delightful sense of the dramatic, Nyberg links the ideas from confluent education, values clarification, and humanistic curricula with group-dynamics theory, and presents a philosophical base for the more research-oriented and applied contributions of the next two texts.

Group Processes in the Classroom (2nd Ed.)
by Richard A. Schmuck and Patricia A. Schmuck.
Dubuque, Iowa: William C. Brown, 1975. 217 pp., $4.95.

Our recent revision picks up where Nyberg leaves off in building a link past group-dynamics theory toward classroom practice. Written as a practical text for teachers, the book presents a series of concepts, research findings, and action ideas on such group-process topics as interpersonal expectations, leadership, attraction, norms, communication, cohesiveness, and developmental stages. Its strength lies in bringing the theory and practice of group dynamics together in one place for humanistic educators.

Joining Together: Group Theory and Group Skills
by David Johnson and Frank Johnson.
Englewood Cliffs, N.J.: Prentice-Hall, 1975. 470 pp., $5.95.

The central contribution of this volume lies in its very thorough and extensive compilation of interpersonal instruments, group exercises, and classroom games that are directly applicable to school situations. For the practitioner who is already familiar with the group-dynamics concepts presented in the previous two books, this volume offers an unlimited number of experiences that could benefit classroom groups from kindergarten to college.

HUMANIZING THE SCHOOL ENVIRONMENT

That aspects of the school environment—its organization and community—affect classroom processes is by now a generally agreed-upon working assumption. And a large amount of attention is now being given to how the organizational attributes of the school relate to humanistic education programs. These four books represent different examples, each highlighting the relevance of the school's social psychological environment to humanization.

The School Book:
For People Who Want to Know What the Hollering Is About
by Neil Postman and Charles Weingartner.
New York: Delacorte Press, 1973. 308 pp., $7.95.

This is a handy, easy-to-use source book for understanding contemporary jargon in humanistic education, especially as it relates to organizational functioning and the change of total school programs. Included are a historical overview, from Sputnik I and Rickover to the "educational romantics"; a functional description of a school as a social institution; the functions that parents and students can take in trying to influence school dynamics; a list of philosophical assumptions associated with controversies in education; a list of many people who are involved in school change; and a summary of legal decisions about taxation and integration. The book's contents attest to the large diversity of thought that now exists in public education.

The School in Rose Valley: A Parent Venture in Education
by Grace Rotzel.
Baltimore, Md.: The Johns Hopkins University Press, 1971. 147 pp., $8.95.

A case study of humanistic education in action, this is an amazing story. The school in Rose Valley was created in 1929 and still exists today. Reading this book can therefore be a very humbling experience. The development of a living organization like Rose Valley takes time; it is consoling to know that many ardent, dedicated people have worked together to make this school what it is.

The purpose of Rose Valley School, as a parent venture in education, was to answer basic questions: Who are we? What are we? What should we do with our lives? And how do we want to organize? The parents created a school to help search for answers in hopes that "understanding can and will combat the only real threat to humanity—man himself. If this hope is not to be in vain, then education must be designed to help children face these questions and seek answers on their own levels" (p. xii).

It took the popularization of humanistic education in the 70's to create a market so that the story of Rose Valley School might be known. Although the school was commenced in 1929, its story was not published until 1971.

The Faculty Team: School Organization for Results
by David Mahan and Gerald H. Moeller.
Palo Alto, Calif.: Science Research Associates, 1971. 241 pp., $4.95.

This book presents a clear design for helping the administrators and teachers of a school to establish their own goals, decision-making procedures, plans for an instructional program, and assessment devices to study the impact of the program as it is tried. The authors use the description "faculty team" to denote a tightly knit group of teaching colleagues who are committed to solving their own organizational problems collaboratively. In the form of a concrete case study, the book deals clearly with accountability, the measurement of organizational effectiveness, decision making, and the productive involvement of students within the faculty team.

A Humanistic Psychology of Education:
Making the School Everybody's House.
by Richard A. Schmuck and Patricia A. Schmuck.
Palo Alto, Calif.: Mayfield, 1974. 388 pp., $5.95.

Like our other book reviewed earlier, this one is a blend of theory and practice. We argue that humanistic relationships in schools will not persist without systemic changes in the school's culture—its behavioral and programmatic regularities. A change of particular teachers, administrators, or student groups will not be sufficient for humanistic education to be realized. The Gestalt must be altered. From the "system perspective," the most powerful tool for developing humanized learning climates for the classrooms as well as for the faculty lies in reforming the norms that influence the interpersonal relationships among all school participants. Over half of the book is constituted of practical suggestions for implementing such normative change in schools.

CONCLUSION

We are more optimistic in 1975 than we were in 1970 about the strength and effectiveness of humanistic education. The tenuousness of alternative education during the 60's seems by now to have been overcome. Many public school districts now reserve a part of their budget for bona fide, humanistically oriented programs. And the range and quality, the reasonableness and practicality of publications on humanistic education are also representative of the strength and durability of the movement. We are, of course, concerned about some piece-meal perspectives and the narrowness of many humanistic educators. Confluent education, individualization, values clarification, group dynamics, team teaching, etc., taken by themselves, we think, will not be sufficient for sustained, humanistic change. We must put much more effort into building comprehensive strategies for integrating most aspects of school life so that all the school's processes carry the humanistic *Zeitgeist*. The taking of roles, the books that are or are not used, the passing in the halls, the occasional human touch—these and many more daily phenomena are what make humanistic education real.

REFERENCES

Bruner, J. *The process of education.* Cambridge, Mass.: Harvard University Press, 1961.

Freire, P. *Pedagogy of the oppressed* (M. B. Ramos, Trans.). New York: Herder and Herder, 1970.

Glasser, W. *Schools without failure.* New York: Harper & Row, 1969.

Herndon, J. *The way it spozed to be.* New York: Bantam Books, 1965.

Illich, I. *Deschooling society.* New York: Harper & Row, 1970.

Kohl, H. *36 children.* New York: New American Library, 1967.

Kozol, J. *Death at an early age.* Boston: Houghton Mifflin, 1967.

Miles, M. *Learning to work in groups.* New York: Teachers College Press, 1959.

Moustakas, C. *The alive and growing teacher.* New York: Ballantine, 1959.

Neill, A. S. *Summerhill.* New York: Hart, 1960.

Rogers, C. *Freedom to learn.* Columbus, Ohio: Charles E. Merrill, 1969.

Silberman, C. E. *Crisis in the classroom.* New York: Random House, 1970.

Thelen, H. *Education and the human quest.* New York: Harper and Brothers, 1960.

Patricia A. Schmuck, Ph.D., is an educational consultant in Eugene, Oregon. She is currently consulting with the Northwest Regional Educational Laboratory and is developing proposals for a training center for women in school administration. Ms. Schmuck's background is in public school teaching, teacher training, consulting with schools, and curriculum development.

Richard A. Schmuck, Ph.D., is a co-director of a research and development program in the Center for Educational Policy and Management and is a professor of educational psychology at the University of Oregon, Eugene. He is currently co-directing a project on documentation and technical assistance for change in urban schools and has authored numerous books and articles on educational change. Dr. Schmuck's background is in the social psychology of education, training in group dynamics, and consultation for organization development in school districts.

VALUES CLARIFICATION:
A REVIEW OF MAJOR BOOKS

Joel Goodman

Values clarification is one branch of the growing humanistic education movement. The past decade has seen a proliferation of books on the topic. What follows is a review from a practitioner's point of view of some of the basic and major contributions to the field.

FOUR ESSENTIAL BOOKS

Values and Teaching
by Louis Raths, Merrill Harmin, and Sidney B. Simon.
Columbus, Ohio: Charles E. Merrill, 1966. 275 pp., $4.75.

This is the book that gave birth to the field. A major stimulus for the book was the increasing amount of values confusion experienced by young people. Bombarded by a myriad of influences (e.g., family, peer group, church, school, media) and enveloped in a world of accelerating change and future shock, many young people were/are experiencing confusion in such values-rich areas as love, sex, friendship, money, work, leisure, family, religion, and politics. The authors see this confusion reflected in such behavior patterns as apathy (listlessness, lack of interest), flight (only fleeting interest), uncertainty (inability to make decisions), inconsistency (incompatible patterns in life), drifting (lack of enthusiasm and planning), overconforming (other-directed with a passion), overdissenting (chronic, irrational dissent), and posing (counterfeit role playing).

Noting that traditional approaches to helping children develop values (e.g., setting an example, persuading and convincing, limiting choices, moralizing, inculcating, establishing rules, appealing to conscience) either do not work, or, in some cases, are inhumane, Raths and his associates have developed an approach that seeks to aid children in feeling value-able (positive, purposeful, enthusiastic, and proud). Thus, unlike many other educational books of the 60's, *Values and Teaching* goes beyond the diagnosis and offers a specific prescription. This is one of the book's (and the movement's) strengths: the values-clarification theory has always had particular appeal in that it is complemented with many practical strategies. At the same time, the authors caution that "this value theory is not a panacea for all that ails children and education . . .[and] it does not pretend to help solve behavior difficulties whose causes lie outside of values issues" (p. 8).

The authors offer a valuing model based on the following definition of a value: (1) it must be chosen freely; (2) it must be chosen from among alternatives; (3) it must be chosen after thoughtful consideration of the consequences of each alternative; (4) it must be prized and cherished; (5) it must be something that one is willing to affirm publicly; (6) it must be acted upon; and (7) it must be done repeatedly, so as to be consistent with other life patterns. Something that does not meet *all* seven criteria is described as a value indicator (e.g., goals, purposes, aspirations, attitudes, interests, beliefs). Although values clarification has evolved in this area (see the review of *Values Clarification: A Handbook of Practical Strategies for Teachers and Students*), these seven criteria provided the original foundation for the theory.

The authors operationalize this theory by presenting numerous practical strategies designed to help students examine their values against the background of the seven criteria. They devote two entire chapters to two basic and incredibly adaptable activities: the clarifying response and the values sheet. The clarifying response is at the heart of processing any values-clarification exercise, while the values sheet is perhaps the easiest way to integrate subject matter and values exploration. The authors provide specific examples of each strategy, along with helpful guidelines for their use. Another chapter in the book introduces eighteen additional strategies.

Not only do the authors offer practical strategies, they also go on to provide support for the teacher just beginning to use values clarification. For example, in the chapter "Getting Started: Guidelines and Problems," Raths, Harmin, and Simon respond to some common questions teachers ask.

Values and Teaching is a primer in the field of values clarification. Because of its background information and its helpful guidelines, as well as its description of some of the basic strategies, I heartily recommend this as a first book to pick up.

Values Clarification:
A Handbook of Practical Strategies for Teachers and Students
by Sidney B. Simon, Leland Howe, and Howard Kirschenbaum.
New York: Hart Publishing, 1972. 397 pp., $5.25.

Recipient of the Pi Lambda Theta "outstanding book" award, this volume has been acclaimed as the most useful collection of values-clarification strategies yet published.

The authors begin with remarks on the values-clarification approach and on ways to use this book. A significant element in this introduction is the move away from emphasizing the seven criteria of a value. Rather, the authors focus on the seven valuing skills or subprocesses (e.g., the ability to choose freely, the ability to consider alternatives and consequences). This change underlines the evolving process (as opposed to content) orientation of values clarification.

The meat of this book is its smorgasbord of seventy-nine values-clarification strategies. The strategies are presented in a very clear and sense-able manner. "First comes the purpose, which always relates to one or more of the seven processes of valuing. Then the procedures are described in detail. Finally, there are notes and tips to the teacher, and additional suggestions if appropriate" (p. 22). These notes and tips often include helpful guidelines for processing the activity, brainstormed ways of adapting the procedure for different age levels, thoughts on sequencing, cautions (related to risk level), as well as numerous examples of the strategy (for example, there are 300 voting questions, over 260 public interview questions, and 170 different rank orders).

The authors emphasize that there is no one right way to use a values-clarification strategy. They encourage the reader to change and adapt the activities, as well as to think of new ones. This suggestion is crucial if the book is to avoid becoming a "cookbook crutch" that is followed blindly.

For those with experience in values clarification (through a workshop, course, or in-service program), this book can be a gold mine of "how to's." Hopefully, the reader will be able to hitchhike on these ideas and further expand the repertoire of valuing strategies.

Clarifying Values Through Subject Matter
by Merrill Harmin, Howard Kirschenbaum, and Sidney B. Simon.
Minneapolis, Minn.: Winston Press, 1973. 146 pp., $3.25.

This easy-to-read book

> offers one approach for making classrooms more relevant to a world of change, confusion, and conflict. It is not the only approach needed, but it is a practical one—something the teacher can use on Monday. Clarifying values through subject matter is a relatively simple method for the teacher to implement in his or her classroom; yet its implications are, we think, revolutionary. (p. 7)

This book is for the teacher who likes the values-clarification approach, but wonders where to fit it in (considering that there is much pressure "to get to 1860" by the end of the semester). The authors propose a three-level teaching model, which suggests that almost any subject matter can be taught on three levels: factual, conceptual, values. The factual level involves the learning of specific information and basic skills (e.g., computation, penmanship). The conceptual level deals with abstractions, making generalizations from facts, examining cause-and-effect relationships. On the values level, students link the facts and concepts of a subject to their own lives. The authors stress that these three levels are interdependent (and not mutually exclusive, as some may assume).

As in their previous work, Harmin, Kirschenbaum, and Simon back up their theory with specific examples and practical suggestions. A major part of the book provides examples of three-level teaching in a wide variety of subject areas (ranging from the 3 R's to the fine arts to physical education to business to home economics to religion). The authors caution that they do not intend "to prescribe a curriculum in each subject. A few examples can hardly do justice to any subject area. But perhaps the examples will suggest a direction in which teachers in various disciplines may go" (p. 43).

In addition to planting seeds about three-level teaching, the authors also include a chapter by Clifford Knapp on using the values strategies with subject matter. Here, Knapp examines ways that fifteen strategies (drawn from *Values and Teaching* and *Values Clarification*) can be integrated within subject matter.

Perhaps the most provocative part of the book is a chapter entitled "Beyond the Third Level: What is Worth Teaching?" The authors pose a series of values-clarifying questions for the teacher:

> Why am I teaching this subject area? Do I really believe my students need to have this knowledge or these skills? If I had no restraints or mandates imposed on me, what would I freely choose to teach? How does each area I am considering teaching relate to my students' lives? What are the real values dilemmas present in the subjects and themes I teach? (p. 107)

The authors proceed to enumerate several approaches to bridging the gap between subject matter and students' lives: the three-level approach, values units, values strategies, self-directed learning, and other humanistic approaches.

Harmin, Kirschenbaum, and Simon conclude with a three-level review of the book itself: they practice what they teach.

Readings in Values Clarification
by Howard Kirschenbaum and Sidney B. Simon (Eds.).
Minneapolis, Minn.: Winston Press, 1973. 383 pp., $6.25.

Kirschenbaum and Simon have gathered here a good blend of conceptual and practical articles on values education. This comprehensive collection of thought-provoking readings is divided into six sections: "Values Clarification and Other Perspectives," "Values Clarification and School Subjects," "Values in Religious Education," "Values in the Family," "Other Applications for Values Clarification," and "An Annotated Bibliography."

The first section provides background on values clarification, paints the values-education context in which it fits, examines the link between values clarification and futuristics, and draws on the expertise of others involved in values education (including Kohlberg, Rogers, and Rokeach), while exploring the cognitive-affective-active dimensions of valuing. The section closes with a very important, evolutionary article by Kirschenbaum: "Beyond Values Clarification." Here, he criticizes and expands on the original theory and suggests the need to integrate values clarification with other humanistic approaches to education.

"Values Clarification and School Subjects" is a good companion to *Clarifying Values Through Subject Matter*. This section includes twelve articles chock-full of ideas for three-level teaching and for using values strategies in a confluent way.

There are an increasing number of religious educators who are excited about using values clarification. The third part of this book addresses that growing interest. Several articles are concerned with the relationship of values clarification to religious education: the need, the role, the application.

"Values in the Family" recognizes the great opportunity available to parents and children to learn from and with one another. Learning can take place around the family dinner table, as illustrated in numerous examples of adaptations of values-clarification strategies. The section ends with an article on listening skills, which are essential to any values clarification process—especially one involving different generations.

The fifth division in the book, "Other Applications for Values Clarification," is a stimulating potpourri of ways/people/places/times in which values clarification has been used. The authors punctuate the versatility of the approach by noting its use in such diverse settings and contexts as a black and Puerto Rican urban junior high school, a freshman dormitory at a rural university, a national women's organization business meeting in Iowa, Girl Scout programs nationwide, and a large public school system-wide training program, among others.

This is a resource-full book. It closes with a resource-full annotated bibliography of articles and books that have been written on values clarification between 1965 and 1973.[1]

OTHER USEFUL TITLES

The four books reviewed above provide a solid foundation of readings in values clarification. In addition to these four, there are a number of publications that have added to the development of the field.

Composition for Personal Growth:
Values Clarification Through Writing
by Robert Hawley, Sidney B. Simon, and David Britton.
New York: Hart Publishing, 1973. 184 pp., $5.25.

This teacher's handbook has a wealth of ideas on ways to develop writing skills and self-literacy simultaneously. The authors present many adaptable activities that aid students in "reading the book within themselves" and then in reflecting these values in composition and/or discussion. A number of schools are using this book in a confluent mode (integrated with a "traditional" English course) as well as congruently (as a course in itself).

Human Values in the Classroom:
A Handbook for Teachers
by Robert Hawley and Isabel Hawley.
New York: Hart Publishing, 1973. 320 pp., $4.95.

The Hawleys view human values as survival skills. In this book, they outline many specific teaching techniques and classroom procedures to enhance the development of valuing skills. Of particular help is the curriculum-development sequence on which they elaborate: orientation—community building—achievement motivation—fostering open communication—information

---

[1]The materials in this bibliography, including many of the books reviewed in this article, are available from the National Humanistic Education Center, 110 Spring St., Saratoga Springs, N.Y. 12866. Telephone: (518) 587-8770. A list of materials and a schedule of values-clarification workshops around the nation are provided on request.

seeking, gathering, and sharing—value exploration and clarification—planning for change. The authors also focus on some issues of interest to those working on valuing in the classroom: grading and evaluation, approaches to discipline, creative problem solving.

Value Clarification as Learning Process: A Guidebook
by Brian P. Hall.
New York: Paulist Press, 1973. 253 pp., $7.95.

As a companion guide to Hall's *Value Clarification as Learning Process: A Sourcebook* (in which value-clarification theory is presented), this volume includes four sections: introduction, exercises in values clarification, conferences, and values strategies in the classroom. The author presents a number of strategies for students, teachers, and professionals through use of the following Pfeiffer-and-Jones-like, structured-experience format: introduction. materials needed, numbers, time, description of exercise, possible outcomes, application. The section on conferences outlines some alternative designs for introductory and advanced programs. Hall hopes that the reader will not blindly follow the strategy recipes and alternative workshop designs. Rather, he wants the book to "be a catalytic agent in helping those who wish to become involved in value clarification to create their own program" (p. 121).

Value Exploration Through Role Playing
by Robert Hawley.
New York: Hart Publishing, 1974. 176 pp., $4.95.

The author presents many helpful guidelines, formats, and examples of ways to use role playing with junior and senior high school students. The book is spiced with numerous ideas for using role plays to focus on values and on decision-making skills. This is an excellent resource for teachers who are looking for the support and the know-how to use role playing in the classroom.

Meeting Yourself Halfway:
Values Clarification for Daily Living
by Sidney B. Simon.
Niles, Ill.: Argus, 1974. 102 pp., $5.25.

This is a catchy handbook/workbook that contains a month's worth of values-clarification activities. Of the thirty-one activities, some are new and some are adaptations of ones appearing in *Values Clarification*. Simon has designed the strategies so that the reader can take a hands-on approach to this book—encouraging personal involvement and interaction with the material.

SUMMARY

The books discussed here are a sampling of some of the important contributions to the developing field of values clarification. In the future, we can expect new books to add to the depth and breadth of the field by focusing on such areas as research in values clarification, applications of values clarification to specific areas of conflict and confusion (e.g., friendship, sexuality, consumerism, health), methodology for values curriculum development, and the development of facilitator skills.

Joel Goodman, Ed.D., is the program coordinator for the National Humanistic Education Center, Saratoga Springs, New York. He is a teacher, consultant, and workshop leader for school systems and organizations throughout the country. He has also authored numerous articles in the field of humanistic education, which have appeared in national journals. Dr. Goodman's background is in humanistic education staff development and curriculum development, values clarification, and creative problem solving.

TRANSACTIONAL ANALYSIS: A REVIEW OF THE LITERATURE

Hedges Capers

As this review indicates, the bulk of good literature on transactional analysis has been written by Eric Berne, Muriel James, Dorothy Jongeward, Thomas Harris, and Claude Steiner. The authors reviewed here are considered alphabetically and each author's titles are listed chronologically.

Since this review was prepared, however, a new good book by Jacqui Schiff and her staff has been published. It is called *Cathexis Reader: Transactional Analysis Treatment of Psychosis* (New York: Harper & Row, 1975). Cathexis Institute is an educational organization that has pioneered in the treatment of incapacitating psychiatric disturbances. The book is a combined effort, detailing what the staff has learned from its patients with their cooperation.

Also recommended as especially good for a quick overview of TA: *The ABC's of PAC*, by Arnold Kambly, M.D.; *Keeping Yourself Together: A TA Primer for the Single Parent*, by Kathryn J. Hallett; *Becoming the Way We Are: A Transactional Guide to Personal Development*, by Pam Levin; *TA for Tots and Grown-Ups Too*, by Alvyn Freed.

Since TA has become such a lively subject, authors are combining it with all sizes and shapes of other material and using the name TA in their titles to attract sales. The reader who wishes accurate information on the credentials of an author discussing TA should check with the official organization of TA: the International Transactional Analysis Association, 1772 Vallejo Street, San Francisco, California, 94123. Telephone: (415) 885-5592. A wealth of small digest and educational material can be secured from Transactional Analysis Publications (a division of the ITAA). The *Transactional Analysis Journal*, the official scientific publication of the ITTA, is published quarterly and is also obtainable through Transactional Analysis Publications.

Transactional Analysis in Psychotherapy: A Systematic Individual and Social Psychiatry
by Eric Berne, M.D.
New York: Grove Press, 1961. 270 pp., paperbound, $3.95.
(Also, New York: Ballantine, 1973, paperbound, $1.95.)

A classic handbook on the principles Berne laid down in his theory of interpersonal relations, this book provides an organized system to understand an individual and his relationship to others. It was written in the late 50's and published during a time when Berne still felt bound to explain a great many things in orthodox psychoanalytic terms. TA literature has grown and there have been many new contributions, but this book still remains the basic textbook for anyone who seriously studies TA. It is particularly good for those who feel that TA is an oversimplified "pop" psychology.

The Structure and Dynamics of Organizations and Groups
by Eric Berne, M.D.
Philadelphia: J. B. Lippincott, 1963. 260 pp., hardbound, $7.50.
(Paperbound edition, New York: Grove Press, 1966, $2.95)

This book offers a systematic framework for examining ailing organizations and therapy groups. Understanding (which can be clearly diagrammed) the internal and external pressures brought to bear on the group can bring these pressures into the open so they can be examined and dealt with. Berne takes the mystery out of what is happening in an organization.

Although this book has been a sleeper, it provides an important, innovative way to look at people's jobs, especially if they are not satisfying.

Games People Play: The Psychology of Human Relationships
by Eric Berne, M.D.
New York: Grove Press, 1964. 192 pp., hardbound, $5.00; paperbound, $1.50.

Intended for TA analysts as a diagnostic tool, *Games People Play* gives an overview of Transactional Analysis and has become a best seller (an occurrence that surprised Berne). The book is written in simple, clear language that makes its information immediately useful to both professional and nonprofessional readers. The book deals with psychological "games"; a game is a series of transactions that lead to bad feelings because they are based on ulterior motives.

Berne discusses the thesis of the game and its antithesis, a way of redirecting or ending the game. Since a great amount of our time is spent playing these games, the book is a valuable tool for those with the training and talent to help themselves and others.

Principles of Group Treatment
by Eric Berne, M.D.
New York: Oxford University Press, 1966. 379 pp., hardbound, $7.50.
(Paperbound edition, New York: Grove Press, 1968, $4.95.)

The textbook for therapists learning how to do group therapy, *Principles of Group Treatment* presents a systematic treatise on the use of TA in a therapy group. Berne discusses the procedures for setting up group therapy programs: how to start a group, what to look for in the group's dynamics, how to diagnose and cure an ailing group. He talks about the important concept of contracts, the therapy relationship, and termination.

The book contains fictionalized examples that illustrate Berne's principles. Of all Berne's books, this one is considered basic for transactional analysts.

A Layman's Guide to Psychiatry and Psychoanalysis
(Updated Version of *The Mind in Action*)
by Eric Berne, M.D.
New York: Simon and Schuster, 1968. 320 pp., hardbound, $6.95.
(Paperbound edition, New York: Grove Press, $1.95.)

This revised book is especially helpful for nonmedical practitioners. In it Berne tells how the brain works, thus helping the reader understand normal and abnormal behavior. His illustrations draw clear pictures of differences in behavior, and his thoroughly medical and Freudian background is translated into language that is comprehensible to a nonmedical reader.

Sex in Human Loving
by Eric Berne, M.D.
New York: Simon and Schuster, 1970. 288 pp., hardbound, $6.95.
(Paperbound edition, New York: Pocket Books, 1971, $1.50.)

A delightful series of lectures put into print, this book reveals Berne as he was with those who knew him—full of humor and straight talk about psychosocial relationships. From time to time, however, he lapses into philosophy and poetic prose.

This book is not a "manual." It is one to share with a close friend, a joy to read aloud. Subjects covered include "What is Sex?," "Male Power," "Female Power," and "How the Sex Organs are Exploited." In "Final Rap," Berne says it well:

> Irresponsible love is an ego trip. If you love mankind but don't dig real cats and chicks, you're loving from your own container. Loving responsibility is real rapping. You've got to get out of the love bag and torque in to the real world of loving. There's plenty of balling on a violence trip, but it doesn't cancel out. If you're freaked out, a groovy smile is only a toothpaste ad. You've got to flip in to look and love what's really there, and that's what's beautiful. What you do after the ball is over is what counts. (p. 241)

What Do You Say After You Say Hello? The Psychology of Human Destiny
by Eric Berne, M.D.
New York: Grove Press, 1972. 457 pp., hardbound, $10.00.
(Paperbound edition, New York: Bantam Books, 1973, $1.95.)

The last book written by Berne and published after his death, this is more gentle and hopeful than some of his previous works. It deals mainly with recent developments in TA—particularly "scripts," the life plans that people play out. It is an advanced book for psychotherapists of any background and yet easily accessible to the general public.

Scripts from prenatal influences to death-time decisions are thoroughly covered. The book includes a very useful script check list and a complete glossary of TA terms. For the dedicated psychotherapist, it is a very useful book, full of insights.

I'm OK-You're OK: A Practical Guide to Transactional Analysis
by Thomas A. Harris, M.D.
New York: Harper & Row, 1967. 278 pp., hardbound, $5.95.
(Paperbound edition, New York: Avon, 1973, $1.95.)

I'm OK-You're OK, written with the close collaboration of the author's wife, Amy Harris, has done more than any other book to popularize the basic tenets of TA. Aimed primarily at the layman, the book covers the basic principles of TA, with its major emphasis on structural analysis. It presents a somewhat different picture of man than that presented by Berne, who believed that we were all born OK, but because of pressures some of us decide we are not OK. Harris, instead, says that all of us start out feeling not OK about ourselves. His chapter (12) on PAC and moral values has caught the attention of churches, where the book is used widely in study programs. Every therapist should read this book; not only have his patients read it, but it is also well written.

Born to Love:
Transactional Analysis in the Church
by Muriel M. James.
Reading, Mass.: Addison-Wesley, 1973. 203 pp., hardbound, $5.95.

Muriel James is a minister in the United Church of Christ, and Born to Love was written for use in the church and for church people. It covers the basic tenets of TA with illustrations employing church settings and problems. Used properly, this book can bring about exciting changes in the lives of church members and in the church.

Born to Win:
Transactional Analysis with Gestalt Experiments
by Muriel M. James and Dorothy Jongeward.
Reading, Mass.: Addison-Wesley, 1971. 297 pp., paperbound, $4.95.

This book combines a thorough knowledge of basic TA principles with Gestalt exercises, in order to explore the feeling level of the material covered. It is a very useful vehicle for study groups because of this combination. The illustrations and examples come from the wide background and experience gained by the two authors in dealing with people and solving problems for more satisfying living. A study guide for group leaders is also available from the same publisher.

Games Alcoholics Play:
The Analysis of Life Scripts
by Claude M. Steiner.
New York: Grove Press, 1972. 202 pp., hardbound, $6.00.
(Paperbound edition, New York: Ballantine, 1974, $1.50.)

This is a very useful book for professionals working with alcoholics and drug abusers. Steiner talks about the TA approach in working with the alcoholic game, as opposed to the medical model, which despairs of a cure for alcoholism. The roles that the alcoholic's associates play in sustaining his not-OK behavior are clearly defined: the alcoholic who is "it"; the "persecutor," who is usually the wife or the husband; the "rescuer" to whom the alcoholic turns for reassurance; the "patsy," who provides money for the alcoholic; and the "fix," who cuts off the source of supply in order to prevent trouble. One of the helpful insights this book gives to the therapist is the way these people can change roles and keep the game going.

Scripts People Live:
Transactional Analysis of Life Scripts
by Claude M. Steiner.
New York: Grove Press, 1974. 332 pp., hardbound, $8.95.

Steiner was a close associate of Berne. This book further develops the concept of life scripts as they are presented in TA. The author's private practice has given him a wealth of information from which to draw his illustrations. He talks about how scripts are formed, how they develop, how they are perpetuated, and how one can take charge of one's own life. The author's view of moving toward "scriptlessness" and into autonomy is hopeful and helpful. A splendid book for dedicated therapists.

Hedges Capers, M. Div., L.H.D., is the president of the San Diego Institute for Transactional Analysis, La Jolla, California. He is a teaching member of the International Transactional Analysis Association, conducts classes and workshops in TA, and has a large private practice. Dr. Capers has thirty years of experience as a counselor and a teacher.

ENCOUNTERING THE WORLD OF DON JUAN

A Review of
Tales of Power
by Carlos Castaneda.
New York: Simon and Schuster, 1974. 287 pp., $7.95.

Journey to Ixtlan: The Lessons of Don Juan
by Carlos Castaneda.
New York: Simon and Schuster, 1973. 315 pp., $6.95.

The Teachings of Don Juan: A Yaqui Way of Knowledge
by Carlos Castaneda.
New York: Simon and Schuster, 1973. 276 pp., $7.95.

A Separate Reality: Further Conversations with Don Juan
by Carlos Castaneda.
New York: Simon and Schuster, 1971. 317 pp., $5.95.

Richard C. Turner

> *Don Juan:* You don't believe that a magical deer talks, do you?
> *Carlos Castaneda:* I'm sorry but I just can't believe things like that can happen.
> *Don Juan:* I don't blame you. It's one of the darndest things.
>
> *Journey to Ixtlan,* p. 1090

Carlos Castaneda's chronicle of his apprenticeship to the sorcerer don Juan Matus has generated extraordinary responses among various academic disciplines and among the general public. The response to the four books has ranged from praise for academic excellence and new knowledge to skepticism about the existence of don Juan and outright rejection of the value of the teachings; from enthusiasm about the books to don Juan's own response when Carlos brought him a copy of the first book: "I better not [keep it]. . . . You know what we do with paper in Mexico" (*A Separate Reality*, p. 8). Much of the controversy has centered on the value of the books as anthropology or as philosophy or as new handbooks on magic and mysticism. Whatever the final decision about the content of Castaneda's contribution, the books present an extraordinary, provocative experience for the reader. The books constantly challenge a reader's assumptions regarding himself and his relation to his world; they never let the reader off that hook.

The Riddle of the "Spot"

Carlos Castaneda begins *The Teachings of Don Juan* with an incident that sets up the terms for the reader's response to all the books. The first chapter focuses on a riddle posed by don Juan to the eager young anthropologist. After talking with Carlos until early evening, don Juan points out that Carlos is tired and sore and that the "proper thing to do was to find a 'spot' (sitio) on the floor" (p. 7) where Carlos could sit without fatigue. Carlos, of course, asks for an explanation; don Juan merely repeats that Carlos must find the "spot" on which he will be at his best and adds that, if Carlos is not ready to solve this riddle, there can be no further conversations about psychotropic plants.

The next seven pages describe Carlos' attempt to find his "spot." Throughout the night Carlos explores an extraordinary combination of spots and postures. He notices that some "spots" seem surrounded by varying luminous hues—greenish-yellow, purple, chartreuse shading off into verdigris. By dawn he narrows his attention to one "spot" that seems to cause an irrational fear in him. Finally, he falls asleep on another, more comfortable spot while trying to figure out why the other spot creates fear in him. When he wakes up, don Juan compliments him on finding the "spot" and congratulates him on passing the test.

This incident with the "spot" establishes a paradigm for the reader's response: (1) it introduces the magical, animistic world of don Juan—what Castaneda calls "states of non-ordinary reality"; (2) it presents the fumbling, comic attempt of Castaneda to deal with this strange world; and (3) it creates the sense of the complex dynamics of the friendship that develops between Carlos and don Juan. The promise of a new insight into reality attracts the reader. The humor of Carlos' fumbling and the warmth/sternness of don Juan entertain the reader and promise a good and charming story. But the incident also challenges the reader's investment in the book. How much credibility surrounds a grown man who spends all night crawling around a porch? The reader is bound to recognize, as Carlos does, the absurdity of such behavior. A more fundamental challenge lies in the reader's response to Carlos' actually finding his "spot" and avoiding the place that was his "enemy." Don Juan explains that "the sheer act of sitting on one's spot created superior strength" and that "the enemy weakened a man and could even cause his death" (p. 16).

Unless predisposed to accept a magical and animistic nature as part of everyday reality, a reader will find don Juan's explanation unbelievable and/or mystifying. Nor will any middle ground alleviate the problem facing the reader. Defining Carlos' experience as psychic projection—i.e., that Carlos found a spot more comfortable than others because he was told he could find one—merely denies the magic of the event by explaining it. Don Juan continually defies Carlos' attempts to explain his experiences; the reader presumably faces the same difficulty in dealing with the events in terms of ordinary reality.

DON JUAN'S SEPARATE REALITY

The fascination of the Castaneda books arises from this constantly precipitous position occupied by the reader. The reader continually fluctuates between awe and contempt, between curiosity and skepticism. In some ways, the turning of each page defines the reader's investment in the book. If don Juan's teachings amount to nothing more than superstition or the strange perspective of an old man who has chewed too many peyote buttons, then there is no point in the reader's continuing with the book. Once a reader discounts the validity and importance of don Juan's world, continued involvement in the book can amount only to a distanced and leisurely interest in the story or the outcome. And the story itself is just not that compelling. But a reader's willingness to entertain the possibility of don Juan's interaction with the world of "power" creates an intense personal involvement in getting to a point of acceptance or rejection of that world. It is a choice point familiar to all group workers and human relations trainers.

The reader's identification with Carlos and the subsequent sharing of the intensity of his encounter with don Juan's world become compelling reasons to continue with the books. At whatever point and for whatever reason a reader stops reading, his involvement up to that point centers on this balance of and fluctuation between the two mutually exclusive worlds—the reader's own world and the "separate reality" presented by don Juan. Few contemporary readers are so sure of their grasp on "reality" that they are likely to reject don Juan's world out of hand in the first chapter. But skepticism and fear about alternative versions of reality create a great barrier to accepting the strange and dangerous world presented by don Juan. Castaneda's works succeed by maintaining in the reader this acute and immediate sense of a tenuous grasp on reality.

The extraordinary dynamics of the Castaneda books elicit extraordinary responses in the reader and so establish a useful starting point for an individual or group examination of attitudes. Faced with the paradoxical situations presented in the books, the reader is forced to delve into his own resources in order to deal with the strange facts of don Juan's world. Furthermore, the reader becomes acutely conscious of responses to and involvement with difficult realities by watching Carlos' encounter with the challenges presented by don Juan. The tensions and ambiguities that surround the interaction between teacher and apprentice in the book suggest the pain and frustration involved in the process of arriving at self-awareness. The model provided by Carlos at least assures the reader that others face extraordinary difficulties, problems, and concerns in reaching new states of awareness.

Despite the reader's frustrations involved in encountering the sorcerer's world, don Juan's description of that world is attractive. At the beginning of *Tales of Power*, don Juan tells Carlos that "what matters to a warrior is arriving at the totality of oneself" (p. 13). He prefaces the statement by admitting the limitations of his language, but his statement still encompasses the nature of the contemporary search for balance and harmony. In his subsequent explanations, don Juan provides a version of human activity that answers the need for unity of perceptions and feelings and holds out the possibility of vital and active involvement in the world. His definition of the "totality of oneself" organizes the modes of perception—reason, talking, seeing, will, dreaming, and feeling—into a vitally connected whole. Don Juan's explanation remains paradoxical and mysterious, but it conveys a promise of a unified sensibility which seems to many beyond their reach.

Don Juan's Alternative Perceptions

Even the most bizarre tenets of don Juan's teachings offer attractive alternatives for readers. Don Juan's description of human appearance constitutes one of the major departures from our usual mode of perception. He tells Carlos in *A Separate Reality* that, when Carlos can "see," he will "see" men as "little fibers of light":

> Fibers, like white cobwebs. Very fine threads that circulate from the head to the navel. Thus a man looks like an egg of circulating fibers. And his arms and legs are like luminous bristles, bursting out in all directions. . . . Besides, every man is in touch with everything else, not through his hands, though, but through a bunch of long fibers that shoot out from the center of his abdomen. Those fibers join a man to his surroundings; they keep his balance; they give him stability. So, as you may *see* some day, a man is a luminous egg whether he's a beggar or a king and there's no way to change anything; or rather, what could be changed in that luminous egg? (*A Separate Reality*, p. 33)

Such a redefinition is bound to cause problems for a reader brought up in a tradition that venerates Michelangelo's statues, the science of anatomy, and the extraordinary knowledge embodied in modern medicine. Comprehending this description raises an especially difficult issue for the reader because it focuses on an immediate sense—the reader's perception of himself and others.

But the description offers two unique possibilities for readers in a tradition plagued by the problem of the one and the many. Don Juan's description posits a description of human beings that identifies all men as being equal. The description establishes the humbling fact that all men are essentially identical, thus complementing don Juan's teachings about losing self-importance. Don Juan's description also offers an acceptable or understandable physics for the union of self with other. The "fibers of light" that touch other things and other people provide a framework for the physical and emotional union of one with another, which has frustrated men since they began to identify their situation as "self" dealing with other "selves," some of whom they wanted to be a lot closer to.

The problems raised by Castaneda in all the books focus on this transcending of ordinary reality—the mystics' concern for centuries. Like most other documents of mystical experience, Eastern and Western, Castaneda's books leave the actual definition of the "separate reality" unexplained because a language developed for ordinary reality cannot comprehend a transcendent reality. But don Juan's physiology of the "luminous web" presents a structure with which the reader can at least conceive of union with others.

286

The "Tonal" and the "Nagual"

Perhaps the most intriguing aspect of the Castaneda books is don Juan's explanation in *Tales of Power* of the *tonal* and the *nagual*, the duality that constitutes the structure of the sorcerer's reality. Don Juan explains that every human being has two sides—the "tonal" and the "nagual." He defines the *tonal* as the "organizer of the world" and elaborates as follows:

> Perhaps the best way of describing its monumental work is to say that on its shoulders rests the task of setting the chaos of the world in order. It is not farfetched to maintain, as sorcerers do, that everything we know and do as men in the work of the *tonal*. . . . I would say then that the *tonal* is a guardian that protects something priceless, our very being. Therefore, an inherent quality of the *tonal* is to be cagey and jealous of its doings. And since its doings are by far the most important part of our lives, it is no wonder that it eventually changes, in every one of us, from a guardian into a guard. (p. 122)

Having defined the *tonal* to include everything that we can know or name, don Juan suggests that the *nagual* is that part of ourselves that we can sense and that influences our behavior, but that we cannot deal with. He says that our lives consist of the tension between the attempts of the *nagual* to intrude on our lives and the efforts of the *tonal* to deny access to the *nagual*. Don Juan's description of the dynamics of personality parallels contemporary definitions, but his suggestion that the *nagual* exists outside as well as inside the personality adds an immediacy to the sense of conflict between the two forces, an immediacy that is lacking from our usual sense of personal involvement in the world.

Despite the difficulties of sorting through and responding to all these strange situations, the reader continually has a sense that something like what don Juan describes must be that elusive point of view that will allow an integrated and satisfying sense of the world. However remote or strange don Juan's explanations and actions may seem, don Juan himself possesses a personal bearing and attitude that suggests a perfectly consistent attitude toward his world. In his terms, he acts "impeccably." That is, he acts without ambiguity, hesitation, or guilt. He approaches all situations with full knowledge of the risks involved and a thoroughly accurate perspective on his situation. Perhaps more than anything else, don Juan's behavior attracts the reader and involves him in the terrifying ambiguities inherent in an encounter with don Juan's world.

The process of involvement and response demanded by the Castaneda books lends itself to a similar involvement in sorting out the paradoxes and mysteries of the reader's own reality. There is much here to capture, involve, excite, and benefit the human relations trainer.

Richard C. Turner, Ph.D., is an assistant professor of English at Indiana University-Purdue University at Indianapolis. He is currently teaching literature in the undergraduate program at IUPUI, offering courses in eighteenth-century British literature and contemporary poetry. He is working on a study of eighteenth-century drama and criticism.

CONTRIBUTORS

Anthony G. Banet, Jr., Ph.D.
Senior Consultant
University Associates
7596 Eads Avenue
La Jolla, California 92037
  (714) 454-8821

Millard J. Bienvenu, Sr., Ph.D.
Professor and Head
Department of Sociology and Social Work
Director of the Family Study Center
Northwestern State University
Natchitoches, Louisiana 71457
  (318) 357-5902

Kenneth H. Blanchard, Ph.D.
Professor of Leadership
  and Organizational Behavior
School of Education
University of Massachusetts
427 Hills North
Amherst, Massachusetts 01002

Hedges Capers, M.Div., L.H.D.
President
San Diego Institute for Transactional Analysis
7636 La Jolla Boulevard
La Jolla, California 92037
  (714) 459-6938

Myron R. Chartier, Ph.D.
Associate Professor of Ministry
Director of the Doctoral Program
The Eastern Baptist Theological Seminary
Lancaster Avenue and City Line
Philadelphia, Pennsylvania 19151
  (215) 877-4200

Cary L. Cooper, Ph.D.
F.M.E. Professor of
  Management Educational Methods
Department of Management Sciences
Institute of Science and Technology
The University of Manchester
P.O. Box 88
Manchester, England M60 1QD
  061-236-3311

James I. Costigan, Ph.D.
Chairman
Department of Speech
Fort Hays Kansas State College
Hays, Kansas 67601

Donald A. Devine, Ph.D.
Program Supervisor
Community Justice Project
5 Appleton Street
Waterville, Maine 04901
  (207) 873-2724

Arthur L. Dirks
Instructor of Communication Arts
Division of the Humanities
Wayne State College
Wayne, Nebraska 68787

Jo F. Dorris, Ed.D.
Associate Dean of Student Affairs
Student Union 369
Oklahoma State University
Stillwater, Oklahoma 74074

A. Donald Duncan
Administrative Assistant for Human Relations
Yonkers Public Schools
145 Palmer Road
Yonkers, New York 10701

Alan C. Filley, Ph.D.
Chairman, Department of Management
Graduate School of Business
University of Wisconsin—Madison
1155 Observatory Drive
Madison, Wisconsin 53706
  (608) 262-1998

John C. Glidewell
Professor of Education and Social Psychology
Department of Education
University of Chicago
Chicago, Illinois 60637
  (312) 753-3829

Joel Goodman, Ed.D.
Program Coordinator
National Humanistic Education Center
110 Spring Street
Saratoga Springs, New York 12866
(518) 587-8770

Kenneth Harrison
Senior Lecturer in Organizational Behavior
Cranfield School of Management
Cranfield, Bedford
England MK43 OAL
0234-750111

Roger Harrison, Ph.D.
Vice President for Overseas Operations
Development Research Associates
c/o Homestead Farm
Mountain Bower
Near Chippenham, Wiltshire
England SN14 7AJ
Marshfield (022124) 616

Stanley M. Herman
TRW Systems Group
One Space Park—E2/7042
Redondo Beach, California 90278
(213) 536-3465

Paul Hersey
Distinguished Visiting Professor
of Organizational Behavior
United States International University
San Diego, California 92131
(714) 271-4300

John E. Jones, Ph.D.
Vice President
University Associates
7596 Eads Avenue
La Jolla, California 92037
(714) 454-8821

H. B. Karp, Ph.D.
Associate Professor
Department of Business Management
Old Dominion University
P.O. Box 6173
Norfolk, Virginia 23508
(804) 489-8000, Ext. 347

Philip Katz, Ph.D.
Clinical Psychologist and Assistant Professor
Department of Secondary Education
University of Bridgeport
Bridgeport, Connecticut 06602

Colleen Kelley
2500-203 Torrey Pines Road
La Jolla, California 92037
(714) 453-8165

Dennis C. King
Internal OD Consultant
1430 Lee Road
Northbrook, Illinois 60062
(312) 278-1502

Jeremy Kisch, Ph.D.
Chief of Psychology
Rockland Psychiatric Center
Orangeburg, New York 10962
and
Assistant Professor of Psychiatry
New York Medical College
1249 5th Avenue
New York, New York 10029

Charles L. Kormanski, Ed.D.
Counseling and Career Development Center
134 Smith Building
Altoona Campus
Pennsylvania State University
Altoona, Pennsylvania 16603
(814) 944-4547

Jacques Lalanne
President, Institut de Développement Humain
3125 Joncas
Quebec 5
Canada
677-4542

Major Robert E. Mattingly, USMC
Assistant Professor
Department of Naval Science
University of Southern California
Los Angeles, California 90007
(213) 746-2674

Holmes E. Miller, Ph.D.
Assistant Professor of
Operations Research and Statistics
Rensselaer Polytechnic Institute
110 Eighth Avenue
Troy, New York 12181

Sherod Miller, Ph.D.
Assistant Professor
Department of Medicine
University of Minnesota Medical School
2001 Riverside Avenue
Minneapolis, Minnesota 55404
   (612) 338-4276

Elam W. Nunnally, Ph.D.
Associate Professor
School of Social Welfare
University of Wisconsin—Milwaukee
3203 North Downer
Milwaukee, Wisconsin 53201

Barry Oshry, Ph.D.
Power & Systems Education
NTL Institute for Applied Behavioral Science
Box 388
Prudential Station
Boston, Massachusetts 02199

Herbert A. Otto, Ph.D.
Chairperson
The National Center for the Exploration of
   Human Potential
976 Chalcedony Street
San Diego, California 92109
   (714) 272-7330

Larry A. Pace
Department of Psychology
University of Georgia
Athens, Georgia 30602

Udai Pareek, Ph.D.
Professor of Organizational Behavior
Indian Institute of Management
Vastrapur, Ahmedabad 380 015
India

Larry E. Pate
Visiting Assistant Professor
Department of Management
University of Nebraska—Lincoln
Lincoln, Nebraska 68508
   (402) 472-3370

J. William Pfeiffer, Ph.D.
President
University Associates
7596 Eads Avenue
La Jolla, California 92037
   (714) 454-8821

Elizabeth Racicot
Ambassade du Canada
BP. 21194 Abidjan
Côte d'Ivoire
West Africa

Gustave J. Rath, Ph.D.
Professor of Industrial Engineering/
   Management Sciences
Director, Design and Development Center
The Technological Institute
Northwestern University
Evanston, Illinois 60201

Anthony J. Reilly, Ph.D.
Senior Consultant
University Associates
7596 Eads Avenue
La Jolla, California 92037
   (714) 454-8821

Jack J. Rosenblum, J.D.
Cliffside Apartments, M-8
Sunderland, Massachusetts 01375
   (413) 665-2971

Patricia A. Schmuck, Ph.D.
1956 Fairmount Boulevard
Eugene, Oregon 97403
   (503) 345-7425

Richard A. Schmuck, Ph.D.
Co-Director
Program on Strategies of
   Organizational Change
Center for Educational Policy
   and Management
Professor of Educational Psychology
University of Oregon
1472 Kincaid
Eugene, Oregon 97401
   (503) 686-5067

Donald T. Simpson
Marketing Education Center
Eastman Kodak Company
343 State Street
Rochester, New York 14650
   (716) 325-2000

Lorrie Collins Trueblood
Director, Santosha Yoga Center
Co-Director, Human Potential Institute
  of Indiana
2060 East 54th Street, Suite No. 1
Indianapolis, Indiana 46220
  (317) 257-4165 or (317) 253-7302

Richard C. Turner, Ph.D.
Assistant Professor of English
Indiana University-Purdue University
  at Indianapolis
925 West Michigan Street
Indianapolis, Indiana 46202
  (317) 264-7362

Daniel B. Wackman, Ph.D.
Associate Professor and
Director of the Communication
  Research Division
School of Journalism and Mass Communication
University of Minnesota
Minneapolis, Minnesota 55455

Julia T. Wood, Ph.D.
Assistant Professor
Division of Speech
115 Bingham Hall
University of North Carolina at Chapel Hill
Chapel Hill, North Carolina 27514
  (919) 933-5096

Copyright © 1976 University Associates, Inc.